Shaping Identity in Canadian Society

Shaping Identity in Canadian Society

Jack Haas
Department of Sociology
McMaster University

William Shaffir
Department of Sociology
McMaster University

Prentice-Hall of Canada, Ltd., *Scarborough, Ontario*

CANADIAN CATALOGUING IN PUBLICATION DATA

Haas, Jack, 1939-
  Shaping identity in Canadian society
Bibliography: p.
ISBN 0-13-808204-9

1. Canada - Social conditions. I. Shaffir,
William, 1945-   II. Title.

HN103.5.H33   309.1'71   C78-001178-3

Prentice-Hall, Inc., Englewood Cliffs, New Jersey
Prentice-Hall of Australia, Pty., Ltd., Sydney
Prentice-Hall of India Pvt., Ltd., New Delhi
Prentice-Hall International, Inc., London
Prentice-Hall of Japan, Inc., Tokyo
Prentice-Hall of Southeast Asia (PTE.) Ltd., Singapore

ISBN 0-13-808204-9
Design: Artplus Limited/Brant Cowie
1 2 3 4 5 W 82 81 80 79 78
Printed and Bound in Canada by Webcom Limited

Contents

To Claire, Chris, Jackie, and Matthew
JACK HAAS

To Rivka, Yael, and Elichai
WILLIAM SHAFFIR

Acknowledgments

We wish to thank Berkeley Fleming and Victor Marshall for their helpful comments. We also greatly appreciate the editorial insights and assistance of MaryLynne Meschino. Finally, we acknowledge the generous support of McMaster University.

Preface

This book attempts to provide an interesting and comprehensible introduction to sociology. We have adopted a particular theoretical orientation, symbolic interactionism, to give a coherent analysis of behavior and identity in Canadian society. We have deliberately selected materials emphasizing the human element that underlies abstract sociological concepts. Our hope is that the reader will begin to develop a sociological perspective by reading material that describes real-life persons and settings.

Our chief concern has been the presentation of a single point of view, and therefore, we have not made comparisons between the symbolic interactionist and other sociological and social psychological perspectives. Attention to this task, though well deserved, would have diverted us from the main job of simply outlining the principal components of one approach to understanding human behavior. Though some may claim that this is a limited view of human conduct rather than a comprehensive theory, we contend that such comprehensive theories of behavior do not exist.

The integrating theme of the book is Canadian identity. We develop that theme by presenting a social psychological approach to understanding the formation of identity, and integrating this approach with an organizational and historical/structural analysis of Canadian society. The book's focus on identity moves back and forth from individual to group, community, organization, social structure, social class, political economy, and societal relationships. The web of relationships important to understanding personal, group, collective, regional, and national identities is inductively described by moving from a micro to a macro analysis.

We have used the concept of identity for two main reasons. First, it allows us to capture the essential elements of the symbolic interactionist perspective. Second, this concept seems especially suitable for analyzing and tying together seemingly unrelated features of everyday life in society. As we will indicate, human behavior is best explained in terms of process, and attempts at understanding such behavior must include an analysis of that process. The concept of identity as formulated within the symbolic interactionist perspective both encourages and enables us to highlight the interconnected processes that underlie our behavior.

We try to demonstrate that the concept of identity and the main tenets of the symbolic interactionist tradition can help us analyze social interaction as it occurs at different levels of society. Accordingly, our analysis of Canadian society begins with a focus on self and identity and then proceeds to examine the groups and structures with which people interact and which influence their behavior—ethnic groups, the work environment, and the larger social structure.

We believe that an important way of learning sociology is to examine the many diverse sources of identity as they are perceived by different Canadians. The major sections of the book emphasize the significance of religious and ethnic identities, occupational and organizational sources of identity, and the role of regionalism, stratification, urbanization, and colonialism in the development of Canadian identity.

This is an ambitious project and as a consequence we have deliberately neglected areas that should be covered by the instructor. For example, attention is not given to the many theoretical or methodological orientations in sociology; nor is the controversy over concept definitions discussed. We have, instead, presented a consistent orientation which the teacher may choose to ignore, refine, or challenge. We have written an analysis that we find holds together conceptually and substantively, and it may be used either as the major text or as a supplement offering just one of several possible ways of understanding our society. In brief, the instructor's preferences and commitments may support or conflict with our analysis, but in either case, the student stands to learn from the consistency or the contradictions in orientation and emphasis.

The book tries to provide a readable approach to understanding Canadian identity and society. It does not read like a text, is not organized like many texts, and does not consider the standard issues in sociology texts. Out of the need for a suitable text, this has emerged. The book meets our purposes and we believe it will be an aid for Canadian students—a book they will read willingly and with understanding.

Introduction

Symbolic Interaction Theory: Personal & Collective Definitions of the Situation

The sociologist . . . tries to "locate" the human being and his conduct in various institutions, never isolating the individual or the workings of his mind from his social and historical setting. He explains character and conduct in terms of these institutions, and of the total social structure which they form. He draws upon the experience of people as social persons rather than upon the physical and organic facts about people as animal organisms. Since he is interested in the social setting and motivations of conduct . . . he does not attempt to explain conduct as if it were the realization of some fundamental condition within the individual. The sociologist tries to explain character and conduct as a fulfillment of social function within an already established, although open-ended, network of social relations. (Gerth and Mills, 1953: 3-4)

GERTH AND MILLS have captured the essence of the sociologist's task; defining and analyzing the social or group bases of human behavior. Man is born into a group, the family; lives and learns in groups and institutions; and dies and is "passed on" in group or organizational contexts. Human life and experience involve others and these others and the structures or patterns of relationships in society affect what we are, what we become, and how we see ourselves and "our" world.

In order to understand social life we must understand its basic processes: communication, interaction and socialization into the various groups, role-playing, and development of values and cultures that form the social structures of everyday life. These processes take place in particular contexts and are affected by concrete events and *a priori* historical circumstances.

This book attempts to introduce the reader to the sociological perspective by emphasizing the individual's relationship to society. The concept of self-identity as well as the images and interpretations that lie at the heart of all interactions is examined in several contexts as a means of relating sociology to our own lives and experiences. We have deliberately chosen materials that give emphasis to the human drama of society. To begin, we will introduce the overriding theoretical orientation that guides this analysis and approach.

3

Introduction to Symbolic Interaction Theory

The symbolic interactionist perspective in sociology and social psychology was not systematically formulated by one person but has developed gradually. It can be traced back to the writings of sociologists W. I. Thomas, Florian Znaniecki, C. H. Cooley, and Robert Park, and two philosophers, John Dewey and George H. Mead. Sociologists such as Ernest W. Burgess, Herbert Blumer, Everett C. Hughes, and Louis Wirth have made significant contributions. Others, including Howard S. Becker, Tamotsu Shibutani, Alfred Lindesmith, and Anselm Strauss, have further refined the symbolic interactionist perspective in their writings.

As Blumer has stated, the term "symbolic interaction" refers to the distinctive character of interaction as it occurs between human beings. The distinction lies in the fact that "human beings interpret or 'define' each other's actions." (Blumer, 1962: 180) Symbolic interactionists contend that human behavior is the product of communication; it is not regarded merely as a direct response to environmental stimuli, inner organic needs, or cultural forces. While they recognize the existence of these phenomena, symbolic interactionists believe that people's conduct is basically formed in the course of interaction with others as they judge and interpret their own actions and those of other people.

Human behavior is not thought of simply as the result of a direct response to stimuli, but as a process in which humans act toward and in response to objects depending upon the meaning of those objects. The meanings are derived through social interaction. Objects (chairs, cats, groups, people, actions) can be given a variety of meanings because language symbols are produced and used to describe them. These language symbols and their shared meanings depend upon individuals interacting with each other and their environment. The meanings of objects, their symbols, and our actions toward them evolve largely out of the contexts of our interactions with others. Social interaction is crucial to the meanings we construct, whether the objects referred to are things, people, acts, or ideas. This interaction takes place in situations defined by the participants themselves.

All group life consists of cooperative activity wherein each individual ascertains the intention of others and responds on the basis of that intention. Human conduct is determined primarily by defining the situations in which a person acts.

Human behavior is not directly related to any biologic or innate capacity, but is predicated on an acquired ability to communicate symbolically. The distinctive attributes of human behavior develop from man's participation in various social structures that necessarily depend on communication. Man is the only animal who manipulates symbols and whose social life is based on symbolic structures and processes that guide, check, define, and interpret actions.

Human Action is Symbolic We are not, of course, automatically and inevitably human. We become human by learning a social heritage and culture through our interactions with others. Robert E. Park describes this process when he says "man is not born human. It is only slowly and laboriously, in fruitful contact, cooperation, and conflict with his fellows, that he attains the distinctive qualities of human nature." (Park, 1915:9)

The important role others play in the development of human characteristics is dramatized in accounts of isolated and feral children (Bettelheim, 1959; Davis, 1947; Singh and Zingy, 1942). These descriptions of children who have never had contact with people point out the importance of human association in the development of human qualities. The young child responds to isolation or to growing up with wild animals by acting like an animal, rather than becoming a socialized human being.

Such children are deprived of language, which is essential to the organization of man's behavior. An important difference between animal and human life is in fact this distinctively human capacity to learn, use, and interpret symbolic communication. Human language, the use of symbols with shared meanings, provides us with the basis for communication. Symbolic interactionists believe that the distinctive attributes of human behavior grow from man's immersion in a cultural environment that depends on the existence of language and the creation and manipulation of signs and symbols. Language is the vehicle by which culture is transmitted from generation to generation, and through it, individuals are able to organize their actions within a framework of mutual expectations. Communication through symbols makes the formation of human groups possible and gives them continuity in time and space. The learning of symbols initiates and facilitates the evolution and transmission of traditions, skills, goals, tactics, rules, and procedures.

Peter and Brigitte Berger describe the significance of language when they say:

> Language provides the lifelong context of our experience of others, of self, of the world. Even when we imagine worlds beyond this one, we are constrained to put our intimations or hopes in terms of language. Language is the social institution above all others. It provides the most powerful hold that society has over us. (Berger and Berger, 1972:75)

Mead further points out the importance of language in forming identity and in the social control of behavior when he says:

> Through the use of language, through the use of the significant symbol, then, the individual does take the attitude of others, especially these common attitudes, so that he finds himself taking the same attitude toward himself that the community takes. (In Strauss, 1956:35)

Defining the Situation Human behavior is understood as the conscious and rational interpretation of symbolic as well as physical stimuli in the environment. Individuals define and construct their social situations, using sets of cultural meanings and understandings as the bases for these interpretations. In such interactions, individuals convey to one another what they ought, or are expected, to do. By symbolically communicating a series of definitions and expectations to one another, they define the situation. As individuals interact with one another, each tries to anticipate what the others are likely to do. By making inferences about others' intentions or by taking another's point of view human beings are able to act together. These actions can be coordinated successfully only because conventional norms and expectations are imposed upon individuals from infancy, thus familiarizing them with the conduct appropriate to given situations. Because people share similar orientations toward their environment, they learn to take part in a common culture and develop similar beliefs and patterns of behavior.

The members of any sociological group share understandings about various objects, symbols, and situations, and the proper ways of responding to them. They agree on normative expectations and on rules of conduct, such as whether or not people ought to be approached. In other words, the society's or group's culture provides individuals with a set of boundaries within which their actions should take place.

The many cultures we become familiar with in this complex, physically and socially mobile Canadian society provide us with a set of ideas and practices that directs our actions. These guides create a certain stability and security in our lives providing shared, time-honored ways of believing and behaving. We can be secure in the knowledge that specific, culturally defined actions will evoke certain reactions.

As we come into contact with more cultures, we expand the range of our possible beliefs and actions, ideas and practices, and we are freed from the tyranny of a single culture. Paradoxically, we are finding that in more "advanced", complex industrial societies, people become very insecure because of the tension of competing demands and expectations.

Cultures are not static, nor are our relationships with other people. Culture is dynamic and subject to continuous change as people develop new ways of thinking and behaving. The changes in our society and in each culture are so immense and rapid that we now speak of generational or cultural gaps of four or five years, or even less.

Our society is not unicultural, since each social group possesses and develops its own culture. Within each group, members have common understandings and expectations of one another; they share a definition of the way the world works. This common definition allows them to anticipate the actions of others, and prepares them to react in an appropriate manner. As Shibutani and Kwan have written, "Men are able to engage in concerted action because they share common understandings concerning the responsibilities of each participant, and the coordination of diverse contributions becomes possible only when each person is able to anticipate to some extent what the others are likely to do and can make the necessary adjustments." (Shibutani and Kwan, 1965:57)

Definitions of social situations may or may not come to be shared by participants. Individuals and groups must be able to "take the role of the other" in order to share the definition of the situation. The sharing of definitions and meanings is more likely to occur in situations involving extended and continuous interaction; this is particularly true for individuals who occupy similar positions or face the same or similar situations. It is this congruence of individual definitions and conduct that defines a social group.

Taking the role of the other is, as Hewitt describes it, "imagining the other's view of one's own act in terms of its typicality, its likelihood under the circumstances, its relationship to cause and effect, its status as a means to an end, its moral or normative stature, and its congruence with a presumably shared definition of the situation." (Hewitt, 1976:127)

Role-taking is a process in which we "see" or attempt to appreciate the perspective of others in a particular situation. We observe the conduct and reactions of other people and learn their expectations and point of view; at the same time, we are able to interpret our own behavior from their point of view. This distinctively human ability provides us with the opportunity to construct action while taking into account the perspectives of others.

In routine situations we already know others' expectations and roles, and it is easy to act in accordance with those people who share our situation. We have learned through previous experiences how to believe and act.

Social interaction is an obviously complex and multifaceted process. Many situations in which we attempt to learn others' points of view and our own place in the situation are problematic. As we create our roles and as we experience or perceive the roles and expectations of other people we sometimes attempt to influence their conduct by controlling the definition of situation. At the same time, others in the situation may attempt to impose their versions of reality on us. Sometimes there is tension and conflict between competing definitions of situations; other times, there evolves a compromise. At all times, however, there is the possibility of change. Social interaction is not, then, limited to those processes in which people seek consensus and adjustment, but often involves tension and conflict. Role-taking is critically affected by the exercise of power in any given situation.

Power is an important element in all social relationships. Whether micro or macro societal structures are under analysis, power is a constant and impressively direct element in our everyday interactions. It affects how we act and how others treat us. This is obvious to most of us if we notice our behavior (Goffman, 1956) in the presence of "significant" others. For example, our conduct in the presence of a wino, brother or sister, parent, teacher, principal, boss, member of parliament, policeman, or prime minister varies considerably. Depending on the particular situation, our behavior and assessment of the power and authority of these others will change.

Power in social relations is simply the capacity to control the actions of others. It pervades all areas of social life and ranges from exacting obedience from other people to influencing decisions that affect us or others. Max Weber sums up the broader implications of power when he says it is "the chance of a man or a number of men to realize their own will in communal action even against the resistance of others who are participating in the action." (Weber, 1946:180)

It is important to realize that if a person claims to have power or authority (legitimated power) it does not necessarily mean that other people will recognize or respect him as powerful. For example, some classroom teachers who have the authority to direct and control students are in fact controlled by students. Similarly, armed prison guards appear to have great power over prisoners, but research on prisons shows that prisoners control life in the prison and that guards frequently bargain with prisoners and give in to their latent or direct threats (Clemmer, 1958; Cressey, 1961; Sykes, 1965; Ward and Kassebaum, 1965).

The relationships we evolve with others fluctuate constantly and are continually being redefined. For example, think of the way the relationship between lovers changes, from the first meeting, through intimate involvement, to the ultimate dissolution through breakup or death. There are changes in our feelings, levels of involvement, and relations of equality, superiority, or subordination. Defining the situation, then, is continuous and includes a variety of problematics, since the situation is always subject to redefinition. Through communication, the individual attempts to define situations and to calculate an appropriate response. This process of interpretation, of mediating external stimuli, allows humans to indicate to themselves suitable lines of conduct before they act. In other words, they are first able to formulate and assess alternative lines of action.

Even before we enter or become involved with a group, it has defined many sets of expectations and guidelines for behavior. As we try to define ourselves, we recognize and take into account our own personal desires and interests as well as the expectations of others. This may create a sense of personal tension or conflict. W. I. Thomas points out this problem when he says that "there is . . . always a rivalry between the spontaneous definitions of the situation made by a member of an organ-

ized society and the definitions which his society has provided for him."
(Thomas, 1967:316) We are aware of the expectations of other people
because of our unique human ability to take the role of the other. George
H. Mead expresses this point aptly when he says:

> It is only insofar as the individual acts not only in his own perspective,
> but also in the perspective of others, especially in the common perspec-
> tive of a group, that a society arises and its affairs become the object of
> scientific inquiry. The limitation of social organization is found in the
> inability of individuals to place themselves in the perspective of others
> .... This principle is that the individual enters into the perspectives of
> others, insofar as he is able to take their attitudes, or occupy their point
> of view. (Mead, 1932:165)

We are able to understand others because we can imagine how they
feel and think. We do this by empathizing with others, by symbolically
assuming their point of view. Because we can see social situations from
the perspective of others, we are able to anticipate and weigh their
possible reactions to our behavior. We can assay the situation from a
number of viewpoints, consider several alternative lines of action, and act
in ways we think will be most appropriate or most successful.

This process of definition is continuous and dynamic. As we move
through new situations we acquire new definitions; as our relationships
with others change, so does our behavior toward or with them. Throughout our lives we come to learn a host of definitions, meanings, and
expectations, and in a complex, heterogeneous society such as ours, some
of these expectations may conflict. Thus, understanding human behavior
is always problematic.

Motives   Groups not only provide us with definitions, meanings, and
expectations about appropriate beliefs and behavior, but also with the
rationales or vocabularies of justification for actions. As C. Wright Mills
has said, "motives are accepted justifications for present, future, or past
progress or acts." (Mills, 1940:907) This definition is important because
motives are described as "accepted" justifications. Our motive for doing
a particular act may be seen as a socially learned and adopted expression
that provides our audience (others or ourselves) with a reason for our
actions.

It is important, as Alfred Schutz (1967) points out, to distinguish
between "because of" motives, similar to Mills's concept of motives as
rationalizations for behavior, and "in order to" motives, which are plans
of action. When acts are questioned we search our minds for a suitable
explanation. We may have acted unquestioningly, or without a calculated
motive, and are now forced to explain our conduct. The only explanations lie in the body of rationalizations or justifications that we have

learned from other social groups; we may, in fact, have a host of motives that we have learned from a variety of associations.

When considering an explanation or rationalization, it is important to be aware of the motives behind the explanation, and the audience to which it is being directed. A simple example may clarify this point. If your professor asks why you are reading this book, your answer might be: "It's interesting", or "I enjoy sociology", or "I hope to do well in the course". If, however, a fellow student asks the same question you might reply: "It's required", or "We have a test on it", or "I'm not reading it unless it's on the test". Different motives are given for the very same act. The rationale, explanation, or motive used often depends on what we perceive is expected of us.

It is important to distinguish between those motives that are applied after the act and those that are part of the consideration that precedes the act. Some behavior is calculated, motivated, and premeditated; often we anticipate our behavior in situations and decide on a course of action as well as a way of presenting ourselves. Our behavior is motivated to the extent that we determine in advance how to act to achieve our goal. We act "in order to" accomplish our ends.

Socialization and Identity   Our discussion thus far suggests that since we are born into a social group, our understanding of who and what we are must be related to the larger group of which we are a part. By the same token, our self-conception cannot be determined without considering other people we are directly or indirectly involved with in social interaction. The responses of others necessarily play an important part in the construction of our image of ourselves. This image, or self-conception, may be regarded as our identity. Whatever else it may be, identity is connected to the ongoing appraisal made of ourselves by us and others.

Our socialization involves coming to appreciate and/or understand others' points of view so that joint actions are possible. Out of our interactions with others, shared meanings emerge. Our socialization includes the ability to understand meanings created by others and to create meanings that can be understood by others. We have the distinctively human capacity to learn meanings and develop our humanness, because we are born with an undeveloped capacity to communicate by taking the role of others.

The agents important to the socialization of the young include the family, the peer group, the mass media, and the educational system. The family and peer group are thought to be primary agents of socialization because of the extensive, intensive, and enduring relationship we have with them. Their influence in terms of the way we identify and view ourselves is profound. Other sources of learning are generally less important in the formation and expression of our identity.

Children are born into a world that they must come to understand and the family is their first and most influential social relationship. In order to understand the world and their place in it, children learn both symbol and role/status meanings; they learn the means and the meaning of communication. Family members and others in the children's world use objects, and their actions involving these objects come to be interpreted, understood, and used by the youngsters as indications of the meanings the objects have. This knowledge helps children to develop a perspective for defining the world and their place in it.

Children identify with the family, taking on its definitions, roles, and attitudes. Family members are a major source of role models for youngsters to imitate. Social learning, at this stage then, takes place through imitation.

Through their concrete experience with others, children begin to develop a more unified conception of themselves as they face several sets of expectations. As they learn to take into account the possible actions of a variety of other people, they construct roles for themselves. On the basis of group relationships and expectations, children come to view themselves from the position of the group or "generalized other". They not only develop an identification with the people they encounter directly, but also an identity that transcends their immediate world.

The children's world expands as they have new contacts and are influenced by new experiences. They learn, for example, not only the language, values, roles, aspirations, prejudices, morality, and behavior expected by the family, but of other groups that they encounter. They also discover that the family itself gives them a location—a status membership in society to which others react. The meanings that children learn from the family group are combined with the status group memberships (religion, race and ethnicity, occupation, social class) of the family to give them a place *vis-à-vis* other social groupings. Thus there is a developing identity, molding and shaping a sense of location, value, and difference—a sense of self. (Strauss, 1969:9)

Identity is, of course, formed, maintained, and reinforced on a daily basis during and as a result of interaction with other people. Everyone develops a conception of the kind of person they are based on the way they imagine other people react to their behavior. This is what led Cooley to describe a person's sense of personal identity as a "looking-glass self":

> In a very large and interesting class of cases the social reference takes the form of a somewhat definite imagination of how one's self ... appears in a particular mind, and the kind of self-feeling one has is determined by the attitude toward this, attributed to that other mind. A social self of this sort might be called the reflected or looking-glass self: "Each to each a looking-glass reflects the other that doth pass". (Cooley, 1964:183-84)

In anticipating the impression our acts will make on those people involved in the interaction, we attempt to visualize the outcome of our behavior even before we begin to act. We anticipate or preview the way our self-image will be reflected in others' eyes.

Our self-conception, or personal identity, reflects the image we believe others will have of us. It is intimately connected to the reactions imputed to other people. The self is therefore a social product, socially created and maintained. We are highly sensitized to other people's reactions and responses to our actions, since our self-image is a reflection of what we believe others think of us.

Although implied, it is necessary to emphasize that the way we may think others regard us does not necessarily always coincide with the conception they actually have of us. Although people may believe that they have earned the respect of their colleagues they may in fact be considered ridiculous. Former mental patients, for example, who believe that they have gained the acceptance and respect of their families, may suddenly and unexpectedly discover that family members consider them to be extremely dangerous and unstable.

Generally speaking, we are sufficiently sensitive to other people's definitions of us to incorporate their image of us into our self-definition. We learn these definitions and they become an important part of our inner conception of self. As we learn other definitions of the situation and of our role and identity in such situations we come to internalize society. Individually we become, in our inner thoughts, a society in miniature, wherein we engage in a dialogue with a host of interpretations and expectations.

A key tenet of the symbolic interactionist approach is the idea that human beings have a self; that they can be the object of their own actions. People can act toward themselves as they might act toward others, or as they imagine others might act toward them. It is, therefore, not uncommon for people to congratulate themselves, get angry at themselves, argue with themselves, or give themselves explicit instructions ("Now make sure to do this", or "Okay, try not to make the same mistake again"). The process through which the self is formed has been outlined by G. H. Mead and C. H. Cooley. This process is significant because by having a self, individuals are able to exercise control over their behavior and are not directly subject to the stimulation of the environment or an organic condition. This is possible because human beings learn to communicate with themselves and in so doing are able to internalize the very process of interaction and communication. Individuals guide and control their behavior by considering the images they believe others have of them. Their assessment of the situation includes an attempt to define the expectations of others.

The human self arises through our ability to take the attitude of the group to which we belong; this is possible because we can talk to ourselves in terms of the community or "generalized other". Through the use of language, through the use of the "significant symbol", we assume the perspective of others so that we take the same attitude toward ourselves that is taken by the community. This is the principal way we control and organize ourselves.

Since our self-conception is intimately bound to the impressions others have of us, many of us, at different times, try to present a certain image of ourselves. We often attempt to guide and control the impressions our audience will receive. In a calculated way, we determine the kinds of things we may or may not do in order to sustain a particular impression.

Goffman's analysis in *The Presentation of Self in Everyday Life* (1959) shows the various techniques and strategies that are used to project and maintain desired self-conceptions. If, for example, individuals wish to convey an impression of affluence they will carefully select the cars they drive and the clothes they wear. To compensate for the lack of an active social life, boys or girls may talk incessantly about the many friends they have. By carefully controlling our behavior, each of us conveys an image of the character we want to assume and have others recognize.

Identity is a fragile concept—temporal, situational, and constrained and defined by those whom we encounter in our daily interactions. In this respect, cooperative activity, wherein we agree upon and share the definition of the situation, is based on the mutual validation of presented identities.

When presenting ourselves to others we do not usually expect that our proffered image will be openly challenged. We assume that our audience will treat us in a manner befitting the kind of person we claim to be. If our performance is consistent with our presented self-image, others will have little ground for denying our claim to that identity.

When an individual "makes an implicit or explicit claim to be a person of a particular kind, he automatically exerts a moral demand upon others, obliging them to value and treat him in a manner that persons of his kind have a right to expect." (Goffman, 1959:13) In exchange, the individual is obligated to accept others' conceptions of who they are. This working agreement to support each other's self-conception lasts as long as nothing about the performances or no discrediting information threatens the shared understanding. As McCall and Simmons have written:

> It is precisely this leverage on others that allows us to maintain our conceptions of ourselves in some degree, as long as we can avoid tripping ourselves up through our own performances. People are obliged to give us the benefit of the doubt as long as the case against our claim is not established *beyond* reasonable doubt. (McCall and Simmons, 1966:139)

The working agreement may continue indefinitely, with each person accepting the other's claim to an identity. Challenges to a proffered identity are likely to arise when new information about the person, revealed intentionally or unwittingly, leads us to question a person's claim to that particular identity. Since certain kinds of information about us may be detrimental to our relationship with others, we seek to control what is known about us. The parts of our biography that we feel may damage our public identity are kept private. (Goffman, 1963)

Throughout life we necessarily perform for many audiences; deliberately, intuitively, or unconsciously, we always play roles. Our conduct is usually oriented toward a certain audience whose judgment is valued. In our complex society we perform for different audiences depending on the particular activity. To understand behavior, then, it is imperative to determine the audience with which individuals identify in any course of action. The audiences for which the individual performs "may be on the scene or far away; they may be specific other persons, or they may be generalized as to be the equivalent of 'they' or 'the Gods'; or they may be alive or long dead ('what would she have said?') or as yet unborn ('what will they say?')." (Strauss, 1969:34)

We are able to engage in concerted action only because we share common understandings and are able to anticipate others' intentions. We all ascribe meaning and see ourselves from the standpoint shared by the participants in the transaction. This common standpoint may be referred to as a perspective or "an organized view of one's world, what is taken for granted about the attributes of objects, of events, and of human nature." (Shibutani, 1962:130) Once we incorporate the culture of a group, we adopt its perspective and use it to deal with new situations that are encountered.

It is obvious that everyone can develop a variety of perspectives. As William James has written:

> ... we may practically say that (the person) has as many different social selves as there are distinct *groups* of persons about whose opinion he cares. He generally shows a different side of himself to each of these different groups. Many a youth who is demure enough before his parents and teachers, swears and swaggers like a pirate among his "tough" young friends. We do not show ourselves to our children as to our club companions, to our customers as to the laborers we employ, to our masters and employers as to our intimate friends. (James, 1925:128-29)

The structural and social complexity of Canadian society brings many of us, in the various aspects of our lives, into contact with others whose behavior and ways of organizing experiences are different from ours. We are continually introduced into and participate in different social worlds, and as a result, we may recognize a number of reference groups to help us organize our activity in the various situations we encounter. Although these perspectives may lead to conflicting definitions of the situation and make it difficult to decide on the appropriate course of action, our lives in a pluralistic society become compartmentalized, or separated into detached categories. Compartmentalization allows us to shift from one perspective to another as we move through a variety of unrelated transactions. For example, although religious individuals may adhere to a set of religious tenets that forbid them to take advantage of their fellow men they, nonetheless, may learn to rationalize cheating on their income tax returns.

While we are generally able to cope with the contradictory demands and expectations in our lives, we are sometimes caught in situations in which such conflicts cannot be resolved. Regardless of what we do, it is impossible to avoid violating the norms of one reference group. This is often true when we occupy a marginal position between two or more social worlds and have no clearly defined role. The concept of "marginal man" was originally developed for discussions of ethnic and minority groups, but it is also applicable to situations concerning other reference groups. This concept is described by Everett Stonequist when he says:

> The marginal man . . . is one who is poised in psychological uncertainty between two (or more) social worlds; reflecting in his soul the discords and harmonies, repulsions and attractions of these worlds, one of which is often "dominant" over the other; within which membership is implicitly if not explicitly based upon birth or ancestry (race or nationality); and where exclusion removes the individual from a system of group relations. (Stonequist, 1961:8)

A "conflict of interest" arises when people are involved in two or more groups. For example, the child of an immigrant (Park, 1950) and the factory foreman (Wray, 1949) both play roles that are particularly susceptible to incompatible expectations. Stouffer's discussion of the noncommissioned officer illustrates the dilemma of a person who plays this role. The "noncom":

> . . . had the role of agent of the command and in case the orders from above conflicted with what his men thought was right and necessary, he was expected by his superiors to carry out the orders. But he was also an enlisted man, sharing enlisted men's attitudes, often hostile attitudes, toward the commissioned ranks . . . the system of informal controls was such as to reward him for siding with the men in a conflict situation and punish him if he did not . . . on the other hand, open and flagrant disobedience by him of an order from above could not be tolerated by the command. (Stouffer, 1949:707)

Such dilemmas and contradictions in status force us to choose between reference groups. Several researchers (Festinger, 1952; Merton, 1957:288-92) have considered the basis on which such a choice is made. A symbolic interactionist view suggests that the choice of definitions is determined by the importance we attach to those individuals regarded as representatives ("significant others") of reference groups. We are more likely to adopt one group's perspective if we have favorable feelings toward its members. If we are treated in a friendly and sincere manner by a group and, with time, come to identify with its members, we feel obligated to comply with its ways under most circumstances.

Religious conversion is an excellent example of the process in which the perspective of one reference group is substituted for the viewpoint of another. Although only mildly interested in the new group at first, religious recruits find themselves becoming increasingly involved in a new set of activities. Those who share their new interests are either members of the group or other newcomers. The conversion is usually marked by a period of frustration and conflict, and as a result, the converts often reject their families and friends. As new group members, the recruits learn to reclassify their experiences. They form new concepts of themselves and see themselves from the perspective of the new reference group (Festinger *et al.*, 1956; Lofland, 1966; Shaffir, 1974).

It is important to stress the fact that our identity is actively shaped and reshaped. It is not something acquired solely at birth, remaining fixed and static. Identity is rooted in other people, situations, and places, and as these change, so do our self-conception and the image others have of us. Erikson put this aptly when he said that a sense of identity 'is never gained nor maintained once and for all. Like a good conscience, it is constantly lost and regained. . . . " (Erikson, 1954:57)

Unlike psychoanalytic theories, which focus on personal change and development and regard these as being essentially rooted in our early childhood, a sociological approach or, more specifically, a symbolic interactionist perspective, more willingly takes into account the way in which our sense of identity changes as we are affected by our interpretation of experiences in different social situations. Symbolic interactionists focus on the changes in our social contacts and experiences which culminate in modifications in our sense of identity.

While the symbolic interactionist perspective recognizes that we determine our actions, the influence and power that others have over us must not be understated. We are not concerned here with describing the unequal influences in social relationships, but the implications of these aspects of social life are nevertheless important in any discussion of identity transformation. While some people try to project a certain identity but discover that others only respond to it reluctantly, others discover that in spite of their resistance their identity is transformed and they come to be seen as different from what they were.

Another point which needs emphasis is that self-identity and group identity are constructed. They are made and remade, altered and refined, disrupted and negotiated through the interactional process. Through our interactions, identities are forged and validated, but always with the threat and/or promise of change or reconstruction.

The construction and management of personal identity is a continuous concern to us all, but certain people are more immediately confronted with the need to define themselves than are others. We can understand this more clearly if we focus our attention on those who find themselves, more frequently than most, trying to maintain, restore, and reconstruct their identity. The identity problem of physically handicapped people is an appropriate example.

In a useful paper, Fred Davis analyzes the initial encounters between visibly handicapped people (crippled limbs, a hunched back, blindness, a scarred face) and "normals" (1961). The latter are so uncomfortable during the encounter that they display a variety of disturbed reactions. Unless the handicapped person has developed a set of tactics to deal with the reactions of the normal people, the interaction between them becomes strained. As Davis has shown, the visible handicap has a "tendency to become an exclusive focal point of the interaction". Handicapped people soon realize that the infirmity poses a threat to any social relationships. They are always seen as "different", "odd", "estranged from the common run of humanity", and in short, "other than normal". (Davis, 1961: 122) In attempting to develop normal social relationships, the handicapped must see to it that other people recognize their "normal" attributes. But, as Davis claims, "there is frequently felt to be an unsettling discordance between these and the handicap. Sociable interaction is made more difficult as a result because many normals can only resolve the seeming incongruity by assimilating or subsuming (often in a patronizing or condescending way) the other attributes to that of the handicap...." (Davis 1961:122)

Defined and treated as though they were basically different people, the handicapped try to construct and maintain a stable identity in their interactions with others. Unlike most of us, their claim to be a certain kind of person and desire to be regarded in a particular way is met with considerable resistance. As a result, they are faced with the ever-present problem of assuming a personal identity and hoping that it will be ratified by others.

The physically handicapped try to disavow their abnormalities and want others to respond to them as they would to those individuals not so defined. However, if "normal" people are considered deviant in some way, they may also be treated as special kinds of people, different from the rest of us. Because they are tagged with a deviant label such as "fairy", "crazy", or "dope fiend", they are seen and treated differently than they want to be. Labeled, defined, and treated as deviant, such people are virtually forced to alter their personal identity to correspond with the image projected by the reaction of others. They then come to see themselves as they believe they are seen by others.

The deviant status is a "master" status; once identified, it becomes the controlling factor in the way we recognize people. The persons are first identified as deviant regardless of the other qualities or skills they may have. Hughes distinguishes between master and auxiliary statuses (1945: 353-59); by this he means that some statuses in our society override other statuses.

Hughes also contends that while most statuses have one key trait that distinguishes those who belong from those who do not, there are also a number of informally expected characteristics. He cites as an example the fact that in American society a doctor is expected to be white, male, upper-middle class, and Protestant. Becker borrows these distinctions from Hughes, to show that a similar process occurs in the case of deviant statuses. As Becker writes, "Possession of one deviant trait may have a generalized symbolic value, so that people automatically assume that its bearer possesses other undesirable traits allegedly associated with it." (Becker, 1963:33) As many sociological studies (Becker, 1963; Lemert, 1951; Ray, 1961) have shown, "treating a person as though he were generally rather than specifically deviant produces a self-fulfilling prophecy. It sets in motion several mechanisms which conspire to shape the person in the image people have of him." (Becker, 1963:34)

In our society, as in others, the task of dealing with people who are designated as different, or as outsiders, has been given over to specialized agencies. Our society maintains a host of public institutions that remove unwanted individuals from the public view. Many of these institutions are responsible for resocializing and rehabilitating their charges so that they may return to society as productive people. Often during this process the staff of these institutions attempts to reconstitute the person's self-concept. The institutional life itself strongly affects the inmate's identity. As Goffman has written:

> The recruit comes into the establishment with a conception of himself made possible by certain stable social arrangements in his home world. Upon entrance, he is immediately stripped of the support provided by these arrangements. In the accurate language of some of our oldest institutions, he begins a series of abasements, degradations, humiliations, and profanations of self. His self is systematically, or often unintentionally mortified. He begins some radical shifts in his *moral career*, a career composed of the progressive changes that occur in the beliefs that he has concerning himself and significant others. (Goffman, 1961:14)

Garfinkel's work on the institutional procedures that can reduce and degrade an individual through moral indignities shows how identity transformation and reconstitution has come to be systematically organized (1956). His study suggests the way in which a successful denunciation must be organized to be most effective, and draws attention to the consequences for the denounced person:

> The work of the denunication effects the recasting of the objective character of the perceived other: the other person becomes in the eyes of his condemners literally a different and *new* person. It is not that the new attributors are added to the old "nucleus". He is not changed, he is reconstituted. The former identity, at best, receives the accent of mere appearance. In the social calculus of reality representations and tests, the former identity stands as accidental; the new identity is the "basic reality". What he is now is what, "after all," he was all along. (Garfinkel, 1956:421-22)

Social deviants are defined, labeled, and treated as if they were different. This may not lead only to a reconstruction of self; as they are denied success, status, and a sense of belonging to conventional groups in society, deviants may come to accept the deviant identity and become committed to a deviant career.

Career, Status, and Identity The concept of career is important in understanding both deviant and conventional behavior. Its greatest value, for our purposes, lies in the link it forms between individuals and social organizations. It ties the individual and the self to society and its organizations and institutions.

A career is the movement of individuals through the structure of society. The various stages signal people's changing status and identity (such as graduation and marriage) and enable them to see themselves as moving along a continuum. Objectively, a career consists of the passage through various statuses, roles, and positions. Subjectively, a career is made up of people's perceptions of themselves as they move through different groups, organizations, and institutions (Hughes, 1958; and Strauss, 1972).

Careers take place in organizational frameworks, where people are processed and the processing and socializing into roles and statuses affect their self-images. Many careers take place in bureaucratic settings or "people-processing institutions", such as schools or work organizations. These institutions deliberately attempt to influence people's beliefs and actions.

As our society becomes increasingly differentiated and secularized, we more often are given a social identity by official agents and institutions. We are moved through school and work organizations which rate and evaluate us, and certify us with an institutionally approved identity. In a "credential" society these institutional badges are labels or passports defining who we are and what we are meant to be.

Individuals are linked to the social order and their sensitivity and consciousness of self are shaped by their social position—the statuses ascribed to them as part of their birthright (sex, religion, ethnicity, social class), the statuses and roles they subsequently assume, and those social worlds in which they participate. People live and define their lives and selves in terms of the subjective definition of situations that evolve out of the interactions they have with others. Out of the mutual process of defining and redefining the meaningful elements of situations, they evolve social structures and self-conceptions.

Persons who occupy a common rank generally tend to relate to one another and dissociate themselves from those of higher or lower statuses. They set themselves apart, limiting their participation in certain activities and restricting their associations to certain people; as they establish and maintain these differential relationships they tend to constitute a status group. These status groups operate within a structure of social classes, and a hierarchy of power and authority that divides them into many overlapping groups and categories.

Stratification systems are defined in terms of the mobility within and between class and status groups and the clarity of the boundaries between the different groups. Open societies possess a relatively free movement of individuals within a class structure that is based primarily on competition and achievement or merit. Closed societies are character-ized by their restricted opportunities of social mobility, with placement depending primarily on ascribed or inherited qualifications.

Social class and status-group membership provides potential bases for distinctions between groups leading to differences in behavior, group consciousness, identification, and collective action. Karl Marx believed that the sharing of experiences and interests would lead to class con-sciousness and political action because of the conflicting interests of capitalists and workers.

The extent of class consciousness depends on the particular period in a nation's history. Workers are more likely to develop a sense of collec-tivity when threatened, as, for example, during deflationary and depres-sion years. Membership in other groups, however, cuts across both class membership and status identification, creating conflicting groups of refer-ence. Regional, religious, ethnic, social, occupational, and community loyalties modify or minimize the primacy of class or status interests and blur or suppress class consciousness.

The relationship of status, role, and identity is important. Status is the rank or position of an individual in a group, or of a group in relation to other groups. Role is the behavior expected of a person who occupies a certain status, and involves enacting the duties and privileges of a status. Both status and role are integral components of identity.

Our society emphasizes the idea that status and role can be attained through merit, and overlooks the importance of ascribed status to careers. In this hypothetically free and open system, success, as measured in material worth, is equivalent to merit, and consequently, self-worth is largely predicated on economic success.

An examination of identity in Canadian society must take into account the myriad of sources of association and identification. Our self-image and identity are two concepts intricately intertwined in the interactions we have with those around us and in a complex society such as ours, the construction of identity is a complicated matter. There are, of course, some perceived sources of identification that are more important than others. Chief among these sources are our identifications with important reference groups. The primary reference group associations are those with which we identify closely and, as such, are important in terms of our self-image.

To broaden our awareness of the importance of reference group orientations to behavior and identity two orientations have been chosen for closer study: ethnicity, which is ascribed (granted at birth), and occupation, an achieved source of identity. At the same time we will be introduced to an appreciation of the way these institutions—ethnic culture and work—relate to and are part of other social structures of the community and society.

Through a discussion of individual and group identities in these institutions, we should begin to have both a theoretical and practical understanding of the dynamics of identity construction within the social structure of the institutions of which we are a part.

Ethnic Groups, Assimilation, and Identity

The concept of identity is important to the study of ethnic groups, and the concept of ethnic group is equally important to the study of Canadian identity. We begin our understanding of ethnic groups by emphasizing that human beings interact more in terms of the conceptions that they form of themselves and others than in terms of what they actually are. (Shibutani and Kwan, 1965:38) As W. I. Thomas indicated long ago, what people do depends on their definition of the situation, and it follows that what people believe to be real becomes real in its consequences. For example, some people believe in the significance of genetic inheritance, by which "various modes of thought and action are believed to be inherited from one's ancestors." (Shibutani and Kwan, 1965:39) People who believe they are genetically related often assume that they are alike and can understand each other in ways that outsiders cannot.

An ethnic group, by definition, consists of people who conceive of themselves as belonging to a special group and sharing particular attributes. This idea is reflected in the following statement from the *Report of the Royal Commission on Bilingualism and Biculturalism: The Cultural Contribution of the Other Ethnic Groups:*

> What counts most in our concept of an "ethnic group" is not one's mother tongue, but one's sense of belonging to a group, and the group's collective will to exist. Ethnic origin, be it French, British, German, Italian, or any other category, implies only biological affiliation and ancestry: an individual's loyalty to a group should . . . depend far more on his personal identification with it. To stress ethnic origin as a basic principle for shaping society would create closed groups based on accidents of birth. An "ethnic group" is consequently much more than a statistic based on one's ethnic origin; much more than the total number of individuals of the same origin; it is a force which draws its vitality from its members' feeling of belonging to the group. (1969:7)

A discussion of ethnicity and personal identity from a symbolic interactionist perspective recognizes that a person's ethnic self-conception evolves in the course of interaction with others. Similarly, an understanding of the way in which an ethnic group maintains a certain image among its members implicitly involves an analysis of the group's position in the larger community. Although numerous studies focus on the culture of the ethnic group, they often neglect the fact that ethnic groups are involved in a common social system, and that what happens to each group must be understood in the context of inter-ethnic contacts. During, and as a result of inter-ethnic contacts, a system of ethnic stratification evolves. This often results in ethnic groups that direct themselves or are directed into particular kinds of work and living areas. On the basis of their limited contacts with members of ethnic groups, members of the dominant society form views and impressions of ethnic groups. Regardless of their accuracy, these impressions are an important base from which the ethnic group's social organization evolves. As members of the ethnic group are exposed and become attuned to outsiders' beliefs about them, and as the evolved system of ethnic stratification becomes self-sustaining, a commonly held set of beliefs about the group is developed. These beliefs critically affect the image that members of the ethnic group form of themselves.

In all systems of ethnic stratification, people are divided into categories on the basis of their presumed similarities of character and background, and whole categories of people (an ethnic group) are ranked in an economic and status hierarchy. Although systems of ranking are often based on exploitation, the institutional arrangements continue to be maintained in many cases because they rest on a socially derived consensus. Out of these social interactions evolve sets of expectations, norms, and rules governing the relationship between the members of the different categories. The literature describing the development and maintenance of such systems of ethnic stratification is considerable and focuses on the dynamics of stereotyping, prejudice, and discrimination. As Vallee has written, this literature is "... concerned mostly with how difficult it is for stigmatized groups to narrow the gap between themselves and a dominant group because of the heavy weight of misunderstanding and dislike bearing down upon them." (Vallee, 1975:191) This research emphasizes that people's actions depend on their definition of the situation.

Human beings not only classify objects and events, but they also place both themselves and others in categories.* Human beings are generally classified into social types and they use these types to try to anticipate what the people they encounter are likely to do. Examples of commonly recognized social types include the student, the businessman, the entertainer, and the delinquent. Each social group has its own repertoire of social types.

Ethnic stereotypes are social types whose meanings have been shaped in social interaction. They are over-simplified, standardized, and in some respects distorted images that are applied to the entire ethnic group. "People in a well-established ethnic group develop a distinctive culture," write Shibutani and Kwan, "and outsiders pick out conspicuous traits and exaggerate them to construct a shorthand depiction of them." (Shibutani and Kwan, 1965:86)

It has been shown that there is usually, though not always, a high degree of agreement on the stereotypes that are assigned to a specific group. In a pioneer study, Katz and Braly (1933) recorded the consensus among American college students who were asked to characterize various ethnic groups and nationalities. The Irish, for example, were seen as very religious, quick-tempered, pugnacious, witty, and honest. Jews, on the other hand, were regarded as industrious, shrewd, ambitious, intelligent, and grasping. When students, in one of the author's courses on ethnic relations, were recently asked to describe how various ethnic groups were typically viewed in the larger society, responses, numbering approximately two hundred, were highly consistent. The adjectives most frequently used to characterize Canadian Indians included: poor, alcoholic, lazy, shiftless, and present-oriented. Italians were seen as manual laborers, affiliated with the underworld, loud and fiery-tempered, whereas persons from Pakistan were thought of as smelly, lazy, lacking in ambition, and involved in marginal work.

Ethnic stereotypes may be regarded as a set of beliefs about an ethnic group. In his study of prejudice, Ehrlich suggests that "stereotypes provide a common language of discourse for prejudiced persons." (Ehr-

---

*Much of the discussion on stereotypes is adapted from Shibutani and Kwan, Ethnic Stratification: A Comparative Approach (New York: Macmillan, 1965), Ch. 4.

lich, 1973:21) Stereotypes or categorical judgments about others are learned as are attitudes of prejudice. Stereotypes, prejudice, and discrimination lie in an unholy alliance, each serving to reinforce the others and justify differential behavior toward the minority group.

In its most common usage, prejudice is defined as an unfavorable ethnic attitude. Literally, the word means "prejudgment", but prejudice is hardly an informed judgment; rather, it is based on emotion and bias. According to Louis Wirth, prejudice is "an attitude with an emotional bias." (Wirth, 1944:303)

Prejudice is an attitude, learned through socialization. As they are commonly used today, the terms ethnic and racial prejudice refer to several distinct elements that are emphasized by writers on the subject. Many have insisted that a prejudiced attitude is mainly irrational, rigid, and immutable. Marden and Meyer define prejudice as "an attitude unfavorable or disparaging of a whole group and all the individual members of it based upon some elements of irrationality" (Marden and Meyer, 1962:31), and Simpson and Yinger claim that it is "an emotional, rigid attitude toward a group of people." (Simpson and Yinger, 1965:13)

Prejudice must be distinguished from discrimination. Whereas the former refers to subjective feelings, the latter deals with overt behavior. Discrimination refers to the unequal treatment of people or groups. In the words of Robin Williams, discrimination is "the differential treatment of individuals considered to belong to a particular social group." (Williams, 1947:39) Prejudice and discrimination, however, are not perfectly correlated. Although our attitudes and overt behavior may sometimes be consistent, there is often a discrepancy between our words and actions. In his presidential address to the Society for the Study of Social Problems, Deutscher stated that "no matter what one's theoretical orientation may be, he has no reason to expect to find congruence between attitudes and actions and every reason to expect discrepancies between them." (Deutscher, 1966:247) It is, therefore, possible to be prejudiced but not translate that prejudice into discriminatory behavior. For example, prejudiced people may believe that Métis are inferior and highly unreliable, but because of a commitment to democratic ideals they are prepared to allow Métis to live in their neighborhood and join associations to which they belong. The reverse is also possible; there can be discrimination without any feelings of prejudice. For example, in spite of their humanitarian ideals, building superintendents may be forced to deny accommodation to black families because of expected reactions from other tenants. In spite of the imperfect relationship between prejudice and discrimination, many forms of discrimination are the simple outcome of prejudice. Most often, equality of treatment is based on an unprejudiced view, and discrimination is related to varying levels of prejudice.

An ethnic group's ability to maintain itself and be seen in a positive way by its members is related to the image of the group formed by outsiders. It is in this sense that the previous discussion of stereotypes, prejudice, and discrimination is important. The tenability of the ethnic group is in some measure influenced by the nature of its relationship with a larger society. If the group and its members are viewed negatively, then the response of some of the group members to stereotyping and discrimination may be self-hatred. (Lewin, 1935:186-200) Realizing that they are identified with an ethnic minority having negative characteristics and a subordinate status determined by the large society, members become ashamed of their own group; they may even despise it, and try to eliminate or deny having the incriminating characteristics.

A less extreme adaptation to minority status is acculturation, whereby members of the ethnic group try to acquire the culture of the dominant group in the society. During the acculturation phase, the individual continues to regard his ethnic group as the point of reference from which to interpret events and define situations. Acculturation may, in time, give way to assimilation, whereby the values of the dominant group are acquired and the ethnic group is seen from an outside standpoint. The decisive change that occurs in assimilation is the displacement of reference groups. (Shibutani and Kwan, 1965:504)

Several writers have pointed to the different kinds of responses ethnic and minority groups can make as they react to the derogatory conceptions and differential treatment accorded them by the larger society (Elliot, 1971; Kurokawa, 1970). The specific response is strongly related to the society's tolerance for people with different customs and traditions. The extent of this tolerance greatly affects the ethnic group's ability to maintain itself as well as to cultivate a distinctive and shared ethnic identity among its members.

The way in which individuals identify themselves is significant, for their actions are directly related to their self-conception. An individual's self-conception, however, is not constructed in isolation from others, but is, as we have argued, closely connected to the approval of others or to the ratification of the individual's self-concept. Although a group of people may wish to be recognized as belonging to a particular ethnic group, established members of that group may deny them access and reject their ethnic self-conception. Alternatively, there may be people who wish to dissociate themselves from a particular ethnic category but discover that outsiders continue to view them as members. Our conception of an ethnic group must take these dimensions into account. As Shibutani and Kwan argue, "an ethnic group consists of those who conceive of themselves as being alike by virtue of their common ancestry, real or fictitious, and who are so regarded by others." (Shibutani and

Kwan, 1965:47) Similarly, Glazer and Moynihan define an ethnic group as follows:

> Concretely, persons think of themselves as members of that group, with that name; they are thought of by others as members of that group, with that name; and most significantly, they are linked to other members of that group by new attributes that the original immigrants would never have recognized as identifying their group, but which nevertheless serve to mark them off, by more than simply name and association in the third generation and even beyond. (Glazer and Moynihan, 1963:13)

Identity Maintenance and the Transformation of Ethnic and Religious Communities As immigrants who believed they were part of a distinctive group with uniquely shared attributes migrated to and settled in Canada, ethnic and religious communities were formed. Immigrants with the same latent identities tended to live together and form neighborhoods and communities where they could speak their own language and follow their customs. These cultural ghettos, or ethnic enclaves, helped to protect the newcomers from the strangeness of the new society. They also helped to preserve and protect the old culture. (Kramer, 1970) It was only in the ghetto, among people of their own kind, that newcomers could retain their time-honored and earned identity and self-respect. In contacts with strangers in the larger society, individuals met with frustrations and discrimination, but in the ethnic colony they could maintain their group's traditions and ways of life. They could, for example, communicate in their native language, find food shops that served traditional dishes, and receive local and old-country news and gossip. The importance of the ethnic colony to the immigrant is described by Zorbaugh:

> In the colony he meets with sympathy, understanding and encouragement. There he finds his fellow-countrymen who understand his habits and standards and share his life experience and viewpoint. In the colony he has a status, plays a role in a group. In the life of the colony's streets and cafes, in its church and benevolent societies he finds response and security. In the colony he finds that he can live, be somebody, satisfy his wishes—all of which is impossible in the strange world outside. (Zorbaugh, 1929:141)

The insulation of the ethnic colony promotes a sense of ethnic identification, even for those individuals whose ties with the group are weak. In the early stages of the community's development, there is a group consciousness among people who are classified together and who see themselves as being alike. This feeling of unity arises as they recognize resemblances among themselves and differences from outsiders, and as the minority community reacts to the dominant society's discrimination and prejudice. This awareness is increased by readily evident means of identification such as the similarity of physical attributes, distinctive modes of dress, a common language, or special kinds of smells associated with particular foods. (Shibutani and Kwan, 1965:42)

A group consciousness involves a sympathetic identification with others in the same category. It is assumed that our own feelings and emotional reactions will be shared by others. We use the concept of social distance to describe degrees of intimacy and separation between individuals and groups. Social distance refers to the interactional barriers that may encourage or detract from social interaction. (Park, 1950:256-60) When social distance is small" ... people can enter imaginatively into one another's minds and share their experiences: they are able to sympathize with one another's pains, joys, sorrows, hopes and fears. Those who feel close to each other are more relaxed and tend to be less defensive, for each feels that he can understand those around him." (Shibutani and Kwan, 1965:42-43) Sharing a group consciousness can also lead to the conviction that outsiders are basically different and should be thought of and treated as such.

The ethnic community becomes an important reference group for new immigrants, and the community's underlying sentiments and ideology define their frame of reference. Members of the group perceive certain aspects of the world from the community's standpoint and this perspective is assumed by the other community members they meet in their everyday lives. Where a group consciousness exists, an individual's quest for recognition is largely confined to this distinct group. The community becomes an effective agency of social control. The extent to which individuals feel pressured to conform to the community's practices reflects the degree to which they identify with it. By identification we mean the person's subjective orientation to the community. A high degree of identification indicates that individuals will become what the community wants them to be. The more people identify with the community, the more control it has over them; the less people identify with the community, the less control the group has over their motivations, beliefs, and actions.

As members of the same ethnic group band together in immigrant colonies that grow with the influx from the old country, they form an almost autonomous society within the large society. The ethnic community, with its own cultural, religious, economic, and social institutions, develops a distinctive way of life.

An examination of ethnic communities indicates that while the normative goals and standards of the old country guide the behavior of the first-generation arrivals, these standards lose their importance by the second and third generations. The immigrants' children and grandchildren begin to take advantage of the educational and occupational opportunities for which their parents and grandparents were less equipped. In time the ethnic group is transformed.

In *The Urban Villagers*, a study of an Italian community in Boston, Gans discusses the new opportunities available to the second and third generation West Enders and notes that "they...will make it more difficult to maintain some of the traditional ways of life." (Gans, 1962:214) The assimilative influences of the new society, especially on the young, have been described in numerous studies (Gottlieb and Ramsey, 1964; Hapgood, 1966; Shibutani and Kwan, 1965; Whyte, 1943; Wirth, 1928).

Of the many societal institutions that help to assimilate ethnic minority group members into the larger culture, none, perhaps, is as effective as the public school. As children attend the dominant society's schools, they become more assimilated and in time the minority group members redefine themselves. The young become increasingly sensitive to the dominant society's values and try to become accepted by their new reference group (Shibutani and Kwan, 1965:504). As a result of the school's curricular and extra-curricular influences, the minority group members may begin to view their own people's ideas and customs as different, even odd or embarrassing.

In contrast, religious communities have been generally more successful at resisting assimilation into the larger society (Hostetler, 1968; Peters, 1971; Redekop, 1969; Shaffir, 1974). A common feature of religious communities is the attempt that members make to insulate themselves, both socially and culturally, from the larger society. Social and cultural insulation can be accomplished in a number of ways. The community may be physically isolated from urban areas, which helps to minimize the members' contact with outsiders. Groups, such as the Amish, may resist new scientific and technological innovations that they see as threats to their established way of life. The community may also try to keep sufficient control over the secular curriculum so that graduates will not face the strain of choosing between different sets of values and expectations.

Most religious communities attempt to organize and shape members' identities; community members are socialized to define themselves as certain kinds of people. While each religious community retains its own unique characteristics, most groups adopt similar strategies to ensure the community's persistence. One important and common practice in religious communities is the wearing of distinctive styles of dress, which fosters in members a symbolic identification both with the past and with the other people in the group.

In general, the strategies religious communities use to maintain their identity depend on insulation from the surrounding culture. Insulation is considered necessary to counteract the group's fear of gradual assimilation and eventual dissolution. By insulation we mean not only spatial separation but also a lack of social and cultural contact with individuals and ideas foreign to the group. While this strategy appears to be used by most religious communities, some have been more successful than others.

Some religious communities have tried to insulate themselves physically from the larger community by settling in rural areas, and in some cases, taking up agriculture. Insulation need not, however, involve complete isolation from city life, but the degree of social and cultural contact between members of the religious group and outside influences must be controlled. This is the case with a Jewish orthodox community, the Lubavitcher: its members have settled in cities, but the contact they have with the non-Lubavitch Jews and Gentiles is limited.

A comparison between the strategies that religious and ethnic communities use to preserve their distinctive ways of life provides useful insights into their relative success in identity maintenance. The extent to which the members are aware of and are actively involved in counteracting potential assimilative influences is important. Some religious communities have developed a series of strategies intended to help maintain their distinctive identity. Because they deliberately try to remain separate, religious communities are relatively successful at resisting the assimilative influences of the larger culture, and group members are better socialized and integrated into the community's way of life. Although ethnic communities may not actively try to become assimilated into the larger society, they are organized for persistence rather than resistance. To put it another way, the two kinds of communities can be distinguished by their *active* and *passive* attempts to forestall assimilation. The active response includes the organization of a series of institutions and activities to resist both the individual's and the community's immersion in the surrounding culture. This type of resistance is characteristic of religious communities. The passive response involves deliberate efforts of individuals or families not to adopt the dominant culture. Unlike religious communities, ethnic groups are not usually striving actively to ensure their survival.

Ethnic communities are usually assimilated into the larger society. While immigrants still retain much of the way of life of their native country, this life style becomes progressively less firmly grounded in the later generations. (Shibutani and Kwan, 1965) As the immigrants' children begin to take advantage of opportunities not available to their parents, the ethnic group is gradually transformed. Religious communities, however, may strictly limit the educational and occupational opportunities open to their young and are thus able to exert greater control over them. This helps ensure that succeeding generations will not differ markedly from previous ones.

The religious communities' continuance may be attributed to the *portability* of religious identity. Whereas ethnic identity tends to be grounded in the culture and life style of the home country and is thus more difficult to retain in a new land, the religious community's identity is firmly rooted in doctrinal belief, supported by an explicit ideology regulating everyday behavior, regardless of geographical location. As a result, immigrant communities are more likely to find it difficult to define and retain their characteristic identity as succeeding generations become less familiar with and less able to develop an intuitive rapport with the old country and its customs.

It is a curious fact, however, that some ethnic communities are more successful than others at maintaining a sense of identity among their members. While many ethnic groups maintain their distinctiveness over generations, others persist in form only, unable to hold the allegiance of the younger generation. These communities have a higher rate of assimilation, and community members become attracted to and influenced by the ways of the society's dominant group. This is not to say that the entire community is simultaneously overtaken by a wave of assimilation, but rather that certain individuals and families become increasingly unconcerned about and less committed to perpetuating the group's distinctive ways.

The degree to which ethnic communities are able to maintain their identity is related to assimilation. Assimilation, as we have already noted, includes a mental process in which the person experiences a change of reference groups. For example, when a person of Italian ancestry no longer thinks of himself as an Italian, but rather as a Canadian, he is on the way to becoming assimilated. Such a person gradually acquires the perspective of the dominant group, identifies with it, and performs for an audience other than the ethnic group. (Shibutani and Kwan, 1965:479) When the assimilation process occurs on a large scale within a minority group, the dominant society sometimes opposes it. Although the person wishing to assimilate may place little importance on his ethnic background, the social group into which he wishes to be accepted may reject his efforts and continue to identify him as a member of a particular group. For example, an Italian wishing to assimilate changes his name from Giovanni to Jones, moves into a fashionable upper middle class neighborhood, and surrounds himself with material possessions comparable to his neighbors', but discovers that these people still identify him as a "greasy wop".

To understand the factors that help accelerate or retard an ethnic group's assimilation, sociologists often focus on the group's social organization. An examination of ethnic groups and their communities in this country reveals that they are organized differently. Some ethnic communities are highly organized, giving members little reason for contact with outsiders: such groups are able to satisfy the members' various needs and desires within the community boundaries. Other ethnic communities, however, are less organized. While they may provide their members with certain facilities and satisfy some of their needs, their limited institutional facilities force members to turn to the larger society for a variety of goods and services.

In attempting to understand the way certain ethnic communities successfully maintain themselves and preserve an ethnic identity, Breton has introduced the concept of "institutional completeness". This concept refers to the degree to which the ethnic community can provide the services required by its members. If an ethnic community's institutional facilities were complete, members "would never have to make use of native institutions for the satisfaction of any of their needs, such as education, work, food, and clothing, medical care, or social assistance." (Breton, 1964:194) On the basis of data collected among immigrants from thirty different ethnic groups, Breton concludes that those ethnic communities with a high degree of institutional completeness are more successful in reinforcing ethnic interpersonal associations among their members, thus decreasing the need to develop personal contacts with members of the larger society. In other words, the more institutions an ethnic group possesses, the better are its chances of maintaining its membership and identity.

Breton's concept of institutional completeness is useful in analyzing the structure and persistence of ethnic communities, for it directs the researcher's attention to the community's structural organization. A study of the community's institutional facilities may lead to an explanation of the different degrees of success that ethnic groups have in maintaining a distinctive identity. It also provides a base from which the researcher may examine the social organization of other communities.

In contrast to the American ideal of the melting pot, in which ethnic groups are eventually absorbed into American life, Canada has adopted the ideal of the mosaic, which encourages ethnic diversity. The melting-pot view envisages the complete mixture of the various ethnic groups through intermarriage, resulting in the emergence of a new cultural being, the American. (Gordon, 1964) In Israel Zangwill's drama, *The Melting Pot*, one of the characters describes this process:

> America is God's crucible, the great Melting Pot where all the races of Europe are melting and re-forming! Here you stand, good folk, think I, when I see them at Ellis Island, here you stand in your fifty groups, with your fifty languages and histories, and your fifty blood hatreds and rivalries. But you won't be long like that, brothers, for these are the fires of God you've come to—these are the fires of God. A fig for your feuds and vendettas! Germans and Frenchmen, Irishmen and Englishmen, Jews and Russians—into the Crucible with you all! God is making the American. (Zangwill, 1909:37)

The Canadian concept of an ethnic mosaic implies, at the very least, a tolerance for ethnic diversity. While blending into the Canadian nation and contributing to a distinct national identity, ethnic groups are given the opportunity and encouragement to preserve their own cultural heritages and identities. The presence of many ethnic groups with well defined cultures is seen as an enrichment that Canadians can neither afford nor wish to lose. The following excerpt from the fourth book of the *Report of the Royal Commission on Bilingualism and Biculturalism* reflects this idea:

> The dominant cultures can only profit from the influence of these other cultures. Linguistic variety is unquestionably an advantage, and its beneficial effects on the country are priceless. We have constantly declared our desire to see all Canadians associating in a climate of equality, whether they belong to the Francophone or Anglophone society. Members of "other ethnic groups," which we prefer to call cultural groups, must enjoy these same advantages and meet the same restrictions. Integration, with respect for both the spirit of democracy and the most deep-rooted human value, can engender healthy diversity within a harmonious and dynamic whole. Finally, the presence of the other cultural groups in Canada is something for which all Canadians should be thankful. Their members must always enjoy the right—a basic human one—to safeguard their languages and cultures. The exercise of this right requires an extra effort on their part; for which their fellow Canadians owe them a debt of gratitude. Their presence facilitates communications between Canada and the rest of the world. Their cultural values find expression not only in popular traditions but also in arts and letters. In our opinion, these values are far more than ethnic differences; we consider them an integral part of the national wealth. We are, therefore, justified in our concern for "the cultural contribution of the other ethnic groups," and having studied it in some detail, proposing ways in which the cultural, social, economic, and political institutions of the country can respond to the legitimate aspirations of the members of the other cultural groups and provide them with opportunities for full development in a dynamic and prosperous Canada. (1969:14)

It is important for researchers to test the ideas expressed in this passage against empirical findings. Quoting again from the same report, we are told:

> ... there are a number of cultural groups in Canada with a clear sense of identity. They want, without in any way undermining national unity, to maintain their own linguistic and cultural heritage. They have their own associations, clubs, parishes, and religious organizations; they maintain their own schools and express their collective views through their own press. Some have formed highly active organizations—for example, the Canadian Jewish Congress and the Canadian Polish Congress. These organizations act as spokesmen for the group, may use the group's ancestral language, and create, as far as possible, a climate propitious to the maintenance of the group's own culture. (1969:8)

Further research on specific ethnic and minority groups will reveal the ability and desire of these groups to maintain themselves in the face of a dominant culture that threatens to absorb them.

Before concluding the discussion of ethnic groups and identity, it is important to note that if an ethnic community has an elaborate and complex formal organization, this does not necessarily imply that it will be successful in guarding against dissolution into the larger society. For example, an ethnic community's institutions and facilities may remain long after they have ceased to serve their original purpose. At the same time, third and fourth ethnic generations, whose involvement in ethnic institutions may be minimal and whose life style involves them in personal relations outside the ethnic community, may show strong interests in, and sincere feelings for their ancestral heritage. As we indicated at the outset, we need a clearer understanding of ethnic community life, including the process by which such communities are maintained or dissolved. Such an understanding will result primarily from studies in which the researcher attempts to gain an understanding of the ways the people under study attempt to organize the perspectives which help to order their everyday lives.

Occupational Careers and Identity

> ...A man's work is one of the more important parts of his social identity, of his self; indeed, of his fate in the one life he has to live, for there is something almost as irrevocable about choice of occupation as there is about choice of mate. (Hughes, 1958:314)

In a highly industrialized society there is perhaps no single more important claim to status, prestige, power, and identity than a person's job. Occupational identification is a most important source of self and collective images and attributes, and is the main factor that a capitalist society uses to rank and distinguish its members. The study of work or occupations is important in understanding identity because most people spend a large proportion of their time working; a high value is placed on work in our society; money, power, status, and esteem are derived from work; and work contributes to the development of personal and collective attributes and identities.

Studies of occupations have reaffirmed the symbolic interactionist principle that personal identity is not fixed and permanent, but is constantly and often subtly changing (Becker, 1968; Blankenship, 1973; Geer, 1973; Hughes, 1927; Salaman, 1971). Socialization continues throughout the life cycle. (Becker and Strauss, 1956; Brim, 1966) We change as we develop new associations with significant others and as we learn the distinct occupational cultures of which we become part. As we are socialized into an occupational career, we come to see ourselves from a new standpoint, as possessing certain occupational attributes.

Our work is one of the main factors by which we are defined and judged. It is not mere coincidence that upon meeting someone for the first time we are interested in finding out what work they do. Our jobs serve as identity badges that inform others about us. It follows, then, that work is one of the more significant means of judging ourselves and others.

The importance of these identity badges is evident in the labels people use to describe the kind of work they do. Examining this idea, E. C. Hughes writes:

> Hear a salesman, who has just been asked what he does, reply, "I am in sales work," or "I am in promotional work," not "I sell skillets." School teachers sometimes turn schoolteaching into educational work, and the disciplining of youngsters and chaperoning of parties into personnel work. Teaching Sunday School becomes religious education, and the Y.M.C.A. Secretary is "in group work." Social scientists emphasize the science end of their name. These hedging statements in which people pick the most favorable of several possible names of their work imply an audience. And one of the most important things about any man is his audience or his choice of available audiences to which he may address his claim to be someone of worth. (Hughes, 1951:313)

As Hughes suggests, we should remember that people's work is an important aspect of their social identity. Realizing that they will be judged by what they say they do for a living, people may attempt to describe their work in the most favorable terms possible.

Often we make judgments about others based on occupational stereotypes. These stereotypes or categorical judgments extend into our definitions of individuals, and often provide us with the initial bases for dealing with others. In his article, "Dilemmas and Contradictions of Status" (1945), E. C. Hughes considers the way we initially judge others based on the work they do. Drawing a distinction between master and auxiliary status traits, Hughes notes that most statuses have one key trait distinguishing those who belong from those who do not. For example, whatever else they may be, surgeons are people with a certificate stating that they have fulfilled certain requirements and are licensed to practice medicine. This, then, is the master trait. However, as Hughes points out, we expect, informally, that surgeons in our society will possess a number of auxiliary traits: most people expect them to be upper middle class, male and white. We assume that certain auxiliary traits naturally follow from the master status trait. The assignment of traits or stereotypes is learned in the course of socialization.

Although the stereotypes assigned to members of occupational categories may be inaccurate, and are largely a product of ignorance, they do serve a function in social life. Stereotypes, as we have described in our discussion of ethnic groups, allow us to construct a shorthand picture of people about whom we have little information. This gives a preliminary structure and stability to ambiguous social settings and interactions. Judgments based on occupational stereotypes make it possible for people to organize their world and anticipate more effectively the beliefs and actions of the people they encounter. Although the stereotypes may be inaccurate, the fact that they are familiar to all facilitates interaction at one level of understanding.

The images that certain occupations conjure up in our minds become part of the initial and superficial classifications that provide background expectations for defining other people. These images enable us to align our own actions with the interests and perspectives of others. Alfred Schutz gives us an example of this process when he writes:

> If I observe, or even hear about, a man tightening a nut, my first interpretive scheme will picture him as joining together two parts of an apparatus with a wrench. The further information that the event has taken place in an automobile factory permits me to place the operation within the total context of "automobile manufacturing". If I know in addition that the man is an auto worker, then I can assume a great deal about him . . . . (Schutz, 1967:192-93)

Because we live in a symbolic environment in which objects are classified and labeled, we are able to interact with strangers simply by placing them in the proper category. When the knowledge that the participants have of one another is impersonal, social interaction can occur only where the social structure is well established and where conventional roles are clearly defined.

We have noted that sociologists use the term "social distance" to describe relationships varying from the very intimate to the superficial. Where social distance is great, knowledge of the other party is highly specialized. People are approached or avoided on the basis of being seen as members of a particular category; they come to be known only as performers of certain roles. For example, we initially know very little about the tellers at a bank except that this is what they do for a living. Similarly, the bartender to whom we regularly nod is known to us only as a bartender. We are able to enter into collective action with these people precisely because we have placed them in the proper category and we know what to expect of them. In each instance, however, the personal qualities of the other party remain irrelevant or of minor importance. The transaction between us and the other person unfolds smoothly simply because we resort to categorizations and know how the other should be addressed and treated.

As our knowledge about a particular category of workers, such as bus drivers, becomes more personal and direct, the social distance may be reduced. If we come to know a bus driver more intimately, we recognize the person as having a unique set of characteristics. Whereas in the past this bus driver was regarded solely in terms of the service he provided, and as a representative of a class, we now realize that he is an individual. We are able to establish an identification with others and regard them as human beings as opposed to objects with a function precisely when our knowledge about their personal characteristics increases.

The perceptions and secondary (impersonal) relations we have with a host of workers, such as medical doctors, clergymen, lawyers, politicians, teachers, policemen, professional criminals, car salesmen, or janitors, often reflect our necessary reliance on stereotypes and expected role performance. This secularization of social roles is characterized by impersonal relations with others and is becoming a feature of modern industrial life. Occupational images and stereotypes have a heightened importance because they are the basis for our actions with these distant, bureaucratic, and impersonal people.

We not only have conceptions about the nature or personality of people in certain occupations but we also assign them status, prestige, power, obligations, and responsibilities. Occupations provide us with roles in life and ready-made but changing sets of relationships with others. These relationships with other individuals and groups are often affected and influenced by the relative prestige and status of occupations.

Occupational Stratification By "division of labor" sociologists refer to an arrangement found in societies in which people perform different but interrelated tasks. The division of labor is also a common basis for social stratification in which people are classified in certain groups. Although stratification and the division of labor are features common to all societies, they vary in their degree of complexity. In preliterate societies, for example, the differentiation of workers is rudimentary, whereas in a modern industrial society such as Canada's, the division of labor is complex.

Not all occupations are equally desirable. Agents of socialization and of the media present some occupations in a favorable light, so that we learn that certain occupations are valued more highly than others. There are several rationales that help sustain occupational hierarchies. First, we are led to believe that some occupations require certain personal characteristics and skills that, in our society, are considered desirable. For instance, the status of the university professor is high because it is assumed that one must be intelligent to teach complex subjects to others, and intelligence is highly valued in our society. The status of a service station attendant is low because such work is not considered to require much intelligence but rather tolerance for boring routine—a quality we do not value highly.

Secondly, some kinds of work require a greater amount of formal preparation and training than others. A dentist, for instance, must have a number of years of specialized training, whereas a garbage collector needs no specialized education. We find that those occupations accorded the highest status are often those which call for the longest or most intensive preparation.

Another factor related to the social ranking of occupations involves their perceived social importance. Certain kinds of work are considered more important than others. Our society values the role of the physician more than that of the nurse, and rewards it much more substantially in prestige, income, and power. There is a remarkably high consistency in the prestige associated with occupations in different countries. In general, high evaluations and prestige accrue to professional occupations, or to jobs that involve decision-making responsibilities, whereas unskilled jobs receive low prestige rankings. (Blishen, 1971; Pineo and Porter, 1967)

Social philosophers have always been concerned with the "ideal" system of social stratification. Whereas Aristotle believed that some human beings were by nature slaves and others freemen, Rousseau, the French philosopher, felt that all men were free and equal until civilization corrupted the natural order. Since people's education, health, politics, and everyday life are affected by social inequalities, sociologists are interested in trying to understand this phenomenon.

The concept of social stratification, referring to structured social disparity, defies simple definition. Some sociologists contend that it is a system of structured inequality in the things that count in any given society. (Heller, 1969:4) Other sociologists refer to social stratification as the ranking of categories of people who share unequally in the distribution of power, prestige, and wealth. Sociologists differ in their definitions, and sociological opinion about the existence of systems of stratification is divided. The following two theoretical views that have guided sociological thought and research will illustrate the problem of defining stratification.

The article by Davis and Moore, "Some Principles of Stratification" (1945), presents the functionalist claim for the universal necessity of stratification, and explains why positions are ranked as they are in any particular system. Davis and Moore assert that social inequality is "an unconsciously evolved device by which societies insure that the most important positions are conscientiously filled by the most qualified persons." (Davis and Moore, 1945:243) Every society, they argue, has certain social positions that are functionally more important than others for that society's preservation and survival. These positions require different amounts of training and sacrifice. To ensure that the most important positions, which, according to the functionalists, require the greatest skill, will be filled, sacrifice and training are matched with the highest social rewards. In this way people are motivated to undertake the required training for these important roles. The uneven distribution of material rewards and prestige is functionally necessary because "every society needs a mechanism inducing people to occupy positions which are socially important and require training." (Davis and Moore, 1945:243)

Generally in Western societies, the status or prestige of an occupation is proportionate to the monetary reward. With some notable areas of exception (professional sports, entertainment, family inheritance), the ranking of prestige is presumably related to the functional importance of the work. Generally, within a work organization, people's positions in the hierarchy are directly related to the rewards they receive. In Canadian society, money is the symbolic measure of value and worth. The assumption that social inequality is a necessity has, of course, resulted in criticism of the functional explanation of stratification.

Sociologists, for example, have questioned whether it is even possible to rate positions by their social importance. Can we definitively state that dentists and lawyers are functionally more important than garbage collectors and street cleaners? Other critics have argued that social position is determined more by inheritance than by performance. Still other criticisms deal with the fact that some highly rewarded members of our society, like the pimp or gangster, are not seen by many as contributing to societal welfare, while other members who are relatively poorly remunerated, such as the social worker and teacher, undertake extensive study and are highly valued. Tumin (1963) argues that systems of social stratification function to limit the possibility of discovery of the full range of talent available in a society. The reason for this is that not everyone has the same access to motivation, channels of recruitment, and centers of training.

A second school of sociology leans heavily on the ideas of Karl Marx to explain capitalist societies' systems of stratification. According to Marxist theory, conflict underlies the stratification process. The upper classes strive to maintain their privileged and powerful positions by preventing the lower classes from appropriating the society's resources for themselves. By virtue of their position in the economic order, members of each class share common experiences as well as certain political and economic interests. The owners of the means of production (bourgeoisie) and the laborers (proletariat) are inevitably led to conflict because of their contradictory interests. The essential discord lies in the fact that the bourgeoisie exploits the proletariat, and the proletariat resists such exploitation. The conflict, as Marx sees it, is an unequal one since the owners control the system of supply and demand and are thus able to manipulate the workers. In spite of this inequality, the workers are seen as eventually winning the conflict. As they come to realize their common exploitation, the workers develop a class consciousness and band together to overthrow the owners and seize control of the means of production, thus ushering in a new form of social organization—the classless society.

Criticism of Marx's theory centers on his incorrect predictions, particularly the failure of the workers to organize themselves and see themselves as an exploited class. The polarization of classes has not taken place in Western society: it has been offset by changes in the society's organization. Instead of becoming progressively impoverished, the working class has seen an increase in its standard of living. The experience of several socialist nations in the twentieth century also conflicts with elements in the Marxian analysis. For instance, socialism in the Soviet Union has failed to prevent inequalities in wealth, power, and prestige; the experience of the kibbutz (collective settlement) in Israel has demonstrated that despite the absence of private ownership, hierarchies of prestige and power nonetheless emerge. These examples suggest that the abolition of private ownership may simply replace old disparities with new ones. Position in the division of labor is the chief determinant of status and identity for most people.

For many of us, our most important links with the social structure involve our career in the institutional and organizational structures of the society. An examination of institutional careers sheds light not only on people's views of their movement through the hierarchies, but also tells us something about the social structure of the society. According to Hughes:

> . . . a study of careers—of the moving perspective in which persons orient themselves with reference to the social order, and of the typical sequence and concatenations of office—may be expected to reveal the mature "working constitution" of a society. Institutions are but the focus in which the collective behaviour and collective action of people go on. In the course of a career the person finds his place within these forms, carries on his active life with reference to other people, and interprets the meaning of the one life he has to live. (Hughes, 1958:140)

There are considerable variations in the importance of occupation to identification, status, and commitment. The professions are conventionally thought to involve high levels of commitment, identification, and status because of their prestige and difficulty of entrance. At the other extreme, low status jobs, such as factory assembly line work, garbage pickup, maintenance, and cleaning, are considered dirty work and therefore involve low personal commitment, status, and identification. Generally speaking, those occupations that require the longest and most intensive socialization affect identities most strongly.

Work is experienced and defined in different ways. Peter and Brigitte Berger (1972:236-37) delineate three major ways in which individuals may experience work. Work is sometimes thought of as a vocation with which individuals identify and in which they experience a measure of human fulfillment. In opposition to the vocation is the type of work that involves human suffering and poses a threat to the individual's self-esteem. Most jobs fall somewhere in between; they are seen as tolerable but not particularly fulfilling.

Later in this book we examine the views that a variety of different workers have of themselves and their work. Some are committed to their work and place a high value on their activity and the self-esteem they derive from it. Others find little or no meaning in their work, as it affronts their dignity and moral worth. The effects of work on identity and sense of worth are profound because of the ever-present and invidious comparisons that are made with other individuals. For many, work is unpleasant, a coercion that people learn to accept. The more work is mechanized, dull, and routine, the more workers see it as satisfying only in terms of what they receive in exchange. The only visible basis for evaluation is the collection of objects that they own or use which gives them status. In this respect, some work is losing its importance as a means of defining identity. In its place is the money received in exchange for work, which in turn is used to obtain the visible objects of self-worth (status symbols).

In our society, a job, or the lack of a job, is often a stigma, a degradation, and we actively or passively deny that our personal worth is reflected in demeaning work or in our inability to find employment. Many people who work are degraded because they cannot do fulfilling work. Often they attempt to disclaim their lack of worth in the economic or occupational order by seeking other sources of identity and value in avocational pursuits or in the accumulation of status symbols. There are those job holders, such as auto workers, who resign themselves to working lives of misery but who rationalize their continual degradation as a sacrifice for their children, who thus will never have to pay such a price. (Chinoy, 1952) With the thousands of specialized occupations in our society the meaning of work, satisfaction with work, and identification and commitment to an occupation involve a host of contingencies, including work autonomy, prestige, reward, monotony, responsibility, tenure, working conditions, length of training, colleagues, employee benefits, advancement, and aspirations.

A society's division of labor may reflect other divisions in the society. Canada is a good example of this. Canada is a multi-ethnic society and an examination of the division of labor reveals that members of ethnic groups are not equally distributed throughout the occupational categories of the society. Certain ethnic groups are highly represented in certain categories but virtually absent in others. For example, according to the 1971 Canadian census, while only 10 percent of the Canadian male labor force was employed in the "construction trades occupations", 22 percent of the Italian male workers and 10 percent of the Polish workers were employed in this area. Only .03 percent of the Jewish male labor force was engaged in such work. Jewish male workers are concentrated mainly in the "managerial", "professional and technical", and "sales" categories, while Ukrainians are more often found in occupations relating to agriculture, the crafts, or factory work.

The concentration of ethnic groups into certain occupational categories is a feature common to all societies in which there are ethnic groups. There is usually some kind of allocation of tasks; arduous or unpleasant jobs are assigned to certain minority groups. In an attempt to organize historical and ethnographic accounts of the contacts among ethnic groups, Robert Park proposed a "race relations cycle" (1950). The essential argument advanced by Park is that first, groups come into contact; there invariably follows competition; eventually some kind of adjustment or accommodation is made; and, finally, there is assimilation. During the accommodation stage, the competition for jobs among people of various ethnic origins causes ethnic groups to move into different kinds of work. For example, in New England during the years between the world wars, a disproportionately large number of French Canadians were employed in cotton and wool mills, Poles in iron foundries, Italians in heavy ditch-digging jobs, Greeks in restaurant businesses, and Chinese in laundries, while "Yankees" operated the banks and brokerages. (Anderson, 1937)

Once an ethnic division of labor is established, people come to believe that certain kinds of people are naturally attracted to and suited for certain kinds of work. (Shibutani and Kwan, 1965) In reality, though, experiences in their countries of origin will determine the work done in the new land. Since 1945, most groups of immigrants to Canada have included relatively large numbers of the educated and skilled. Because of their backgrounds and familiarity with urban life, these immigrants may have less difficulty settling in Canadian society. However, many immigrants from economically less advanced countries such as Italy, Greece, and Portugal still come largely from rural areas, villages, and towns. The hardships that they meet resemble those of earlier immigrants from peasant backgrounds who settled in Canada.

Immigrant Italians with little formal education, for example, usually have to make drastic and dramatic changes as soon as they arrive. (Boissevain, 1970) Very few Italians can continue to be farmers or farm laborers, occupations they pursued in their native country. The labor market draws them to the cities to become day laborers in the industrial, construction, and transportation sectors of the economy. In this way, then, ethnic groups become associated with particular jobs.

In most cases the immigrant group eventually becomes acculturated and assimilated into the new society. Acculturation and assimilation involve, as we know, a profound change in the values and self-concepts of individuals. One way members of ethnic groups handle this conflict in values and identities is to take jobs that are controlled by members of their own ethnic group or that serve their group. Such work enables them to be among people with whom they can identify, among whom they can relax, and on whom they can count for sympathetic support. (Shibutani and Kwan, 1965:12) For instance, chassidic Jews who are not self-employed try to work for orthodox Jews who will understand their observance of Jewish holidays and give them the necessary time off. Individuals can preserve their ethnic identity by choosing occupations that will put them into contact with people of their own kind.

Some types of work evolve specifically to meet the particular wants and needs of an ethnic group. Ethnic enterprises help group members adjust to an alien environment, maintain their identity, and resist the assimilative forces of the larger society. Such services are discussed in the fourth volume of the *Report of the Royal Commission on Bilingualism and Biculturalism*:

> Often a substantial portion of a cultural group is employed in serving the particular wants of that group. They may provide goods and services that only members of their own ethnic group desire (such as Matzos and Kosher wine); or that the host society is hesitant to supply (such as haircuts for Negroes); or that the members of the group do not want to receive from strangers (such as religious or medical services); or that are especially related to immigration (such as travel agencies that help immigrants bring their relatives to Canada). Those who supply such goods and services often also furnish jobs for other members of the same group and teach them skills in the process, so that while they rise to middle-class status they also help others to rise. (1969:52)

Members of ethnic groups may resolve identity conflicts by entering either ethnic occupations or occupations in the dominant society. Processes of ethnic self-selection, and minority group discrimination or exploitation may affect the kind of economic or occupational relationship the immigrant has with the ethnic culture or the dominant society. Discrimination may prevent people from entering certain areas of employment because of their ethnic origin. For instance, the experience of the Jews illustrates this:

> Two cultural groups that have been the targets for discrimination, although they rank high in occupational status, are the Jewish and the

Japanese. The Jews also rank high in income, partly because many are self-employed business owners or professionals, and because members of the Jewish group are generally well educated. These high levels of self-employment and education are to some degree responses to discrimination. Of the Jewish non-agricultural male work force, 42 per cent are self-employed, compared to between 9 and 15 per cent self-employed for the British, French, Germans, Italians, Ukrainians, and all other origins taken together. Because they are self-employed, Jews tend to remain in the work force until late in life; 47 per cent of Jewish males 65 and over are in the labour force, compared to 28 per cent of Italians. They also enter the labor force late, because of their concern with education.

* * *

In the past certain occupations, including engineering and teaching, were considered to be virtually closed to Jews and as a result very few Jews even tried to become engineers or teachers. Since World War II most of these older barriers seem to have broken down, but research suggests that discrimination, or anticipation of discrimination, still influences the occupational distribution of Jews. Jews have specialized successfully as sub-contractors in the mechanical trades in Montreal, because Jewish engineers feel they have difficulty progressing as professionals and therefore turn to other applications of their training, such as mechanical contracting. Their firms then profit from being headed by persons with advanced professional training. The predominance of Jews in real estate development is also due in part to the impression that senior management positions in companies controlled by members of the predominant British or French groups are closed to them. (*Report of the Royal Commission on Bilingualism and Biculturalism*, Book IV, 1969: 66 and 63)

In sum, certain occupations attract and are filled by a disproportionately large number of people from particular ethnic groups. Once an ethnic division of labor emerges, it may be used to demonstrate that certain kinds of people are naturally suited for specific kinds of work. An unforeseen consequence of this division is that it reinforces and solidifies ethnic identity, and at the same time reinforces discriminatory attitudes among ethnic groups, and between ethnic groups and the dominant society.

Social Structure and Identity

People act within a larger network of other individuals, groups, and organizations. An important part of the sociological perspective is understanding the patterns and regularities of our constructed worlds. Concepts such as culture, social structure, and society emphasize the interdependent nature of individuals, groups, organizations, and institutions.

Any society develops mechanisms that coordinate different lines of activity and resolve or manage conflicting perspectives. The coordination of individual and group activities depends on collective definitions of reality and social order, and the way in which these definitions are maintained.

Social structure is created by people when they construct and fit lines of action into meaningful and regularized patterns. Society is organized when individuals and groups enter into reciprocal relations with one another. The structure or set of understandings about expected relationships exists as long as participants take it, and one another, into account. The structure is negotiated as the basis of coordinated activity shifts. New members and novel situations produce changes in which old definitions are reformulated and altered.

There are, of course, several conflicting constructions of social reality. Individuals view the social order through their own particular lenses. Their views are developed largely through the interactions they have had in the past with "significant others".

Social reality and identity then, are bound in perceptions, which themselves are colored by different experiences. One of the broader complexes of experiences that describe different sets of relationships with other groups in society is the social class. This concept is important for developing an understanding of social behavior and identity.

To understand the dynamics of Canadian society and identity, it is necessary to comprehend the patterns of conflict, cooperation, competition, and accommodation among various groups. Our conception of society depends on the active construction of reality, and the conduct of groups and individuals within these shared or disputed realities. The concept of a Canadian identity is, for example, real and continuous for some, but exists intermittently, rarely, or not at all for other people. The concept is heightened at some periods, confused or disrupted at others: it is an amorphous, changing phenomenon affected by situations, expectations, values, and historical events.

This section deals with three perceived attributes affecting personal and group identity. Firstly, we discuss socioeconomic positions, and the way that identity is affected by the disparity among these positions. Secondly, we discuss gender as a major source of identity, since sex roles are critical to the formation of personal and group identity. Lastly, we discuss the relationship of schooling to identity. Educational institutions are important "processors" that differentiate young people, and provide them with a base for self-comparison, a notion of success or failure, and a powerfully enforced and reinforced view of themselves.

Social Class and Identity To understand behavior and identity in Canadian society, it is useful to examine social inequality, and the important effects it has on the definitions of our selves and our social worlds. Social inequality is a feature of all capitalist societies, which are based on rewards, inequality, and social stratification. The economic or material inequities that characterize our society have important consequences in the patterns and degrees of influence and power possessed by individuals and groups at different socioeconomic levels.

Social stratification is a form of differentiation in which individuals are grouped into classes according to economic, social, and political criteria. A class, by definition, then, is a group of individuals with similar amounts of money, occupational prestige, and political and economic power. Members of a social class also share the same amount and quality of education. These shared situations lead to the development of similar norms, values, and life styles at the different levels of society.

Although membership in a social class usually includes indicators other than occupation, social class in the Canadian capitalist society is grounded in the division of labor. This complex society has many workers, managers, and owners with varying degrees of skill, authority, and reward. Social prestige and power are usually accorded to individuals in the more highly ranked social and occupational positions, and these positions are frequently passed on to descendants. As Porter (1965) and Clement (1975) have shown, Canadian society is being controlled by a political and economic elite that is self-perpetuating and restrictive. Ascribed (determined at birth) status is more important than achieved (earned) status for membership in the upper circles. Our place in the social hierarchy at birth, a position which is based on the status and prestige of our parents, determines the experiences and opportunities we will have. There is, therefore, an objective reality in class relationships.

Canadian society, however, emphasizes the possibility that status and roles can be achieved through merit, and de-emphasizes the importance of ascribed status to our career opportunities. There is an overall presumption that the system is based on the competition of individuals with equal opportunities and rights. In this idealized open system, success as measured by material worth is equivalent to merit, and consequently, self-worth is largely predicated on economic success.

A dominant myth is that Canada is both democratic and egalitarian. Obvious differences in wealth and power are explained by some sociologists as being related to the different contributions people make to the society. This thesis argues that members of a society are distributed throughout the labor market and must be motivated to perform their tasks competently. If all positions were of equal importance and equally rewarded, it would make little or no difference who performed the various jobs. Because this is not the case, "structural-functionalists" argue that a society must offer different rewards to motivate individuals to take on important tasks. Social inequality is thus a device by which societies ensure that important positions are conscientiously filled by qualified people. (Bendix and Lipset, 1966).

Social class differences then, are a reality that divides our society. The members of a class may or may not be sensitive to the fact that their economic interests and circumstances are similar. One possible consequence of their perception of a shared class situation is the development of a solidarity, a class consciousness. In such situations, members come to recognize that they share the same interests and problems, and develop similar beliefs about the world around them.

The existence and cogency of class consciousness in Canadian society seem to be limited, for the most part, to intermittent periods of crisis and depend upon the shared perception of individuals regarding their common position and problems. Although the feeling of class solidarity is sporadic for most Canadians, the underlying perception of class distinction is nevertheless a basic part of Canadians' perceptions.

The most basic and important disparity is economic. Inequality in economic power is reflected in the authority system of the work environment. Workers take orders; owners or managers give them. Economically superior people are also superior in status, while economic inferiors have a lower status. The status system is created by and reflects the class system, and it serves to insulate and protect the economically dominant from those beneath them.

In general, the working class has a dual perception of social reality. For the most part, Canadian workers accept the dominant culture and operate from a conservative political standpoint. In times of crisis, however, Canadian workers develop a more militant and collectivistic consciousness. (Gardner, 1976; Lipton, 1968; and Jamieson, 1968)

Many class differences in Canadian society are blurred and seen as cultural distinctions. The cultural mosaic philosophy of Canadian society tends to overlook class similarities and the disadvantages of minority groups, and emphasizes instead the richness, rarity, and societal integration of minorities in Canadian life. Minority groups tend to resist any collective approaches to resolving their class-based problems because of the emphasis on cultural diversity.

There is also a close relationship between class position and rank in the status hierarchy in Canada. A status group can be distinguished from a social class because it evolves as a group, and solidifies itself by restricting membership and monopolizing the status symbols that distinguish it from others. This dominant group sometimes excludes individuals who meet the group's criteria for membership economically, but who may not meet other standards. For example, wealthy and successful Jews may be denied full participation in W.A.S.P. clubs and organizations and often establish their own status hierarchy including exclusive residential areas, country clubs, and resorts.

Another important dimension of social stratification is the power structure. The unequal distribution of economic rewards in Canadian society is closely paralleled by the unequal distribution of power. Canadian society is unique in having both an external and internal elite that share similar economic interests. This relationship and some of its consequences are described by Leo Johnson when he says:

> ... the Canadian capitalist class consists of a small group of enormously powerful men whose structural relations are undergoing rapid change. Caught up in the ideology of growth and multi-nationalism, the small capitalist accepts being swallowed up by a large Canadian or foreign (especially American) corporation as an inevitable process in which his disappearance as an autonomous capitalist is compensated for by his participation as a very junior partner of the very powerful.
>
> The process of consolidation of capitalism is very far advanced, but on a multinational, not a national, basis. The huge American, British, German, French, and Japanese capitalist structures all reach into Canada, while a few equally powerful capitalist structures originating in Canada reach into other countries. The ideology of multi-nationalism therefore has Canadian as well as foreign beneficiaries and advocates. The power of these giants, both foreign and domestically based, is greatly enhanced by their close association with government, to say nothing of their ownership and control of the media, university boards of governors and other aspects of the national ideological apparatus. In their search for international economic power, they are quite willing to accept (and indeed to advocate) the economic dismemberment of Canada and the rape of raw materials and natural resources. (Johnson, 1972:162)

Different classes and interest groups in Canadian society openly compete for political power, but it is fair to say that decision-making in the country is largely controlled by an elite few. The major debate revolves around whether there is competition among several elites in Canada, or whether the financial elite is paramount in political decision-making.

There are two important variables that relate to social class identification—sex and education. These may be used as examples distinguishing ascribed and achieved status, but they can only be understood by examining the ideas and practices of society. The importance of sex as an ascribed status determinant is, in Western society, changing immensely. Our discussion of sexual identity focuses on the cultural dynamism that surrounds sex and sex roles, status, and identity.

Sex and Identity   It is difficult to write about sexual identities in an age of "sexual revolution", a revolution with ramifications that are unclear in breadth and scope. Most researchers agree that sexual attitudes have changed; there is, however, less agreement and evidence about the actual changes in behavior. These changes in attitude revolve around the increased frequency of premarital sex, the gradual erosion of male dominance, greater economic equality between the sexes, and a conception of sex as a recreational, rather than a procreational, activity. (Bell and Gordon, 1972; Petras, 1973; and Reiss, 1971)

Appropriate sex role behavior varies from culture to culture. In all societies the sex role is one of the first and most important ones learned and each society socializes the sexes differently, leading to differences in the ways boys, girls, men, and women perceive themselves. Sex role behavior becomes "scripted" conduct, played in accordance with limited expectations. (Simon and Gagnon, 1970)

Early sex role differentiation and training begins in the family and these differential expectations are reinforced by other reference groups and social institutions. Education and the media are particularly important for perpetuating sex stereotypes. Concepts of appropriate masculinity or feminity are further reinforced by the division of labor where sex discrimination in hiring and employment is rooted in culturally based stereotypes.

Sex roles are defined by each individual within the context of learned sets of expectations and meanings. It is a fact that the sex of a human being is biologically determined; there are, however, a number of concepts related to sex roles whose origins are cultural, and not biological, as commonly believed. For example, there exists a notion that men are by nature aggressive, while women are passive.

The cultural prescriptions of appropriate sex role behavior—male dominance and female submissiveness—are incorrectly linked to biological concepts of difference (superiority and inferiority). Women are treated as a minority group by the male-dominant society. (Hacker, 1951) The cultural stereotypes of women are based on traits that are presumed to be biologically determined: dependency, inability to reason, emotionalism, and physical and mental inferiority. These beliefs have and continue to be incorporated into expectations about suitable sex role behavior. Femininity depends upon male approval; women must be perceived as appropriately submissive.

These ideas about masculinity and femininity are undergoing drastic change and reevaluation. The definitions of sex roles that we have taken for granted are being challenged, changed, and separated from assumptions about biological makeup. There are obvious biological differences between the sexes but the most important differences are those that are socially acquired. Culturally defined differences which are learned through human interaction always affect the way others see us and the way we see ourselves.

Sexual identity is, no doubt, a complex, changing, and empirically uncertain concept; in a society that ideologically represses sexuality, there is bound to be a tremendous amount of insecurity about appropriate sexual behavior. This fact is compounded by changing mores, brought about particularly by the Gay and Women's Liberation movements. Complicating such new dimensions is the pervasive sexuality that is so much a part of everyday life; sex permeates the media, advertising, entertainment, sport, politics, life itself. It is an age of sexual uncertainty, even neuroticism.

The scientific research on sexuality done by Alfred C. Kinsey (1948 and 1953) and Masters and Johnson (1966) brought the study of sex behavior into the public domain. Kinsey's work centered on asking people to report on their past and present sexual activities, which pointed out discrepancies between their expressed sexual norms and actual behavior. Masters and Johnson observed volunteer subjects during sexual activity. These studies, and others, point to a widespread confusion and dissatisfaction with human sexuality; the problem is compounded by the studies themselves, which implicitly suggest that people indeed have reason for concern.

The scientific study of sexuality and the diminishing role religions play in determining appropriate sexuality have combined to produce a situation of moral and personal ambiguity. Religion no longer provides the authoritative basis for interpreting sexuality, and in its place is scientific research which furnishes members of society with new attitudes and standards of behavior.

There exists in Canadian society a tremendous variation in responses to a large number of sexual identities. In most Canadian cities live a host of people with their own life styles and different, even conflicting notions of acceptable sexual identities and activities. At the same time society severely restricts the range and style of legal or prescribed sexuality. The official censorship of sexual materials by school and government, the criminal laws used to discourage prostitution and homosexuality, and the intermittent law enforcement binges effected by churches, politicians, and the police, testify to the schizophrenic character of North American sexuality.

If there is anything to conclude about the sexual revolution and its effect on sexual identity it is that the alternatives have been increased, and so also the uncertainty about appropriate behavior. We observe that although the revolution has liberated us by providing a broader range of options, it has at the same time created a personal and collective insecurity because of the myriad of competing expectations. Sexual identities, both masculine and feminine, now appear to run a broader gamut. Sexual identities and roles are more variable, and less stereotypic and predictable; ironically, they are also more problematic.

Education and Identity Education plays an important role in the organization and consolidation of a national or cultural identity. For our society to continue, it must transmit its values, attitudes, and accumulated knowledge to each new generation. Our educational institutions serve, both formally and informally, to socialize the individuals within them into the economic, social, and political sectors of the larger society. By doing so they contribute to the persistence of an organized social life. Durkheim, the French sociologist, observed that education is "above all the means by which society perpetually recreates the conditions of its very existence." (Durkheim, 1956:123)

In their attempt to analyze the social functions of education, sociologists have examined the accomplishments of schools in the post-industrial society. Sociological analyses of education have emphasized the transmission of culture theme. Sociologists have also observed, however, that by their organization and curricula, our educational institutions have fashioned persons to fit the requirements of the larger society. In addition to being a primary socializing force, schools have supplanted the family as the screening mechanism for occupational recruitment and allocation, and have come to serve as occupational processing centers.

An important feature of an industrial society like Canada's is the selective and allocative functions of the educational system. The increased demands for professional and/or scientific skills have made educational qualifications critical links to occupational structures and opportunities. The importance of formal education to social mobility has also increased, but only modestly. The more obvious function of schooling is to sort the new generation into their future roles and statuses.

The school is an important gatekeeper in social selection and a significant determinant of the individual's position in the class structure. The school serves as the mediator between the "class origin" and "class destination" of young people. (Pike and Zureik, 1975:5-9) It stratifies the young, and directs them into various channels which correspond to future roles. At school, the child develops a social identity, as he orients himself to the expectations of others. Not only are students sorted into various categories and statuses where they learn specific skills necessary to their placement, but they are exposed to a pervasive and sometimes subtly reinforced conception of appropriate values, motivations, and perceptions of self. The child begins to learn his place by conforming to the expectations of others around him.

The sifting and sorting function of schools is complemented by an evaluation system that creates and defines identities in the school world. Part of this reputation-building process comes from the students and may be part of the student culture. The school and its agents make evaluations of a different kind, against which the student body may rebel. Many of the perspectives which are part of the student culture evolve, in fact, out of the interactions students have about problems created by the school's evaluative system. (Becker, *et al.*, 1961; Becker and Geer, 1958; and Haas and Shaffir, 1977)

The family into which a child is born is one of the major determinants of his subsequent scholastic success. The family gives the individual a set of identifying characteristics which affect educational placement and success. The background and home experiences of students, and the composition of the school's student body explain the variance in achievement to a greater extent than do school facilities, characteristics of the teachers and the curriculum, and other features of the internal educational system. The pervasive influence that socioeconomic status has on school success is summarized by Boocock when he says:

> The family characteristic that is the most powerful predictor of school performance is socioeconomic status (SES): the higher the SES of the student's family, the higher the academic achievement. This relationship has been documented in countless studies and seems to hold no matter what measure of status is used. . . . It holds with a variety of achievement-aspiration variables, including grades, achievement test scores, retention at grade level, course failures, truancy, suspensions from school, dropout rates, college plans and total amount of formal schooling. It holds, moreover, even when the powerful variables of ability and past achievement are controlled. (Boocock, 1972:36)

People's socioeconomic backgrounds influence the length and quality of their education. This education will, in turn, determine opportunities for employment, income, and status. Both socioeconomic background and education, therefore, play an important role in shaping people's social and personal identities.

Another important consequence of education in a pluralistic society such as Canada's is the help it provides in transforming potentially divisive ties and allegiances—class, ethnic, and religious—into a sense of common identity. As we have already noted, our population is a heterogeneous one, and without some kind of cohesion and integration, our society would consist of a multitude of independent factions. By teaching us all the same language, education helps to provide the integration that contributes to our social organization.

Language, the core of any culture, enables us to communicate our thoughts to others as well as understand others' intentions toward us. Those who speak a different language, then, are unable to communicate effectively. In a country with an ethnic diversity like ours, not all children entering the public schools speak the same language. A crucial outcome of our educational process, then, is that by the time the young graduate from public school they are able to speak and understand English and/or French.

In addition to a common language, our educational system provides us with a set of shared experiences. Though the curricula of public schools may differ from province to province, all school children are exposed to some form of organized education. In all schools textbooks are read, homework is assigned, tests are administered, and evaluations are made. Of equal importance, however, is the fact that we are all exposed to the same informal learning that occurs within the formal classroom setting. We are taught, for example, that honesty is a virtue and that we ought to save money rather than spend it at once. Thus in addition to the training they give, schools are instrumental in imparting and thus increasing our awareness of many of our culture's definitions.

More specifically, however, those people attending the same schools, especially private institutions, share a number of experiences which lead to similar attitudes and perspectives. Numerous ethnic groups in this country, feeling that their language and culture will not be transmitted to succeeding generations by the public schools, have established private schools which, on a full-time or part-time basis, pass the ethnic heritage on to the students. The influence of private schools in shaping the attitudes and manners of the Canadian elite has been documented sociologically by Porter (1965), Clement (1975), and Podmore (1976). A more popular treatment of this influence appears in Newman's account of the Canadian establishment:

> Perhaps because it comes early, when personalities are still malleable, no influence is more cohesive, no bond more lasting, than the time spent at the private schools and other institutions that instill Establishment values. Those early impressions, absorbed through willing pores, set lifetime priorities, prejudices, presumptions, and above all, personal partnerships. At a subconscious level, they perpetuate the idea that privilege exists and that it should be exercised; that rebellion, however fleetingly attractive, is ultimately self-defeating. (Newman, 1975:347)

Our ability to share attitudes and experiences with others in our society is crucial to the development of a national identity. Although ethnic groups are encouraged to maintain their identities, it is nonetheless hoped that all citizens and landed immigrants will learn to identify with this country's history, heroes, symbols, and traditions. While such identification is not centrally coordinated by any official body, our sense of patriotism is manipulated by our societal institutions. Although other groups, including the family, the mass media, and the church, are also responsible for creating and maintaining a national cultural identity, the schools, more than any other institutions, are organized to familiarize students with their cultural heritage and instill in them a sense of Canadian identity.

*   *   *

In this general study we have examined some of the main features of symbolic interactionism, and seen that behavior and identity may be understood within a framework of individual and group relationships. This developmental analysis gives primacy to the group and its influence through symbolic communication, and also stresses people's views of the world and themselves. The readings that follow elaborate on various points discussed in the introduction. These articles have been grouped so that we first look at the behavior and identity of the individual, and the ways in which the individual is affected by contact with others. Subsequent sections deal with identity formation in progressively larger groups: ethnic groups, occupational groups, and social classes.

Readings

Personal & Collective Definitions of the Situation

TWO VERY IMPORTANT foci of the symbolic interactionist's approach to understanding human behavior and meaning are structure and process. By structure, we mean those arrangements, understandings, and expectations that are part of the situation. The process by which these definitions of the situation are developed, shared, enacted, and changed is understood by observing group interaction. Through observation and participation we learn how to define others and ourselves in the emerging context or situation. We are socialized into the ways of the group and come to take its standpoint. Behavior, sociologically speaking, is group based and oriented and involves individuals interacting with each other, taking each other into account, deriving and sharing meanings, and acting within the emerging definition of the situation.

The symbolic interactionist approach argues that in order to understand the perspectives of other people, we must take their role, literally or figuratively. We must observe and participate with others in order to assume their point of view. Understanding human behavior requires being socialized, to some extent, into the groups we desire to understand. Only in this way can we learn the symbols and referents of the group, and share in its meanings.

Many of the situations described in the following articles are experienced by participating with others, and by coming to understand their lives through sharing in their definitions of the situation. We begin the book with three articles that emphasize the importance of the "situation" for understanding behavior.

The first article, an excerpt from *The Unadjusted Girl* by W. I. Thomas, discusses the various indications that are involved in thought processes. That human beings behave on the basis of their "definition of the situation" is, of course, axiomatic for the symbolic interactionist perspective. The next article, by Chappell, examines, in a different context, the importance of shared definitions to the construction of a validated social reality. In this study, the researcher-author interacts with the "senile", and this contact leads her to describe senility as including conflicting definitions of the situation. The following selection, by Turowetz and Rosenberg, dramatizes professional wrestlers' manipulation of social reality and definitions of the situation by creating a moral drama in which the audience can participate and share meanings.

The first three articles in the section, then, focus on perceptions or definitions of the situation that are learned in social contexts, both from and with others. However, our behavior and self-conception are intimately related to our socialization into and adoption of other people's perspectives. The last article emphasizes the relationship between our socialization and our ability to organize an appropriate definition of the situation. Kleinman examines the contingencies that women perceive as justifications for deciding to forego or participate in premarital sex. Coloring these perceptions and changing definitions of the situation is the desire of all the women interviewed to protect their moral certitude.

The Definition of the Situation

WILLIAM I. THOMAS

ONE OF THE most important powers gained during the evolution of animal life is the ability to make decisions from within instead of having them imposed from without. Very low forms of life do not make decisions, as we understand this term, but are pushed and pulled by chemical substances, heat, light, etc., much as iron filings are attracted or repelled by a magnet. They do tend to behave properly in given conditions—a group of small crustaceans will flee as in a panic if a bit of strychnia is placed in the basin containing them and will rush toward a drop of beef juice like hogs crowding around swill—but they do this as an expression of organic affinity for the one substance and repugnance for the other, and not as an expression of choice or "free will." There are, so to speak, rules of behavior but these represent a sort of fortunate mechanistic adjustment of the organism to typically recurring situations, and the organism cannot change the rule.

On the other hand, the higher animals, and above all man, have the power of refusing to obey a stimulation which they followed at an earlier time. Response to the earlier stimulation may have had painful consequences and so the rule or habit in this situation is changed. We call this ability the power of inhibition, and it is dependent on the fact that the nervous system carries memories or records of past experiences. At this point the determination of action no longer comes exclusively from outside sources but is located within the organism itself.

Preliminary to any self-determined act of behavior there is always a stage of examination and deliberation which we may call *the definition of the situation*. And actually not only concrete acts are dependent on the

From The Unadjusted Girl by I. Thomas. Copyright 1923 by Little, Brown and Company.

definition of the situation, but gradually a whole life-policy and the personality of the individual himself follow from a series of such definitions.

But the child is always born into a group of people among whom all the general types of situation which may arise have already been defined and corresponding rules of conduct developed, and where he has not the slightest chance of making his definitions and following his wishes without interference. Men have always lived together in groups. Whether mankind has a true herd instinct or whether groups are held together because this has worked out to advantage is of no importance. Certainly the wishes in general are such that they can be satisfied only in a society. But we have only to refer to the criminal code to appreciate the variety of ways in which the wishes of the individual may conflict with the wishes of society. And the criminal code takes no account of the many unsanctioned expressions of the wishes which society attempts to regulate by persuasion and gossip.

There is therefore always a rivalry between the spontaneous definitions of the situation made by the member of an organized society and the definitions which his society has provided for him. The individual tends to a hedonistic selection of activity, pleasure first; and society to a utilitarian selection, safety first. Society wishes its member to be laborious, dependable, regular, sober, orderly, self-sacrificing; while the individual wishes less of this and more of new experience. And organized society seeks also to regulate the conflict and competition inevitable between its members in the pursuit of their wishes. The desire to have wealth, for example, or any other socially sanctioned wish, may not be accomplished at the expense of another member of the society— by murder, theft, lying, swindling, blackmail, etc.

It is in this connection that a moral code arises, which is a set of rules or behavior norms, regulating the expression of the wishes, and which is built up by successive definitions of the situation. In practice the abuse arises first and the rule is made to prevent its recurrence. Morality is thus the generally accepted definition of the situation, whether expressed in public opinion and the unwritten law, in a formal legal code, or in religious commandments and prohibitions.

The family is the smallest social unit and the primary defining agency. As soon as the child has free motion and begins to pull, tear, pry, meddle, and prowl, the parents begin to define the situation through speech and other signs and pressures: "Be quiet," "Sit up straight," "Blow your nose," "Wash your face," "Mind your mother," "Be kind to sister," etc. This is the real significance of Wordsworth's phrase, "Shades of the prison house begin to close upon the growing child." His wishes and activities begin to be inhibited, and gradually, by definitions within the family, by playmates, in the school, in the Sunday school, in the community, through reading, by formal instruction, by informal signs of approval and disapproval, the growing member learns the code of his society.

In addition to the family we have the community as a defining agency. At present the community is so weak and vague that it gives us no idea of the former power of the local group in regulating behavior. Originally the community was practically the whole world of its members. It was composed of families related by blood and marriage and was not so large that all the members could not come together; it was a face-to-face group. I asked a Polish peasant what was the extent of an "okolica" or neighborhood—how far it reached. "It reaches," he said, "as far as the report of a man reaches—as far as a man is talked about." And it was in communities of this kind that the moral code which we now recognize as valid originated. The customs of the community are "folkways," and both state and church have in their more formal codes mainly recognized and incorporated these folkways.

The typical community is vanishing and it would be neither possible nor desirable to restore it in its old form. It does not correspond with the present direction of social evolution and it would now be a distressing condition in which to live. But in the immediacy of relationships and the participation of everybody in everything, it represents an element which we have lost and which we shall probably have to restore in some form of cooperation in order to secure a balanced and normal society—some arrangement corresponding with human nature.

Very elemental examples of the definition of the situation by the community as a whole, corresponding to mob action as we know it and to our trial by jury, are found among European peasants. The three documents following, all relating to the Russian community or *mir*, give some idea of the conditions under which a whole community, a public, formerly defined a situation.

25. We who are unacquainted with peasant speech, manners and method of expressing thought—mimicry—if we should be present at a division of land or some settlement among the peasants, would never understand anything. Hearing fragmentary, disconnected exclamations, endless quarreling, with repetition of some single word; hearing this racket of a seemingly senseless, noisy crowd that counts up or measures off something, we should conclude that they would not get together, or arrive at any result in an age.... Yet wait until the end and you will see that the division has been made with mathematical accuracy—that the measure, the quality of the soil, the slope of the field, the distance from the village—everything in short has been taken into account, that the reckoning has been correctly done and, what is most important, that every one of those present who were interested in the division is certain of the correctness of the division or settlement. The cry, the noise, the racket do not subside until every one is satisfied and no doubter is left.

The same thing is true concerning the discussion of some question by the *mir*. There are no speeches, no debates, no votes. They shout, they abuse each other, they seem on the point of coming to blows. Apparently they riot in the most senseless manner. Some one preserves silence, silence, and then suddenly puts in a word, one word, or an ejaculation, and by this word, this ejaculation, he turns the whole thing upside down. In the end, you look into it and find that an admirable decision has been formed and, what is most important, a unanimous decision.[1]

26. As I approached the village, there hung over it such a mixed, varied violent shouting, that no well brought-up parliament would agree to recognize itself, even in the abstract, as analogous to this gathering of peasant deputies. It was clearly a full meeting today. . . . At other more quiet village meetings I had been able to make out very little, but this was a real lesson to me. I felt only a continuous, indistinguishable roaring in my ears, sometimes pierced by a particularly violent phrase that broke out from the general roar. I saw in front of me the "immediate" man, in all his beauty. What struck me first of all was his remarkable frankness; the more "immediate" he is, the less able is he to mask his thoughts and feelings; once he is stirred up the emotion seizes him quickly and he flares up then and there, and does not quiet down till he has poured out before you all the substance of his soul. He does not feel embarrassment before anybody; there are no indications here of diplomacy. Further, he opens up his whole soul, and he will tell everything that he may ever have known about you, and not only about you, but about your father, grandfather, and great-grandfather. Here everything is clear water, as the peasants say, and everything stands out plainly. If any one, out of smallness of soul, or for some ulterior motive, thinks to get out of something by keeping silent, they force him out into clear water without pity. And there are very few such small-souled persons at important village meetings. I have seen the most peaceable, irresponsible peasants, who at other times would not have thought of saying a word against any one, absolutely changed at these meetings, at these moments of general excitement. They believed in the saying, "On people even death is beautiful," and they got up so much courage that they were able to answer back the peasants commonly recognized as audacious. At the moment of its height the meeting becomes simply an open mutual confessional and mutual disclosure, the display of the widest publicity. At these moments when, it would seem, the private interests of each reach the highest tension, public interests and justice in turn reach the highest degree of control.[2]

27. In front of the volost administration building there stands a crowd of some one hundred and fifty men. This means that a volost meeting has been called to consider the verdict of the Kusmin rural commune "regarding the handing over to the [state] authorities of the peasant Gregori Siedov, caught red-handed and convicted of horse-stealing." Siedov had already been held for judical inquiry; the evidence against

him was irrefutable and he would undoubtedly be sentenced to the penitentiary. In view of this I endeavor to explain that the verdict in regard to his exile is wholly superfluous and will only cause a deal of trouble; and that at the termination of the sentence of imprisonment of Siedov the commune will unfailingly be asked whether it wants him back or prefers that he be exiled. Then, I said, in any event it would be necessary to formulate a verdict in regard to the "non-reception" of Siedov, while at this stage all the trouble was premature and could lead to nothing. But the meeting did not believe my words, did not trust the court and wanted to settle the matter right then and there; the general hatred of horse-thieves was too keen. . . .

The decisive moment has arrived; the head-man "drives" all the judges-elect to one side; the crowd stands with a gloomy air, trying not to look at Siedov and his wife, who are crawling before the *mir* on their knees. "Old men, whoever pities Gregori, will remain in his place, and whoever does not forgive him will step to the right," cries the head man. The crowd wavered and rocked, but remained dead still on the spot; no one dared to be first to take the fatal step. Gregori feverishly ran over the faces of his judges with his eyes, trying to read in these faces pity for him. His wife wept bitterly, her face close to the ground; beside her, finger in mouth and on the point of screaming, stood a three-year-old youngster (at home Gregori had four more children) . . . But straightway one peasant steps out of the crowd; two years before some one had stolen a horse from him. "Why should we pity him? Did he pity us?" says the old man, and stooping goes over to the right side. "That is true; bad grass must be torn from the field," says another one from the crowd, and follows the old man. The beginning had been made; at first individually and then in whole groups the judges-elect proceeded to go over to the right. The man condemned by public opinion ran his head into the ground, beat his breast with his fists, seized those who passed him by their coat-tails, crying: "Ivan Timofeich! Uncle Leksander! Vasinka, dear kinsman! Wait, kinsmen, let me say a word. . . . Petrushenka." But, without stopping and with stern faces, the members of the *mir* dodged the unfortunates, who were crawling at their feet. . . . At last the wailing of Gregori stopped; around him for the space of three *sazen* the place was empty; there was no one to implore. All the judges-elect, with the exception of one, an uncle of the man to be exiled, had gone over to the right. The woman cried sorrowfully, while Gregori stood motionless on his knees, his head lowered, stupidly looking at the ground.[3]

The essential point in reaching a communal decision, just as in the case of our jury system, is unanimity. In some cases the whole community mobilizes around a stubborn individual to conform him to the general wish.

28. It sometimes happens that all except one may agree but the motion is never carried if that one refuses to agree to it. In such cases all endeavor to talk over and persuade the stiff-necked one. Often they

even call to their aid his wife, his children, his relatives, his father-in-law, and his mother, that they may prevail upon him to say yes. Then all assail him, and say to him from time to time: "Come now, God help you, agree with us too, that this may take place as we wish it, that the house may not be cast into disorder, that we may not be talked about by the people, that the neighbors may not hear of it, that the world may not make sport of us!" It seldom occurs in such cases that unanimity is not attained.[4]

A less formal but not less powerful means of defining the situation employed by the community is gossip. The Polish peasant's statement that a community reaches as far as a man is talked about was significant, for the community regulates the behavior of its members largely by talking about them. Gossip has a bad name because it is sometimes malicious and false and designed to improve the status of the gossiper and degrade its object, but gossip is in the main true and is an organizing force. It is a mode of defining the situation in a given case and of attaching praise or blame. It is one of the means by which the status of the individual and of his family is fixed.

The community also, particularly in connection with gossip, knows how to attach opprobrium to persons and actions by using epithets which are at the same time brief and emotional definitions of the situation. "Bastard," "whore," "traitor," "coward," "skunk," "scab," "snob," "kike," etc., are such epithets. In "Faust" the community said of Margaret, "She stinks." The people are here employing a device known in psychology as the "conditioned reflex." If, for example, you place before a child (say six months old) an agreeable object, a kitten, and at the same time pinch the child, and if this is repeated several times, the child will immediately cry at the sight of the kitten without being pinched; or if a dead rat were always served beside a man's plate of soup he would eventually have a disgust for soup when served separately. If the word "stinks" is associated on people's tongues with Margaret, Margaret will never again smell sweet. Many evil consequences, as the psychoanalysts claim, have resulted from making the whole of sex life a "dirty" subject, but the device has worked in a powerful, sometimes a paralyzing way on the sexual behavior of women.

Winks, shrugs, nudges, laughter, sneers, haughtiness, coldness, "giving the once over" are also language defining the situation and painfully felt as unfavorable recognition. The sneer, for example, is incipient vomiting, meaning, "you make me sick."

And eventually the violation of the code even in an act of no intrinsic importance, as in carrying food to the mouth with the knife, provokes condemnation and disgust. The fork is not a better instrument for conveying food than the knife, at least it has no moral superiority, but the situation has been defined in favor of the fork. To smack with the lips in eating is bad manners with us, but the Indian has more logically defined the situation in the opposite way; with him smacking is a compliment to the host.

In this whole connection fear is used by the group to produce the desired attitudes in its member. Praise is used also but more sparingly. And the whole body of habits and emotions is so much a community and family product that disapproval or separation is almost unbearable.

NOTES

1. N. Engelgardt: "Iz Derevni: 12 Pisem" (From the Country, 12 Letters"), p. 315.
2. N. N. Zlatovratsky: "Orcherki Krestyanskoy Obshchiny" ("Sketches of the Peasant Commune"), p. 127.
3. "V. Volostnikh Pisaryakh" ("A Village Secretary"), p. 283.
4. F. S. Krauss: "Sitte und Brauch der Südslaven," p. 103.

ONE WAY OF dramatizing the importance of a basic feature of social life is to study situations from which the feature is missing and observe the consequences of its absence. Shared interpretations of the situation are extremely important prerequisites for organized or collective activity. If individuals do not share the same reality, or communicate with the same set of meanings, organized social life is impossible. If they do not understand the meaning of each other's actions, they will neither be able to share ideas, nor understand each other's points of view.

If we deny others trust and the assurance that their constructed actions are rational and purposeful, we effectively deny their reality and their place in group life. Such denials amount to a rejection of their humanness.

In life there are many examples of cruelty, barbarism, violence, eccentric behavior, and idiocy that seem inexplicable to us. Unable to take the role of the other, we are forced to label such behavior sick, pathological, or demented.

It may be that we fail to appreciate the reasons for people's actions because we don't understand their views of the world. If we could see and understand situations from their perspectives, we would certainly move closer to grasping the interpretations and motives that are an integral part of their actions.

The article, "The Senile: Problems in Communication", brings into question the discrediting interpretations "normal" people attach to the senile's construction of reality. We can imagine the frightful consequences of being denied credibility, of being defined and treated as "out of touch." Those of us who believe we are "in touch" with reality arrive at that conclusion because of the social affirmations of others. The reality of those labeled senile and mentally ill is denied, and these people are isolated, physically and symbolically, from those of us who share legitimated reality.

This article highlights the importance of shared and affirmed constructions of reality in group life. It also suggests that many people who are thought to be "out of touch" have a right to their perceptions, and that communication with the senile can be reestablished.

Senility: Problems in Communication

NEENA CHAPPELL

SENILITY IS COMMONLY referred to as a mental infirmity of old age and those described as senile are often said to be confused and irresponsible. Contrary to this view, which can be labeled a medical or disease model of senility, the present paper applies the assumptions of a symbolic interactionist perspective in its search for an approach to the rehabilitation of the senile. Within this perspective, reality is considered largely subjective; what is defined as real is real in its consequences. Everyone is assumed to have his own reality and communication is possible through shared meanings. From this point of view, senility can be considered a lack of normal communication between individuals. This paper considers some of the possible reasons for a breakdown in communication, such as the lack of shared meanings or the absence of a belief in the existence of shared meanings, and attempts to reestablish the bases for communication. The works of several authors are drawn upon: Mead's definition of irrationality as a lack of communication; Schutz's discussions of interpersonal trust and faith as necessary prerequisites for communication; and Simmel's concept of sociability as a particular type of interaction which has the potential for reestablishing the basis of communication.

While this paper[1] adopts a symbolic interactionist approach to mental illness, and to senility in particular, its primary purpose is not to provide yet another account of this perspective. Rather, it attempts to integrate some of our existing knowledge on the importance of communication between individuals, and to illustrate the ways in which an understanding of this concept can be applied to social problems in the "real" world. It leaves unanswered the larger ethical question of whether or not we should try to rehabilitate or reintegrate senile persons into the paramount social reality of others.

It should be noted at the outset that the findings reported here were serendipitous to a larger study.[2] Consequently, the empirical data are not

Neena Chappell is an Assistant Professor, Department of Sociology, University of Manitoba.

conclusive but only suggest the possibilities of this approach. Further evidence awaits future research.

Irrationality as a Lack of Communication

Irrationality need not refer to a trait inherent in an individual. Within a social behaviorist perspective it refers to a type of interaction between individuals in which each individual involved does not understand the meaning of the other's behavior (in this research the two individuals involved are the "senile"[3] person and the researcher). Neither person takes the attitude of the other nor controls his own or the other's actions by these attitudes. In other words, only a person who can interact in meaningful conduct with others is rational. (Mead, 1934:7,44-45,334-335) In Mead's words, rationality

> implies that the whole group is involved in some organized activity and that in this organized activity the action of one calls for the action of all the others. What we term 'reason' arises when one of the organisms takes into its own responses that attitude of the other organism involved. It is possible for the organism so to assume the attitudes of the group that are involved in its own act within this whole co-operative process. When it does so, it is what we term 'a rational being'.... If the individual can take the attitude of the others and control his action by these attitudes, and control their actions through his own, then we have what we can term 'rationality'. (Mead, 1934:334)

Similarly, the phenomenologist Alfred Schutz refers to rationality as involving not one person in isolation but rather one person in relation to another. (Schutz, 1971:23-34) According to Schutz:

> We may say that a man acted sensibly if the motive and the cause of his action is understandable to us, his partners and observers.... If an action seems sensible to the observer and is, in addition, supposed to spring from a judicious choice among different courses of action, we may call it reasonable.... Rational action however presupposes that the actor has clear and distinct insight into the ends, the means, and the secondary results.... (Schutz, 1971:27-28)

Both authors agree that rationality (and consequently irrationality) refers to interaction involving more than one person in which each understands the actions of the other (or does not understand the actions of the other). The very essence of the definition then, includes the concept of communication among individuals.

A senile person can be considered irrational to the extent that either he or the one attempting to interact with him does not take the attitude of the other or does not understand the other. If communication does not take place, rationality does not exist. This is not an unusual description of mental illness; some authors suggest that what people now call mental illness is for the most part a lack of communication, or a lack of acceptable communication (see for example Szasz, 1960). However, it should be noted that within the approach expounded here the "sane" person is also irrational during the situation in which he is attempting to communicate with the senile person, since neither understands the other.

While it is not the task here to elaborate either on the various pressures in the social environment that may lead to a lack of meaningful interaction, or on those circumstances which result in a person being labeled senile or mentally ill, other authors have investigated this area. Goffman (1961:130-136) and Brown (1974), for example, argue that behaviors which come to be seen as mental illnesses are the result of the situations in which people find themselves. Whether or not a person's behavior does in fact become so labeled depends on what Goffman calls the person's "career contingencies": socioeconomic status, visibility of the behavior, proximity to a mental hospital, treatment facilities available, community regard for the type of treatment offered, and the social distance between those doing the labeling and those being labeled. (Krim, 1961)

Similarly, the place of the physician or psychiatrist in the labeling process has been well documented. Cameron (1974) and Sampson (1962) are but two authors who have illustrated the way family and friends readily accept the label once it has been applied by members of the medical profession. Marshall and Hughes (1974) reveal that such persons possess absolute legal powers to define the mentally ill.

Our aim, however, is to gain a greater understanding of the irrationality that characterizes the senile person so that we can discover an approach to rehabilitation. It should be noted that since we cannot "know" what the senile person is thinking, to say he is irrational does not mean that he cannot or does not control his own actions or attitudes. Nor does it mean that he does not understand the conduct of those around him. It does mean that those around him do not understand his actions and cannot take his attitude, and that communication does not take place or is limited to a greater extent than is normal.

Furthermore, a lack of communication need not imply that the senile person does not live in reality or that his world is less real than that of others. Although his reality may be different from that of others (and presumably it is since others cannot understand it), it need not be less correct in any ultimate or moral sense of the word. If he lives in a different reality than most others, it need not follow that he is confused or irresponsible as is commonly claimed. Indeed, it is argued below that he can be seen as simply living in a different reality. The importance of this interpretation lies in the possibility of another entering his reality, taking his underlying attitude, understanding his meanings, and thereby communicating with him. The senile person is no longer characterized as irrational, and the possibility of rehabilitation presents itself.

Multiple Realities

The concept of multiple realities is not new. Schutz bases his discussions of the concept on the subjective nature of reality. Any object x is real if it is believed to be real and any object x is believed to be real if it remains uncontradicted by another stronger belief. This is similar to Thomas's famous statement: "Situations defined as real are real in their consequences." (Thomas and Thomas, 1970) We can and do live in realities that differ from those of others. For example, a hairdresser may not share the world of aerospace technology with a scientist. In addition, we all live in multiple realities, some of which we share with others and some of which we do not. We all live in the different worlds of dreams, fantasy, and the wide-awake state. (Schutz, 1954;1945) Although our hairdresser and aerospace scientist may not share their occupational worlds, both may hike and both may garden; thus they may share some of the realities in which they live.

Among the multiple realities there is one paramount reality which most of us take as our home base. This is the world of working[4] in which we have a "wide-awake attitude". It is here that we accept the world as it appears to be, and use spontaneous bodily movements geared to the outer world with the intention of bringing about a projected state of affairs. We experience this work self as our total self and experience sociality as the common intersubjective world of communication and social action. Our time perspective is one of anticipating future repercussions based on past experiences. This paramount reality is the one that *practical* experiences point to as real and irrefutable. It is the one which seems *natural* to us. (Schutz, 1940)

This work world or paramount reality is the culturally dominant reality of the society (or the particular subculture of which we are members). This is evident in Schutz's writings on Don Quixote. (Schutz, 1954) Quixote is seen as taking the world of fantasy rather than a stratum of the paramount reality as his home base. He is not described as living in a different stratum of the paramount reality despite the fact that his reality meets all of the criteria for the dominant reality which Schutz lists. Instead, Quixote is described as a homecomer to the paramount reality when he leaves his world of fantasy and returns to the wide-awake state.

Although most of us share the paramount reality, we are not equally interested in all strata of the working world. We are interested only in those aspects relevant to our situation. In this way Schutz accounts for different strata of the paramount reality. Sufficient deviation, however, leads to a reality other than the paramount reality, referred to as a subuniverse of meaning. Considering Schutz's exposé on Quixote, a senile person can be seen as living in a subuniverse of meaning rather than simply in a different stratum of the paramount reality. He does not share the reality of most others in his society and does not communicate within that universe of meaning. He does, however, have a biographical history containing particular experiences and therefore a subjectively defined reality.

If an outsider can enter the senile person's subuniverse of meaning, share at least part of his reality, or find a juncture at which his reality and either the paramount reality or the reality of the outsider exist concomitantly, communication should take place. In order to do this, the prerequisites from which communication (a universe of discourse or a system of common or social meanings, Mead, 1934:89-90, 156-158, 269) proceeds must be present. If they are not present, they must be established. Schutz provides an elaboration of the bases of communication.

The Prerequisites for Communication

Before any communication can be established the person (in this case the senile person) must have the desire to interact with the other (in this case the researcher). Without this willingness no communication is possible, even if shared meanings already exist. The lack of desire to interact can result from the person's belief that the other does not credit him with the ability to define reality. As Schutz points out, a person's lack of faith in the other's acceptance of his ability to define reality prevents communication:

> Intersubjective experience, communication, sharing something in common presupposes, thus, in the last analysis faith in the other's truthfulness . . . ; it presupposes that I take for granted the Other's possibility of bestowing upon the innumerable subuniverses the accent of reality, and on the other hand, that he, the Other, takes for granted that I, too, have open possibilities for defining what is my dream, my phantasy, my real life. . . . Only mutual faith in the Other's terms of reality guarantees intercommunication. . . . (Schutz, 1954:155-156)

The very labeling of a person as "senile" is a withdrawal of mutual faith. It indicates that others do not believe the person is capable of defining his own reality. (The following section elaborates on this point in relation to the sample studied here.) Anyone attempting to communicate with these persons is therefore wise to assume that this mutual faith does not exist and to try to establish it.

Even if this mutual faith in another is present, the senile person may not believe he shares his reality with others, and so, communication cannot take place. To quote from Schutz again:

> Our relationship with the social world is based upon the assumption that in spite of all individual variations the same objects are experienced by our fellow-men in substantially the same way as by ourselves and vice versa, and also that our and their schemes of interpretation show the same typical structure of relevances. If this belief in the substantial identity of the intersubjective experience of the world breaks down, the very possibility of establishing communication with our fellow-men is destroyed. (Schutz, 1954:142-143)

Much literature suggests that those labeled senile may well come to believe that they no longer share their reality with others. Our self-conceptions and definitions of reality emerge from interaction with others and the situations we experience. If others do not validate our identities but label us otherwise, we come to see ourselves as others see us. (Kinch, 1968; Denzin, 1970; Stone, 1970) In other words, if a person is defined as senile and placed in this status, he begins to play the role of the senile person and may come to see himself in this way. (Scheff, 1966) The researcher attempting to establish a universe of discourse with senile persons should be aware of this possibility and be prepared to have to establish the belief that he and the other do share the same reality.

Since it seems reasonable to assume that a senile person may believe the researcher does not have faith in his terms of reality, or that he does not share the same reality as that of the researcher, both bases of communication may need to be established when attempting to interact with these persons. The following research was approached with these ideas in mind.

The Sample

The data was collected among long-term hospital patients aged 60 and over (in the summer of 1972). The hospital is located in a southern Ontario city with a population of approximately 300,000. All 128 elderly patients in the hospital required extensive medical care and few were expected to leave before their death. All of these patients were approached for a lengthy interview, which comprised the larger study. Following Mead's definition of rationality and Schutz's discussion of the paramount reality, any patient with whom the researcher could not communicate, or could not communicate in "standard" ways, was classified as senile. A patient then, was classified here if: he did not respond when approached; he spoke words which could not be interpreted as answers to questions; his words were meaningless to the researcher; he did not answer questions about his name, age, or the length of time spent in the hospital; or he gave objectively incorrect or contradictory answers to questions. Typical examples of initial contact with these persons follow:

Respondent 900 said she was visiting a friend for the weekend and would return home tomorrow. She would not acknowledge that she was in the hospital or that she had been there for several months.

Respondent 841 insisted that he was living on his farm which he and his sister bought recently. He said he was not in any hospital and invited me to stay for dinner and meet his sister.

Respondent 818 said she had no children and no one came to visit her. The hospital staff said, and her records showed, that she did have children and the staff reported that they came frequently to visit her. She did not know her name or age.

Except for a few patients it took only one or two moments to classify a particular person as senile or not. Usually they would not answer one of the questions mentioned above in an "appropriate" manner. As the medical librarian said when asked how the staff knew patients were senile or "confused": "*Oh we know* shortly after they get here; all you have to do is talk to them." In all but two cases those classified as senile by the researcher were also referred to as senile by the staff. Three patients classified as senile by the staff were not so classified by the researcher since they successfully completed an hour-and-a-half interview. Fifty-nine (46% of the original 128 patients) were classified as senile.

Most of these patients resided in hospital wards, with a few in semiprivate and private rooms. None had many visible personal belongings. The rooms were typical hospital rooms furnished with little but beds and dressers. The patients had a few of their own clothes and some had one or two ornaments on their dressers. In other words, the "stripping process" of which Goffman talks was in evidence. Depersonalization was indicated by the lack of personal belongings, everyday comforts, privacy, and personal autonomy. (Goffman, 1961) In addition, over the period of eight months in which the researcher frequented the hospital, members of staff were seen interacting with these patients only to perform their hospital chores. On occasion, when some of the patients were in the sunporch for the afternoon, the staff behaved in a way that could be interpreted as "teasing" or "condescending". Only infrequently would relatives or friends be seen visiting the senile patients, and during such an encounter they would typically "correct" what the patient was saying or agree as if with a child. That is to say, people's behavior toward patients in the hospital was affected by the label "senile". (Rosenhan, 1974; Kaplan, *et al.*, 1968 also discuss this point.) Such observations tend to support the earlier suggestion that someone labeled senile (especially in the environment of a total institution) may well believe that others do not credit him with the ability to define his reality and that he does not share the same realities as others.

Since the patients and the researcher could not communicate and it seemed evident that the patients did not share the same reality as the researcher, the patients themselves were left to provide cues and signs for establishing communication. The conversations were therefore open and unstructured.

Establishing Universes of Discourse

There were varying degrees of success in establishing universes of discourse with the senile patients. Patients were finally placed in one of three catagories. Category I contains those patients with whom any attempt at communication was unsuccessful, including those from whom no responses were elicited and those who gave unintelligible responses. An example of such an encounter is reported below.

Respondent 820, male, 87 years old, admitted 1969. The respondent was lying in his bed when I entered the ward. His eyes were *wide* open, and he was saying, "O.K., O.K., O.K., . . . " loudly and clearly. He was looking elsewhere. I went to his bed and said, "Hi, what's your name?" He looked at me but kept saying, "O.K., O.K., good."
RE (researcher): "What's good?"
PA (patient): "O.K., O.K., O.K.,. . . . "
RE: "Great! "O.K., O.K., O.K. Good isn't it?"
PA: "O.K., O.K., O.K."
RE: "Marvellous, O.K., O.K., can you hear me?"
PA: "O.K., O.K.,. . . "
I could elicit no other response from this patient. Presumably he could hear since he looked at me only after I spoke to him. I said goodbye and left. Since he was in a ward, I was in the room numerous times after this encounter to speak to other patients. While I was talking to someone else he would often look over at me and say something similar. For example one time he said, "O.K., O.K., yes, no, O.K." On any of these following occasions attempts to establish a universe of discourse with him were as unsuccessful as the first attempt. (Many of the respondents classified here uttered no sounds at all. Others were uttering when the researcher entered and continued during the visit but the sounds could not be understood, nor could any meaning be attached to them.)

Twenty-four or 40.7% of the 59 senile patients were classified here.

Since no universe of discourse was established, little can be said other than they did not share the paramount reality. These encounters were terminated by the researcher when no signs of success were visible.

All other patients did give meaningful responses. The conversations in Category II generally consisted of brief but understandable responses. Twenty, or 33.4%, of the patients were classified here. An example of such a conversation is listed below.

Respondent 917, male, 82 years old, admitted 1972. This respondent was lying in his bed when I entered the ward. He seemed to be saying something but I could not hear him clearly enough to understand the words. I went over to his bed. He looked at me and said, "Wash my back, nurse, wash my back."
RE: "I'm not a nurse. Do you want me to call one for you?"
PA: "Oh, my back, it's awful, my feet, oh. . . . "
RE: "I'll go and get a nurse, O.K.?"
PA: "I'm dying, this is it, it's terrible."
RE: "You're dying?"
PA: "Oh it hurts, my back, my feet, I'm dying."
RE: "You're dying?"
PA: "Yes."
RE: "Is dying terrible? Is that what's terrible or is dying alright?"
PA: "Dying is good, yes, it's good, but my back—oh my back, *it's* terrible, terrible (calling) n-u-r-s-e."
RE: "I'll get a nurse for you."
I went to the nursing station on that floor. I told them about the patient and asked if one of them could come down to his room. One of them said, "Oh, Mr. H . . . , he's alright. Just ignore him, he's always making a noise." I said I thought one of them could have a look at him just in case and one of the nurses said she would be down later on. I then returned by myself and said to the patient, who was just lying there, "Mr. H . . . , it's me again, the girl who was just here. A nurse will be down in a little while, but I think you'll have to wait before one comes. How are you feeling now?"
PA: "Wash my feet, wash my back. . . . "
RE: "I can't. I'm not a nurse, but one of them will be down later on."
PA: "I'm dying."
RE: "Yes, you told me. Do you want to talk about it?"
PA: "I don't know."
RE: "Why do you say you're dying?"
PA: "I don't know?"
RE: "How old are you?"
PA: "I don't know."
RE: "How long have you been here?"

PA: "I don't know."

RE: "What's it like to be dying?"

PA: "It's good."

RE: "Yes? Can you tell me what it's like? I'd like to know."

PA: "I don't know, it's just good."

RE: "You mean you feel good? You're glad?"

PA: "I don't know."

RE: "Why do you want your feet and back washed?"

PA: "Wash my feet, oh, wash my back. . . . "

Additional responses were similar to the above. He answered "I don't know" to all questions unless they referred to washing his feet or back or to dying but even those answers were not elaborate. I spoke to this man on July 25, 1972, at 2:30 p.m. and he died on August 1st, 1972.

Those classified in Category III also gave meaningful replies. However, their responses were extensive. Although they did not share the paramount reality, another subuniverse of meaning was found in which to communicate. Fifteen, or 25.4%, of the patients were classified here. An example of such an encounter is listed below.

Respondent 840, female, 88 years old, admitted 1971, married. This respondent was lying in her bed when I entered the ward. I was impressed by her alertness and the energy in her voice.

RE: "Hi, my name is Neena. How are you feeling today?"

PA: "I'm going to the States tonight. Can you tell me how much the fare is?"

RE: "I don't know how much the fare is. Why are you going to the States?"

PA: "Oh I'm going to live there."

RE: "Why, is your husband or someone there?"

PA: "No, but I have friends. I'm going to live it up and have a good time . . . I was never married you know."

RE: "Why not?"

PA: "That man might just want my money. I have to be careful. . . . "

Apparently she has little money now. She is in a public ward in the hospital and the government pays for most of her stay.

RE: "Aren't you Mrs. S . . . ?"

PA: "They call me Tilly. It's really Matilda but they call me Tilly."

RE: "But aren't you *Mrs.* Tilly S . . . ?"

PA: "Uh-huh. . . . "

RE: "Then were you married once?"

PA: "Oh yes, for quite some time."

RE: "Are you married now? Is your husband still living?"

PA: "I don't know, I haven't seen him in quite some time."

RE: "Are you divorced or separated?"

PA: "No."

RE: "Well where's your husband? Is he dead?"

PA: "I don't know, I haven't seen him for a long time."

RE: "Do you have any children?"

PA: "Oh yes, two or three I think."

RE: "Do you see them often?"

PA: "I have to get up now. I'm going to the States tonight."

RE: "Before you go can I stay and talk to you for a while?"

PA: "Well alright but don't be too long. I haven't much time."

I thought perhaps she might be able to answer some of the questions on the interview schedule which was part of the larger study so I explained it to her. She consented and we proceeded but I soon had to discard it. The first question on the schedule was the Twenty Statements Test, to which she replied: "I am Tilly S. . . . I am perfect. I am good. I don't like being bad."

RE: "Anything else?"

PA: "No."

RE: "How long have you lived at . . . (the hospital)?"

PA: "Where? I don't remember."

RE: "Why did you leave your former home?"

PA: "I don't know."

RE: "Why did you come to live at . . . (the hospital) rather than going elsewhere?"

PA: "I don't know."

She continued to answer "I don't know" or "I don't remember" to the interview questions, so I discontinued.

RE: "Well, what would you like to talk about now?"

PA: "I'm going to the States tonight. I must get up."

She tried to get up but physically she was too weak and could hardly lift her head. This did not seem to bother her though; she just kept trying and finally put her head back down.

RE: "Why don't you want to stay here?"

PA: "Oh I just stopped here for the night. It's a nice place you know, but I'm going to the States."

RE: "What are you going to do when you get there?"

PA: "I'll make out alright; I have friends there. When are you going down?"

RE: "I'm not going down. I have to stay here in . . . (the hospital city)."

PA: "Oh, you should come. It's a lively place, lots of fun. When are the young couple going?"

RE: "What young couple's that?"

PA: "You know, that one that just got married."

RE: "No, I don't know who you mean. Who?"

PA: "The one that just got m-a-r-r-i-e-d."

RE: "But who's that? I don't think I know them."

PA: "Yes, the one who just got m-a-r-r-i-e-d." (She was getting rather angry at this point.)

RE: "The ones who are so happy?"

PA: "Well . . . I g-u-e-s-s so. You know they j-u-s-t got m-a-r-r-i-e-d."

RE: "Isn't that nice for them! Shouldn't they have gotten married?"

PA: "I suppose so, if that's what they want. They're going to the States too. When are they leaving? . . . Well I must get up now; I have to go to the States."

She tried again, but couldn't get up so she lay back.

PA: "Do you know anyone else who's going down?"

RE: "No I don't, sorry. Why are you so anxious to go to the States? You must like it there. How are you going to manage when you get there? I wouldn't want to go by myself."

PA: "Oh, I can look after myself, but you have to watch the men. They may be just after money. But I have to go now so if you're not going I have to leave anyway."

RE: "O.K. I'll be off now, but I'll come and see you again. O.K.?"

PA: "O.K. Goodbye. Find out when that couple are leaving and let me know, will you?"

RE: "I'll try. Bye now."

The next time I visited this respondent she had been moved to another ward on the same floor. She was lying in her bed again and still looking alert.

RE: "Hi Tilly, remember me? I spoke to you a week or so ago when you were in the other room."

PA: "Oh?"

RE: "You were going to the States. Did you go and have a nice trip?"

PA: "Oh?"

RE: "The States, did you go to the States?"

PA: "What have you got there?"

She reached for the interview schedules I had with me.

RE: "They're interview schedules. I interviewed you, remember?"

PA: "Oh?"

RE: "They tell me you used to make the best homemade apple pies in the area." (One of the staff had told me this since the last time I spoke with her.)

PA: "I still do. I'll make you one some time. I make the best apple pies anywhere."

RE: "You do? Great, I'm looking forward to it."

She then grabbed one of the side rails on her bed and tried to pull herself up but was too weak. She lay back and said, "Get me my slippers. I'm getting up."

I looked for her slippers but there were none. "I can't find them, they aren't here."

PA: "They're under the bed. *Look.*"

RE: "No they aren't."

PA: "Oh let me look, they're under the bed." She tried to get up again but couldn't.

RE: "Where are you going?"

PA: "I'm getting up. Get me my slippers, they're under the bed."

At this point a nurse came in with supper so we "argued" a bit about the slippers and I said goodbye, I'd let her eat her supper. She said, "Goodbye, look for my slippers will you?"

RE: "O.K. Bye now."

An attempt was made to analyze the conversations with those people in Categories II and III, since some success in communication was achieved. The content of the conversations differed from person to person. No two persons seemed to share a subuniverse of meaning, and no pattern or uniformity seemed to characterize them. Furthermore, the range of topics was relatively small; conversations usually included one, or at most, two or three topic(s). The topic dominating one conversation did not necessarily extend to a different conversation with the same person. Attempts made by the researcher to change the topic during the conversation were usually fruitless. The patients themselves usually specified the topic of the conversation by not talking about anything else. Finally, the termination style encountered varied from patient to patient. Sometimes the researcher terminated it when the patient became redundant; sometimes the respondent terminated it with seeming deliberateness; and sometimes the patient "drifted off" or diverted his attention elsewhere. Differentiating the conversations along any of these dimensions proved unrewarding. The only difference between the conversations of persons in Categories II and III was in the extent of the universe of discourse that was established.

In an effort to further distinguish between these categories, they were compared for age and sex distributions. No statistically significant relationships emerged, only trends. Males were most prominent in Category I and least so in Category II. However, only 8 of the 59 persons were male. The proportion of persons between the ages of 60 and 79 (the youngest age category) decreased from Category I through to Category III. In other words, the more success in establishing a universe of discourse with the patient, the more over-represented the older age group in that category. Additional information was unavailable, preventing further analyses.

If the above analyses reveal unsatisfactory results, what can be said about the conversations with the senile persons? It is suggested below that Simmel's concept of sociability provides a meaningful interpretation of this data.

Making Sense of the Conversations

Words can be spoken without communication taking place. Similarly, communication can take place without those involved believing the meaning of the words spoken. Individuals can also interact even though the purpose of their relationship is not communication. Simmel refers to this latter form of interaction as sociability. (Simmel, 1909, 1950)

Sociability is that form of interaction in which individuals interact for the sake of interaction and not as a means to an end. It approximates pure interaction and exists for its own sake. Members derive satisfaction from the feeling of being sociated. In other words, this form of behavior gains its own life apart from the individual contents or personal interests of the members. It is called the play form of sociation because it is composed of individuals who have no desire other than to create "wholly pure interaction".

Because sociability has no purpose other than interaction itself, its success depends on the personalities of those involved and more specifically, on the tactful expression of those personalities. In Simmel's own words:

> The conditions and results of the process of sociability are exclusively the persons who find themselves at a social gathering. Its character is determined by such personal qualities as amiability, refinement, cordiality, and many other sources of attraction. But precisely because everything depends on their personalities, the participants are not permitted to stress them too conspicuously. . . . Without the reduction of personal poignancy and autonomy brought about by this form, the gathering itself would not be possible. *Tact*, therefore, is here of such particular significance: where no external or immediate egoistic interests direct the self-regulation of the individual in his personal relations with others, it is tact that fulfills this regulatory function. (Simmel, 1950:45, emphasis original)

Even though communication is not the purpose of sociability, a topic of conversation is nevertheless the indispensable medium through which the individuals relate. While the content of the conversation must not become significant in its own right, it must be interesting, fascinating, and even important. Simmel stresses this point:

> For since the topic is merely a means, it exhibits all the fortuitousness and exchangeability that characterize all means as compared with fixed ends. . . . Sociability presents perhaps the only case in which talk is its own legitimate purpose. . . . It thus is the fulfillment of a relation that wants to be nothing but relation—in which, that is, what usually is the mere form of interaction becomes the self-sufficient content. (Simmel, 1950:53)

It is suggested here that the interaction between the researcher and the senile persons was precisely sociable interaction as described by Simmel. Because the researcher was attempting to enter their realities without knowing anything about their subuniverses of meaning, a style of interaction had to be adopted that would allow the patients to define the universe of discourse and at the same time would reveal the researcher's desire to interact with the patients. Sociable interaction permits both, and also allows the researcher to show willingness to recognize the reality of the patients, a reality that need not differ from that of the researcher. By allowing the patients to define the reality and by showing them the researcher's desire to interact, sociability can serve to establish the bases of communication of which Schutz spoke (if indeed, as suggested previously, they are not already present). Especially in an environment such as the one in which the patients who were interviewed lived, there seems to be no reason why the patients should believe the researcher will grant them credibility in their terms of reality, especially if no one else they encounter does so. Sociability provides a mechanism for researchers to establish another relationship and show the patients that they are not interacting with them as others do. The only thing necessary for sociable interaction is a willingness on the part of the patients to interact.

A reviewing of the conversations with the senile patients illustrates the sociable nature of these encounters. Words were used as the medium for this interaction, but as the preceding analyses of the three categories revealed, the content of these conversations was not significant in itself. Indeed, many of the respondents were willing to continue the interaction even though their words had become redundant. Similarly, the lack of logical order in many of the conversations can also be seen as the patients' desire to interact simply for the sake of interacting. A patient would often respond with a remark that was unrelated to the topic being discussed, but would still be willing to converse. Others would return to previous points even though they were unrelated to the immediate conversation. There is space for only one example here.

Respondent 891, female, 86 years old, admitted 1972, married. This respondent was in a ward. I had previously interviewed one patient there a few days earlier. When I returned few patients were in the room but those who were there included this respondent and the one who had been interviewed earlier. I went over to this respondent, and the previous respondent, who knew of my interviewing at the hospital for the larger study, said, "Oh, she can't talk, you're wasting your time." I said I wanted to visit with her anyway and said to the respondent, "Hello, Mrs. G . . . ?" She said nothing and was not looking at me. "Can you talk Mrs. G . . . ?" She looked at me for a couple of moments then spoke.

PA:"Sure I can, see? *She* said I couldn't but I can."
She was difficult to understand but she *could* talk.
RE: "Sure you can."
PA: "She said I couldn't." (She sounded upset.)
RE: "That's alright, don't let her bother you. How old are you?"
PA: "I'm not sure, but I'm in my 80s." (She was right.)
RE: "Are you? That's very good."
PA: 'Yes, and I have children."
RE: "Good. Do they come and visit you?"
PA: "Yes. . . . I have a sore back; I fell on it."
RE: "I see. You must be careful then."
An announcement was heard over the PA system.
PA: "What's that?"
RE: "They're calling a nurse."
PA: "Well let them then. If they want to call her, let them."
RE: "Sure."
PA: "Are you going to see Aunt Liz?"
RE: "No."
PA: "Where are you going?"
RE: "Afterwards, I'm going downtown."
PA: "To see Aunt Liz?"
RE: "No, I'm going to do some shopping."
PA: "Shopping! Oh, I need some clothes."
RE: "You need some clothes? Well, I'll see what I can do. Who's Aunt Liz?"
PA: "I don't think you should go. You may get hurt."
RE: "Get hurt? How?"
PA: "You may get hurt."
RE: "Why would I get hurt?"
PA: "You may get hurt."
RE: "No, I'll be O.K., I know my way around."
PA: "O.K. then."
She kept trying to take the sheet off but said nothing about it. A nurse came in and told her to leave it on (nicely). The nurse covered her up. The respondent said nothing but continued trying to take it off.
RE: "It's O.K. if I go downtown then?"
PA: "When are you going to work?"
RE: "Not until tomorrow. Why?"
PA: "Is Jim at work?"
RE: "I don't know Jim; is he your son?"
PA: "O.K. . . ."
She said something else but I couldn't understand the words.
RE: "Pardon me, I didn't hear you?"
PA: "O.K. then, go shopping."

RE: "O.K. I'll go shopping, but I don't have to go right now. Why don't we chat for a while?" (She said nothing.) "It's hot in here today, isn't it?"
PA: "I can talk."
RE: "You certainly can."
She closed her eyes and seemed to either go to sleep or to "drift off" elsewhere. I could get no more responses from her. I had been in this ward previously and had never heard her say anything. I had previously gone over to her but could get no response and had assumed she was asleep. After this conversation however, I returned to this ward two more times to speak with other patients. When I entered the room she would start talking out loud and keep talking provided someone else was talking (not necessarily to her). Sometimes she would say "I can talk, I can talk." I spoke to her on these two following occasions and she would always respond. Unfortunately, her speech was too difficult to understand and not clear enough to enable recording the conversations.

This willingness to converse then, is interpreted as a desire to interact.[5] Within Mead's terminology the patients' underlying attitude would be one of wanting to interact for the sake of interacting. Within Schutz's terminology, the subjective interpretation of the patients would be one of interacting for the sake of interacting.

Sociability as a means of entering different realities and communicating with others is especially useful when the members of the population being studied do not share a subuniverse of meaning among themselves. Sociability stresses flexibility in interaction and the use of different personality traits with different persons. Since, as the data revealed, the patients did not share their reality with other senile patients, the importance of this flexibility is evident.

Furthermore, the potential usefulness of this concept extends far beyond the limits of the empirical data reported here. For example, it can be considered a first step toward understanding senile persons. After a common subuniverse of meaning has been established, and communication proceeds within it, it is possible to speak of expanding these subuniverses of meaning and then of returning these persons to the paramount reality. This is speculative at present, but if such an approach were viable, it could serve as a technique for rehabilitation. The data for this sample comprise only initial attempts (two or three conversations with each person) to enter the realities of the senile and describe only the first steps to be taken in this program. Intensive research is obviously needed to determine the success of such an approach. Nevertheless, the conceptual frameworks of Mead and Schutz provide the basic tools for such a scheme and the data reported here suggest that the majority of senile patients at the hospital (35 or 58.8%) did have the desire to interact, the first condition necessary for sociable interaction.

Before closing, some of the possible reasons for the lack of success with those classified in Category I and the less than complete success with those in Category II will be discussed. Many reasons exist which are compatible with the interpretation of subjective and multiple realities given here. Some of them support the argument in favour of sociable interaction as a means of rehabilitating the senile, and all of them point to the complexity of the subject matter with which we are dealing.

Obstacles to Sociable Interaction

The reasons for not achieving more success than was attained are unknown. Senility is often attributed to physical malfunctions such as brain damage. (Busse, 1971) Available evidence, however, is far from conclusive, since medical measures of brain damage often contradict autopsy investigations.[6] Furthermore, as Szasz (1960) has argued, if mental illness were caused by a brain disease it should be manifested in blindness, paralysis, or some other bodily malfunction rather than as a psychosocial problem. That is to say, there is no convincing evidence to prove that brain damage is the reason for the failure to establish universes of discourse. This of course does not deny a relationship between physiological, psychological, and social processes. Much more interdisciplinary research is needed before any conclusions can be drawn.

Drug medication had an unknown effect on the patients. All of them were given drugs and most of the people received different kinds several times a day. The kinds of medication each patient received, the dosage, and the frequency per day were all recorded from the patients' charts. Unfortunately, the medical pharmacist could not even estimate the effects when he realized the multiple combinations of the different kinds of drugs. Although current research is investigating the effects of drugs (Webb, 1971), our state of knowledge is still in its initial stages.

It is also possible that shared meanings did not exist. Without a minimal consensus of meanings, it would be impossible to interact with these persons. (Miyamoto, 1959) Or, as suggested earlier, the patients could have lacked faith in the researcher's acceptance of their ability to define their reality. Perhaps they did not believe that they shared the same reality as the researcher. It is certainly possible that the brief and temporary encounters with the researcher were insufficient to reestablish this belief for many. Much more time with each patient is needed to test the implications of the approach suggested in this paper. Presumably some patients would require more time than others. For example, one Category III respondent continually spoke of being afraid and feared for her own as well as the researcher's safety. By the third visit she showed signs of recognizing the researcher ("You're the girl with the long hair and brown eyes"), and no longer expressed the same fear. However, most respondents did not show signs of recognition even after three visits. (This particular respondent was atypical insofar as her conversations centered on the same topic during all three visits, that of fear.) Another respondent who was classified as senile on the first two visits successfully completed the interview which was part of the larger study on the third visit. She was released from the hospital a few weeks later.

The variations among patients highlight Simmel's contention that the type of tact and the personal qualities employed must change from person to person. Presumably one researcher would have success with one patient where another researcher would not. Although the written word is not the best medium for conveying the idea that the researcher is "taking the underlying attitude of the other" (tape recorders and movie projectors may be helpful for this purpose), attempts were made to assume the attitude of the patient. For example, if the patient was serious, happy, or afraid, the researcher tried to portray similar attitudes in an attempt to share that reality. Obviously the attitude could have been misinterpreted, or attempts to convey a similar attitude to the patient could have failed.

Considering these difficulties, the main conclusion to be drawn from this study seems to be the need for continued research. The problems requiring study are numerous, and include the following: the effects of drug medication, the relationship between physiological, psychological, and social processes, the feasibility of the sociability approach, effects of the institutional environment on perceptions of reality, and the whole question of whether or not we should even try to rehabilitate the senile. Some people suggest that senility is not considered a deviant status but is seen instead as a normal consequence of aging. (Baizerman and Ellison, 1971) With more people living longer, perhaps increased efforts will be devoted to preventing senility and/or rehabilitating the senile.

Discussion

This paper has attempted to analyze the results, both objective and impressionistic, of efforts to communicate with hospitalized senile patients. The existence of senility has been neither questioned nor "argued away" by redefinition. Rather, the approach used in the study starts with an acceptance of the phenomenon and asks, "What is it and what can be done about it?" It has been argued here that the answer to the second question is to be sought in the answer to the first; one solution to the problem is to be found in the symbolic interactionist and phenomenological perspectives. From this point of view, senility can be considered an absence of shared meanings and a subsequent breakdown in communication. As such, existing knowledge about the reconstruction of shared meanings and about the "taken-for-granted" background within which communication takes place can be applied to develop a method for the rehabilitation of the senile. In other words, if senility is a "failure" within the social process, then the solution should also be sought at that level, within the world of interaction with others, rather than in the physiological or biochemical spheres. This paper, then, has not focused on senility as a lack of shared meanings; rather, it has centered on the possibility of using our knowledge about communication between individuals to discover a means of rehabilitation.

The data presented in this study were a preliminary effort to test the symbolic interactionist approach. Viewed in this light, the incomplete success with the patients can be interpreted more as a reflection of the complexity of the problem, than as the failure of the technique. Indeed, the partial success which was achieved in such a short period of time might well indicate the potential success of this approach.

NOTES

1. This is a revised version of a paper entitled, "Entering a Different Reality: Conversations with the Senile," presented at the Canadian Association on Gerontology, first General Biennial meeting, Ottawa, Ontario, 1973.

2. This paper is drawn from a larger study entitled "Future Time Perspective among the Hospitalized Elderly and a Phenomenological Interpretation of Senility," M.A. thesis, McMaster University, Hamilton, Ontario, 1973.

3. The term "senility" is not intended to convey any judgment of the persons involved. Rather, it is used to refer to those labeled as such in the hospital where the data were collected.

4. In Schutz's world of working, the word "working" is not synonymous with the word "job" or "occupation". Rather it refers to "getting things done".

5. It is not known whether or not the patients actually did have an objective purpose or ulterior motive for interacting or if they conversed for other reasons than those suggested here. The interpretation of the interaction as sociable is therefore necessarily a subjective judgment of the researcher. The basis for this judgment lies with the other's ability to take the underlying attitude of the patient.

6. Source: conversation with the medical director of the hospital, June, 1972.

BIBLIOGRAPHY

Baizerman, M., and D. L. Ellison. "A Social Role Analysis of Senility." *The Gerontologist*, 1971, Summer, pp. 163-170.

Brown, C. "Memoirs of an Intermittent Madman: A Declaration of Rebellion Against a Therapeutic Tyranny that Threatens All Who Find Their State of Consciousness in Conflict with the Norm," in *Decency and Deviance*, eds. Haas and Shaffir. Toronto: McClelland and Stewart, 1974, pp. 179-195.

Busse, E. W. "Biologic and Sociologic Changes Affecting Adaptation in Mid and

Late Life." *Annals of Internal Medicine*, 1971, pp. 115-120.

Cameron, D. "Tim Crawford Meets the Mind Police," in *Decency and Deviance*, eds. Haas and Shaffir. Toronto: McClelland and Stewart, 1974, pp. 167-178.

Denzin N. K. "The Methodologies of Symbolic Interaction: A Critical Review of Research Techniques," in *Social Psychology through Symbolic Interaction*, eds. Stone and Farberman. Toronto: Ginn-Blaisdell, 1970, pp. 447-465.

Goffman, E. *Asylums*. New York: Doubleday, 1961.

Kinch, J. W. "A Formalized Theory of the Self-Concept." *American Journal of Sociology*, Vol. 68 (1963), pp. 481-486.

Kaplan, H. B., I. Boyd, and S. E. Bloom. "Patient Culture and the Evaluation of Self," in *Deviance, The Interactionist Perspective*, eds. Rubington and Weinberg. New York: Macmillan, 1968, pp. 355-367.

Marshall, V., and D. Hughes. "Nothing Else But Mad: Canadian Legislative Trends in the Light of Models of Mental Illness and Their Implication for Civil Liberties," in *Decency and Deviance*, eds. Haas and Shaffir. Toronto: McClelland and Stewart, 1974, pp. 146-166.

Mead, G. H. *Mind, Self and Society*, ed. C. W. Morris. Chicago: Phoenix Books, 1934.

Miyamoto, S. F. "The Social Act: Re-Examination of a Concept." *Pacific Sociological Review*, 1959, pp. 51-55.

Rosenhan, D. L. "On Being Sane in Insane Places," in *Decency and Deviance*, eds. Haas and Shaffir. Toronto: McClelland and Stewart, 1974, pp. 43-63.

Sampson, H., S. L. Messinger, and R. D. Towne. "Family Processes and Becoming a Mental Patient," in *Deviance, The Interactionist Perspective*, eds. Rubington and Weinberg. New York: Macmillan, 1968, pp. 41-50.

Scheff, T. J. *Being Mentally Ill*. Chicago: Aldine, 1966.

Schutz, A. "Phenomenology and the Social Sciences," in *Philosophical Essays in Memory of Edmund Husserl*, ed. Farber. Cambridge: Harvard University Press, 1940. Also in *Collected Papers I*, ed. Natanson. The Hague: Martinus Nijhoff, 1971, pp. 118-140.

――――. "The Problem of Rationality in the Social World." *Economica*, Vol. X (1943), pp. 130-149. Also in *Collected Papers II*, ed. Brodersen. The Hague: Martinus Nijhoff, 1964, pp. 64-88.

――――. "On Multiple Realities." *Philosophy and Phenomenological Research*, Vol. V (1945). Also in *Collected Papers I*, ed. Natanson. The Hague: Martinus Nijhoff, 1971, pp. 229-234.

――――. "Don Quixote and the Problem of Reality," *Dianoia, Yearbook of the Department of Philosophy*, University of Mexico, 1954. Also in *Collected Papers II*, ed. Brodersen. The Hague: Martinus Nijhoff, 1964, pp. 135-159.

――――. "Rational Action within Common-Sense Experience," *Collected Papers I*, ed. Natanson. The Hague: Martinus Nijhoff, 1971, pp. 27-34.

Simmel, G. "The Problem of Sociology," trans. A. E. Small. *American Journal of Sociology*, Vol. XV (1909), pp. 289-320.

――――. *The Sociology of Georg Simmel*, trans. K. Wolff. New York: The Free Press, 1950.

Stone, G. P. "The Play of Little Children," in *Social Psychology through Symbolic Interaction*, eds. Stone and Farberman. Toronto: Ginn-Blaisdell, 1970, pp. 545-553.

Szasz, T. "The Myth of Mental Illness." *American Psychologist*, Vol. 15 (1960), pp. 113-118.

Thomas, W. I., and D. S. Thomas. "Situations Defined as Real are Real in their

Consequences," in *Social Psychology through Symbolic Interaction*, eds. Stone and Farberman. Toronto: Ginn-Blaisdell, 1970, pp. 154-155.

Webb, W. L. "The Use of Psychopharmacological Drugs in the Aged." *Geriatrics*, 1971, pp. 95-103.

PEOPLE ARE ROUTINELY called upon, either individually or collectively, to order and make sense of their experiences. The world of professional wrestling permits us to examine the manner in which audiences are manipulated to collectively define situations.

The following article provides a systematic symbolic interactionist account of professional wrestling. It is instructive, because the authors relate the wrestling situation to everyday life experiences and understandings. All people—wrestlers, physicians, astronauts—are alike in that their activities and understandings are built up out of the interactions and expectations of everyday life. Past analyses, in which wrestling is seen as no more than "ritual", fail to do justice to the symbolic interactionist perspective. As this article shows, symbolic interaction can be used to comprehend the dynamic of any situation without resorting to other explanations.

Symbolic interactionists typically locate the emergence of social identity within an ongoing process of interaction. As Goffman has shown, however, not all identity-forming occurs within reciprocally interactive situations. Interactive situations may be "directed" or "presentational" as in performances before others in the theatre, in a classroom, or at wrestling matches. Those individuals whom Goffman sees as being managed are referred to as the "audience".

To view a situation solely in these terms, however, is to accept the point of view of only one participant in the situation (the actor) while ignoring the viewpoint of the others (the audience). From a symbolic interactionist perspective, it should be obvious that the actor is also constrained by the audience. The success of the presentation depends on whether or not it fits in with the audience's own experiences and range of understanding. The actor must therefore first take the role of the other —the typical audience member—in determining his performance.

It is necessary, then, to examine the nature and processes of audience expectations and understandings in order to analyze directed situations. Wrestling proves to be a good subject for this study, because the audience experiences the activity as an exaggerated form of everyday life. Through its exaggerations, wrestling conveys the expectations of different life situations in a form easily understood.

The identification of the wrestling fan is not the interactive identity of face-to-face encounters, but the more abstract identification built around the symbols of group membership. Aside from some seminal work by Blumer (1953) and Strauss (1969), symbolic interactionist studies have rarely dealt with the formation and maintenance of such collective identities. While interactive identity creates and sustains action within a specific situation, group membership has the additional characteristic of categorization; at the same time as it identifies members within the group, it dissociates those who are not members. Again, wrestling is shown to be a particularly instructive example of the dynamic of this group identification/dissociation process.

Exaggerating Everyday Life: The Case of Professional Wrestling

ALLAN TUROWETZ/MICHAEL ROSENBERG

Introduction

SYMBOLIC INTERACTION HAS made substantial contributions to the sociological understanding of such diverse areas of social life as deviance (Becker, 1963; Schur, 1965), dying (Glaser and Strauss, 1967), occupational socialization (Geer, 1972; Hughes, 1958), and above all, the subtleties of everyday life (Blumer, 1969; Goffman, 1959). There can be little doubt, then, that this perspective has developed to the point where it can be used to examine and make sense of a variety of social relationships. In this paper, we shall attempt to develop a symbolic interactionist account of professional wrestling as a social relationship.

Wrestling has already been analyzed by one of the foremost symbolic interactionists, Gregory P. Stone (1971); interestingly enough, however, Stone makes only partial use of the symbolic interactionist perspective. He also attempts to account for certain characteristics of this form of entertainment in terms of the mentality and class culture of the audience. According to the study, the wrestling audience tends to be above average in age, below average in education, from a low socioeconomic stratum, and composed of a high proportion of women. Using concepts derived from Lipset's discussion of "working-class authoritarianism" Stone proposes that the wrestling audience is concerned with "the immediately perceivable", is "susceptible to staging", and tends to view the world in the simplistic terms of a struggle between good and evil. Wrestling's emphasis on morality, Stone concludes, is a partial result of the high proportion of female fans, since women "attach significantly greater importance" to morality than do men.

Allan Turowetz and Michael Rosenberg teach at the Department of Sociology, Dawson College, Montreal.

In our opinion, the relationship between wrestling and its audience is far more complex than Stone's cultural explanation suggests. Not all wrestling fans are working-class people nor do all working-class people enjoy wrestling. Its distinction between good and evil is no less sophisticated than that found in the typical television show or the average motion picture. As to the "simplicity" of the wrestling audiences' perceptions, Stone himself indicates that the wrestling fan need not and usually does not believe in the action but in the performer. This is illustrated by his quotation, overheard from a fan:

> I don't give a damn if it is a fake! Kill the son-of-a-bitch! (in Stone, 1971:301)

We contend that people's enjoyment of wrestling does not depend on "mental set", "cultural predispositions", or "working-class naiveté"; wrestling is popular because it fits in with persons' experiences of everyday life and permits them to identify with and participate in the activity. Wrestling is an exaggeration of everyday life experience. It reflects this experience in that the ideas, conflicts, and personality types are those recognizable in daily life. However, in wrestling, the men are stronger, the drama of situations is greater, and people are either heroes or villains. By examining the ways in which wrestling as a social activity comes to acquire meaning for its audience, we can uncover the social processes of identification and participation that are central in the everyday lives of audience members.

Identification in Everyday Life

Identification is a communication process emergent in everyday life interaction. In his analysis of socialization, Mead (1934) shows that identification begins as the form of self-indication called "taking the role of the other". By taking the role of the other, persons are able to orient their behavior toward each other by interpreting the impressions, gestures, and verbalizations given off by each of them. It is this mutual process of role-taking that generates shared social meanings as an interpretive context for social interaction and identification. (Stone, 1962) Identification with others, then, is an interpretation process centered around symbolic interaction.

Identification, however, is a two-fold process. On the one hand, we identify with others through participation in shared social relations. When we chose to identify with a certain person, however, we in a sense dissociate ourselves from some "other" person. All identification thus implies dissociation. The choice is based on a standard repertoire of shared social identities all of which are recognized through the symbolic character assigned to each identity.

The work of sociologists such as Goffman (1959, 1961, 1963), who uses the dramaturgical model to study identity, has shown that the symbolic character of identity permits and, in fact, usually requires the manipulation and management of those symbols. The individual is not passive but, rather, involved in presenting and maintaining definitions of self and others. Stone (1962) has further focused on appearance as the symbolic means by which persons establish the "identifications" of one another. Appearance is communicated in gestures, clothing, discourse, names, and all the other means of self-presentation that act as symbols of an individual's identity.

Viewed in this way, an individual's identity "is established when others place him as a social object by assigning him the same words of identity that he appropriates for himself or announces." (Stone, 1962:93) Identity announcements and placements become evident through participation in social relations. Such participation is both an indication and a result of the degree of fit between announcements and placements. In the case of wrestling, the audience participates in the interaction by placing upon the wrestlers those identities of group membership (Strauss, 1959) which the wrestlers announce through the staging of appearances. Wrestling dramatizes and exaggerates the standard symbols of appearance, and its staging transforms identification and dissociation into drama. This drama is successful when the audience participates as members in the relationship; the staged action becomes a form of interaction for the fans. We will now examine in detail the ways in which wrestling both creates appearances and manages staging within this social relationship.

Dynamics of Audience Identification

The creation and manipulation of dramatic appearance is based upon a symbolic repertoire which has become familiar to the wrestling audience. It is by acting in terms of these identities that wrestlers make their behavior understandable to that audience. Consequently, to become a wrestling fan, it is necessary to learn this repertoire of dramatic appearances.

There have been several attempts to determine the dimensions of the dramatic identity portrayed by wrestlers (Henricks, 1974; Smith, 1974). By focusing on dramatic appearance, we have uncovered four dimensions in terms of which audience members identify with wrestlers: morality, sexuality, ethnicity, and athletic prowess. Through the staged exaggerations of everyday life activity, these dimensions of dramatic appearance serve as identification and dissociation symbols.

A. Morality Dramatic appearance is set up dichotomously through the symbols of "good" and "evil". In the private language of the wrestling world, the roles based upon these symbols of good and evil are referred to as "Babyface" and "Heel" respectively, and these roles focus on the display of certain character attributes. One such attitude is inherent in the nature of games; games are governed by rules and players can be evaluated in relation to how they play the game.

The Babyface is seen as a "clean" wrestler in that he follows what are supposed to be, and what the audience perceives to be, the rules. The Heel is a wrestler who breaks these rules in order to gain what the audience should consider an unfair advantage. For example, he will surreptitiously use "brass knuckles" or a pencil, which he conceals in his wrestling trunks, or commit such "illegal" moves as pulling his opponent's hair or punching below the belt.

An audience member, however, need not wait for a match to begin in order to determine whether a given wrestler is a Heel or a Babyface, for wrestlers will exhibit their dramatic role in every aspect of their appearance and behavior. The Babyface presents himself as cleanshaven, serious but polite, good-looking, and articulate. The Heel is violent and uncontrolled, inarticulate, and possesses some peculiarity which sets him apart, such as an unkempt or immaculate appearance, a scar, or a nervous twitch. The purpose of such exaggerated appearances and behavior is not simply to make the wrestler recognizably good or evil but to enhance the process of audience identification and dissociation.

Names and nicknames may also be used to convey a wrestler's identity. Names such as "Abdullah the Butcher", "Mad-Dog Vachon", "Gorilla Monsoon", "Killer Kowalski", and George the "Animal" Steele, indicate that their bearers are the Heels. In contrast, Babyfaces do not carry definite labels of "goodness" with such minor exceptions as Jean Ferré, the "Friendly Giant", or Igor, the "Gentle Polish Strongman".

B. Sexuality   Sexuality is yet another component of dramatic appearance. Heels are usually presented in a way that permits the audience member to label them as sexually deviant. This dimension of dramatic appearance is evident in symbols of sexual "otherness"; pink velvet jackets, teased blond hair, and baby-blue tights. Such dress styles are enhanced by an effeminate gait and by such names as "The Love Brothers" or "The Hollywood Blonds". Roland Barthes uncovers some of the symbolic meanings contained in sexual appearance:

> Thauvin, a fifty year-old with an obese and sagging body, whose type of asexual hideousness always inspires feminine nicknames, displays in his flesh the character of baseness ... [and] in addition ugliness as wholly gathered into a particularly repulsive quality of matter: the pallid collapse of dead flesh (the public calls Thauvin la Barbaque, 'stinking meat'). (Barthes, 1973:17)

C. Ethnicity One of the major dimensions of dramatic appearance in North American wrestling is ethnicity. The attributes displayed through ethnicity are determined by the typical ethnic membership of the audience. For example, in Montreal, those wrestlers presented to audiences as Germans, Japanese, Russians, and Arabs are cast as Heels, while French Canadians and Italians are cast as Babyfaces.

In 1958, a match was staged at the Montreal Forum between "Baron" Fritz Von Erich and "Rabbi" Raphael Halpern. Advance publicity resulted in a large Jewish audience. Baron Fritz Von Erich was presented as a Nazi from Germany. Sporting a swastika on his arm and wearing high black boots, the Baron stomped into the ring screaming obscenities in German and raising his arm in a Hitlerian salute. Pointing to members of the audience, the Baron promised to send his opponent back to Auschwitz. Following the Baron's five minute pre-match performance his opponent, "Rabbi" Raphael Halpern, ran into the ring, prayer book in hand, skullcap on head, and wearing a blue and white costume covered with Stars of David. The crowd roared its approval. On this occasion the forces of defined good prevailed and the "Rabbi" was victorious.

The New York circuit is another where the symbols of ethnic membership are predominant. Pedro Morales, a Puerto Rican and former World Wrestling Federation champion, was carried in from the dressing room on the shoulders of four fans to the cheering and flag-waving of the Puerto Rican fans. Responding to the audience, Morales began to wave two miniature flags, Puerto Rican and American, which had previously been concealed in his robe.

Once again, the ethnic character of the wrestler is often contained in his name. For example, "The Golden Greek", "The Sheik", and "The Kangaroos" are names that identify wrestlers to the audience as members of a particular ethnic group.

D. Athletic Prowess Athletic prowess has received little attention from previous analysts of wrestling. This is primarily due to the fact that athletic prowess is so closely linked to morality. For instance, it is the athletic prowess generally exhibited by the Babyface that will overcome the unfair advantage of the Heel. Such athletic prowess becomes confused with the "moral goodness" of the Babyface. Yet Heels such as "Killer Kowalski" are also capable of exhibiting athletic prowess. Prowess, then, does not depend on the morality of the wrestler, but may be found in both the Babyface and the Heel.

Some wrestlers specialize in the presentation of athletic prowess, a fact usually announced by their names or nicknames. Because athletic prowess provides the least opportunity for the symbolic manipulation of dramatic appearance, one might say that the scripts of such wrestlers' performances are contained in their names. For example, iron-stomached

Tony Marino usually appears in main events with those villains who are noted for their punching ability. The match begins with Marino standing in the middle of the ring and watching with scientific detachment as the villain punches him repeatedly in the stomach. After several minutes of this apparently severe beating, the villain, in mounting frustration, begins to kick Marino in the same area. Tony gradually becomes angry, and urged on by the audience, begins his attack.

In any wrestling match, the audience member should have no doubt about which side to support. For, when the Babyface beats the Heel, the lumberjack defeats the Russian, or the hero beats the homosexual, the audience does not regard the outcome as the victory of some abstract quality over another; rather, it is "us beating them". The wrestling match is always the battle between "us" and "them", in which the actual wrestlers are the concrete representatives of that group struggle.

Hidden behind the blatant distinctions of dramatic appearance is the inarticulated set of dimensions of group membership. Wrestling exemplifies the ways in which persons differentiate themselves from others. That is, wrestling embodies a system of positive and negative identifications which is, in fact, a system of identification and dissociation. The Heel's evil is exaggerated, not to make him an embodiment of an abstract quality, but to *guarantee* that the typical audience member will not identify with him.

Not only does wrestling make use of conventional stereotypes by its staged exaggeration of these qualities, but it also invites the audience to *participate* in the action. This participation is referred to by wrestlers as "audience heat". Ideally, everyone should react to the "Nazi" as one audience member did:

> Fucking Nazi, we'll kill you once and for all. No more Auschwitz. The allies got you and now Johnny will. Give him hell.

It is the tension produced by the staged exaggeration in wrestling that generates audience heat. Should the hero lose, then this is everyone's loss and everyone is equally disturbed and frustrated by it, especially when that loss is "undeserved" or "unnatural". This tension is not always successfully diffused by a sense of moral victory. Some Heels are so effective in their presentation, or some outcomes are so frustrating to the audience, that the fans overreact, often placing a wrestler in serious danger:

> I remember one time in Marseille after I beat the wrestler. They put a fire to the ring. You know, I braved the people and then the people turned on me. You know that the French are pretty wild at times.
> After the fight some guy runs at me. I applied the abdominal stretch.

They carried him away. You know, some of those people get carried away and since they think that I am small, they try to take advantage of me. But that doesn't work; I can usually take care of myself.

Managing the Staging of Wrestling

Identification is not a static condition, but a symbolic process emergent in social interaction. Like any other form of social interaction, wrestling is a staged event. According to Goffman, appearances are not merely internalized expectations which are acted out, but are subject to the manipulation and control of the actors. With such a perspective, Goffman is able to describe everyday life in its implicit dramaturgical terms. So, for example, the waiter in a restaurant will convey an air of politeness while in the presence of his customer (the front region) but will let out his irritation at a poor tipper when he is in the kitchen area (the backstage). We can also speak of the "setting", and its importance in interactions. For example, we take friends out to an expensive restaurant in order to make a good impression or to sustain a definition of ourselves as the kind of people who should be in such a restaurant. These self-presentations which vary according to region or audience are examples of impression management. Goffman suggests that this process is continuous even if we are rarely aware of it.

Such impression management creates interactive settings within which identities and identifications are mobilized. In the case of wrestling, the staging is conscious, elaborate, and entertaining. It is the audience member's participation in, or active response to this form of entertainment that makes wrestling an enjoyable experience.

A. The Setting A wrestling event is termed a "match". This is usually set to vary in time from 15 to 30 minutes, although some of the matches have no specific time allotment and are fought until the referee decides that one of the wrestlers is "victorious". The match ends with a fall, which may be either a pin (keeping an opponent's shoulder on the mat for three seconds) or a submission hold (holding an opponent in a position which forces him to concede the match).

There are different kinds of matches staged on any given night. A regular match is fought between two opponents and is usually won in one fall, although some matches are won by two out of three falls. Other kinds of events include the "tag-team match" (four wrestlers fight in teams of two with only one member from each team allowed in the ring at one time), the "Battle Royal" (a match among a number of wrestlers with one final winner), and the "cage match" (a "grudge match" in which the ring is surrounded by wire meshing six feet high to prevent either wrestler from "escaping").

The wrestling ring is set up in the center of the arena, and the arena as a whole becomes the front region during the match. Ringside seats are reserved for media representatives, friends of the wrestlers, representatives from the municipal athletic commission, the timekeeper, and the circuit promoter. All of these individuals are characterized by the seriousness with which they attend to the match; neatly and somewhat formally dressed, they are the apparent agents of authority whose presence is used to confirm the "authenticity" of the wrestling match. In appearance and demeanor, then, they are sharply differentiated from both the wrestlers and the audience.

The athletic commissioners are supposedly there to see that the "rules" are not "violated".* The commission is appointed by the municipality (or, in the U.S.A., by the state) and consists of judges, lawyers, doctors, and other reputable "high status" individuals. Apart from their symbolic, legitimating function, these people do not participate in the wrestling match.

The ringside physician also functions to legitimize activity. The physician is supposed to provide medical aid to a wrestler "injured" during a match, but few, if any, of these physicians have a medical license. Such staged legitimacy is organized not only to make the match believable, but also to make the setting complete.

B. Audience Identification and Participation   Audience identification and participation is best examined by describing a typical wrestling match. The wrestlers approach the ring from opposite sides of the Montreal Forum. The champion is Pierre, a French Canadian Babyface and his opponent is the Caliph, an Arab Heel, who is followed by Gamul Ptolomy, his manager. Pierre's approach to the ring is relaxed and friendly. He acknowledges the cheers by waving to the audience, shaking hands with friends and smiling genially. The Caliph is at first aloof and disdainful of the audience. However as the audience begins to jeer him, he yells insults back at them.

Once the lights are dimmed, a set of bright spotlights hits the ring. The ring announcer, dressed in a black tuxedo, introduces the combatants with great formality, making note of their weights and places of residence. As the Caliph is announced, the audience boos, jeers, and throws objects at the ring; the introduction of Pierre provokes

---

* Rules vary from city to city but the following rules are typical: ring ropes may not be used to strangle, entangle, or gain extra leverage; the wrestler is forced to break his hold if his opponent is able to touch any of the ropes surrounding the ring; use of equipment or any objects, such as chairs, chains, and metal objects is forbidden; blows with a closed fist, finger jabs to the eyes, forearm smashes to the head, or the pulling of hair are prohibited.

enthusiastic applause while the announcement of the referee is treated with indifference.

The officials continue to conduct the event with great formality. The combatants meet the referee in the center of the ring where he explains the "rules". They then return to their respective corners, remove their robes and hand them over to their valets. The ringing of the bell by the timekeeper signals the start of the match.

Before the match begins, the Caliph already indicates his feelings of violence and aggression toward Pierre; he taunts, threatens, and can barely restrain himself from attacking his opponent. Yet, once the bell sounds, the Caliph suddenly begins an elaborate ceremonial prayer to "Allah". Pierre initially appears as perplexed by this ceremony as the audience, but he soon begins to mock and mimic it, thereby showing the audience that he is "one of them". Throughout the match, Pierre presents himself as the man who follows the rules. He waits for the bell to ring and then he begins to fight to the "best of his ability". Pierre appears to bear no personal animosity toward the Caliph; like all of us, he is "merely doing his job". In contrast, the Caliph appears uncontrolled and semihuman. His aggression is ongoing and directed at everyone; he appears to take a perverse pleasure in breaking the rules. From the point of view of the typical fan, even the Caliph's prayer is not a legitimate ritual, but a persistent and stubborn attempt to delay the proceedings and frustrate the audience.

Pierre attempts to entrap the Caliph with a submission hold throughout the match, but the Caliph succeeds in avoiding this by jabbing Pierre in the forehead with a foreign object. As the audience knows this is "illegal", they yell to the referee who "by chance" is facing the other way when the act is committed. When the referee hears the fans he turns to face the scene, but by this time the Caliph has hidden the object in his trunks. The referee warns the beleaguered Pierre, who seems about to answer the Caliph's action with an "illegal punch"; every time the audience now yells, the referee acts as if he assumes that they are indicating that Pierre is violating the rules.

The role of the referee, as Henricks points out, is related to the social type "fool":

> While the failure of the official to effectively control the villain occa-
> sionally may take on ludicrous overtones (e.g. he may get knocked on
> the seat of his pants by a misdirected punch), generally he appears as
> the fairly colourless representative of ineffective justice. His position is
> discounted; no one expects that he will be able to control the wrestlers.
> (Henricks, 1974:184)

What this means is that institutional authority as represented by the referee is both ineffectual and foolish. The referee is well-meaning; he tries to do things right, but in the process he overlooks true merit and frustrates both the hero and the audience.

As the match progresses, Pierre is subjected to progressively greater degrees of torment and humiliation. Sticking stubbornly to the rules, he is thwarted in his attempt to gain any advantage, and so is forced to give up his obedience to institutional order and break the rules in the name of the higher order of morality. Once the decision is made, Pierre, with the enthusiastic approval of the audience, now begins to beat his opponent savagely and skillfully. The Caliph is now transformed from an inhuman aggressor to a cringing coward. The audience continues to vilify the Caliph and exhort Pierre.

The hero is then caught delivering an "illegal" punch and is disqualified by the referee; the Caliph, apparently cowering in terror in his corner, is declared the winner. Pierre's loss, however, is the audience's loss, and everyone is equally disturbed and frustrated by it. The next week, these fans will be back in the hope that they and Pierre will be vindicated and the Caliph, "that ugly son-of-a-bitch", will finally be "killed".

C. The Media   The ability of wrestling to mobilize audience identification and participation is further increased by skillful use of the mass media. The media maintain audience interest between matches and provide the interested fan with news, ratings, and scenarios for upcoming events. The fact that most of the media reject wrestling as a legitimate sport, however, is a problem. Newspapers will accept advertisements but will rarely report outcomes; famous wrestlers will not be profiled in *Sports Illustrated*; CTV's *Wide World of Sports* will not televise professional wrestling championships. As a result, wrestling circuits have been forced to create their own magazines and to pay for their own telecasts.

Especially important in wrestling are the magazines which relate the latest news to their supporters. Wrestling magazines are similar in text to movie-fan magazines. Their stories are exaggerated and often completely fallacious; photographs of bloody faces and injured bodies help to promote desired impressions. The following are typical examples of the media's creation and manipulation of dramatic appearances.

> Anyway, the trouble with New York authorities occurred for the Bruiser near the beginning of his third year as a pro. An overflow crowd of 20,000 in the old Madison Square Garden on Eighth Avenue was incited to mass hysteria by the Bruiser's antics in the ring. . . . They [the fans] left via handy exits to escape dozens of melees in the main arena following the Bruiser's appearance. The Bruiser had to be escorted by a Cordon of Police. . . . They [the police] had to flail at people with clubs, while the people were flailing at the Bruiser who wasn't idle by a long

shot. He was trying to break through the Police Cordon to get at the fans. (*Wrestling World*, Vol. 8, No. 5 (February 1970), p. 51)

It wasn't too long after the match began that Kolof demonstrated how strong he really is. He picked up Sammartino and dropped him to the mat with a body slam. He continued to match strength with Bruno and later opened a gash across Sammartino's forehead. It was an ugly thing which caused the blood to flow freely down the champion's face. The referee called time, examined Sammartino and then signaled a halt to the match. . . . Both Kolof and Angelo were angered by the referee's ruling. . . . They were bitter and Kolof maintained that it was another capitalist trick, so typical of American policies. (*Wrestling World*, Vol. 9, No. 2 (1970), p. 64)

I call it my "coup de grace", he said. In reality it is a full Nelson. But, the way I use it makes it hard to duplicate. I put so much pressure into it that sometimes my fingers get locked into place, and I can't break the hold. Quite often the referee doesn't believe me and he disqualifies me. Usually it takes two people to pry my fingers loose. (*Wrestling World*, Vol. 8, No. 5 (1970), p. 44)

Television plays an even more significant part in the creation and manipulation of these dramatic appearances. Televised matches are taped, a fact that permits both the media and wrestling organizers to manipulate the events. The wrestling commentary is not usually provided by a member of a television sports department; on one Montreal station, the wrestling commentator had been a weather reporter. The commentator, however, is usually accompanied by an analyst who is either a current or retired wrestler. Commentaries during the match, which are presented as purely technical and refer to holds and ring strategies, appear to legitimate the authenticity of the match:

That's a good side head lock that grinds away at the ears of Marconi and Marconi tries to take him off balance and does. . . . This style of wrestling that you are witnessing of course is growing in popularity throughout the world mainly because there is so much action and so much body contact; such clever wrestlers with such innovative holds that it has replaced some of the older established styles.

Good holds and counterholds exchanged in rapid succession by the two men. The Chief finally with the hammerlock nicely applied to McNie. . . . Well, that's unlike McNie to use the ropes for an escape but this situation of course called for it. . . . Of course, the fans are in a dilemma; they're not quite sure whom to support. . . . A close call that time as the Chief went for the sleeper. . . . This Chief is a very stylish individual, an Indian with loads of class, and of course his scientific exploits are well known to audiences; an international performer who travels far and wide to demonstrate his skills, and leg work.

The televised interviews between matches are designed to promote forthcoming events. The tone of such interviews shifts from commentary to promotion:

INTERVIEWER: Do you think that you can handle Kowalski?

MAD-DOG: On Monday night I am going to tear Kowalski's ear off. He had better get an undertaker because when I get through with him, he'll need a coffin. I am going to beat him into a pulp and then eat his ear in front of the fans. This is it. His career is over.

Tomorrow night wrestling fans throughout Canada, you're looking at the new World's Heavyweight champion. All you've got to do is show up and you're going to see them put the belt around the middle of Harley Race. I have chased Funk throughout our world of wrestling, through Australia, Japan, all across the continental United States and now into Canada. But tomorrow night, right here in the Maple Leaf Gardens you're seeing history being made. . . . Harley raises his hand in victory as the new champion and I'm telling you now that I can beat anybody in the world whether it's in that squared circle or whether it's out in your street; I am the dominant figure in wrestling, the absolute supreme. When it comes to what I do, I do better than anyone else on the face of God's green earth and I'm going to prove it to you tomorrow night in Toronto.

Conclusion

Regardless of social class or sex, people who enjoy professional wrestling are moved by it, and participate in the activity. For these people, the appearance of wrestling is familiar. The notions of good and evil, the typifications of ethnic identity, and the glorification of athletic prowess are not simply the products of the wrestling world. Rather, they are the products of the biases, the desires, and the hopes of ordinary people. Wrestling capitalizes on these notions through the symbols of identity found spontaneously in everyday life conflict; symbols of fair play, decency, skill, and group membership. If we can recognize the wrestler for what he presents himself to be, it is only because we are able to recognize each other as what we present ourselves to be.

We have not attempted a causal explanation of wrestling's characteristics or popularity in terms of mental set, or cultural dispositions. In keeping with the labeling theory (Becker, 1963), we have sought to examine professional wrestling as a social relationship.

Symbolic interaction provides a theoretical perspective for uncovering the interaction processes underlying any social relationship.

BIBLIOGRAPHY

Barthes, Roland. *Mythologies*. St. Albans: Paladin, 1973.

Becker, Howard S. *Outsiders: Studies in the Sociology of Deviance*. New York: The Free Press, 1963.

Blumer, Herbert. *Symbolic Interactionism*. New Jersey: Prentice-Hall, 1969.

Dunning, Eric, ed. *Sport: Readings From a Sociological Perspective*. Leicester: University of Leicester Press, 1971.

Geer, Blanche. *Learning to Work*. Beverly Hills: Russell Sage Foundation, 1972.

Glaser, Barney, and Anselm Strauss. *Awareness of Dying*. Chicago: Aldine, 1967.

Goffman, Erving. *The Presentation of Self in Everyday Life*. Garden City: Doubleday Anchor, 1959.

————. *Asylums*. Garden City: Doubleday Anchor, 1961.

————. *Encounters*. New York: Bobbs-Merrill, 1963.

Henricks, Thomas. "Professional Wrestling as Moral Order." *Sociological Inquiry*, Vol. 44, No. 3. (1974), pp. 177-188.

Hughes, Everett C. *Men And Their Work*. New York: Free Press, 1958.

Mead, George H. *Mind, Self, and Society*. Chicago: University of Chicago Press, 1934.

Schur, Edwin. *Crimes Without Victims*. Englewood Cliffs, New Jersey: Prentice-Hall, 1965.

Smith, M. Dwayne. "Patterns and Functions of Ethnicity in Professional Wrestling," paper presented at the annual meetings, Southwestern Sociological Society, March 27-29, San Antonio, Texas, 1974.

Stone, Gregory P. "Appearance and the Self," in *Human Behavior and Social Processes*, ed. Arnold M. Rose. Boston: Houghton-Mifflin, 1962.

————. "Wrestling—The Great American Passion Play," in *Sport: Readings From a Sociological Perspective*, ed. E. Dunning. Leicester: University of Leicester Press, 1971.

Strauss, Anselm. *Mirrors and Masks*. New York: The Free Press, 1959.

THE PREVIOUS ARTICLES have focused on the part that definitions of the situation play in shaping human behavior. These definitions outline for us the roles and expectations that are operative in the particular social setting, and assist us in organizing our actions and reactions.

As we have suggested earlier, the process by which individuals learn the ways of a given society may be conceptualized as socialization. While originally referring to the way in which the biological organism becomes fully human, this concept has assumed a broader meaning and refers to "all the processes by means of which both children and adults are incorporated into groups of all types and sizes, and by means of which the norms, perspectives and values of such groups are acquired by the individual." (Lindesmith and Strauss, 1968:5)

Because of the important effect that childhood or primary socialization has on all succeeding phases of socialization, much of the traditional work in this area in sociology and psychology has been devoted to this early phase. Socialization is not, however, restricted to the childhood years. The process occurs throughout life in various settings and in interaction with many people, and thus it may be viewed in terms of its agents—the groups and settings in which the socializing occurs. Depending upon the stage of socialization the agents vary.

The family is usually the most important agent in childhood socialization although play and peer groups have a part even in this early phase. In later phases of the process, such as adolescence and adulthood, the socializing effects of peer groups, friends, and work groups strongly influence the person's social conduct. As people enter new groups and develop different friendship networks they continue to be socialized, and at times experience discrepancies between earlier and more immediate socialization.

Some sociologists have suggested that in modern Western societies the peer group has become an extremely important socializing agent. In his book *The Lonely Crowd* (1966), David Riesman concludes that for many people the approval of a peer group is the most important motivating factor in human behavior. Peer groups provide and define models for behavior, and when groups adopt new standards and practices, individuals are left in a state of uncertainty as to the appropriate manner of response in particular social situations. The changing attitudes and behavior regarding premarital sexual relations exemplify this point.

The author of "Female Premarital Sexual Careers" describes both the moral and situationally based views of the self as centering on the relationship between personal morality and premarital sexual activity. It is worth noting the extent to which such conceptions of moral worth have changed in the context of a moral revolution. A very short time ago, women who were thought to engage in premarital sex faced the real possibility of moral censure and stigma. Men, on the contrary, were expected to have premarital sexual relations, and were accorded status for doing so.

The so-called sexual revolution has presumably changed the moral field in which such activity takes place. Kleinman's article, however, shows that the sexual revolution has created a situation of moral ambiguity for women, and has increased the range of dilemmas and possible sanctions faced by those who engage in premarital sex. Women are now caught in a double bind where they are damned if they do, and damned if they don't. In the context of a more liberal rhetoric about sexual activity, women find that some reference groups critical of premarital sexual relations conflict with other groups emphasizing a more "liberated" set of activities. Skillfully, the author describes the ways women perceive this dilemma in a framework of numerous, competing expectations and views of self.

Female Premarital Sexual Careers

SHERRYL KLEINMAN

Introduction

THE SEXUAL REVOLUTION has received widespread attention in the mass media, as well as in popular and social scientific literature. The question, "Has a sexual revolution come about?", is complicated by the difficulties that arise when one attempts to provide a clear definition of the phenomenon. One thing, however, is evident; the term "sexual revolution" is both ambiguous and multidimensional.[1] It denotes numerous sexual life styles and lines of activity, each of which is accorded varying degrees of approval by the community.

The fact that the notion of approval-disapproval exists indicates that sexual behavior is not considered to be an amoral matter by members of the community. That is, decisions as to which sexual activities one should participate in may be characterized by moral speculation and doubt; in addition, all disclosed sexual behavior will meet with a degree of approval or disapproval by others. Has the sexual revolution removed sexual activity from the moral realm? The answer to this question entails an examination of changes in sexual behavior, as well as in attitudes toward sex.

Traditionally, men have unofficially acquired the license to be permissive in their premarital relationships with women. That is, the male is expected to engage in premarital intercourse before he marries, and may pursue such activity with many partners. The major "moral limitation" to the male's sexual behavior has been his choice of partner; the "moral man" could not expect to have premarital intercourse with a woman whom he respected or intended to marry. Women, on the other hand, were expected to remain virgins until marriage. As Ehrmann (1959b:158) states, this double standard of sexual morality "contains a logical inconsistency because, if men are permitted to have premarital sexual intercourse, but women are not, and this code is rigidly obeyed, there would be no women with whom the men could have coitus." However, he further notes that in *practice*, the double standard created two classes of women: the "bad" women with whom men engage in premarital sex but do not marry; and the "good", with whom men refrain from having sexual intercourse and whom they marry.

Has the double standard persisted? In a study by Kaats and Davis (1970), the authors found that half of the males in their sample held a double standard, "particularly when the woman in question was a sister or potential spouse." (1970:398) This led them to suggest that "while

Sherryl Kleinman is a Ph.D. candidate, Department of Sociology, University of Minnesota.

male attitudes may be changing, they may not be changing as rapidly as the sexual behavior of college women." (1970:395) That sexual behavior is less a matter of moral concern for men than for women is shown by data on the way college students think various reference groups would feel about their having engaged in sexual intercourse when in love and with a casual date. (Kaats and Davis, 1970:396) The authors discovered that the males regarded "family and societal groups as only slightly to moderately disapproving" of their behavior, and felt that close friends would approve. (1970:398) Females, on the other hand, perceived that all groups, including close friends, would disapprove of their actions, "even when they [were] in love with the person." (1970:398) There are data to suggest, then, that males are less likely to anticipate or experience the disapproval of others (regarding their participation in sexual activities) than females; men are permitted to engage in casual sexual encounters, and are aware of their "license" to do so.

A number of recent studies indicate that the rate of premarital intercourse for females has increased during the 1960s and 1970s (Bell and Chaskes, 1970; Christensen and Gregg, 1972; Davis, 1971; Hunt, 1974; Kaats and Davis, 1970). In Hunt's (1974) survey of 982 males and 1044 females, a sample which "closely parallels the American population of persons 17 years old and over" (1974:16), he found that

> in the 18-24 age group 70% of the single white females and 80% of the married white females had had at least some premarital coital experience ... nearly 2 to 3 times as many unmarried females are having coitus in their late teens and early twenties as did a generation ago. (Hunt, 1974:150, 168)

Does this imply that women, in fact, regard sex as a casual, amoral matter? In Hunt's study, although two thirds of the younger female sample (ages 18-34) had had premarital intercourse, more than half (51%) of these women had had only one partner. (1974:151) According to Hunt, "Males, on the other hand, typically have a handful of coital partners before marriage, and in many cases at least some of these relationships have been casual." (1974:153) There are other indicators which support the contention that sexual behavior is not perceived to be an amoral matter by women. Christensen and Gregg (1972:61) and Hunt (1974:157) point out that although feelings of guilt and remorse regarding participation in sexual activities have been reduced, females are more likely to regret their behavior than males. The evidence suggests that women accept premarital coitus more readily when the female is involved in a love relationship with her partner (Christensen and Gregg, 1972:60; Davis, 1971; Ehrmann, 1959a, Ch. 4; Reiss, 1967:114). As Davis notes, "for women, the development of a sense of themselves as sexual creatures is still strongly rooted in the experience of affection, love, and romance." (1971:130) Although Hunt's data (1974:153) indicate that more males are participating in sexual relations within a love relationship than formerly, Ehrmann (1959b:164) found that "love is *inversely* related to sexual behavior among males with a double and males with a liberal standard."

The literature suggests that despite the sexual revolution, sexual behavior remains a moral, rather than a pragmatic concern for many women.[2] Although the rate of female premarital coitus has significantly increased, this change has not been concomitant with a "violent overthrowing of all cultural values concerning sexuality." (Hunt, 1974:154) The woman who decides to engage in a particular sexual activity must also deal with the additional moral issues generated by that decision. As Rains (1971:12) states:

> Even an open and genuine acceptance of premarital sexual intercourse does not eliminate all sources of moral conflict in premarital sexual relations; such a position simply opens a new set of moral issues—for example, the exclusiveness of one's sexual relationships.

The woman is concerned about others' definition of the kind of person she is (Rains, 1971:14) as well as her own judgment of her planned or actual behavior. Premarital sexual activity may therefore be defined as marginal or unofficial deviance (Matza, 1969:11-12): "[it is] subject to disapproval in certain segments of the community but [is not] legally proscribed." (Briedis, 1975:480)

This paper describes the moral career of one group of marginal deviants—women who participate in premarital sexual activities.[3] "Career" here refers to "changes over time that are basic and common to the members of a social category." (Goffman, 1961:127) The moral aspect of premarital sexual careers includes "the regular sequence of changes that career entails in the person's self and in [her] framework of imagery for judging [herself] and others." (Goffman, 1961:128) The "deviant" aspect of the woman's career is illustrated by her experience of moral conflict and doubt as she makes decisions about participating in premarital sexual activities, and reflects on (judges) her actions of the past. The experience of *marginal* deviance is demonstrated by the ambivalence and fluctuations which characterize the woman's evaluation of her activities. As Rains states (1971:13) [see also Reiss, (1970:80)]:

> The central feature of premarital sexual careers is the experience of coming to view as acceptable what was previously viewed as unacceptable, of acting in ways which are not yet acceptable to oneself but which will come to be acceptable.

The stages of premarital sexual careers include the following: commitment to virginity, tension between remaining a virgin and desiring to gain experience, definition of the situation as appropriate to losing one's virginity, commitment to premarital sex, disillusionment with the sex with love perspective, acceptance of sex for pleasure, and a return to sex for love.[4]

This paper is informed by the symbolic interactionist perspective (Blumer, 1969). Sexual careers are not, then, understood and examined as simple progressions through various stages of physical activity. Rather, this study focuses primarily on the meanings people assign to their participation (or lack of participation) in particular activities. Mead's notion of the prospective-retrospective character of the self (1934) will also be applied here. According to Mead, the individual is able to understand the meanings of others, indicate the responses of others to herself, and act upon the responses of herself and others in the organization of future activity.

Commitment to Virginity

All of the women in the sample had been committed to virginity at an earlier time in their lives. This does not imply that none of the respondents were virgins when interviewed (3 were). What this does imply is that these 3 women were no longer committed to the *idea* of remaining virgins until marriage.

Even the woman who believes she should not engage in premarital intercourse must make decisions regarding which activities she should participate in, and with whom. Rains (1971:18) notes that as the woman progresses through various stages of physical activity, she experiences each act as a "qualitatively more permissive activity." Consider the following quotations from interviewees:

> It was the first time I was really kissed. Not just little pecks, but a real passionate kiss. This guy started turning me on and he started pressing himself against me and I had never felt that before . . . but nothing below the waist had happened. He started making moves below the waist but then I kind of pushed him away. I really wasn't aware of that yet.

> So we French-kissed—probably for half a second. I don't even remember it except that we both went 'Yech' . . . so we continued to do what we always did—press lips and bodies close together, and I think that at the time if I had known why I was getting so excited I would have worried; because, if you shouldn't French-kiss, you really shouldn't do anything with your sexual organs—which, in a sense we were doing with this friction thing. But, because I didn't know where it was coming from it was okay.

Although each woman has a slightly different pattern of progression through the stages of sexual activity, the boundaries in terms of perceived degree of permissiveness tend to be symbolized by certain activities. These include light kissing, heavy kissing, having one's breasts fondled, manual stimulation of the genitalia, being unclothed in the presence of a male, genital apposition, and sleeping nude in a bed with a male. Each activity is likely to be accompanied by ambivalence:

He had never done anything to me below the waist and of course I had never touched him below the waist because to me, the penis didn't exist —figuratively—and all of a sudden . . . he stimulated me down there . . . I was just really embarrassed about the whole thing . . . I guess I did have this thing that it was kind of dirty or something.

Anyway, we necked and petted. He was the first guy who touched me below the waist. It was a big deal when it happened.

The interview data are compatible with Reiss's finding (1967, chapter 7) that guilt reactions are present at all levels of premarital sexual activity. The data also support what Reiss (1970:80) describes as the "typical path of sexual development":

[This path involves] initial feelings of guilt at the first kiss and then a reduction in guilt as kissing behavior [continues] through time. Then movement into a more advanced form of sexual intimacy such as breast or genital petting, and then guilt reactions which in turn are eliminated by repeated behavior, and so on until one either gets married or reaches the maximum level of permissiveness.

Tension between Remaining a Virgin and Desiring to Gain Sexual Experience

Literature on sexual behavior (Christensen and Gregg, 1972; Hunt, 1974; Reiss, 1967: chap. 7) and the present data indicate that women do not regard their participation in sexual activities in an amoral fashion. How is it, then, that they become sexually active? The sexual revolution does not "force" women to have sexual relations, but by emphasizing sexuality and presenting alternative life styles, it gives the woman the opportunity to entertain the vision of herself as a different kind of *moral* person—one who might become sexually active out of wedlock.[5] When the individual is in a situation in which she knows the activity is going on, and the participants are significant others, it is even more difficult for her not to take notice of the activity and regard it as important.

In twelfth grade, when I was 17, my closest girlfriend fell in love with a guy from our high school. This was probably my first close contact with

anybody's, any peer's, sexual experience...and hearing about her
experience I think it was as if I had had a boyfriend—I could see
thinking about going to Europe with him, I could see sleeping with him,
making love with him.

And, during the summer I think the virginity thing started bothering me
more because I thought John and Sylvia had this fantastic relationship.
There they were—living together, loving together; I thought it was
terrific.

Through interaction with significant others, these respondents are
learning about the situations in which premarital intercourse is
considered to be appropriate, and about the rationale (love) and motives
for engaging in such activity.[6]

Although the sexual revolution emphasizes numerous codes of sexual
conduct (see note 1), the respondents understood the term to imply
premarital intercourse beginning in the teenage years.

R: ...now I say, 'oh, God, I'm so old.' It makes me nervous just to think
about the subject.

I: What do you mean?

R: It's really the embarrassment of virginity at this age. I think that it's
come to the point that if I were in a situation where it would come to
that [intercourse], I'd be embarrassed enough about my virginity to
retain it.

I: When did you first feel this way?

R: Somewhere between the ages of 18 and 19. I just thought that one
should lose one's virginity by then. It's a little funny. I sometimes feel
that I'm the oldest virgin in Montreal.

I: How old are you?

R: Twenty-one-and-a-half. Right after high school my best friend was
living with someone—that's since she was about 18 or 19—and my other
friends are also non-virgins. To some degree it's a feeling of being
different, of being left out.

The impact of the sexual revolution is important not in the extent to
which more teenagers are engaging in full sexual relations, but rather in
that individual females believe that most single women are not virgins by
the age of 20. The woman who is a virgin at this age considers herself to
have a deviant sexual career (by not yet having experienced sexual
intercourse); she may feel that other women "gratuitously" choose to
engage in sex and are immune to the ambivalence that characterizes *her*
feelings about engaging in full sexual relations. She may think that it is
"easy" for others to lose their virginity, but "difficult'" for her. The
virgin therefore sees herself as deviant in two ways. First, she has not yet
done what she should have done (lost her virginity). Second, she is

incapable of solving her problem, because the importance that she attributes to losing her virginity is, to her mind, an unnecessary complication in her decision-making. Virgins, then, are likely to be in a situation of pluralistic ignorance. (Schank, 1932) Because personal sexuality is a taboo topic for public discussion (Kaats and Davis, 1970:397), there tends to be a discrepancy between the individual's perceptions of the sentiments of the group (young women) and the *actual* feelings of group members about their participation in premarital intercourse. Therefore, the virgin mistakenly believes that other women are not only sexually active, but are committed to their actions.

The virgins interviewed felt that, because of the sexual revolution, their inexperience was a stigma. As Densmore notes, "our 'right' to enjoy our own bodies has not only been bestowed upon us: it is almost a *duty*." (1973:110, my emphasis) Everyday interaction sometimes becomes problematic for the woman who believes that certain others may suspect that she is a virgin. By sensing herself as transparent[7] and consequently, attempting to prevent disclosure, the woman's experience of deviance is intensified.

> Now it's [virginity] something I feel I have to conceal in discussions ... they say you can smell a virgin a mile away. Sometimes, I feel that's true. As one guy once said to me 'with some girls you can tell they're virgins because it's embroidered on their arms in pink.' I know I'm sexually naive and I think it shows.

These women supposedly wish to conceal their inexperience, but when they do find themselves in a relationship, they pointedly state that they are inexperienced at the time they anticipate the initiation of sexual contact by the male. Expressing embarrassment over their inexperience can in fact be a means of exploiting the advantages of virginity. The woman is then excused from being nervous, inhibited, or from not being aggressive or sexually aroused. If the woman continues her relationship with the same man, he may have reservations about attempting further sexual activities because of the woman's initial embarrassment. Therefore, when the "inexperienced" woman feels that she is ready to progress through further stages of sexual activity, her partner may be reluctant to initiate the contact. Her original embarrassment may also make it difficult for her to express a desire for increased sexual contact because this expression would involve a radical shift in her presentation of self.

> ... I was lying against him, and he went to put his hand on my shoulder, and he accidentally put his hand on my breast. He pulled it away like fire, it was so funny. And I remember thinking, 'God, what an idiot,' because at that point I was really ready to have his hand there.

> I remember at one point when we were kissing and doing what we were usually doing, I really wanted him to do more—at least put his hand on my breast—*something*—and he didn't do it. I didn't feel that I could say 'do more' or put his hand there.

The tension between the desire for experience and the desire for self-respect (by retaining virginity) is reflected in the woman's concern for her reputation. The woman who stays overnight in the same bed as her boyfriend, without engaging in intercourse, may say that she hopes others will assume she has had full sexual relations:

> I liked it that other people thought we were sleeping together.

> I wasn't crazy about being a virgin . . . I liked to think that they thought we were sleeping together.

However, the virgin's apparent acceptance of the imputed reputation and the moral implications that it may involve does not reflect her own acceptance of the behavior, partly shown by the fact that she does not actually engage in sexual intercourse. However, her statements are not lies; she wishes to be temporarily relieved of the stigma which she feels is attached to virginity, while at the same time abstaining from an activity of which she disapproves.

Definition of the Situation as Appropriate to Losing Virginity

The sexual experiences of the women interviewed are characterized by ambivalence, and therefore it appears that while females are able to participate in certain activities they are, at the same time, not committed to their actions. In order to engage in sexual activity, the woman develops a rationale to justify her behavior both to herself and to others. According to Sykes and Matza, although such justifications are usually viewed by sociologists as following deviant behavior, "there is also reason to believe that they precede deviant behavior and make deviant behavior possible." (1957:666) Love is the condition that serves to neutralize the conflicting feelings experienced by sexually active women. (Rains, 1971:15) The women adopt love, one of the justifications for marital intercourse, to justify premarital relations.[8] Since the emotional involvement of both partners in a marriage is considered to validate full sexual relations, unmarried people who "are in love" may feel that they have "reason" to engage in sexual activity. The language of love allows the woman to rephrase the question "Am I the kind of girl who will engage in premarital intercourse?" to "Am I the kind of person who will be intimate with the man I love?" Thus, the emphasis is placed on love, and premarital intercourse comes to be accepted as its natural expression.[9]

The woman who remains in what she defines as a love relationship over an extended period of time comes to think that the feelings of affection which both she and her boyfriend share justify sexual intercourse. However, her decision is not likely to be one to which she is totally committed. Women experience conflicting feelings about their intended course of action. Until the women engages in intercourse, she is able to define herself as respectable, since technically she is a virgin. Thus, while she may have experienced many other forms of sexual activity, she can consider herself to be respectable.

R: Tom and I were sleeping together sporadically.

I: By 'sleeping together' you mean . . .

R: Clitoral stimulation, sleeping nude, kissing all over the body, oral intercourse—everything but the actual sexual intercourse . . . I was still into
the head that I wanted to pick the person I had intercourse with and not
vice versa. Like, I wanted to say, 'you're the man I want to lose my
virginity to.' Tom was ready at any time that I was ready. But, in
sophomore year [one year later], even *then* I was getting doubts.

One particular stage of physical activity is crucial to the woman's emerging definition of the situation as appropriate to engaging in premarital intercourse for the first time. Sleeping nude in a bed with a male, with or without sexual activity, signifies a growing intimacy and trust which usually provide the woman with qualitatively enough "love justification" to consider having intercourse during one of her next sexual encounters (with the same man).

. . . It wouldn't have been intercourse with the Belgian that soon. I would
have had to have seen him longer than that to have had intercourse with
him. I wanted to sleep with him, though, nude and all that.

After seven or eight months I decided that the relationship had come to
the point where we should sleep together . . . so we went to the hotel and
I knew that we weren't going to have intercourse. After that time, we
decided that the next time we were going to have intercourse.

It is interesting to note that the length of time considered necessary to define a relationship in terms of love, and therefore to justify sexual activity, differs when the woman is outside her home environment. A relationship of two or three weeks "on holiday" is defined as a "long" one and therefore permits a more rapid progression through the stages of sexual activity than would occur during the same period of time at home.

However, because the possibility of permanency (continuation of the relationship) is smaller, the length of the relationship is not deemed sufficient time to justify full sexual relations. Thus, while the woman can temporarily alter her definition of love's relationship to time, she cannot eradicate it.

> My next experience was when I was in Israel on a kibbutz, and I had just turned 18. I met this guy and we became very close very quickly and so within about 3 weeks we were living together. Sexually, we did 'everything *but*' [intercourse] because I wouldn't sleep with him.

> I thought he liked me. Who else would put up with everything *but* for 3 weeks . . . and he was seeing me even 3 or 4 times a week! . . . Like it went sour for me that night. I was lying there naked thinking 'what am I doing?' . . . I mean, I did *like* him, but not enough. I didn't *love* him; I don't know. I guess it was more that there was no future in it.

Commitment to Premarital Sex

Commitment to premarital intercourse develops *after* the woman loses her virginity, when she continues to have sexual relations with her boyfriend. The woman comes to accept her behavior as a legitimate expression of love for her partner.

The woman's commitment to her own actions, however, does not neutralize her concern about others' actual or anticipated reactions to her conduct. Concerns about her reputation play an important part in the woman's sexual career and in her experience of being deviant. Since she considered women who engaged in premarital intercourse to be immoral when she was younger, and shared this view with others, she can hardly escape thinking about the way others will now judge her behavior. Even the woman who engages in sexual activities within the context of a love relationship is careful about the people who know her activities. Some individuals may be allowed to learn of a few details, whereas all facts must be concealed from certain others:

> After I slept with him the first time, I was really wary about telling my friends. . . . I live at home and my parents don't know of his existence.

Concern about her reputation or "the definition of the kind of person she is" (Rains, 1971:14) is experienced by the woman in her relationship with her parents. One important aspect of the parent-daughter relationship is the parents' belief in the moral "goodness" of their child. In order to maintain the relationship, the woman acts in ways that sustain her parents' definition. Because most parents disapprove of premarital sexual intercourse, and therefore of those who engage in it, the woman tries to conceal the fact that she is sexually experienced. Often, she volunteers information concerning her emotional involvement with a particular male but avoids discussing or alluding to the sexual aspects of her relationship.

> Well, I don't tell her [mother] any sexual details, just feelings.

Since the parents also have an interest in retaining an image of their daughter as sexually inexperienced, they may interact with the woman in such ways as to evade a direct confrontation. (Briedis, 1974) The parents make indirect comments or jokes which are intended to convey to the woman their disapproval of persons who have premarital relations; yet they do not directly question their daughter about her sexual activity even if they suspect she is engaging in sexual intercourse.

> . . . She has this idea that I'm going to go there to visit him, he's older than me, I'm starry-eyed, I'll have a few drinks, I'll lose control and the next thing I'll be in bed with him . . . she made her point, she does not want me to sleep with him . . . but she doesn't want to know because she never at any point asked me point blank, 'did you sleep with him?'.

> Also like she would sometimes give me these ridiculous digs . . . she used to bother me about what I'm doing sexually, without really asking me what I'm doing . . . but I don't think it really matters what she says to me because she still thinks I'm pure and she would never really ask me specifically what I had done with anybody.

When the parents are confronted by the fact that their daughter is having sexual relations, they may still avoid making explicit references to it.

> And when my sister was living with her boyfriend my mother would say 'she's living in his house' rather than 'she's sleeping with him'.

Even women in the sample who discussed some details of their sexual experiences with their parents felt they must limit the kind and amount of information conveyed. These women (2) may have been able to discuss more sexual details with their parents than most women because the nature of their parents' occupations allowed them to discuss sexual matters in the special language of the profession. The woman who consulted her physician-father when she experienced side effects from contraceptive pills was ostensibly seeking medical advice, while also communicating to him the fact that she was engaging in sexual intercourse. Another example is illustrated by the woman who recognized the advantages of having a mother who was a psychiatric social worker.

> Being a clinician, she's had to belong to therapy. So, she's talked about

me in therapy with the other people . . . my mother deals primarily with high school students. The stuff she hears in the groups . . . well, my stuff is miniscule compared to theirs. All my traumas are little compared to girls pregnant with four kids at age 16 . . . I'm seen as being mature and having good sense.

By speaking in the language of the profession rather than in the parent-daughter language, certain sexual details become neutralized; that is, they are temporarily defined as professional, rather than moral matters.

Commitment to premarital intercourse and the concept of love are also related to concerns about contraception. While the women interviewed use the language of love to describe their relationship with the first person with whom they have intercourse, the women who doubt the sincerity of their partner's emotional involvement do not use contraception the first time they experience full sexual relations. These findings coincide with those of Kirkendall (1961:285): "An examination of the data indicates that contraceptive measures are more likely to be taken in relationships where there is a definite degree of attachment than in relationships where there is little or no attachment." Why is this so? A woman is not likely to conceive of herself as the "kind of person" who engages in premarital intercourse, but she may accept herself as the kind of person who engages in intimacy within a love relationship. The woman who doubts the presence of mutual love lacks proper justification for engaging in intercourse and is therefore less likely to use contraception. As Pohlman and Pohlman (1969:353) note: "to make contraceptive plans is to admit to oneself an intention which, in the thinking of many unmarried individuals, is sinful." Therefore, the woman who sees herself in a relationship of mutual love is likely to be more committed to her actions, and consequently, more likely to take appropriate contraceptive measures.

Disillusionment with Sex with Love, Sex for Pleasure, a Return to Sex with Love[10]

The woman's commitment to premarital intercourse is based on love. Therefore, she may lose this commitment when she can no longer use the language of love to describe her feelings for her lover. When this happens, although the woman may still experience sexual pleasure with her partner, her definition of the activity as "sex without love" usually accompanies a cessation of the relationship and the activity. That is, once the technique of neutralization—love—can no longer be used, the activity comes to be viewed with moral disapproval and thus cannot involve commitment on the part of the woman.

This becomes most apparent when the relationship is brought to an end by the male not long after the couple has begun to participate in full sexual relations. The woman is susceptible to losing a definition of herself as respectable at this point because she has not yet had sufficient time to develop a commitment to the activity based on love. Also, because the male has ended the relationship, implying that he no longer loves her, she is open to doubt that mutual love existed during the short time before the breakup when sexual intercourse occurred. The absence of mutual love implies the absence of the justification for sexual intercourse. Thus, while any woman is potentially open to doubting her boyfriend's love for her and therefore losing her self-image of respectability, the woman who is not yet committed to the act of sleeping with someone she loves would experience more ambivalence toward the act, and would be even more likely to doubt the morality of her behavior. In retrospect, then, the woman whose loved one has left her defines her experience of sexual intercourse as alienating:

R: . . . But, he had slept with everybody and everybody knew it anyway. I guess a jock is someone who has sex on the brain and doesn't care who it's with. Like an animal, I guess.
I: How did you feel about your experience with him?
R: At the time I didn't realize how much of a jock he was. I thought there was more sincerity in it.

Paradoxically, at this time when she is the least committed to her action and the most doubtful about her respectability, the woman acts in ways that maintain an image of herself as unrespectable. That is, she begins to engage in sexual intercourse with men with whom she is not in love, thus lacking the technique of neutralization that would allow her to define her actions as morally acceptable. How is it, then, that she does not? The woman who loses her virginity within a relationship lacking mutual love conceives of herself and her action as unrespectable. The way in which she temporarily regains an image of herself as respectable is by changing her definition of respectability. She challenges the view that love is the necessary requirement for engaging in sexual intercourse, and proposes instead that sex needs no justification except for the pleasure it gives.

By accepting the perspective of "sex for pleasure" as respectable, the woman is able to redefine her original action as respectable. She then proceeds to provide herself with evidence for the respectability of that view by having sexual relations with men whom she does not love. Her behavior, however, does not "prove" to the woman that she is the kind of person for whom love is unrelated to sexual activity. Her lack of commitment to her actions reveals itself after a number of sexual encounters without love, when she finally rejects the view that sexual activity is amoral. At this time, how does she accept her behavior of the immediate past? The woman claims that she was "really" searching for a relationship with a male rather than sexual pleasure, thereby redefining her actions within a framework of love and allowing herself to regain a degree of respectability.

> When I came here I felt that I'd gone through a lot of pain and that it was time to get over him [the man she loved who left her], and that I was responsible for myself and my actions. I was going to try and have good relationships and not try to marry, because that had been our whole problem—or get some sort of commitment out of anyone I met, and I decided that I was just a free agent . . . I think attraction was what dictated my actions. I'm attracted to that person, I want him, and we'll see how the relationship goes . . . [after 1 year of engaging in sexual intercourse with men whom she did not love]. In retrospect I condemn my activities of the last year . . . I was really looking for some kind of relationship, none of them fit the bill, I didn't enjoy them after they ended.

The data are compatible with Hunt's findings (1974:154):

> Recreational sex . . . does not clearly appear as a separate entity in our data or in most of our interviews because for most people it is not a viable alternative way of life. Instead, it is a . . . temporary escape . . . that meets the needs of many people during special and sharply delimited periods of their lives—at the conclusion of which they move on to, or return to, the romantic philosophy of sex.

The woman whose relationship is terminated by the male and who proceeds to have intercourse within the context of casual relationships eventually acquires a diaphragm or contraceptive pills. Until that time, these women rely on the man's discretion, which sometimes results in unprotected intercourse. After several sexual encounters, it becomes increasingly difficult for the woman to think of herself as other than sexually experienced, although she may disapprove of her actions. However, she may still not take the necessary steps to obtain a contraceptive device until a friend or lover points out that she is in danger of getting pregnant, and "supports and organizes her attempt to acquire contraceptive means." (Rains, 1971:22) The woman therefore comes to recognize a need for contraception.

> I got on the Pill because I saw that you can really get into the situation where he might ejaculate, so I'd better get responsible. There was this guy at the time and he told me that I was really stupid not to be on it.

Conclusion

The present study suggests that female premarital sexual careers are marginally deviant. Women participate in activities that they initially view with disapproval, but that they come to regard as acceptable. Although more women are having full sexual relations than in previous times, sexual involvement, for women, is not divorced from moral concerns. Women question their own participation in sexual activities and are concerned about the projected and/or actual responses of others toward their behavior. Every premarital sexual activity, and sexual intercourse in particular, is considered to be most acceptable within a love relationship. Therefore, women define the moral parameters of sexual behavior in terms of the degree of affection shared by both partners.

Although the sexual revolution has brought the subject of sexuality into the open, it has perhaps also created new anxieties for women. Because the sexual revolution publicly introduced a multiplicity of sexual standards and life styles, the individual is confronted with many moral standards from which to choose. This lack of moral consensus creates a social climate which is experienced by the women as one of moral ambiguity. (Briedis, 1974, 1975) By providing varying definitions of acceptable action, the complex network of competing moral positions complicates both the woman's judgment of her own actions, and other people's evaluation of her behavior.

This study outlines the stages of premarital sexual careers for those women who do not remain committed to the "sex for pleasure" perspective. The data suggest that women do not consider casual sex to be a viable alternative to sex with love.

NOTES

1. For example, individuals may understand sexual liberation to imply losing one's virginity before marriage, being an "aggressive" lover, having sexual relations with a loved one, or engaging in full sexual relations with many people (free love), to mention a few.

2. This is not meant to suggest that women do not participate in "recreational sex". Hunt (1974:152) notes that "casual or promiscuous sex ... in our sample ... is not typical of the great mass of single young people." Davis (1971:142) found that "a small (5-15%) but not insignificant number of college women find full sexual intercourse acceptable even if there is no particular affection between partners."

3. The data are derived from an exploratory study of nine college women, living in Montreal, ages 19-23. Each three-hour, tape-recorded interview was conducted in an informal and open-ended style.

4. None of the interviewees was committed to the sex for pleasure perspective.

5. For further discussion of affiliation, "the process by which the subject is *converted* to conduct novel for him but already established for others", see chapter 6 in *Becoming Deviant* (Matza, 1969).

6. The "appropriateness" of premarital sex and the rationale for engaging in it are discussed in the next section.

7. In *Becoming Deviant* David Matza (1969) uses the concept of transparency to refer to the deviant's fear that others are aware of his deviancy: "the concerns underlying the fear of transparency are quite ordinary and are based on the common understanding that social communication occurs through inadvertent cues, gestures and expressions as well as plain talk, on the common sense that the subject may 'give himself away'." (1969:150-151)

8. Although love provides a rationale for engaging in premarital sex, this is not meant to suggest that these women are not *actually* "in love". Rather, this technique of neutralization simply assumes that "most people remain sensitive to conventional codes of conduct (sex only within marriage) and must deal with their sensitivities in order to engage in a deviant act for the first time." (Becker, 1963:28)

9. As Reiss (1970:84) notes, "love experience is one of the best predictors of which females will have premarital intercourse."

10. These three stages focus on a few members of the sample and are therefore discussed together. Some women, perhaps most women, continue to engage in premarital intercourse with a loved one. (Hunt, 1974) These women do not become disillusioned with "sex with love" and therefore are not likely to develop a "sex for pleasure" perspective. Also, some women (not in the present sample) become *committed* to the sex for pleasure outlook and do not return to the sex with love perspective. Hunt (1974) and Davis (1971) found that these women constitute a minority.

    Hopefully, this section also illustrates the symbolic interactionist view of self as process: "an important part of the self is the memory of past events (or personal history) that everyone carries with him and uses as a partial reference for new decisions." (Wiseman, 1976:13)

BIBLIOGRAPHY

Becker, H. S. *Outsiders.* New York: Free Press, 1963.

Bell, R. R. and J. B. Chaskes. "Premarital Sexual Experience Among Coeds, 1958 and 1968." *Journal of Marriage and the Family,* Vol. 32 (February, 1968), pp. 81-84.

Blumer, H. *Symbolic Interactionism.* Englewood Cliffs, New Jersey: Prentice-Hall, 1969.

Briedis, C. "Staying Respectable—Managing the Moral Repercussions of Teenage Sex and Pregnancy." Master's Thesis, McGill University, 1974.

———. "Marginal Deviants: Teenage Girls Experience Community Response to Premarital Sex and Pregnancy." *Social Problems,* Vol. 22, No. 4 (April, 1975), pp. 480-493.

Christensen, H. T. and C. F. Gregg. "Changing Sex Norms in America and Scandinavia," in *Sex and Society,* ed. J. N. Edwards. Chicago: Markham, 1972, pp. 46-63.

Davis, K. E. "Sex on Campus: Is There a Revolution?" *Medical Aspects of Human Sexuality,* Vol. 1 (January, 1971), pp. 128-142.

Densmore, D. "Independence from the Sexual Revolution," in *Radical Feminism,* eds. A. Koedt and E. Levine. New York: Quadrangle, 1973, pp. 107-118.

Ehrmann, W. W. *Premarital Dating Behavior.* New York: Holt, Rinehart and Winston, 1959.

———. "Premarital Sexual Behavior and Sex Codes of Conduct with Acquaintances, Friends, and Lovers." *Social Forces,* Vol. 38 (December, 1959), pp. 158-164.

Goffman, E. "The Moral Career of the Mental Patient," in *Asylums.* New York: Doubleday, 1961, pp. 125-169.

Hunt, M. *Sexual Behavior in the 1970's.* New York: Dell, 1974.

Kaats, G. R. and K. E. Davis. "The Dynamics of Sexual Behavior of College Students." *Journal of Marriage and the Family,* Vol. 32 (August, 1970), pp. 390-399.

Kirkendall, L. A. *Premarital Intercourse and Interpersonal Relationships.* New York: Gramercy, 1961.

Matza, D. *Becoming Deviant.* Englewood Cliffs, New Jersey: Prentice-Hall, 1969.

Mead, G. H. *Mind, Self and Society.* Chicago, Illinois: University of Chicago Press, 1934.

Pohlman, E. "Contraception In and Out of Marriage," in *The New Sexual Revolution,* eds. L. A. Kirkendall and R. N. Whitehurst. New York: Donald W. Brown, 1971, pp. 183-196.

Pohlman, E. and J. M. Pohlman. *The Psychology of Birth Planning.* Cambridge, Massachussetts: Schenkman, 1969.

Rains, P. M. *Becoming an Unwed Mother.* Chicago: Aldine, 1971.

Reiss, I. *The Social Context of Premarital Sexual Permissiveness.* New York: Holt, Rinehart and Winston, 1967.

————. "Premarital Sex as Deviant Behavior: An Application of Current Approaches to Deviance." *American Sociological Review,* Vol. 35 (February, 1970), pp. 78-87.

Schank, R. L. A. "A Study of a Community and its Groups and Institutions Conceived as the Behavior of Individuals." *Psychological Monographs,* Vol. 43, No. 2 (Whole Number 195, 1932).

Sykes, G. M. and D. Matza. "Techniques of Neutralization: A Theory of Delinquency." *American Sociological Review,* Vol. 22 (December, 1957), pp. 664-670.

Wiseman, J. P., ed. *The Social Psychology of Sex.* New York: Harper and Row, 1976.

Ethnic Groups, Assimilation, & Identity

THE STATUS OF ethnic groups in Canada is closely related to the federal government's endorsement of multiculturalism. According to the government, Canadian society should be able to accommodate people of different backgrounds. Ethnic diversity is believed to have definite advantages for the overall structure and organization of our society, and ethnic groups are encouraged to maintain a degree of distinctiveness and still blend into the larger society.

Our society includes a number of ethnic groups to whom the maintenance of a distinct identity is important. These groups wish to retain their unique linguistic and cultural heritages, and have organized cultural institutions including religious organizations, schools, and the press to achieve this end. A recent resurgence in ethnicity in this country has resulted in both new and intensified efforts by the leaders of ethnic communities to revive and retain the essential elements of their groups' heritages and to ensure their transmission to succeeding generations.

As we have already suggested, the processes of identity formation and maintenance are central to the symbolic interactionist perspective. It is unfortunate that researchers in the area of ethnic relations have not utilized the themes emerging from this perspective more frequently. Analyses of ethnic groups and communities, which focus on the processes of identity maintenance and its relationship to self-evaluation and social control, would greatly help us to understand ourselves and our society.

While the articles in this section cannot do justice to the rich ethnic diversity of this country, they do attempt to deal with the relationship between ethnicity and identity. The common theme is the idea that ethnic identity is not a fixed and permanent feature but rather, a process which is shaped by efforts to deal with the assimilative influences of the larger society. Each selection addresses itself to a particular cultural feature with which ethnic groups in this country have had to come to terms while attempting to maintain a distinct way of life.

Our first selection is Tamotsu Shibutani's "Reference Groups as Perspectives". Shibutani analyzes the various ways in which the concept of reference group has been employed and suggests that the psychological application is the most useful of all. This concept is particularly relevant to our study of the social and cultural transformation experienced by members of ethnic groups as they acculturate and assimilate the customs of the larger society. The following two selections by Lamy and Paris deal with the role of language and the retention and preservation of ethnic identity. Both authors suggest that language shapes our thinking by providing or failing to provide appropriate words and concepts for communication, and they also indicate that among the aspects of culture that facilitate assimilation none are as effective as language.

While assimilation may become a source of concern to the particular ethnic community or to the larger ethnic group, it may, on the other hand, be welcomed by some as a solution to their groups' subordinate status. In the selection by Cardinal we see the way that the stereotyping of Indians has influenced their self-conception as a people. As a result of stereotyping, prejudice, and discrimination, the Indians in Canada are faced with the prospect of occupying a marginal status in their own land, and many have advocated assimilation as a solution to their difficulties.

In contrast to this approach, the ethnic group may adopt other patterns of interaction with the larger society to mitigate its subordinate status. The selections by Lévesque and Shaffir offer examples of such alternate patterns. Lévesque discusses Quebec's separation from Canada as a means of maintaining the French language and culture in the province, while Shaffir examines a religious community that has voluntarily elected to segregate itself from the social and cultural influences of the outside world. For both groups, the respective strategies are deemed necessary to maintain cultural boundaries which will help to consolidate a distinct identity and to offset assimilation.

Reference Groups as Perspectives

TAMOTSU SHIBUTANI

ALTHOUGH HYMAN COINED the term scarcely more than a decade ago, the concept of reference group has become one of the central analytic tools in social psychology, being used in the construction of hypotheses concerning a variety of social phenomena. The inconsistency in behavior as a person moves from one social context to another is accounted for in terms of a change in reference groups; the exploits of juvenile delinquents, especially in interstitial areas, are being explained by the expectations of peer-group gangs; modifications in social attitudes are found to be related to changes in associations. The concept has been particularly useful in accounting for the choices made among apparent alternatives, particularly where the selections seem to be contrary to the

T. Shibutani, *"Reference Groups as Perspectives."* From the American Journal of Sociology, LX (May, 1955), pp. 562-569, by permission of the University of Chicago Press. Copyright 1955 by the University of Chicago.

"best interests" of the actor. Status problems—aspirations of social climbers, conflicts in group loyalty, the dilemmas of marginal men—have also been analyzed in terms of reference groups, as have the differential sensitivity and reaction of various segments of an audience to mass communication. It is recognized that the same generic processes are involved in these phenomenally diverse events, and the increasing popularity of the concept attests to its utility in analysis.

As might be expected during the exploratory phases in any field of inquiry, however, there is some confusion involved in the use of this concept, arising largely from vagueness of signification. The available formal definitions are inconsistent, and sometimes formal definitions are contradicted in usage. The fact that social psychologists can understand one another in spite of these ambiguities, however, implies an intuitive recognition of some central meaning, and an explicit statement of this will enhance the utility of the concept as an analytic tool. The literature reveals that all discussions of reference groups involve some identifiable grouping to which an actor is related in some manner and the norms and values shared in that group. However, the relationship between these three terms is not always clear. Our initial task, then, is to examine the conceptions of reference group implicit in actual usage, irrespective of formal definitions.

One common usage of the concept is in the designation of that group which serves as the point of reference in making comparisons or contrasts, especially in forming judgments about one's self. In the original use of the concept Hyman spoke of reference groups as points of comparison in evaluating one's own status, and he found that the estimates varied according to the group with which the respondent compared himself. Merton and Kitt, in their reformulation of Stouffer's theory of relative deprivation, also use the concept in this manner; the judgments of rear-echelon soldiers overseas concerning their fate varied, depending upon whether they compared themselves to soldiers who were still at home or men in combat. They also propose concrete research operations in which respondents are to be asked to compare themselves with various groups. The study of aspiration levels by Chapman and Volkmann, frequently cited in discussions of reference-group theory, also involves variations in judgment arising from a comparison of one's own group with others.[1] In this mode of application, then, a reference group is a standard or check point which an actor uses in forming his estimate of the situation, particularly his own position within it. Logically, then, *any* group with which an actor is familiar may become a reference group.

A second referent of the concept is that group in which the actor aspires to gain or maintain acceptance: hence, a group whose claims are paramount in situations requiring choice. The reference group of the socially ambitious is said to consist of people of higher strata whose status symbols are imitated. Merton and Kitt interpret the expressions of willingness and felt readiness for combat on the part of inexperienced troops, as opposed to the humility of battle-hardened veterans, as the efforts of newcomers to identify themselves with veterans to whom they had mistakenly imputed certain values.[2] Thus, the concept is used to point to an association of human beings among whom one seeks to gain, maintain, or enhance his status; a reference group is that group in which one desires to participate.

In a third usage the concept signifies that group whose perspective constitutes the frame of reference of the actor. Thus, Sherif speaks of reference groups as groups whose norms are used as anchoring points in structuring the perceptual field,[3] and Merton and Kitt speak of a "social frame of reference" for interpretations.[4] Through direct or vicarious participation in a group one comes to perceive the world from its standpoint. Yet this group need not be one in which he aspires for acceptance; a member of some minority group may despise it but still see the world largely through its eyes. When used in this manner, the concept of reference group points more to a psychological phenomenon than to an objectively existing group of men; it refers to an organization of the actor's experience. That is to say, it is a structuring of his perceptual field. In this usage a reference group becomes any collectivity, real or imagined, envied or despised, whose perspective is assumed by the actor.

Thus, an examination of current usage discloses three distinct referents for a single concept: (1) groups which serve as comparison points; (2) groups to which men aspire; and (3) groups whose perspectives are assumed by the actor. Although these terms may be related, treating together what should be clearly delineated as generically different can lead only to further confusion. It is the contention of this paper that the restriction of the concept of reference group to the third alternative—that group whose perspective constitutes the frame of reference of the actor—will increase its usefulness in research. Any group or object may be used for comparisons, and one need not assume the role of those with whom he compares his fate; hence, the first usage serves a quite different purpose and may be eliminated from further consideration. Under some circumstances, however, group loyalties and aspirations are related to perspectives assumed, and the character of this relationship calls for further exploration. Such a discussion necessitates a restatement of the familiar, but, in view of the difficulties in some of the work on reference groups, repetition may not be entirely out of order. In spite of the enthusiasm of some proponents there is actually nothing new in reference-group theory.

Culture and Personal Controls

Thomas pointed out many years ago that what a man does depends largely upon his definition of the situation. One may add that the manner in which one consistently defines a succession of situations depends upon his organized perspective. A perspective is an ordered view of one's world—what is taken for granted about the attributes of various objects, events, and human nature. It is an order of things remembered and expected as well as things actually perceived, an organized conception of what is plausible and what is possible; it constitutes the matrix through which one perceives his environment. The fact that men have such ordered perspectives enables them to conceive of their ever changing world as relatively stable, orderly, and predictable. As Riezler puts it, one's perspective is an outline scheme which, running ahead of experience, defines and guides it.

There is abundant experimental evidence to show that perception is selective; that the organization of perceptual experience depends in part upon what is anticipated and what is taken for granted. Judgments rest upon perspectives, and people with different outlooks define identical situations differently, responding selectively to the environment. Thus, a prostitute and a social worker walking through a slum area notice different things; a sociologist should perceive relationships that others fail to observe. Any change of perspectives—becoming a parent for the first time, learning that one will die in a few months, or suffering the failure of well-laid plans—leads one to notice things previously overlooked and to see the familiar world in a different light. As Goethe contended, history is continually rewritten, not so much because of the discovery of new documentary evidence, but because the changing perspectives of historians lead to new selections from the data.

Culture, as the concept is used by Redfield, refers to a perspective that is shared by those in a particular group; it consists of those "conventional understandings, manifest in act and artifact, that characterize societies."[5] Since these conventional understandings are the premises of action, those who share a common culture engage in common modes of action. Culture is not a static entity but a continuing process; norms are creatively reaffirmed from day to day in social interaction. Those taking part in collective transactions approach one another with set expectations, and the realization of what is anticipated successively confirms and reinforces their perspectives. In this way, people in each cultural group are continuously supporting one another's perspectives, each by responding to the others in expected ways. In this sense culture is a product of communication.

In his discussion of endopsychic social control Mead spoke of men "taking the role of the generalized other," meaning by that that each person approaches his world from the standpoint of the culture of his group. Each perceives, thinks, forms judgments, and controls himself according to the frame of reference of the group in which he is participating. Since he defines objects, other people, the world, and himself from the perspective that he shares with others, he can visualize his proposed line of action from this generalized standpoint, anticipate the reactions of others, inhibit undesirable impulses, and thus guide his conduct. The socialized person is a society in miniature; he sets the same standards of conduct for himself as he sets for others, and he judges himself in the same terms. He can define situations properly and meet his obligations, even in the absence of other people, because, as already noted, his perspective always takes into account the expectations of others. Thus, it is the ability to define situations from the same standpoint as others that makes personal controls possible.[6] When Mead spoke of assuming the role of the generalized other, he was not referring to people but to perspectives shared with others in a transaction.

The consistency in the behavior of a man in a wide variety of social contexts is to be accounted for, then, in terms of his organized perspective. Once one has incorporated a particular outlook from his group, it becomes his orientation toward the world, and he brings this frame of reference to bear on all new situations. Thus, immigrants and tourists often misinterpret the strange things they see, and a disciplined Communist would define each situation differently from the non-Communist. Although reference-group behavior is generally studied in situations where choices seem possible, the actor himself is often unaware that there are alternatives.

The proposition that men think, feel, and see things from a standpoint peculiar to the group in which they participate is an old one, repeatedly emphasized by students of anthropology and of the sociology of knowledge. Why, then, the sudden concern with reference-group theory during the past decade? The concept of reference group actually introduces a minor refinement in the long familiar theory, made necessary by the special characteristics of modern mass societies. First of all, in modern societies special problems arise from the fact that men sometimes use the standards of groups in which they are *not* recognized members, sometimes of groups in which they have never participated directly, and sometimes of groups that do not exist at all. Second, in our mass society, characterized as it is by cultural pluralism, each person internalizes several perspectives, and this occasionally gives rise to embarrassing dilemmas which call for systematic study. Finally, the development of reference-group theory has been facilitated by the increasing interest in social psychology and the subjective aspects of group life, a shift from a predominant concern with objective social structures to an interest in the experiences of the participants whose regularized activities make such structures discernible.

A reference group, then, is that group whose outlook is used by the actor as the frame of reference in the organization of his perceptual field. All kinds of groupings, with great variations in size, composition, and structure, may become reference groups. Of greatest importance for most people are those groups in which they participate directly—what have been called membership groups—especially those containing a number of persons with whom one stands in a primary relationship. But in some transactions one may assume the perspective attributed to some social category—a social class, an ethnic group, those in a given community, or those concerned with some special interest. On the other hand, reference groups may be imaginary, as in the case of artists who are "born ahead of their times," scientists who work for "humanity," or philanthropists who give for "posterity." Such persons estimate their endeavors from a postulated perspective imputed to people who have not yet been born. There are others who live for a distant past, idealizing some period in history and longing for "the good old days," criticizing current events from a standpoint imputed to people long since dead. Reference groups, then, arise through the internalization of norms; they constitute the structure of expectations imputed to some audience for whom one organizes his conduct.

The Construction of Social Worlds

As Dewey emphasized, society exists in and through communication; common perspectives—common cultures—emerge through participation in common communication channels. It is through social participation that perspectives shared in a group are internalized. Despite the frequent recitation of this propostion, its full implications, especially for the analysis of mass societies, are not often appreciated. Variations in outlook arise through differential contact and association; the maintenance of social distance—through segregation, conflict, or simply the reading of different literature—leads to the formation of distinct cultures. Thus, people in different social classes develop different modes of life and outlook, not because of anything inherent in economic position, but because similarity of occupation and limitations set by income level dispose them to certain restricted communication channels. Those in different ethnic groups form their own distinctive cultures because their identifications incline them to interact intimately with each other and to maintain reserve before outsiders. Different intellectual traditions within social psychology—psychoanalysis, scale analysis, *Gestalt*, pragmatism—will remain separated as long as those in each tradition restrict their sympathetic attention to works of their own school and view others with contempt or hostility. Some social scientists are out of touch with the masses of the American people because they eschew the mass media, especially television, or expose themselves only condescendingly. Even the outlook that the *avant-garde* regards as "cosmopolitan" is culture-bound, for it also is a product of participation in restricted communication channels—books, magazines, meetings, exhibits, and taverns which are out of bounds for most people in the middle classes. Social participation may even be vicarious, as it is in the case of a medievalist who acquires his perspective solely through books.

Even casual observation reveals the amazing variety of standards by which Americans live. The inconsistencies and contradictions which characterize modern mass societies are products of the multitude of communication channels and the ease of participation in them. Studying relatively isolated societies, anthropologists can speak meaningfully of "culture areas" in geographical terms; in such societies common cultures have a territorial base, for only those who live together can interact. In modern industrial societies, however, because of the development of rapid transportation and the media of mass communication, people who are geographically dispersed can communicate effectively. Culture areas are coterminous with communication channels; since communication networks are no longer coterminous with territorial boundaries, culture areas overlap and have lost their territorial bases. Thus, next-door neighbors may be complete strangers; even in common parlance there is an intuitive recognition of the diversity of perspectives, and we speak meaningfully of people living in different social worlds—the academic world, the world of children, the world of fashion.

Modern mass societies, indeed, are made up of a bewildering variety of social worlds. Each is an organized outlook, built up by people in their interaction with one another; hence, each communication channel gives rise to a separate world. Probably the greatest sense of identification and solidarity is to be found in the various communal structures—the underworld, ethnic minorities, the social elite. Such communities are frequently spatially segregated, which isolates them further from the outer world, while the "grapevine" and foreign-language presses provide internal contacts. Another common type of social world consists of the associational structures—the world of medicine, of organized labor, of the theater, of café society. These are held together not only by various voluntary associations within each locality but also by periodicals like *Variety*, specialized journals, and feature sections in newspapers. Finally, there are the loosely connected universes of special interest—the world of sports, of the stamp collector, of the daytime serial—serviced by mass media programs and magazines like *Field and Stream*. Each of these worlds is a unity of order, a universe of regularized mutual response. Each is an area in which there is some structure which permits reasonable anticipation of the behavior of others, hence, an area in which one may act with a sense of security and confidence.[7] Each social world, then, is a culture area, the boundaries of which are set neither by territory nor by formal group membership but by the limits of effective communication.

Since there is a variety of communication channels, differing in stability and extent, social worlds differ in composition, size, and the territorial distribution of the participants. Some, like local cults, are small and concentrated; others, like the intellectual world, are vast and the participants dispersed. Worlds differ in the extent and clarity of their boundaries; each is confined by some kind of horizon, but this may be wide or narrow, clear or vague. The fact that social worlds are not coterminous with the universe of men is recognized; those in the underworld are well aware of the fact that outsiders do not share their values. Worlds differ in exclusiveness and in the extent to which they demand the loyalty of their participants. Most important of all, social worlds are not static entities; shared perspectives are continually being reconstituted. Worlds come into existence with the establishment of communication channels; when life conditions change, social relationships may also change, and these worlds may disappear.

Every social world has some kind of communication system—often nothing more than differential association—in which there develops a special universe of discourse, sometimes an argot. Special meanings and symbols further accentuate differences and increase social distance from outsiders. In each world there are special norms of conduct, a set of values, a special prestige ladder, characteristic career lines, and a common outlook toward life—a Weltanschauung. In the case of elites there may even arise a code of honor which holds only for those who belong, while others are dismissed as beings somewhat less than human from whom bad manners may be expected. A social world, then, is an order conceived which serves as the stage on which each participant seeks to carve out his career and to maintain and enhance his status.

One of the characteristics of life in modern mass societies is simultaneous participation in a variety of social worlds. Because of the ease with which the individual may expose himself to a number of communication channels, he may lead a segmentalized life, participating successively in a number of unrelated activities. Furthermore, the particular combination of social worlds differs from person to person; this is what led Simmel to declare that each stands at the point at which a unique combination of social circles intersects. The geometric analogy is a happy one, for it enables us to conceive the numerous possibilities of combinations and the different degrees of participation in each circle. To understand what a man does, we must get at his unique perspective— what he takes for granted and how he defines the situation—but in mass societies we must learn in addition the social world in which he is participating in a given act.

Loyalty and Selective Responsiveness

In a mass society where each person internalizes numerous perspectives there are bound to be some incongruities and conflicts. The overlapping of group affiliation and participation, however, need not lead to difficulties and is usually unnoticed. The reference groups of most persons are mutually sustaining. Thus, the soldier who volunteers for hazardous duty on the battlefield may provoke anxiety in his family but is not acting contrary to their values; both his family and his comrades admire courage and disdain cowardice. Behavior may be inconsistent, as in the case of the proverbial office tyrant who is meek before his wife, but it is not noticed if the transactions occur in dissociated contexts. Most people live more or less compartmentalized lives, shifting from one social world to another as they participate in a succession of transactions. In each world their roles are different, their relations to other participants are different, and they reveal a different facet of their personalities. Men have become so accustomed to this mode of life that they manage to conceive of themselves as reasonably consistent human beings in spite of this segmentalization and are generally not aware of the fact that their acts do not fit into a coherent pattern.

People become acutely aware of the existence of different outlooks only when they are successively caught in situations in which conflicting demands are made upon them, all of which cannot possibly be satisfied. While men generally avoid making difficult decisions, these dilemmas and contradictions of status may force a choice between two social worlds. These conflicts are essentially alternative ways of defining the same situation, arising from several possible perspectives. In the words of William James, "As a man I pity you, but as an official I must show you no mercy; as a politician I regard him as an ally, but as a moralist I loathe him." In playing roles in different social worlds, one imputes different expectations to others whose differences cannot always be compromised. The problem is that of selecting the perspective for defining the situation. In Mead's terminology, which generalized other's role is to be taken? It is only in situations where alternative definitions are possible that problems of loyalty arise.

Generally such conflicts are ephemeral; in critical situations contradictions otherwise unnoticed are brought into the open, and painful choices are forced. In poorly integrated societies, however, some people find themselves continually beset with such conflicts. The Negro intellectual, children of mixed marriages or of immigrants, the foreman in a factory, the professional woman, the military chaplain—all live in the interstices of well-organized structures and are marginal men.[8] In most instances they manage to make their way through their compartmentalized lives, although personal maladjustments are apparently frequent. In extreme cases amnesia and dissociation of personality can occur.

Much of the interest in reference groups arises out of concern with situations in which a person is confronted with the necessity of choosing between two or more organized perspectives. The hypothesis has been advanced that the choice of reference groups—conformity to the norms of the group whose perspective is assumed—is a function of one's interpersonal relations; to what extent the culture of a group serves as the matrix for the organization of perceptual experience depends upon one's relationship and personal loyalty to others who share that outlook. Thus, when personal relations to others in the group deteriorate, as sometimes happens in a military unit after continued defeat, the norms become less binding, and the unit may disintegrate in panic. Similarly, with the transformation of personal relationships between parent and child in late adolescence, the desires and standards of the parents often become less obligatory.

It has been suggested further that choice of reference groups rests upon personal loyalty to significant others of that social world. "Significant others," for Sullivan, are those persons directly responsible for the internalization of norms. Socialization is a product of a gradual accumulation of experiences with certain people, particularly those with whom we stand in primary relations, and significant others are those who are actually involved in the cultivation of abilities, values, and outlook.[9] Crucial, apparently, is the character of one's emotional ties with them. Those who think the significant others have treated them with affection and consideration have a sense of personal obligation that is binding under all circumstances, and they will be loyal even at great personal sacrifice. Since primary relations are not necessarily satisfactory, however, the reactions may be negative. A person who is well aware of the expectations of significant others may go out of his way to reject them. This may account for the bifurcation of orientation in minority groups, where some remain loyal to the parental culture while others seek desperately to become assimilated in the larger world. Some who withdraw from the uncertainties of real life may establish loyalties to perspectives acquired through vicarious relationships with characters encountered in books.[10]

Perspectives are continually subjected to the test of reality. All perception is hypothetical. Because of what is taken for granted from each standpoint, each situation is approached with a set of expectations; if transactions actually take place as anticipated, the perspective itself is reinforced. It is thus the confirming responses of other people that provide support for perspectives.[11] But in mass societies the responses of others vary, and in the study of reference groups the problem is that of ascertaining *whose* confirming responses will sustain a given point of view.

The Study of Mass Societies

Because of the differentiated character of modern mass societies, the concept of reference group, or some suitable substitute, will always have a central place in any realistic conceptual scheme for its analysis. As is pointed out above, it will be most useful if it is used to designate that group whose perspective is assumed by the actor as the frame of reference for the organization of his perceptual experience. Organized perspectives arise in and become shared through participation in common communication channels, and the diversity of mass societies arises from the multiplicity of channels and the ease with which one may participate in them.

Mass societies are not only diversified and pluralistic but also continually changing. The successive modification of life-conditions compels changes in social relationships, and any adequate analysis requires a study of these transformational processes themselves. Here the concept of reference group can be of crucial importance. For example, all forms of social mobility, from sudden conversions to gradual assimilation, may be regarded essentially as displacements of reference groups, for they involve a loss of responsiveness to the demands of one social world and the adoption of the perspective of another. It may be hypothesized that the disaffection occurs first on the level of personal relations, followed by a weakening sense of obligation, a rejection of old claims, and the establishment of new loyalties and incorporation of a new perspective. The conflicts that characterize all persons in marginal roles are of special interest in that they provide opportunities for cross-sectional analyses of the processes of social change.

In the analysis of the behavior of men in mass societies the crucial problem is that of ascertaining how a person defines the situation, which perspective he uses in arriving at such a definition, and who constitutes the audience whose responses provide the necessary confirmation and support for his position. This calls for focusing attention upon the expectations the actor imputes to others, the communication channels in which he participates, and his relations with those with whom he identifies himself. In the study of conflict, imagery provides a fertile source of data. At moments of indecision, when in doubt and confusion, who appears in imagery? In this manner the significant other can be identified.

An adequate analysis of modern mass societies requires the development of concepts and operations for the description of the manner in which each actor's orientation toward his world is successively reconstituted. Since perception is selective and perspectives differ, different items are noticed and a progressively diverse set of images arises, even among those exposed to the same media of mass communication. The concept of reference group summarizes differential associations and loyalties and thus facilitates the study of selective perception. It becomes, therefore, an indispensable tool for comprehending the diversity and dynamic character of the kind of society in which we live.

NOTES

1. H. H. Hyman, "The Psychology of Status," *Archives of Psychology*, XXXVIII (1942), 15; R. K. Merton and A. Kitt, "Contributions to the Theory of Reference Group Behavior," in R. K. Merton and P. F. Lazarsfeld (eds.), *Studies in the Scope and Method of "The American Soldier"* (Glencoe, Ill.: Free Press, 1950), pp. 42-53, 69; D. W. Chapman and J. Volkmann, "A Social Determinant of the Level of Aspiration," *Journal of Abnormal and Social Psychology*, XXXIV (1939), pp. 225-38.

2. *Op. cit.*, pp. 75-76.

3. M. Sherif, "The Concept of Reference Groups in Human Relations," in M. Sherif and M. O. Wilson (eds.), *Group Relations at the Crossroads* (New York: Harper & Bros., 1953), pp. 203-31.

4. *Op. cit.*, pp. 49-50.

5. R. Redfield, *The Folk Culture of Yucatan* (Chicago: University of Chicago Press, 1941), p. 132. For a more explicit presentation of a behavioristic theory of culture see *The Selected Writings of Edward Sapir in Language, Culture and Personality*, ed. D. G. Mandelbaum (Berkeley: University of California Press, 1949), pp. 104-9, 308-31, 544-59.

6. G. H. Mead, "The Genesis of the Self and Social Control," *International Journal of Ethics*, XXXV (1925), pp. 251-77, and *Mind, Self and Society* (Chicago: University of Chicago Press, 1934), pp. 152-64. Cf. T. Parsons, "The Super-ego and the Theory of Social Systems," *Psychiatry*, XV (1952), pp. 15-25.

7. Cf. K. Riezler, *Man: Mutable and Immutable* (Chicago: Henry Regnery Co., 1950), pp. 62-72; L. Landgrebe, "The World as a Phenomenological Problem," *Philosophy and Phenomenological Research*, I (1940), pp. 38-58; and A. Schuetz, "The Stranger: An Essay in Social Psychology," *American Journal of Sociology*, XLIX (1944), pp. 499-507.

8. Cf. E. C. Hughes, "Dilemmas and Contradictions of Status," *American Journal of Sociology*, L (1945), pp. 353-59, and E. V. Stonequist, *The Marginal Man* (New York: Charles Scribner's Sons, 1937).

9. H. S. Sullivan, *Conceptions of Modern Psychiatry* (Washington, D.C.: W. H. White Psychiatric Foundation, 1947), pp. 18-22.

10. Cf. R. R. Grinker and J. P. Spiegel, *Men under Stress* (Philadelphia: Blakiston Co., 1945), pp. 122-26; and E. A. Shils and M. Janowitz, "Cohesion and Disintegration in the Wehrmacht in World War II," *Public Opinion Quarterly*, XII (1948), pp. 280-315.

11. Cf. G. H. Mead, *The Philosophy of the Act* (Chicago: University of Chicago Press 1938), pp. 107-73; and L. Postman, "Toward a General Theory of Cognition," in J. H. Rohrer and M. Sherif (eds.), *Social Psychology at the Crossroads* (New York: Harper & Bros. 1951), pp. 242-72.

THE CONCEPT OF reference group can be especially useful in the study of ethnic and minority groups, particularly when considering the transformation of such groups. One of the transformation processes frequently considered is assimilation, which involves the transformation of an individual's self-conception. From a macro view, assimilation may be regarded as a process in which different cultural groups come to share a common culture; a more social psychological approach focuses on the way people who are being assimilated acquire the dominant group's values and the way they see the minority group from the new standpoint.

A decisive change that occurs during the course of assimilation is the displacement of reference groups. The people being assimilated by the larger society are exposed to and learn an alternate point of view from which to define the situation; over time, they substitute the perspective of the dominant group for the one traditionally used by members of their own group. As individuals adopt the standards of the larger society, they come to judge themselves in those terms. (Shibutani and Kwan, 1965:505) If certain features of their ethnic group are ridiculed, they become particularly sensitive and try to eliminate those characteristics in themselves. Children of immigrants, for example, become extremely conscious of their foreign accent and different dress, and try to minimize their distinctiveness in various ways. When their efforts are unsuccessful or when they do not receive more favorable reactions from their new associates, some people come to despise their identification with an ethnic minority. Some writers have referred to this phenomenon as minority group "self-hatred". (K. Lewin, 1948:186-200; Sartre, 1960:92-100)

When reference groups are changed, individuals wishing to assimilate try to enhance their virtue in the eyes of the dominant group. In the process, the meaning of ethnic symbols and the pattern of communication between these individuals and other members of the ethnic group become transformed. When they choose a new reference group, the individuals' conduct may change. They may come to express certain opinions and engage in courses of action that are shocking and repugnant to other members of the ethnic group.

In the previous article Shibutani suggests that, if we are interested in studying the processes by which people in our complex society select reference groups, we should focus attention on the communication channels they use. As mentioned earlier, human beings are able to communicate symbolically, and in doing so they create and transmit specific meanings. As the philosopher John Dewey put it, "Society not only continues to exist *by* transmission, *by* communication, but it may fairly be said to exist *in* transmission, *in* communication." (Dewey, 1921:5) By this he means that language as well as other means of communication is not only a group product but is also a necessary medium without which human groups cannot exist.

All human societies have language. Like other aspects of a group's social heritage, language is passed on from one generation to the next and must be learned. Since languages differ from society to society, and among different social groups within the same society, events may be classified and categorized differently in the various languages. Some linguists contend that the same objects and events are categorized in the same way in all languages; different labels are simply attached to this pre-existing reality. Others maintain that languages construct and define reality for us. (Hodges, 1971:42) The language we speak alters our perceptions and sensitizes us to culturally defined aspects of the world around us, pointing out and highlighting certain things, while overlooking others. Thus different conceptions of reality are conveyed by a language and our perceptions, categorizations, and definitions are directly influenced by the linguistic symbols we use.

The view that language conveys a particular reality or idea is in line with our conception of man as actively engaged in defining and organizing his experiences. Language does not predefine experience, but is created and manipulated so that we can perceive, order, and organize our environment. Clyde Kluckhohn points to the connection between symbol and cultural meaning when he writes:

> Every language is also a special way of looking at the world and interpreting experiences. Concealed in the structure of each different language are a whole set of unconscious assumptions about the world and life in it. (Kluckhohn, 1964:123)

The cultural significance of language forms the very basis of the Quebec Government's language legislation. Its "White Paper on Language" discusses this idea:

> In Quebec, the French language is not just a means for expression, but a medium for living as well. . . . Because of their common language, people realize that they are part of the same group and that their feelings are similar to those of others; language shapes both dialogue and argument. Language, therefore, is a real and concrete medium, and not just a means of communication. Awareness of the state of a language, care for its health and its precision, as well as work to develop it, are actions which follow from the consideration of language as one of the principal ingredients of the "quality of life". ("Full Text of White Paper on Language." *Montreal Star*, April 2, 1977, p. B1)

It follows that learning a new language exposes us not merely to a new set of linguistic symbols, but also to attitudes with which these symbols have, over time, become associated. In the course of learning a new language, we undergo a change in our self-concept: we come to see ourselves, and are seen by others, as a different person. Mead claims that learning a new language inevitably results in a "readjustment" of views:

A person learns a new language and, as we say, gets a new soul. He puts himself into the attitudes of those that make use of language. He cannot read its literature, cannot converse with those that belong to the community, without taking on its peculiar attitudes. He becomes in a sense a different individual. You cannot convey a language as a pure abstraction; you inevitably in some degree convey also the life that lies behind it. And this result builds itself into relationship with the organized attitudes of the individual who gets this language and inevitably brings about a readjustment of views. (Mead, 1962:283)

When reading the following two selections it is useful to give some thought to the desire of the Parti Québecois to separate from Canada, and to the legislation in that province making French the official language. Both these phenomena reflect concerns about the preservation not only of the French language but also of the French Canadian culture, which is interpreted through that language. Lamy and Paris argue that becoming bilingual involves a change in the way people identify themselves as individuals, and as members of an ethnic group. If this argument is valid, then we might better understand French Canada's apprehensions about the apparent dominance of the English language in a province populated mainly by people of French descent.

It should also become obvious that language serves as the basic building block of any culture, and if it is not passed from one generation to the next, efforts to perpetuate the culture are futile. It is not then merely by coincidence, but by careful planning, that leaders of ethnic groups attempt to include the group's native language in the curriculum of the public schools and universities. It is also for this reason—preservation of culture—that ethnic groups organize language classes for the young.

Bilingualism & Identity

PAUL LAMY

Introduction

EFFORTS TO STUDY the effects of bilingualism on the individual have often been accompanied by controversy since the results of such studies can and have been used (and sometimes produced) for political purposes. German researchers in the years immediately preceding World War II began investigating the effects of bilingualism on Germans living outside their country's frontiers; they reached the conclusion that bilingualism was bad for them in that it causes "deëthnization".[1] Other researchers

Paul Lamy is an Assistant Professor, Department of Sociology, University of Ottawa.

have asserted that bilingualism causes stuttering, left-handedness, schizophrenia, lower intelligence, and dual ethnic identities.[2] Over the past two decades, many of these earlier studies have been repeated using more careful procedures. The first studies reporting lower intelligence among bilinguals, for instance, tended to compare socially disadvantaged first-generation immigrants with unilinguals who were better off. The intelligence tests used often measured only verbal intelligence, and the particular test administered was often written in the language in which the bilingual was least proficient. Two social psychologists in Montreal, Elizabeth Peal and Wallace E. Lambert, carried out a very careful study of the effects of bilingualism on intelligence in which both verbal and non-verbal tests of intelligence were used and in which the dominant language of the bilingual was taken into account. In addition, care was taken to control for age, sex, educational background, and socioeconomic status (since intelligence test scores vary with these factors). It was found that bilinguals actually performed better on both verbal and non-verbal tests of intelligence. One should not interpret these results as indicating that bilingualism causes higher intelligence; it seems more appropriate to ask why one would expect bilingualism to have any impact on intelligence at all (since, as yet, there appear to be no compelling theoretical reasons for assuming that bilingualism should have any direct impact on intelligence).[3]

Empirical studies on bilingualism and identity report a relationship between these two variables, and there is a respectable theoretical tradition that can be drawn upon to explain its existence. Christophersen maintains that "nobody can know a language perfectly without associating himself to a large extent with the people who speak it;"[4] Pieris claims that a "bare colloquial smattering of a foreign national language gives the speaker a sense of identification with the culture that language symbolizes."[5]

These views are compatible with those of George Herbert Mead, to whom the "symbolic interactionist" tradition in sociology can be traced. Mead maintained that one's unity of self comes from the taking on the attitudes of what he called the "generalized other". This is done by acquiring the language of the group. The self is not there at birth but arises only with the internalization of language.[6] If this is so, then learning another language must have some impact on one's self. Mead thought this to be the case; he states that "A person learns a new language and . . . gets a new soul."[7]

Schutz, a theorist who accepted basic symbolic interactionist principles, looked upon language as serving functions similar to those of a map.[8] In Schutz's view, to get our bearings on a new map (the new language) whose symbols are foreign to us, it is necessary to throw away the old one. While some of the symbols on the new map may be more or less equivalent to some of those on the old one, this equivalence won't help much because the map is organized differently. So we discard the old map and try to understand and use the new one. Since the meanings of these foreign symbols can be learned and since they form a meaningful pattern (just like the symbols on the old map can be learned and form meaningful patterns) we can eventually use the new map just as well as the old one. At this point, Schutz says, if we don't replace the old map with the new one altogether, we remain "a cultural hybrid on the verge of two patterns of group life, not knowing to which of them [we belong]."[9]

At first glance, all of this appears plausible. But what about multilinguals? Where do they situate themselves *vis-à-vis* their various language groups? The case of the multilingual is particularly problematic because if learning a second language "inevitably brings about a readjustment of views" as Mead says, the multilingual would be a unique individual. Yet we are sometimes surprised to find that persons who seem to be no different from the other English Canadians or French Canadians we know are accomplished linguists; they speak two, three, or more languages almost as well as they speak their mother tongue.

Apart from multilinguals, we might wonder about those people who speak dead languages (such as Latin) fluently. Then, of course, there is the problem presented by the CIA or KGB agents who learn the enemy's language well enough to hide their real identity from large numbers of native speakers of the language. This kind of thing happened on a large scale at one point during the Second World War when Germans who spoke English very well were sent behind Allied lines dressed in American uniforms. These men were so difficult to detect that the Americans had to ask those who aroused their suspicion questions which only individuals familiar with the American culture could answer (such as questions related to baseball and football). So there seems to be plenty of room for doubt about the effect of bilingualism on ethnic identity.

Searching for Answers

We have two questions to deal with: do bilinguals identify with both their language groups rather than with one or the other? If this is so, is it because they are bilingual or because of other factors? To try and find answers to these questions we will analyze a study of ethnic relations in Canada carried out for the Royal Commission on Bilingualism and Biculturalism in 1965.[10] This study was chosen because the people who were interviewed were asked about their level of fluency in the other official language (a measure of bilingualism) and whether they felt closer to English or French Canadians (a measure of ethnic identity). The people who were interviewed were selected by a procedure that permits us to generalize about the Canadian adult population. A large number of people were interviewed (4071); this number is important because only a small proportion of Canadians are bilingual in English and French (only 12% according to the 1971 census). When the people who were interviewed were asked about their level of fluency in the other official language, their responses were of three kinds: most said they did not speak the other official language (unilinguals); others said they spoke the other official language, but not as well as their mother tongue (bilinguals); a small group said they spoke both official languages equally well (equilinguals).[11] When the people interviewed were asked whether they felt closer to English or French Canadians, most people said they felt closer to their own language group; others said they felt equally close to the two groups. If the person was of English mother tongue and felt closer to the English, or of French mother tongue and closer to the French, that person was labeled "feels closer to mother tongue group".[12] All other persons were labeled "feels as close to each or between both groups". To find out whether bilinguals identify with both their language groups rather than with one or the other, the computer was asked to make six categories and sort the people interviewed into these categories as follows: all the unilinguals who feel closer to their mother tongue group go into one category, and all the unilinguals who feel equally close to the two groups go into another; the same is done for bilinguals and for equilinguals. These results are presented in Table 1, where percentages rather than the actual numbers of people are given.

From Table 1, we see that in Canada only 14.6% of the unilinguals, as compared to 25.1% of the bilinguals and 57.3% of the equilinguals, feel close to both language groups (i.e. English Canadians and French Canadians). There is certainly a relationship between degree of bilingualism and ethnic identity. It is also apparent that the relationship between degree of bilingualism and ethnic identity varies from one mother tongue group to the other: 15.5% of the English unilinguals, 44.7% of the English bilinguals, and 59.2% of the English equilinguals feel close to both groups; the proportions of the French in these categories are 12.4%, 22.4%, and 57.2%, respectively. While we can see that more anglophones in all categories say they identify with both language groups than do francophones, this does not mean that the relationship between degree of bilingualism and ethnic identity is stronger among the English. As an assessment of the strength of the relationship, a measure of association called Pearson's r will be used.

Pearson's r assumes that the measures (degree of bilingualism and ethnic identity) are interval—that is, it assumes that the difference between unilinguals, bilinguals, and equilinguals is fixed and clearly defined, like the difference between units of money.[13] If none of the unilinguals, half of the bilinguals, and all of the equilinguals said they felt equally close to the two groups, the r would attain its maximum value of 1.00, because there would be a perfect linear relationship

Table 1
Ethnic Identity in Canada by Mother Tongue and by Degree of Bilingualism (in %)

Ethnic Identity	Degree of Bilingualism		
	Unilingual	Bilingual	Equilingual
CANADA			
Feels closer to mother tongue group	85.4	74.9	42.7
Feels as close to each or between both groups	14.6	25.1	57.3
Total	100.0	100.0	100.0
N	(2781)	(290)	(98)
	Chi-square = 138.2, 2 df, p .001 (r = .20)*		
ENGLISH			
Feels closer to mother tongue group	84.5	55.3	40.8
Feels as close to each or between both groups	15.5	44.7	59.2
Total	100.0	100.0	100.0
N	(1978)	(36)	(9)
	Chi-square = 33.5, 2 df, p .001 (r = .13)*		
FRENCH			
Feels closer to mother tongue group	87.6	77.6	42.8
Feels as close to each or between both groups	12.4	22.4	57.2
Total	100.0	100.0	100.0
N	(803)	(255)	(90)
	Chi-square = 112.9, 2 df, p .001 (r = .29)*		

* r is statistically significant at .01 level

between degree of bilingualism and ethnic identity. If half of all unilinguals, bilinguals, and equilinguals said they felt close to both groups, the r would attain its minimum value of 0.00 because there would be no relationship at all between degree of bilingualism and ethnic identity.

Looking at Table 1 again, we see that the relationship between degree of bilingualism and ethnic identity in Canada is not very strong— the r is a modest .20; among those of English mother tongue it is .13, as compared to the r of .29 among those of French mother tongue. The relationship between degree of bilingualism and ethnic identity is not strong because some unilinguals feel close to both groups and a lot of bilinguals and equilinguals do not. Moreover, the relationship between degree of bilingualism and ethnic identity is stronger among those of French mother tongue ($r = .29$) than among those of English mother tongue ($r = .13$). This is not what one would expect if bilingualism actually does cause people to identify with both their language groups (if bilingualism is the cause, why does the strength of the relationship vary so much from one mother tongue group to the other?).

We have found that the relationship between degree of bilingualism and ethnic identity is not very strong and that it varies from one mother tongue group to the other in Canada. Thus bilingualism does not seem, in itself, to have much of an impact on ethnic identity.

Two other researchers who are critical of the notion that bilingualism itself causes people to identify with both their language groups have made the following points: first, there will be no relationship between bilingualism and identity among those learning a second language in a monocultural setting;[14] and second, the relationship itself is due to antagonistic acculturative pressures on the bilingual emanating from each of his language communities.[15] To illustrate these points, we can sort our subjects into two categories according to the number of speakers of the other language in their neighborhood, city, and province, and according to the amount of contact they personally have with members of the other language group. According to the researchers we will find that among those people who have very few speakers of the other language in their area and who have little contact with members of the other language group, there will be *no* relationship between the degree of bilingualism and ethnic identity. Put another way, if we hold demographic context and intergroup contact constant, the r will be 0.00.

There is a way of doing this statistically through partial correlations. A partial correlation is a measure of the strength of the relationship between two variables, such as degree of bilingualism and ethnic identity, with some third factor, such as intergroup contact, held constant. So now we are going to call the r's (which measure the strength of the relationship between degree of bilingualism and ethnic identity) "zero-order correlations." If you look at Table 2, you will see in the "zero-order" column the same correlations that appear in Table 1. What we want to know is whether or not, with intergroup contact and demographic context held constant, there is much of a relationship between degree of bilingualism and ethnic identity.[16] Remember, the zero-orders are .20 in Canada, .13 among those of English mother tongue, and .29 among those of French mother tongue. When intergroup contact is held constant, the correlation between degree of bilingualism and ethnic identity is only .13 in Canada, .10 among those of English mother tongue, and .14 among those of French mother tongue. When demographic context is held constant, the correlations are only .14 in Canada, .07 among those of English mother tongue, and .21 among those of French mother tongue. With both intergroup contact and demographic context held constant, the correlations between degree of bilingualism and ethnic identity are now only .10 in Canada, .07 among those of English mother tongue, and .10 among those of French mother tongue.[17] Therefore, with both intergroup contact and demographic contact held constant, there is almost no relationship between degree of bilingualism and ethnic identity.

Table 2
Partial Correlations between Ethnic Identity and Degree of Bilingualism with Intergroup Contact and Demographic Context Held Constant

Controlling for	Sample Characteristic		
	CANADA	ENGLISH	FRENCH
Zero-order	.20	.13	.29
Intergroup contact	.13*	.10*	.14*
Demographic context	.14*	.07	.21*
Intergroup contact and demographic context	.10*	.07	.10*

* *r* is statistically significant at .05 level.

Conclusions

We have tried to discover whether the frequently observed tendency of bilinguals to identify with both language groups is due solely to the acquisition of a second language, as some theorists suggest, or due to other factors. It was found that in Canada, among persons of either English or French mother tongues, the tendency to identify with both official language groups increases as fluency in the second language increases. However, the relationship between bilingualism and ethnolinguistic identity is not very strong and it is therefore doubtful that it is bilingualism itself that explains this relationship. Further, those bilinguals who tend to identify with both language groups are usually those who have interpersonal relationships with members of the other language group in settings where the other language group constitutes a majority at the local and/or regional level (i.e. anglophone bilinguals in Quebec and francophone bilinguals everywhere else in the country). Bilinguals who have little contact with the other language group and who are in social contexts where the other language group constitutes a minority (anglophone bilinguals in Ontario, for instance) are much less likely to identify with both language groups. Put another way, when intergroup contact and demographic context are taken into account, the relationship between bilingualism and identity is extremely weak. Bilingualism itself, then, has very little direct impact on ethnolinguistic identity.

NOTES

1. Uriel Weinreich, *Languages in Contact* (The Hague: Mouton, 1968), pp. 117-118.

2. *Ibid.*, pp. 116-122.

3. Elizabeth Peal and Wallace E. Lambert, "The Relation of Bilingualism to Intelligence," *Psychological Monographs*, Vol. LXXVI, No. 27 (1962), pp. 1-23.

4. Paul Christophersen, *Bilingualism* (London: published for the University College, Ibadan, by Methuen, 1948), p. 8.

5. Ralph Pieris, "Bilingualism and Cultural Marginality," *British Journal of Sociology*, Vol. 2 (1951), p. 321.

6. George Herbert Mead, *On Social Psychology*, edited and with an introduction by Anselm Strauss (Chicago: University of Chicago Press, 1964).

7. *Ibid.*, p. 258.

8. Alfred Schutz, *Collected Papers, II* (The Hague: Martinus Nijhoff, 1964).

9. *Ibid.*, pp. 104-105.

10. This study, the Ethnic Relations Study, was carried out by the Social Research Group. The sample was selected by means of a multistage, stratified, area random procedure from the electoral lists for the 1963 federal elections. The Yukon and the Northwest Territories were excluded. The weighted case base of 23,459 was down-weighted to 4,070.

11. The measure of bilingualism was constructed from responses to two questions in the Ethnic Relations Study. Cf. Paul Lamy, "Language and Ethnicity: A Study of Bilingualism, Ethnic Identity, and Ethnic Attitudes," Ph.D. Thesis, McMaster University, 1976, ch. III.

12. Mother tongue was not asked in the Ethnic Relations Study, though respondents were asked which language their parents spoke at home. If both parents spoke English at home, English was assigned as the respondent's mother tongue. All other cases were dropped from the analysis.

13. Those who have a keen interest in knowing why level of measurement assumptions were violated and why these particular statistical procedures are used should refer to Lamy, *op. cit.*, ch. III.

14. James P. Soffietti, "Bilingualism and Biculturalism," *Journal of Educational Psychology*, Vol. 46 (1955), p. 222-227.

15. A. Richard Diebold, Jr., "The Consequences of Early Bilingualism in Cognitive Development and Personality Formation," in *The Study of Personality*, eds. Edward Norbeck *et al.* (New York: Holt, Rinehart, and Winston), pp. 218-245.

16. Intergroup contact was measured by means of two questions; one dealt with how recently the respondent had had contact with the other group, whereas the second measured frequency of contact but failed to distinguish between past and present contact. Demographic context is a control for both ethnic composition of the electoral district and linguistic composition of the region.

17. The partials for both intergroup contact and demographic context are second-order. The partials for both intergroup contact and demographic context combined are fourth-order.

The Bilingual Problem: How Do You Identify Yourself to Yourself?

ERNA PARIS

I'VE BEEN SPEAKING French every day for nine years, and still I have language problems. I went to France in 1960, became bilingual, stayed three years, married a Frenchman, and then came back to Canada with him. Long ago I acquired the ability to switch back and forth from French to English, sometimes without even being aware I'm doing so. And yet the problems persist. I can say almost anything I want to in French; but when I speak French, "I" am not completely there. The real me, the cultural me that spent twenty-two years growing up in Toronto, remains on the outside, watching.

This was most acute during my years in France when all my relationships, including my marriage, were in French. It was as though an essential part of myself was missing, hidden to those I knew and loved. So I have some strong feelings about bilingualism, and the sort of things that happened to me while I was getting there and even after I got there. I went to Quebec recently to check out my own experience, and I found it held true for others. So these notes are on bilingualism, from the inside and from the outside.

France came as a shock. I had grade 13 French from Ontario, plus a couple of university courses in the subject, and I thought I knew French. I soon realized that I could speak a little but couldn't understand anyone who didn't speak with an English accent. For a while I lived in agony lest anyone ask me a question. I took some courses at the Sorbonne, where you had to listen from the hall if you didn't get there an hour early. I read dictionaries for pleasure. I soon developed more of an ear. But I became increasingly aware that I was speaking French words, striving to mimic the French context in which I heard those words spoken around me, succeeding, in fact, making contact—but losing "myself" in the process. My idiom, my own particular way of being me, just couldn't be translated. As a result, I had to accept a level of communication that enormously frustrated me. I also had to accept the humiliation of realizing that people judged me by what I said and the way I said it.

Linguistically, I kept improving. But a rather different personality was emerging. The French "me" was far weightier and more serious than her English counterpart, for humor is so quick and so involved with culture that it is one of the last things a bilingual acquires, if he ever does. I once

Erna Paris, *"The Bilingual Problem: How Do You Identify Yourself to Yourself?"* Reprinted from Saturday Night, *February 1970, pp. 24-26.*

tried to translate a joke for my young French nieces, and when I'd finished they just stared at me curiously until their father courteously changed the subject.

My French-language self also had considerable paranoid tendencies. French shopkeepers are not known for their amiability. The customer, French or foreign, is often suspect, and should she not make a purchase, borderline tolerance dissolves into open contempt. I was asked once to leave a shoe store and never return simply because I had purchased nothing. I wondered what I would have done had such a scene occurred in English. At least I would have been able to reply and retain my self-respect; here I was defenceless. This incident further diminished my sense of self and, no matter how good my French became, I was rarely able to meet this sort of occasion to my own satisfaction.

After seven or eight months I began to think and dream in French. My accent improved, too, until the French thought it was French—not Parisian, but from somewhere out in that distant land of the "provinces" or the "colonies." Once, during the Franco-Algerian war, I was openly insulted by a grocery shop proprietress who thought I was a *pied-noir*, a colonial from Algeria. But I still made occasional mistakes in syntax and grammar, and soon found, paradoxically, that some people thought I was a poorly educated French-woman rather than an educated foreigner speaking a newly acquired second language. It became important to state early in all relationships, even the most superficial, that I was an English-speaking Canadian. Only then could I relax, and feel proud rather than ashamed of the way I spoke French.

About this time, my English began to slip. Canadian friends would occasionally drop in while they were visiting Paris. There were often long pauses while I searched for words. I would speak English using French constructions and they would stare at me, incredulous. My French wasn't perfect, and my English was no longer up to par. I couldn't take any one thought process far enough in either language without blocking on vocabulary. It was hell.

Fifteen months after my arrival, I married, and we took a flat in a working-class section of Montmartre. This was not an area frequented by tourists. To the concierge, the shopkeepers, and all those I had to deal with daily, I was French. My name itself was now French and the government had even bestowed citizenship upon me as the wife of a national. Sometimes I longed to shout aloud in English; but the words always came to mind in French. Even the intimate moments of marriage were in French: my husband knew no English. The whole set-up seemed unreal, though my former self, and its reality, were fast slipping into obscurity.

When I had been in France almost three years, I made friends with an American woman, and gradually recovered some fluency in English.

With indescribable relief, I slowly, as if recovering, rediscovered my identity as an English-speaking Canadian. I hadn't fully realized, until then, how much I had lost.

Back in Canada, I became an English teacher. I feel almost apologetic about that as I write it, but in 1964 the teaching of high-school French consisted mostly of explaining grammar and drilling verbs, and that was not for me. But sometimes in class I would stop point-blank in the middle of a sentence and search for the word I needed. A French one might have come instead or, as often happened, I just went blank and no word came at all.

I gave up hope of recovering my former command of English, for in spite of the fact that we now lived in Toronto, and I worked in English, our language at home was French. I lived and still live my daily life in both languages. Approximately one year ago, I began writing professionally, and I saw that my English expression of eight years previous was returning. Though I'm not there yet, I no longer feel hopeless. We speak more English than French at home these days. My husband is now bilingual.

* * *

SALLY-ANN LAPOINTE is in her mid-twenties, a Montreal advertising executive; mother, Irish; father, French-Canadian. We're sitting in a lounge at the top of Place Ville-Marie, looking over the lights of her city. We're talking in French, but when things get serious and I start taking notes, she switches into English. I ask her why and she looks surprised and says she did it because the article will be in English, so why not talk in English? I'm grateful and impressed, too. She must be confident about the language or she wouldn't choose it for our interview.

In fact, her English is excellent, though there is the slightest trace of a French-Canadian accent. She appears to be a truly bilingual and bicultural individual, but then her whole life has been one long attempt to integrate both languages and cultures into some sort of cohesive whole she could call herself. Her early life was English, but she was sent to a French elementary school: by age ten she belonged to both cultures.

"At fifteen, along with other adolescent problems, I also had to contend with an identity crisis. I didn't know what I was. This is the age when most children from mixed homes usually opt for one language or the other. I didn't. I decided to reinforce both languages. Today I speak to my father in French to show my respect for his language. I speak to my mother in English."

Now in her mid-twenties, she thinks she has been successful in creating that "cohesive whole," and feels richer for it, but the result is still a duality of personal identity. In her work, she daily, even hourly crosses cultural lines; she tends to fade into the environment of the moment.

"When I speak English, I speak as an English person. I mean I communicate in their way because culturally, I know them. It's one thing to understand the grammar of a second language and adapt yourself to the vocabulary, but it's quite another thing to adapt what you're thinking to another scale of social and individual values and do it with all the zest of that other person and in a way that he understands. I have not simply learned two languages. I have become bicultural."

"But how do you identify yourself to yourself?"

She hesitates. Then she says that she's alone in the middle of the two groups and can become either at will, but there's an intangible core at her centre that remains constant when she changes. That immutable point of reference is her "self." But she's never exactly like either group. Accepted by both, yes, but never totally belonging.

"As a kid I'd hear *'les maudits Anglais'* and I'd think, 'that's me,' and then I'd hear 'those frogs,' and I'd think, 'that's me, too.' I always had to defend both groups."

But after a while, being slightly removed brings its own particular perspective. Politically, that means that you see both sides of the coin. And for that reason, Sally-Ann has not joined René Lévesque's Parti Québecois.

"I want the best for Canada and the best for Quebec, too," she says, emotionally. "Perhaps, straddling the fence as I do, I see it more objectively. I'm always questioning myself. I try to read *La Presse, Gazette, Le Devoir,* and the Montreal *Star* when I can. I don't know yet which side I will opt for politically."

Socially, she dates French and English Canadians and finds them quite different from each other; she finds that she's different too, depending on whom she's with. With her French friends she's more relaxed. They take time to laugh and sing, and are more openly emotional and subjective. With her English friends she's more serious and subdued. Sally-Ann calls it "walking a tight-rope," and says it doesn't really matter now, but that it will when she marries and has a family. She'll have to choose one language in which to relate to her children. And marriage is a problem in itself. Sally-Ann's husband will have to be bilingual. If he isn't completely so, she'll have to give up a vital part of herself.

This is why she tends to prefer what she calls "international" men. Men whose travels have exposed them to different cultures. Men who know that approaching another person's language is only a part of the game. Meeting his culture is what really counts.

"When I meet a German, for instance, I listen to his words last. First, I look at his eyes and I watch how he behaves with his friends. I'm trying to understand him and communicate non-verbally, because translation never works. Eventually, I try to find the words he uses in a particular context. I'm learning his language but I'm also learning to understand him. I'd rather add a third language and culture than marry a unilingual, unicultural man."

"Bilingualism and biculturalism are ridiculous outside Montreal," she tells me heatedly. "Elsewhere in Canada Quebec is French and the rest of Canada is English. Bilingualism is a living thing, not a theory. You have to be fifty-fifty in your daily life, because if you're not, you become sixty-forty, and then it's gone. And it doesn't just happen; it's always a choice. But bilingualism is useless unless people understand what's going on behind the scenes, unless they're bicultural as well."

Sally-Ann possesses biculturalism, that elusive substance mentioned in the title of the Royal Commission. She was born and educated to it.

* * *

PAUL O. TRÉPANIER is in his mid-forties, an architect, former mayor of Granby, Quebec, national vice-president of the Progressive Conservative Association of Canada. We meet at the University of Montreal, in a small corridor that has been converted into a cafeteria. We sit next to each other on a small hard bench that lines the wall. He exudes poise and self-assurance. Longish hair, a stylish jacket, a gold shirt and gold tie give him a "with it" look. But he's also a part-time politician, and as such he chooses his words carefully. He's a federalist, an internationalist, an anti-nationalist; as he is quick to point out. He pauses professionally while I write it all down.

But we are talking in French, and the atmosphere around us is informal, and soon the politician drops his public face. Frequently his ideas appear to contradict one another. He says, "I was brought up with the idea that nationalism was bad; I'm an internationalist." But he also says: "When I leave Quebec, I'm in a foreign country."

He says: "The trend towards bilingualism in Ottawa is very interesting and should produce good results." But he also says: "I spoke in French at the Progressive Conservative convention in Niagara Falls. There was simultaneous translation available, but not ten per cent of the English Canadians present bothered to listen to me. I blew up about it. They're not accustomed to making an effort for us."

He goes on: "We pay a high price psychologically to be Canadian. We would pay a high price economically to be *Québecois*. The conflict is between ideology and material comfort . . . When I began speaking two languages, I lost the ability to express myself in either language. This upsets me. I feel personally diminished. Sometimes I even feel more confident in English because I know my mistakes will be excused."

Paul Trépanier has never seriously thought about the psychological side of bilingualism, he tells me, and my questions seem to disturb him. He was twenty-one years old when he learned to speak English words, but he has never understood their cultural context. And in at the end he seems discouraged and unsure: "No, we can't really understand each other on a personal basis. I can't really communicate with an English Canadian, and he can't communicate with me."

* * *

ANDRÉ MORIN is about thirty, an advertising executive, a separatist "sympathizer." He wears his hair at a respectable length with respectable middle-length sideburns. Until recently, he worked almost exclusively in English, though he now helps to head a French-language agency that has been formed within his company. He trusts me because we are speaking in French and because I, too, know the frustrations of which he speaks. He tells me that because his first language is French, he can't really communicate fully in English. He also tells me that his English isn't as good now as it was several years ago when he was living in Toronto. It was important, then, to feel proficient in English, but as a result he began to forget his French. That was serious for André, because only in French could he establish meaningful relationships. So he returned to Montreal. He then recovered French but forgot a good part of his English.

"It was then that I came to this agency. At my first meeting with English-language clients, I had real problems, though I had been fluent in English only a few months earlier. I lost confidence in myself and I felt stupid in the eyes of the others.

"I have always known that lack of contact with one language, even for a few weeks, would make me lose that language. A few minutes ago, I had to search for a (French) word. Ten years ago, I would have had it and three others besides.

"I have trouble being perfect in two languages. I think most people are like that—with the exception, maybe of Trudeau. I have had to choose, and I have chosen to concentrate on French, even though it might have been more advantageous to choose English. Anyway, I couldn't really have chosen English, because culturally, I am French."

Culture is untranslatable. André Morin could live in English Montreal for the rest of his life and still not become an Anglo-Saxon. He would lose his French, though, and likely even his "Frenchness," as he believes many French-Canadians have done. In their desire to integrate into the English milieu, they abandon their culture, they listen to English radio, buy the morning *Gazette*, work all day in English, buy the evening *Star*, and watch English television at night. This is the group that the young nationalists abhor. André calls himself a *Québecois* rather than a

French-Canadian, and his feelings about his language and his "Frenchness" have a lot to do with his feelings about his province.

As a business student at Laval university, André knew that his English was far from perfect. In Quebec City, that didn't matter, but Montreal was a different story; and that's where the business action was. So, after graduation, he spent a year at the London School of Economics, getting a master's degree and improving his English. That was 1960-61, and it was then that he first sensed what was wrong at home in Quebec.

"I was struck by the fact that the English spoke English in their country, and that the French spoke French in their country, and I thought they were lucky to have an identity. They were at home. They didn't need to cross an ocean to learn another language so that they could live and work at home. I realized that we didn't have a country of our own. It was just coincidence that my personal experience corresponded with the beginning of awareness in Quebec.

"Quebec is French, and the English people must learn that they are not in Canada here, but in a French country. The anglophones in Quebec should have to learn French, but we should not have to learn English, except by personal choice."

Like Paul Trépanier, André Morin is culturally French, though he has learned to function in English. But living in a professional English world has been an "adaptation," as he puts it, and "not actually being." Social relationships are exclusively French, with the exception of one close friend who happens to speak French fluently.

"I spend my life looking for words in two languages. I haven't accepted this, nor what it does to me inside. And I never will."

EVERY SOCIETY IS forced to come to terms with its own problems. While the general nature of these problems may be common to a number of societies, each society's history and its traditional ways of dealing with these problems result in a different approach to establishing an acceptable *modus vivendi*. Specifically Canadian problems are the overall concern of the two official language groups. The previous article dealt with the effect of bilingualism on immigrants' affinity with their ethnic group. Another problem in Canada is the place of Native People in society. The term "Native People" includes both Indians and Inuit, but our concern lies with the role of the Indian.

Just as we classify objects and events, so also do we classify other human beings into social types. We construct these types by fitting together the conspicuous traits that we believe are characteristic of a category of people, and we use them in our everyday lives to anticipate the behavior of people we encounter. (Shibutani and Kwan, 1965:85) Those individuals characterized as belonging to a particular social type are supposed to share common traits. Once stereotypes are learned, they are often reaffirmed as we selectively perceive those characteristics that confirm our expectations and disregard those traits that conflict with our conceptions. Though stereotypes may not be accurate, they do represent the way in which people see each other.

Although all ethnic and minority groups have experienced some form of stereotyping, few stereotypes are as widely publicized and accepted as are stereotypes of the Indians. From childhood on, Canadians learn images of Indians and Indian life through history books and the media. The picture that emerges has been described by one observer as follows:

> ... Indians are shown as a nation of trappers and canoemen, an angry people seeking white scalps, men at war with each other, and of falter-
> ing allegiances easily influenced by White men carrying firewater ... and
> impoverished people with large diseased families in overcrowded homes.
> It is a picture of people who are immoral, lazy, frequently inebriated,
> unambitious and unwanted. (Lagasse, 1955:170)

These stereotypes have surely influenced the personal and collective identities of the Indian people. Because they have been defined as certain kinds of people and treated accordingly, many Indians accept themselves as inferior to white people. The master status of "Indian", which is based on negative stereotypes, overrides the Native People's other statuses.

As the Hawthorn Report shows, the inculcation of a negative self-image begins early in the Indian child's life:

> It is difficult to imagine how an Indian child attending an ordinary
> public school could develop anything but a negative self-image. First,
> there is nothing from his culture represented in the school or valued by
> it. Second, the Indian child often gains the impression that nothing he or
> other Indians do is right when compared to what non-Indian children
> are doing. Third, in both segregated and integrated schools, one of the
> main aims of teachers expressed with reference to Indians is "to help
> them improve their standard of living, or their general lot or them-
> selves" which is another way of saying that what they are and have now
> is not good enough. ... (*A Survey of the Contemporary Indians of Canada: A*
> *Report on Economic, Political, Educational Needs and Policies*, Vol. 2, 1967:142)

Apart from this concern over the outsider's view of Indians, there are also problems created by the government's system of classification. As the following selection by Harold Cardinal emphasizes, the legal and social definitions of Indian status do not necessarily coincide. The legal definitions laid down in the Indian Act are often at odds with the way the people see themselves and the way they are seen by others. The excerpt from Cardinal's *The Unjust Society* points out that it is possible for full-blooded Indians, in the eyes of the law, to be considered non-Indian, while a white woman who marries an Indian may legally be classified as Indian. In addition, the Indian Act does not recognize the Métis, who are of Indian-white descent, as Indians. Problems of identity arise when the person who is not legally recognized as an Indian is nonetheless treated as one by society. The Métis are a case in point.

In dealing with the problems created by their status as Indians, some Indians have attempted to assimilate into the larger society, and have advocated assimilation as a solution to the problem. Accepting the larger society's definition of their people as an inferior minority, many come to despise themselves. They come to view their situation from an alternate perspective and believe that the Indians' difficulties could be eliminated if Indians would change their ways. These people and those who advocate the assimilation of all ethnic and minority groups believe that the minority group deserves the differential treatment it receives, and many scathingly criticize the group. For instance, while Eastern European Jews blamed Gentiles for anti-Semitism, the more assimilated Jews felt that Jews were also responsible, and suggested that the problem might be overcome if they changed their way of life. Many of the Indian advocates of assimilation eventually discover that they are blocked in their efforts to escape their past, for they live in a society that treats them like Indians. (Sartre, 1965-64)

In his article, Harold Cardinal discusses some of the roots of the Indians' identity problems. Indians, we are told, have encountered numerous difficulties in managing both their personal and collective identities because of their subordinate status in Canada. As a consequence, they feel ambivalent about their place in Canadian history and society. While Canada is indeed their native land, the Indians feel that their way of life and their image have been systematically destroyed through their contacts with the larger society. This feeling was sensitively expressed by Chief Dan George at a centennial celebration in Vancouver on Dominion Day, 1967:

How long have I known you – Oh Canada? A hundred years? Yes – a hundred years – and many many years before. Today, when you celebrate your hundred years Oh Canada – I am sad for all the Indian people throughout the land. For I have known you when your forests were mine. When they gave me food and my clothing. I have known you – in your brooks and rivers – where your fish splashed and danced in the sun, and whose waters said, "Come and eat of my abundance." I have known you in the freedom of your winds and my spirit like your winds – once roamed this good land. But in the long hundred years since – the white man came – I have seen my spirit disappear – just like the salmon as they mysteriously go out to sea. The white man's strange ways and customs – I could not understand – thrust down upon me until I could no longer breathe. When I fought to protect my home and my land – I was called a savage. When I neither understood nor welcomed this new way of life – I was called lazy. When I tried to rule my people – I was stripped of my authority. My nation was ignored in your history textbooks. We were less important in the history of Canada than the buffalo that roamed the plains. I was ridiculed in your plays and motion pictures – and when I drank your firewater – I got drunk – very, very drunk – and I forgot. Oh Canada – how can I celebrate with you this Centennial Year – this hundred years? Shall I thank you for the reserves that are left me of my beautiful forests? Shall I thank you for the loss of my pride and authority – even amongst my own people? For the lack of my will to fight back? Shall I thank you for my defeat?

Red Tape

HAROLD CARDINAL

CANADIANS WORRY ABOUT their identity. Are they too English? Are they too American? Are they French Canadians or some other kind of hybrid? Indians worry about their identity, too. For the most part they like to think of themselves as Canadians. But there are towns and cities in Canada, in every province of Canada, where an Indian dares not forget his identity as an Indian. There are towns and cities in Canada where a Canadian Indian simply dares not go.

If that seems a shocking statement to the non-Indian, it shocks Indians even more. There are towns and cities in Canada where simply being an Indian means getting a beating. Indians in such towns and cities have even been dragged out of restaurants into the streets and beaten. In such cases an Indian foolish enough to attempt to bring charges finds *himself* charged with creating a disturbance. No citizen is likely to forget his identity under such circumstances.

For the Canadian Indian the question of identity bears heavily on the kind of life a native may lead. Under Canada's mixed-up legal definition, full-blooded Indians may be classed non-Indian, and full-blooded whites can legally be Indians. The *Indian Act* defines an Indian as "a person who pursuant to this Act is registered as an Indian or is entitled to be registered as an Indian." This simplistic legalism, however, eliminates roughly 250,000 native people who, under the American system, would be recognized as Indian.

This *Indian Act* definition has been and continues to be a divisive force among Canada's natives. If you are legally an Indian, then you and your family can live on reserves and are entitled to certain limited rights. No matter how full-blooded you may be, if you are not a legal Indian, you can forget the reserve. You can't live there.

From The Unjust Society *by Harold Cardinal, pp. 18-26. Edmonton: Hurtig Publishers, 1969.*

The whole silly bit about who is an Indian and who isn't came about as a result of the treaties. On the Prairies, the native people were given a choice at the time of signing as to the status they wanted. If they chose to be Indians under treaty, native people were promised certain treaty rights, including land on a reserve, perpetual hunting and fishing rights, along with myriad lesser pledges, but they were denied the right to vote or access to liquor.

The alternative was to choose script, a legal piece of paper proclaiming the victim's citizenship, providing a sum of money (it varied in different treaties) and a piece of land (the area varied). This choice gave access to liquor and the vote, the same privileges accorded any citizen of Canada.

If a man chose to give up his Indian status, he never could reclaim it. But if a native chose to become a registered or treaty Indian, he still retained a sort of horrible option. He could enfranchise. This meant and still means that a treaty or registered or legal Indian still could and still can give up his special status by applying to Ottawa for enfranchisement. This remains a pretty drastic decision for an Indian. He gains full citizenship rights, the vote, liquor (which he now can get as an Indian, anyhow) and, in theory, becomes a Canadian like anyone else. But he renounces his Indianness: he loses all treaty or aboriginal rights; he gives up forever his right to membership on a reserve and all title to his portion of resources or reserve land. He cannot return to the reserve to take up residence where the rest of his family, his relatives and his friends live.

If the parents make this choice or if an entire Indian family enfranchises, then the children of that family and all subsequent grandchildren and direct heirs lose forever the right to claim title to being Indians, at least legally. The only exception to this loss of identity occurs in maternal lineage. If any woman, Indian or non-Indian, marries a treaty or registered Indian, she automatically becomes a legal Indian; no matter whether she is red, white, yellow or black, married to a legal Indian she becomes one, too. However, it doesn't work the other way around. If an Indian woman marries a non-Indian man, she automatically forfeits her claim to be an Indian.

Just to make it more confusing, when a white or non-Indian woman becomes by reason of marriage legally an Indian, this does not mean that her children necessarily will be Indian. Under section 12, subsection (a) 4 of the *Indian Act*, effective in the 1970s, a person whose mother and paternal grandmother are non-Indian (except by right of marriage) also loses his claim to be an Indian.

This legal hocus-pocus has created many problems for the younger generation. In some instances, where full-blooded Indian families have for one reason or another enfranchised, they and their children are, in the eyes of the law, non-Indian, Métis or even white—in theory. At the same time, in the case of a white woman marrying a registered Indian, she and her children suddenly, in the eyes of the law, are Indians. Among the younger generation where pride of race once again is growing, Indians in all but the law have found themselves classed as non-Indians no matter how much they want to be Indians, because parents enfranchised. Many young Indians today are being denied their birthright because someone else decided to renounce his legal claims to being Indian. They have no recourse; they never legally can reclaim their birthright.

Stan Daniels, president of the Métis Association of Alberta, puts the problem this way: "The question of my identity is hard for me to understand; on one hand, when I consider myself an Indian, and I say this, the Indian says, 'Who do you think you are: you are nothing but a white man.' And when I consider myself a white man, talk or act like one, the white man says to me, 'Who in the hell do you think you are? You're nothing but a damned Indian.' I am a man caught in the vacuum of two cultures with neither fully accepting me."

Legalities continue to play a divisive role among Canadian Indians. Even among those who have a legal right to be Indian, further classifications complicate the matter. There is, for example, a distinction between treaty Indians and registered Indians. A treaty Indian is one whose ancestors signed a treaty with the representatives of the queen and ceded some land rights to the crown in return for specified rights. Treaties have been signed with Indians in Ontario, Manitoba, Saskatchewan, Alberta and portions of the Northwest Territories. A registered Indian is one whose ancestors signed no treaties, such as Indians in the Maritimes, in Quebec, in portions of the Northwest Territories and in British Columbia, but who did choose under the *Indian Act* to be regarded as legal or registered Indians. Maritimes Indians signed "pacts of friendship" with the representatives of the queen. Many treaty Indians fear that association with Indians from non-treaty areas will jeopardize their claims to their treaty rights, while Indians from the non-treaty areas are concerned that association with treaty Indians will compromise their requests for settlement of aboriginal claims. In some cases, even minor differences between treaties can confuse and worry Indians as to their rights when they intermingle. Treaty Six carries a medicine chest promise, which in present-day usage can be considered the right to paid-up medicare. Treaties Seven and Eight, although the question of medical treatment was promised verbally, never followed through on this issue in writing. A Treaty Six Indian conceivably could lose her claims to medical care by marrying a Treaty Seven man.

Sneakier things than that have come from government offices. In fact, the government, specifically the Department of Indian Affairs and Northern Development, seems to enjoy this divisiveness and even, in many cases, to encourage it. Anything that divides the Indians makes the department stronger. No wonder no Indian in his right mind trusts the department.

Some progress is being made toward unity among Canada's native people, but much work remains to be done to tear down this inner Buckskin Curtain. It is self-definition, not this network of inhuman legalities or the recently proposed alternative of assimilation, that will foster Indian unity. All the legal definitions fail to accomplish one thing— they fail to solve the real, human problem of identity. Identity means as much to an Indian as it does to the Québecois in Trois Rivières or the Icelander in Gimli. Obviously this has no meaning for many people. They are the sort who feel that the only future for the Indian lies in assimilation. Such people see all residents of Canada as Canadians, without regard to ethnic background. As far as we are concerned, these melting-pot advocates don't understand the nature of our country, let alone the nature of the native. To all too many, being Canadian simply means, "white is right," or "be Anglo and you'll be happy," or "be like me and all your problems will vanish."

Other people, both Indian and non-Indian, seem to feel that being Indian means being some sort of relic out of the past, a guy with a feathered headdress and beaded buckskin clothes, a buffalo hunter. They feel that Indianness is a thing of the past, with no relevance today. Indians who feel this way can be spotted quickly. They continually apologize for being Indian. They may be extremely successful in the white man's world, perhaps even in Canadian legislative bodies, but they always apologize for being Indian. You don't hear a man like Lincoln Alexander, MP for Hamilton, apologize for being a Negro.

Such Uncle Tomahawks have a compelling urge to go around telling other Indians to pull up their bootstraps. Once they have it made, they seem to develop a case of very bad memory as to how it was with them on the way up. They lose touch and become blind to the circumstances under which their "brothers" are living. They don't command much respect from their own people for very long. Indians can be fooled once, like anyone else, but don't try it twice.

When I attended a white school, there were a very few Indians there. None ever wore articles of Indian apparel. When winter came, I put on my mukluks. Some of the other Indian students came to me and suggested I shouldn't wear them. My mukluks called attention to the fact that I was an Indian. But I continued to wear them, not as any sort of hollow protest and not feeling particularly self-righteous—just warm. The next year more Indian students found the "courage" to wear Indian clothing in which they felt comfortable. By my third year, even the white students who could get them were wearing mukluks.

Now Indian clothing is acceptable. In fact it has become high fashion in some quarters. The only problem now is that an Indian runs the risk of being taken for a hippie if he wears his ordinary clothing.

I wear a buckskin jacket today and have for many years. I wear it first of all because it is one of the most comfortable garments I have, but I also wear it as an example to young Indians. One other reason: I got tired of being asked if I were from China or Japan or India or somewhere like that. I got tired of having people jump to the conclusion that, just because I was educated and could talk like a white man, even though I obviously am not one, that I must be an Asian. I wear my buckskin jacket because it says, "I am a Canadian Indian."

For a long time many, many Indians accepted the white man's evaluation of them as a race and as individuals. So often were they told openly and brutally that they were no good, that they were nothing, that they came to accept this negative image. "What can we do?" one hears an Indian say. "We are just Indians." Or, "How can we talk of equality? We will always be Indians no matter what we do. The government can't just suddenly rule that we are equal and make it a fact. Will the person who hated us yesterday because we are Indian love us tomorrow because the government says he should?"

Young Indians who went off to residential schools were obviously at a disadvantage. The missionary teachers soon made them aware of it if they didn't know it when they came. It doesn't take many times being called "an ungrateful little savage" to impress your difference upon you. And those who went into the white man's schools to be integrated found their little white friends brought their homes to the classroom: "My father says all Indians are drunks; my mother says Indians are dirty and I can't play with you." Indians who went to the cities to try to make their way found themselves isolated, pointed out, penalized for being Indian. Small wonder many Indians sought to hide their Indianness. They had lost their pride. They had overlooked the one thing they had that no white man had or has or can have—Indianness.

Today the trend is the other way. Young Indians are proud of their heritage and are learning more about it. During and after World War II many of our people crossed the colour line. It was a status thing to do. They had lived in a white world; they had fought as well as the white soldier. They were accepted for the time being, at least. Many married across the colour line. Now social pressure swings the other way with Indians, and is against marrying into white society.

Of course no one can deny there still are many negative factors relating, if not to actual Indian identity, then to the popular image of our identity. Indians are sensitive. We know that we may be turned away from the odd hotel because of our colour. We know that available suites at good highrise locations suddenly are taken when we show up. We are careful about the kind of restaurant we go into. But we also know that more and more Indians are suddenly standing straighter, walking with a firmer step and finding new pride in being Indian.

The political aspect of our identity causes misunderstanding. In a meeting with the National Indian Brotherhood, Prime Minister Trudeau seemed concerned that a possible growth of separatism might exist among Indians. It is necessary to emphasize that the question of establishing a positive Indian identity does not mean political separatism —not yet, at least, not if the white man will agree to be reasonable—nor does it mean a desire to return to the days of yesteryear. The fact remains, however, that most Indians firmly believe their identity is tied up with treaty and aboriginal rights. Many Indians believe that until such rights are honoured there can be no Indian identity to take its place with the other cultural identities of Canada.

Our identity, who we are; this is a basic question that must be settled if we are to progress. A native person in Canada cannot describe himself without basically talking about himself as a Canadian. Being Canadian is implied and understood. To an Indian, being Indian in Canada simultaneously and automatically means being Canadian. The German Canadian has a homeland called Germany; the Ukrainian has a homeland; even the French Canadian, although he may have ancestors going back three hundred years in Canadian history, has a homeland called France. The Indian's homeland is called Canada.

The challenge to Indians today is to redefine that identity in contemporary terminology. The challenge to the non-Indian society is to accept such an updated definition.

If I were to accept the bothersome term *Indian problem*, I would have to accept it in light of the fact that our most basic problem is gaining respect, respect on an individual basis that would make possible acceptance for us as an ethnic group. Before this is possible, the dignity, confidence and pride of the Indian people must be restored. No genuine Indian participation in the white world can be expected until the Indian is accepted by himself and by the non-Indian as an Indian person, with an Indian identity.

As long as Indian people are expected to become what they are not— white men—there does not and there will not exist a basis upon which they can participate in Canadian society.

Before we can demand acceptance by the white man, we must earn his respect. Before we can take our place in a larger society, we must regain our own confidence and self-respect. To do this we must be allowed to rebuild our own social institutions, torn down by their white counterparts. We must rebuild our structures of social and political leadership, demoralized and undermined for a hundred years by the Department of Indian Affairs; we must restore our family unit, shaken and shattered by the residential school system; we must rebuild communications between the younger and older generations of our people. We must recognize that the negative images of Indianness are false; the Canadian government must recognize that assimilation, no matter what they call it, will never work. Both Indian and non-Indian must realize that there is a valid, lasting Indian identity.

We are not interested, therefore, in the government's newest definition of who and what an Indian is, or must be. We have ceased to allow our identity to be a paperwork problem for members of the Department of Indian Affairs. Our people are now in the process of discovering what they are in a positive sense; Canadian society must accept us in a positive way before there can be an identification of common purpose and before true citizenship can develop. It is only when men are able to accept their differences as well as their similarities and still relate to each other with respect and dignity that a healthy society exists.

WE HAVE ALREADY suggested that in response to their subordinate status, members of the minority group may advocate assimilation, which involves the transformation of one's self-conception. An alternate response by the members of the ethnic group, however, may be survival as a distinct group.

Elliott's analysis of inter-ethnic contact (1971) traces the various patterns that such contact may assume. She distinguishes between *voluntary segregation*, in which one culture attempts to insulate and isolate itself from the larger society, and *militant separation*, in which a cultural group rejects the dominant culture and attempts to establish an independent order. The latter response typically develops after leaders of the minority group become convinced that their goals cannot be attained under the existing form of government. While perhaps convinced at first of the feasibility of reform, the leaders conclude, sometimes reluctantly, that reorganization within the established political structure is impossible.

As history attests, nationalism has served as an important basis of identification for many cultural groups that have wished to radically change their relationship with the dominant group and its social, economic, and political institutions. An ideal of any nationalistic group is the power to constitute an independent polity and to determine its own destiny. Efforts are therefore made to develop pride within the minority group members, and the group's language is often regarded as a cornerstone of its continued existence. As nationalistic fervor is instilled in the population, group consciousness is intensified.

The growth of French Canadian nationalism in Quebec has demonstrated that identity maintenance and preservation may be advocated by way of political separation. Such political separation and its attendant advantages are seen by members of the Parti Québecois, as well as other French Canadian nationalist groups and associations, as the only viable means of ensuring the preservation of a distinctively Québecois way of life. While opponents of Quebec sovereignty argue that with appropriate constitutional change French Canadian cultural identity can be maintained within the boundaries of Confederation, the leaders of the Parti Québecois have repeatedly emphasized the inevitable failure of such a solution. In the following selection, René Lévesque argues that Quebec's independence is absolutely necessary to the preservation of the French language and culture in Quebec.

An Option for Quebec

RENE LEVESQUE

1. "Belonging"

WE ARE QUÉBÉCOIS.

What that means first and foremost—and if need be, all that it means —is that we are attached to this one corner of the earth where we can be completely ourselves: this Quebec, the only place where we have the unmistakable feeling that "here we can be really at home."

Being ourselves is essentially a matter of keeping and developing a personality that has survived for three and a half centuries.

At the core of this personality is the fact that we speak French. Everything else depends on this one essential element and follows from it or leads us infallibly back to it.

In our history, America began with a French look, briefly but gloriously given it by Champlain, Joliet, La Salle, La Verendrye. . . . We learn our first lessons in progress and perseverance from Maisonneuve, Jeanne Mance, Jean Talon; and in daring or heroism from Lambert Closse, Brébeuf, Frontenac, d'Iberville. . . .

Then came the conquest. We were a conquered people, our hearts set on surviving in some small way on a continent that had become Anglo-Saxon.

Somehow or other, through countless changes and a variety of regimes, despite difficulties without number (our lack of awareness and even our ingorance serving all too often as our best protection), we succeeded.

Here again, when we recall the major historical landmarks, we come upon a profusion of names: Etienne Parent and Lafontaine and the Patriots of '37; Louis Riel and Honoré Mercier, Bourassa, Philippe Hamel; Garneau and Edouard Montpetit and Asselin and Lionel Groulx. . . . For each of them, the main driving force behind every action was the will to

From An Option for Quebec *by René Lévesque, pp. 13-30. Reprinted by permission of the Canadian Publishers, McClelland and Stewart Ltd., Toronto.*

continue, and the tenacious hope that they could make it worthwhile.

Until recently in this difficult process of survival we enjoyed the protection of a certain degree of isolation. We lived a relatively sheltered life in a rural society in which a great measure of unanimity reigned, and in which poverty set its limits on change and aspiration alike.

We are children of that society, in which the *habitant*, our father or grandfather, was still the key citizen. We also are heirs to that fantastic adventure—that early America that was almost entirely French. We are, even more intimately, heirs to the group obstinacy which has kept alive that portion of French America we call *Québec*.

All these things lie at the core of this personality of ours. Anyone who does not feel it, at least occasionally, is not—is no longer—one of us.

But *we* know and feel that these are the things that make us what we are. They enable us to recognize each other wherever we may be. This is our own special wave-length on which, despite all interference, we can tune each other in loud and clear, with no one else listening.

This is how we differ from other men and especially from other North Americans, with whom in all other areas we have so much in common. This basic "difference" we cannot surrender. That became impossible a long time ago.

More is involved here than simple intellectual certainty. This is a physical fact. To be unable to live as ourselves, as we should live, in our own language and according to our own ways, would be like living without an arm or a leg—or perhaps a heart.

Unless, of course, we agreed to give in little by little, in a decline which, as in cases of pernicious anaemia, would cause life to slip slowly away from the patient.

Again, in order not to perceive this, one has to be among the *déracinés*, the uprooted and cut-off.

2.   The Acceleration of History

On the other hand, one would have to be blind not to see that the conditions under which this personality must assert itself have changed in our lifetime, at an extremely rapid and still accelerating rate.

Our traditional society, which gave our parents the security of an environment so ingrown as to be reassuring and in which many of us grew up in a way that we thought could, with care, be preserved indefinitely; that "quaint old" society has gone.

Today, most of us are city dwellers, wage-earners, tenants. The standards of parish, village, and farm have been splintered. The automobile and the airplane take us "outside" in a way we never could have imagined thirty years ago, or even less. Radio and films, and now television, have opened for us a window onto everything that goes on throughout the world: the events—and the ideas too—all of humanity invade our homes day after day.

The age of automatic unanimity thus has come to an end. The old protective barriers are less and less able to mark safe pathways for our lives. The patience and resignation that were preached to us in the old days with such efficiency now produce no other reactions than scepticism or indifference, or even rebellion.

At our own level, we are going through a universal experience. In this sudden acceleration of history, whose main features are the unprecedented development of science, technology, and economic activity, there are potential promises and dangers immeasurably greater than any the world ever has known.

The promises—if man so desires—are those of abundance, of liberty, of fraternity; in short, of a civilization that could attain heights undreamed of by the most unrestrained Utopians.

The dangers—unless man can hold them in check—are those of insecurity and servitude, of inhuman governments, of conflicts among nations that could lead to extermination.

In this little corner of ours, we already are having a small taste of the dangers as well as the promises of this age.

A Balance Sheet of Vulnerability   The dangers are striking enough.

In a world where, in so many fields, the only stable law seems to have become that of perpetual change, where our old certainties are crumbling one after the other, we find ourselves swept along helplessly by irresistible currents. We are not at all sure that we can stay afloat, for the swift, confusing pace of events forces us to realize as never before our own weaknesses, our backwardness, our terrible collective vulnerability.

Endlessly, with a persistence almost masochistic, we draw up list after list of our inadequacies. For too long we despised education. We lack scientists, administrators, qualified technical people. Economically, we are colonials whose three meals a day depend far too much on the initiative and goodwill of foreign bosses. And we must admit as well that we are far from being the most advanced along the path of social progress, the yardstick by which the quality of a human community can best be measured. For a very long time we have allowed our public administration to stagnate in negligence and corruption, and left our political life in the hands of fast talkers and our own equivalent of those African kings who grew rich by selling their own tribesmen.

We must admit that our society has grave, dangerous, and deep-rooted illnesses which it is absolutely essential to cure if we want to survive.

Now, a human society that feels itself to be sick and inferior, and is unable to do anything about it, sooner or later reaches the point of being unacceptable even to itself.

For a small people such as we are, our minority position on an Anglo-Saxon continent creates from the very beginning a permanent temptation to such a self-rejection, which has all the attraction of a gentle downward slope ending in a comfortable submersion in the Great Whole.

There are enough sad cases, enough among us who have given up, to show us that this danger does exist.

It is, incidentally, the only danger that really can have a fatal effect upon us, because it exists within ourselves.

And if ever we should be so unfortunate as to abandon this individuality that makes us what we are, it is not "the others" we would have to blame, but only our own impotence and resulting discouragement.

The only way to overcome the danger is to face up to this trying and thoughtless age and make it accept us as we are, succeeding somehow in making a proper and appropriate place in it for ourselves, in our own language, so that we can feel we are equals and not inferiors. This means that in our homeland we must be able to earn our living and pursue our careers in French. It also means that we must build a society which, while it preserves an image that is our own, will be as progressive, as efficient, and as "civilized" as any in the world. (In fact, there are other small peoples who are showing us the way, demonstrating that maximum size is in no way synonymous with maximum progress among human societies.)

To speak plainly, we must give ourselves sufficient reason to be not only sure of ourselves but also, perhaps, a little proud.

3. The Quiet Revolution

Now, in the last few years we have indeed made some progress along this difficult road of "catching up," the road which leads to the greater promise of our age.

At least enough progress to know that what comes next depends only on ourselves and on the choices that only we can make.

The enticements toward progress were phrases like "from now on," or "it's got to change," or "masters in our own house," etc.

The results can be seen on every side. Education, for us as for any people desirous of maintaining its place in the world, has finally become the top priority. With hospital insurance, family and school allowances, pension schemes, and the beginnings of medicare, our social welfare has made more progress in a few years than in the whole preceding century; and for the first time we find ourselves, in many of the most important areas, ahead of the rest of the country. In the economic field, by nationalizing electric power, by created the S.G.F., *Soquem*, and the *Caisse de Dépôts*[1] we have taken the first steps toward the kind of collective control of certain essential services without which no human community can feel secure. We also, at last, have begun to clean up our electoral practices, to modernize and strengthen our administrative structures, to give our land the roads that are indispensable to its future, and to study seriously the complex problems of our outmoded municipalities and underdeveloped regions.

To be sure, none of this has been brought to completion. What has been done is only a beginning, carried out in many cases without the co-ordination that should have been applied—and far too often in circumstances dictated by urgency or opportunity. All along the way there have been hesitations and, God knows, these still exist. In all these accomplishments mistakes have been made and gaps have been left—and whatever happens, even if we do a hundred times as much, this always will be so.

No One Will Do It For You But in the process we have learned certain things, things which are both simple and revolutionary.

The first is that we have the capacity to do the job ourselves, and the more we take charge and accept our responsibilities, the more efficient we find we are; capable, all things considered, of succeeding just as well as anyone else.

Another is that there is no valid *excuse*, that it is up to us to find and apply to our problems the solutions that are right for us; for no one else can, much less wants to, solve them for us.

Yet another thing we have learned—and perhaps the most important: "The appetite comes with the eating." This is a phenomenon we can see everywhere as soon as a human group decides to move forward. It is called the "revolution of rising expectations."

This is the main driving force at our disposal for continued progress. We must calculate its use as precisely as possible, to avoid costly diversions; but even more we must take care not to stifle it, for without this we shall experience the collective catastrophe of an immobilized society, at a time when those who fail to advance automatically retreat, and to a point which can easily become one of no return.

In other words, above all we must guard against loss of impetus, against the periodic desire to slow down, against the belief that we are moving too quickly when in reality—despite a few wanderings—we are just beginning to reach the speed our age demands. In this, a nation is like an individual: those who succeed are those who are unafraid of life.

The fact is that we are condemned to progress *ad infinitum*.

Not only are we just beginning, but we shall always be just beginning, as far as we can see ahead. On the horizon are further changes and adaptations; on the horizon is the hope that we will be wise enough to make the right choices, with the courage and vitality called for by the ceaseless pursuit of progress and the acceptance of every challenge on the way.

4. The Basic Minimums

On this road where there can be no more stopping are a number of necessary tasks which must be attended to without delay. Neglecting them would endanger the impetus we have acquired, perhaps would slow it down irreparably.

And here we encounter a basic difficulty which has become more and more acute in recent years. It is created by the political regime under which we have lived for over a century.

We are a nation within a country where there are two nations. For all the things we mentioned earlier, using words like "individuality," "history," "society," and "people," are also the things one includes under the word "nation." It means nothing more than the collective will to live that belongs to any national entity likely to survive.

Two nations in a single country: this means, as well, that in fact there are *two majorities*, two "complete societies" quite distinct from each other trying to get along within a common framework. That this number puts us in a minority position makes no difference: just as a civilized society will never condemn a little man to feel inferior beside a bigger man, civilized relations among nations demand that they treat each other as equals in law and in fact.

Now we believe it to be evident that the hundred-year-old framework of Canada can hardly have any effect other than to create increasing difficulties between the two parties insofar as their mutual respect and understanding are concerned, as well as impeding the changes and progress so essential to both.

It is useless to go back over the balance sheet of the century just past, listing the advantages it undoubtedly has brought us and the obstacles and injustices it even more unquestionably has set in our way.

The important thing for today and for tomorrow is that both sides realize that this regime has had its day, and that it is a matter of urgency either to modify it profoundly or to build a new one.

As we are the ones who have put up with its main disadvantages, it is natural that we also should be in the greatest hurry to be rid of it; the more so because it is we who are menaced most dangerously by its current paralysis.

Primo Vivere Almost all the essential tasks facing us risk being jeopardized, blocked, or quietly undone by the sclerosis of Canadian institutions and the open or camouflaged resistance of the men who manipulate them.

First, we must secure once and for all, in accordance with the complex and urgent necessities of our time, the safety of our collective "personality." This is the distinctive feature of the nation, of this majority that we constitute in Quebec—the only true fatherland left us by events, by our own possibilities, and by the incomprehension and frequent hostility of others.

The prerequisite to this is, among other things, the power for unfettered action (which does not exclude cooperation) in fields as varied as those of citizenship, immigration, and employment; the great instruments of "mass culture"—films, radio, and television; and the kind of international relations that alone permit a people to breathe the air of a changing and stimulating world, and to learn to see beyond itself. Such relations are especially imperative for a group whose cultural connections in the world are as evident and important as ours.

Our collective security requires also that we settle a host of questions made so thorny by the present regime that each is more impossible than the next. Let us only mention as examples the integrity of Quebec's territory, off-shore rights, the evident unacceptability of an institution like the Supreme Court, and Quebec's need to be able to shape freely what we might term its internal constitution.

That collective personality which constitutes a nation also cannot tolerate that social security and welfare—which affect it daily in the most intimate ways—should be conceived and directed from outside. This relates to the oft-repeated demand for the repatriation of old-age pensions, family allowances, and, when it comes into being, medicare.

By the same token, and even more so, it relates to the most obvious needs of efficiency and administrative responsibility. In this whole vast area there are overlapping laws, regulations, and organizations whose main effect is to perpetuate confusion and, behind this screen, to paralyze change and progress.

The Madhouse   *Mutatis mutandis*, we find similar situations with equally disastrous results in a multitude of other areas: the administration of justice, jurisdiction in fields such as insurance, corporations, bankruptcies, financial institutions, and, in a general way, all economic activities which have become the most constant preoccupations of all men today and also the aspect of society in which modern states have seen their sphere of action grow most dramatically in the last couple of generations.

On this point, here is how the C.S.N., the F.T.Q., and the U.C.C.[2] describe the situation in their joint memorandum to the Quebec Legislature's Constitutional Committee:

The fact that certain economic tools belong to the federal government, while other powers whose exercise also influences economic life belong to the provinces, creates a difficult problem in the rational planning of economic activity in general. Thinking in terms of a more advanced socialization than that which we know today, this situation, along with opportunity given one government to thwart the actions of other, may lead to conflict, and is in any case of such a nature that it could, at these two levels of government, result in impotence in attacking the economic problems of the country with any kind of resolution or efficiency. Any duplication of institutions should be avoided, moreover, if it leads to a duplication of costs. This situation should demand our attention all the more urgently because of the fact that already (for example, in agriculture) laws and regulations at the two levels of government, and especially their application, because of their overlapping, their duplication, their superimposition of their lack of co-operation, cause many grave difficulties and are often most prejudicial to the citizens involved, especially those of Quebec in view of our lagging behind in a number of areas.

Here again let us limit ourselves to citing the minimums established by the most complete studies of recent years. And so, back to those three organizations and the way in which they define these minimums in the cautious conclusion of their memorandum:

> The Quebec government should exercise its powers by giving direction to the economy, rationalizing its marginal industries, developing secondary industry, etc. The government of Quebec should promote an economic policy frankly favourable to its own population and more demanding *vis-à-vis* the capitalist interest, for it is not enough only to appear to govern in favour of the people in this sector. In particular, the Quebec government must obtain the greatest advantages and royalties it can possibly extract from the exploitation of natural resources, taking account of the reasonable limits of this kind of policy. Activity just as intense and equally devoted to the interests of the people must spread through all departments responsible for economic matters, notably agriculture, industry, and commerce, and so forth.

This outline, which is necessarily incomplete ("and so forth"), hints at a program immediately acceptable to everyone, but it poses at once the question of means.

A Strong State How can it be carried out? Let us mention only what is clearly obvious. Order must be re-established in the chaos of a governmental structure created at a time when it was impossible to foresee the scientific and technical revolution in which we now are caught up, the endless changes it demands, the infinite variety of things produced, the concentration of enterprises, the crushing weight that the greatest of these impose on individual and collective life, the absolute necessity of having a state able to direct, co-ordinate, and above all humanize this infernal rhythm.

In this up-dating of political structures that are completely overtaxed by an economic role they cannot refuse to play, the action demanded of the Quebec government, to be specific, would require at the very least new jurisdictions over industrial and commercial corporations, fiduciary and savings institutions, and all the internal agencies of development and industrialization, as well as the power to exercise a reasonable control over the movement and investment of our own capital.

So as not to belabour the obvious, we shall mention only for the record the massive transfer of fiscal resources that would be needed for all the tasks this State of Quebec should undertake in our name—not counting the tasks it already has, tasks that daily grow more out of proportion to its inadequate means: *i.e.*, the insatiable needs of education, urban problems without number, and the meagreness or tragic non-existence of the tools of scientific and industrial research.

Very sketchily, this would seen to be the basic minimum of change that Quebec should force the present Canadian regime to accept in order to reach both the collective security and the opportunity for progress which its best minds consider indispensable.

We could certainly add to the list. But nothing could be struck from it easily.

For us, this is, in fact, a true minimum.

5.   *The Blind Alley*

But we would be dreaming if we believed that for the rest of the country our minimum can be anything but a frightening maximum, completely unacceptable even in the form of bare modifications or, for that matter, under the guise of the constitutional reform with which certain people say they are willing to proceed with.

Not only the present attitude of the federal government, but also the painful efforts at understanding made by the opposition parties and reactions in the most influential circles in English Canada all give us reason to expect that our confrontation will grow more and more unpleasant.

From a purely revisionist point of view, our demands would seem to surpass both the best intentions displayed by the "other majority" and the very capacity of the regime to make concessions without an explosion.

If we are talking only of revision, they will tell us, our demands would lead to excessive weakening of that centralized state which English Canada needs for its own security and progress as much as we need our own State of Quebec. And they would be right.

And further, they could ask us—with understandable insistence—
what in the world our political representatives would be doing in Ottawa
taking part in debates and administrative acts whose authority and
effectiveness we intend so largely to eliminate within Quebec.

If Quebec were to begin negotiations to revise the present frame of
reference, and persisted in this course, it would not be out of the woods
in the next hundred years. But by that time it is most likely that there
would be nothing left worth talking about of the nation that is now
trying to build a homeland in Quebec.

During the long wait we would soon fall back on the old defensive
struggle, the enfeebling skirmishes that make one forget where the real
battle is, the half-victories that are celebrated between two defeats, the
relapse in to divisive federal-provincial electoral folly, the sorry
consolations of verbal nationalism and, above all, ABOVE ALL ELSE—this
must be said, and repeated, and shouted if need be – above all the
incredible "split-level" squandering of energy, which certainly is for us
the most disastrous aspect of the present regime.

And as for this waste of energy, English Canada suffers from it, too.
And there, too, the best minds have begun to realize this fact, let there
be no doubt of that.

Two Paralyzed Majorities For the present regime also prevents the
English-speaking majority from simplifying, rationalizing, and
centralizing as it would like to do certain institutions which it, too,
realizes are obsolete. This is an ordeal which English Canada is finding
more and more exhausting, and for which it blames to the exaggerated
anxieties and the incorrigible intransigence of Quebec.

It is clear, we believe, that this frustration may easily become
intolerable. And it is precisely among the most progressive and
"nationalist" groups in English Canada, among those who are concerned
about the economic, cultural, and political invasion from the United
States, among those who are seeking the means to prevent the country
from surrendering completely, that there is the greatest risk of a growing
and explosive resentment toward Quebec for the reasons mentioned
above.

And these are the very men among whom we should be able to find
the best partners for our dialogue over the new order that must emerge.

We are seeking at last to carve out for ourselves a worthy and
acceptable place in this Quebec which has never belonged to us as it
should have. Facing us, however, a growing number of our fellow-citizens
of the other majority are afraid of losing the homeland that Canada was
for them in the good old days of the Empire, when they at least had the
impression that they were helping to rule, and that it was all within the
family. Today the centres of decision-making are shifting south of the
border at a terrifying rate.

In this parallel search for two national securities, as long as the search is pursued within the present system or anything remotely resembling it, we can end up only with double paralysis. The two majorities, basically desiring the same thing—a chance to live their own lives, in their own way, according to their own needs and aspirations— will inevitably collide with one another repeatedly and with greater and greater force, causing hurts that finally would be irreparable.[3]

As long as we persist so desperately in maintaining—with spit and chewing gum or whatever—the ancient hobble of a federalism suited to the last century, the two nations will go on creating an ever-growing jungle of compromises while disagreeing more and more strongly on essentials.

This would mean a perpetual atmosphere of instability, of wrangling over everything and over nothing. It would mean the sterilization of two collective "personalities" which, having squandered the most precious part of their potential, would weaken each other so completely that they would have no other choice but to drown themselves in the ample bosom of "America."

6.   The Way of The Future

We think it is possible for both parties to avoid this blind alley. We must have the calm courage to see that the problem can't be solved either by maintaining or somehow adapting the *status quo*. One is always somewhat scared at the thought of leaving a home in which one has lived for a long time. It becomes almost "consecrated," and all the more so in this case, because what we call "Confederation" is one of the last remnants of those age-old safeguards of which modern times have robbed us. It is therefore quite normal that some people cling to it with a kind of desperation that arises far more from fear than from reasoned attachment.

But there are moments—and this is one of them—when courage and calm daring become the only proper form of prudence that a people can exercise in a crucial period of its existence. If it fails at these times to accept the calculated risk of the great leap, it may miss its vocation forever, just as does a man who is afraid of life.

What should be concluded from a cool look at the crucial crossroads that we now have reached? Clearly that we must rid ourselves completely of a completely obsolete federal regime.

And begin anew.

Begin how?

The answer, it seems to us, is as clearly written as the question, in the two great trends of our age: that of the freedom of peoples, and that of the formation by common consent of economic and political groupings.

A Sovereign Quebec   For our own good, we must dare to seize for ourselves complete liberty in Quebec, the right to all the essential components of independence, *i.e.*, the complete mastery of every last area of basic collective decision-making.

This means that Quebec must become sovereign as soon as possible.

Thus we finally would have within our grasp the security of our collective "being" which is so vital to us, a security which otherwise must remain uncertain and incomplete.

Then it will be up to us, and us alone, to establish calmly, without recrimination or discrimination, the priority for which we are now struggling feverishly but blindly: that of our language and our culture.

Only then will we have the opportunity—and the obligation—to use our talents to the maximum in order to resolve without further excuses or evasions all the great problems that confront us, whether it be a negotiated protective system for our farmers, or decent treatment for our employees and workers in industry, or the form and evolution of the political structures we must create for ourselves.

In short, this is not for us simply the only solution to the present Canadian impasse; it also is the one and only common goal inspiring enough to bring us together with the kind of strength and unity we shall need to confront all possible futures—the supreme challenge of continuous progress within a society that has taken control of its own destiny.

As for the other Canadian majority, it will also find our solution to its advantage, for it will be set free at once from the constraints imposed on it by our presence; it will be at liberty in its own way to rebuild to its heart's desire the political institutions of English Canada and to prove to itself, whether or not it really wants to maintain and develop on this continent, an English-speaking society distinct from the United States.

—and a New Canadian Union   And if this is the case, there is no reason why we, as future neighbours, should not voluntarily remain associates and partners in a common enterprise; which would conform to the second great trend of our times: the new economic groups, customs unions, common markets, etc.

Here we are talking about something which already exists, for it is composed of the bonds, the complementary activities, the many forms of economic cooperation within which we have learned to live. Nothing says that we must throw these things away; on the contrary, there is every reason to maintain the framework. If we destroyed it, interdependent as we are, we would only be obliged sooner or later to build it up again, and then with doubtful success.

Now, it is precisely in the field of economics that we feel the pinch most painfully. In our outmoded constitutional texts and governmental structures, we flounder hopelessly over how to divide between our two states the powers, the agencies, and the means for action.

On this subject any expert with the slightest pretension to objectivity must certainly endorse the following statement by Otto Thur, Head of the Department of Economics at the University of Montreal (in a special edition of *Le Devoir*, June 30, 1967): "It is not the wording of a constitution that will solve problems [in the field of economics], but rather enlightened and consistent action, which brings about a progressive betterment of existing reality."

It seems to us, given a minimum of wisdom and, of course, self-interest—which should not be beyond the reach of our two majorities—that in the kind of association we are proposing we would have the greatest chance of pursuing jointly such a course of "enlightened and consistent action" worth more in economic affairs than all the pseudo-sacred documents with their ever-ambiguous inflexibility.

Such an association seems to us, in fact, made to measure for the purpose of allowing us, unfettered by obsolete constitutional forms, to pool our stakes with whatever permanent consultation and flexible adjustments would best serve our common economic interests: monetary union, common tariffs, postal union, administration of the national debt, co-ordination of policies, etc.

And nothing would prevent us from adding certain matters which under the present system have never had the advantage of frank discussion between equals: the question of minorities, for one; and also the questions of equal participation in a defence policy in proportion to our means, and a foreign policy that might, if conceived jointly, regain some of the dignity and dynamism that it has lost almost completely.[4]

We are not sailing off into uncharted seas. Leaving out the gigantic model furnished by the evolution of the Common Market, we can take our inspiration from countries comparable in size to our own—Benelux or Scandinavia—among whom cooperation is highly advanced, and where it has promoted unprecedented progress in the member states without preventing any of them from continuing to live according to their own tradition and preferences.

Making History Instead of Submitting To It   To sum up, we propose a system that would allow our two majorities to extricate themselves from an archaic federal framework in which our two very distinct "personalities" paralyze each other by dint of pretending to have a third personality common to both.

This new relationship of two nations, one with its homeland in Quebec and another free to rearrange the rest of the country at will, would be freely associated in a new adaptation of the current "common-market" formula, making up an entity which could perhaps—and if so very precisely—be called a Canadian Union.

The future of a people is never born without effort. It requires that a rather large number of "midwives" knowingly make the grave decision to work at it. For apart from other blind forces, and apart from all the imponderables, we must believe that basically it is still men who make men's history.

What we are suggesting to those who want to listen is that we devote our efforts, together, to shape the history of Quebec in the only fitting direction; and we are certain that at the same time we shall also be helping the rest of the country to find a better future of its own.

NOTES

1. S.G.F. is *la Société Générale de Financement* (General Investment Corporation), an investment, holding, and management company designed to promote business and industry in the province, and financed by both public and private sectors. *Soquem* is *la Société Québecoise d'Exploration Minière* (Quebec Mining Exploration Co.), government-owned and the largest in the province. The *Caisse de Dépôts* is the investment arm of the Quebec Pension Plan.

2. C.S.N. is the *Confédération des Syndicats Nationaux* (Confederation of National Trade Unions) and F.T.Q. is the *Fédération des Travailleurs du Québec* (Quebec Labour Federation). These are the two largest central labour bodies in the province. The U.C.C. is the *Union Catholique des Cultivateurs*, a major farm organization sometimes known in English as the Catholic Farmers' Union or the Farmers' Catholic Union.

3. See in this connection the remarkable study by Jacques Parizeau, Appendix 3, "Quebec-Canada: A Blind Alley."

4. In this paragraph some people have felt obliged—and others have hastened —to find a far-too-strict limitation imposed on Quebec's sovereignty. This would indeed be true if we proposed really to include Defence and External Affairs in the areas of actual association. These two are among the most important means through which a people can express its personality. But such is not our proposal. The highly conditional form in which it is couched, and the suggestion of preliminary studies, seem to us to indicate clearly enough that we were referring to the possibility of agreements which might be reached, agreements that would be strictly limited in nature (e.g. joint general staffs? Certain common agencies abroad, such as commercial representatives?), which should not a priori be excluded in the free development of countries which are neighbours and partners. This is the sort of thing we had in mind below when we speak of these two distinct societies which "have a crying need now to give each other some breathing space, and to rediscover themselves, freely and without prejudice, creating little by little new points of contact as the need arises."

IN A COMPLEX society such as Canada's, people are exposed and expose themselves to a variety of settings and contacts, and as a result, the personal identities of these individuals are often altered. Problems of identity maintenance are met not only at the individual level but at the community level as well. Ethnic and religious communities must try to preserve a sense of who they were, are, and want to be. As mentioned earlier, ethnic groups have been less successful than religious communities in resisting the assimilative influences of the larger society, and have not been able to direct their members' lives to ensure the perpetuation of the community. While ethnic communities may be slow to die and disappear, the life style of previous generations, including the traditions, normative guidelines, and expectations, is only tangentially shared by the most recent generation.

In contrast to ethnic communities, religious groups such as the Hutterites, Amish, Mennonites, and Chassidim, have been more successful in maintaining their distinct ways of life, and have ensured that the young will be socialized into the community's life style. To accomplish this, these communities create a way of life that is tenable and attractive to the members. The community must effectively impress on its members the idea that the surrounding society's seemingly attractive features are, in fact, potentially harmful to their own life style. Since community members, especially the young, are strongly discouraged from participating in society's popular fads and fashions, the community must offer a suitable replacement. This usually centers on the observance of a set of religious obligations. This observance is the basic unit of the community's reward system and is the central organizing feature of its persistence.

To ensure its continuing existence, the religious community must combat assimilative influences which threaten the young especially. These influences are usually regarded as corruptive and antithetical to the community's way of life. As the secular educational process is seen as a primary way in which the young absorb the surrounding society's culture, efforts are made to control the kind of secular education the children receive and to limit and offset its potentially harmful consequences. This is generally done by streamlining the secular curriculum to avoid areas of conflict with religious beliefs. In other words, religious communities attempt to segregate their children from the larger society and to ensure that a particular identity is instilled in them.

The following article, which is excerpted from the author's study of a Jewish religious community, focuses on the process of religious identity maintenance. Shaffir suggests that different features of community life may contribute to the community's ability to maintain an identity of its own. In the case of the Lubavitcher chassidim*, their identity centers on the members' familiarity with the lives, work, and teachings of their previous leaders. Today this is manifested in the relationship between the

---

The chassidim are a religious movement within the framework of Jewish laws and practices, but with their own customs and traditions. Their everyday life is circumscribed by religious ideas and principles that differentiate them from other Jewish minority groups, both orthodox and non-orthodox.

individual Lubavitcher and the present leader of the chassidic group, the *Rebbe*. This relationship with the *Rebbe* enables the community members to see themselves as alike in one significant respect, and allows a group consciousness to develop.

The last part of Shaffir's article deals with a feature that is unique to the Lubavitcher chassidim. At the same time as they are trying to insulate themselves from the surrounding society, Lubavitcher chassidim engage in a series of proselytizing activities designed to disseminate orthodox Judaism within the larger Jewish community. Such activities may appear to endanger the community's tenability since, in the course of proselytizing, members are exposed to potentially harmful influences; Shaffir suggests, however, that through such contacts with outsiders, Lubavitchers' beliefs are reinforced. In the course of convincing Jews of, for example, the significance of the Torah and the *Rebbe's* accomplishments, Lubavitchers strengthen their own convictions.

Identity Maintenance in a Religious Community

WILLIAM SHAFFIR

Techniques of Identity Maintenance in Religious Communities

ONE TECHNIQUE RELIGIOUS communities use in trying to preserve their identity is to channel their members' lives so that they conform to certain standards or sets of expectations intended to regulate their contact with outsiders. The identifying features that a community can use to make its members feel they belong to a distinct group can range from dress to insulation, language, and history.

Dress   Styles of dress are important identity symbols as they link the community with its past history and provide a visible distinction between community members and outsiders. Unlike certain chassidic groups such as the Satmarer who insist that their members dress as their ancestors did, Lubavitcher have adapted their clothes to Western customs. This is not to suggest, however, that Lubavitcher approve of their members wearing the latest fashions. Women and girls are continually reminded about the importance of a modest appearance, while the men's and boys'

From Life in a Religious Community: The Lubavitcher Chassidim in Montreal *by* William Shaffir, pp. 49-52, 61-72, and 188-193. Copyright © 1974 by Holt, Rinehart and Winston of Canada, Limited.

suits and jackets are expected to be dark coloured and simple. A young man in the community who began to wear the latest fashions was mildly criticized and at times even censured by some Lubavitcher. One of his peers once remarked to him:

> You see what happens when you leave the Yeshiva?[1] (pointing to the wide tie and flared slacks). This is what happens and this is only the beginning. You know it, so what's going to be next? (translated from Yiddish).

However, as the Lubavitch community's attire is not sufficiently uniform always to allow the distinction between insider and outsider, dress is not considered an important identifying feature of the community under study.

Insulation: Physical, Cultural and Social Many religious communities assign a high priority to insulation from the surrounding culture to prevent assimilation. Although insulation is sometimes spatial, it is more often social, aiming at minimal contact with individuals whose behaviour and ideas are discouraged as they are considered potentially threatening to the community.

In the case of chassidic groups, the degree of insulation varies according to the concept the particular group has of outsiders and their estimate of the surrounding society's threat to the continuity of their way of life. Insulation ranges from actual removal from the city to a rural settlement, as exemplified by the Tasher and Squarer chassidim, to strictly enforced cultural and social separation from outsiders, as occurs among the Satmarer, to the Lubavitcher chassidim's more moderate social separation. In fact, the main distinguishing feature between Lubavitch and other chassidic groups is the former's efforts at contacting non-observant Jews and urging them to enter the orthodox fold. The Lubavitcher are thus more exposed to arguments and ideas directly opposed to their world view. While it may be argued that insulation serves to buttress a religious community's distinctive identity, the nature of Lubavitchers' relationship with outsiders suggests this is less the fact in their case than among other chassidim.

Language Learning a new language is of considerable importance for it necessitates a reorganization of experiences and eventual acquaintance with a new world of objects. This is what Hostetler meant when he wrote about the Amish: "Roles and functions tend to organize around each language; thus when speaking English the Amishman tends to think and behave like the English speaking person." (1968:139) As the ideas and perspective of a community are embodied in its language, the children will more easily comprehend and assume for themselves the community's conception of the world if the particular language of the community is their mother tongue. Successful instruction both to the young and newcomers adds to the community's distinctive identity and facilitates the development of shared understandings among the members.

Among chassidim, English will not, in general, be spoken unless the situation demands it. The language of everyday discourse is, for the most part, Yiddish and the Jewish curriculum in the Yeshiva is also in this language. The attitude toward learning an outside language, in this case English, is not uniform among the chassidic groups or even within the groups themselves. Lubavitcher, for example, are likely to be more fluent in English than are the Satmarer as greater attention is paid to secular education in the Lubavitcher Yeshiva.

In all chassidic groups some parents do not permit their children to study secular subjects until a certain age. As a result, it is not uncommon to find chassidic youth who, except at a most elementary level, neither understand nor speak English. A teacher in a Hungarian-Jewish Yeshiva remarked:

> ...first of all, half of the parents didn't approve of their children learning English at all. You have people who are born in Brooklyn, in X (name of city), who can't read and write English. They can't even sign their name. The only language they speak is Yiddish and the second language, if any, is Hungarian. Most of the parents consider it *goyish*,[2] not English....

The number of Lubavitch parents who refuse to allow their sons to study the Lubavitcher Yeshiva's secular curriculum is probably less than among parents in other chassidic groups.

History   The history of any group consists of collective memories of their ancestors' deeds, the difficulties encountered throughout its existence, and the events which have culminated in the group's present situation. (Shibutani and Kwan, 1965:43) However, "...the way in which the history of the group is remembered is far more important than what it has actually been." (Ibid:43) As among other groups, historical events signifying major turnning points for the group are recalled and celebrated by the Lubavitcher. These often centre on incidents relating to Lubavitcher *Rebbeim*[3] and are celebrated at *Farbrengens*,[4] or gatherings of Lubavitcher on days held sacred by them. At these gatherings the *Rebbe* delivers discourses ranging from Lubavitch philosophy to exhortations on how Jews ought to conduct their everyday lives.

Lubavitchers' identity is reinforced by their knowledge of the group's history, especially familiarity with its leaders. Kehot, the Lubavitch Publication Society, continually publishes collections of histories and anecdotes about the lives of previous Lubavitcher *Rebbeim* tracing the origin and development of the Lubavitch chassidic movement. The songs sung by previous generations of Lubavitcher have been carefully compiled and published. The central link uniting Lubavitcher since the founding of the movement is their study of the *Tanya;*[5] written by the first Lubavitcher *Rebbe*, it outlines the principles of the Lubavitcher chassidim. It is this general awareness of the lives, work and teachings of the previous Lubavitcher *Rebbeim* rather than dress, insulation, or language that is the central and unifying feature of the Lubavitchers' self-conception and also the main distinction between them and other orthodox Jews.

Lubavitcher and their Rebbe

As the Yeshiva plays an important role in reinforcing the individuals' self-conception as a Lubavitcher chassid, it can be regarded in many ways as the nucleus of the Lubavitch community. Yet the essence of this community, and of the Lubavitcher chassidim everywhere, is the Lubavitcher *Rebbe*. As one Lubavitcher said:

> 770 (the world headquarters of Lubavitch from where the *Rebbe* carries out his work) spiritually is more important than the Yeshiva. 770 is the heart and soul of every Lubavitcher because the *Rebbe Shleete*[6] (he shall live good long years, Amen) is what Lubavitch is and therefore 770 means very much to every Lubavitcher.

An older Yeshiva student expressed his feelings regarding the *Rebbe* in this manner:

> The *Rebbe* is the head of our generation. The *Rebbe* is the head of *Yiddishkayt*[7] now. As Yeshiva students we have more opportunity of absorbing the *Rebbe* than we will when we are out of the Yeshiva. We don't want to miss any bit of that. We came here to Montreal because it's away from home, but we don't want to be away from the *Rebbe*. And the *Rebbe's Farbrengen* is worth so much to us that we will give up three days of learning to go.

Writing about the Lubavitcher *Rebbeim*, an emissary of the previous Lubavitcher *Rebbe* claimed:

> In his personal greatness and in the greatness of his leadership, every Lubavitcher *Rebbe* in the chain of their descendence has personified those ideas and ideals which Chabad Chassidus presents to mankind. They brought to perfection the ability tot instill in the hearts and the conduct of their disciples, chassidim and students, each according to his abilities and devotion to the study of chassidus, that path which is within the reach of everyone, from the highest chossid to the furthest. (*Di Yiddishe Heim*, Vol. 12, No. 4:9)

The *Rebbe's* centrality to the Lubavitch community is immediately striking to anyone familiar with these chassidim. Evidence of his importance can be gleaned from the frequency with which Lubavitcher refer to him in their everyday conversation, especially with visitors and newcomers. When I first visited the Yeshiva a young man spoke to me about the *Rebbe*:

> He's a tremendous man. I think that as you go on you will understand what the *Rebbe* means to us and why we believe in him so much. I mean, how that one man does so much is beyond understanding. The correspondence he carries on is just fantastic. It has been said, I don't know by whom but I believe it, that the postmaster general has said that the *Rebbe* has the second largest correspondence in the United States. . . . He has a few secretaries but he should really have a dozen because there is so much work to do. It has been said that sometimes the *Rebbe* is in the Yeshiva till three or four in the morning. It's also said, and I can believe it, that sometimes he's even up till six o'clock because he has so much to do. I know. I've seen it. There's a story about the *Rebbe* that when a summer camp opened in New York they asked the *Rebbe* to come and give his blessings. Five years later after they made new improvements in the camp they asked the *Rebbe* to come and see the camp again, and they had a letter from him saying that he still had to catch up on the five hours of work which he lost on his first visit. . . . This just goes to show how busy the man is. It is said that the *Rebbe* has left New York only twice except for his visits to his father-in-law's grave, and there also seems to be more to his visits than meets the eye because it's said that after the *Rebbe* returns different things happen at the places he has been.[8]

I soon discovered that all Lubavitcher display the same high esteem and reverence toward the *Rebbe*. The miraculous stories related about his activities, the efforts made by Lubavitcher to be in New York during Lubavitch celebrations, and the kinds of advice sought from him all testify to his dominating influence among his followers.

Rabbi Menachem Mendel Schneerson, the present Lubavitcher *Rebbe*, is the seventh *Rebbe* in the line of Chabad chassidim founded by Rabbi Schneur Zalman (1745-1812). He is reported by Mintz as being a quiet intense man with a kindly expression, and gives the impression of "a man restraining a well of emotion." (1968:152) Born in 1902, he was a student of mathematics and science at the Sorbonne in Paris and trained in electrical engineering. He assumed the position of *Rebbe* after the previous Lubavitcher *Rebbe*, Rabbi Joseph Isaac Schneerson, his father-in-law, passed away. The position of *Rebbe* is usually inherited, often transmitted from father to son through several generations, but the previous *Rebbe's* family included two married daughters but no sons. Under such circumstances the selection of a new *Rebbe* is determined by following the instructions in the previous *Rebbe's* will, and if such information is unavailable the elders of the movement decide. The most likely candidates to assume the position in this instance were the previous *Rebbe's* two sons-in-law. Menachem Mendel Schneerson was chosen to be the new leader of the Lubavitch movement, while his brother-in-law remained head of the network of Lubavitcher Yeshivas. A newspaper account claimed: "There was no election, but he was the natural candidate on dynastic grounds and on the basis of scholarship and personal qualities." While never officially confirmed, it is often reported that Menachem Mendel only assumed his new position with some reluctance. As Weiner reports:

> For his part Menachem Mendel was genuinely reluctant to assume the leadership. He had taken courses in electrical engineering in Paris, while his wife was studying architecture, and they had planned to earn their living in these professions. It required two years to persuade him to accept the position of rebbe. (1969:151)

From his office situated to the left of the entrance to the Lubavitch headquarters on 770 Eastern Parkway, the *Rebbe*, with the assistance of his small office staff, directs the affairs of the Lubavitch movement throughout the world. In addition to meeting regularly with his followers and answering their inquiries, Lubavitcher claim that all correspondence issued from the *Rebbe's* office is carefully checked by him and must receive his approval. The *Rebbe's* work load is often so heavy that his office hours sometimes last into the early hours of the morning.

Although he has been married since 1929, the *Rebbe* and his wife are childless—a fact of great concern to his followers. Reluctant to discuss the practical implications of this situation for the Lubavitch movement, the *Rebbe's* followers often suggest that a very possible solution to this dilemma will be the Messiah's arrival. When the *Rebbe* was asked who was to be the eighth Lubavitcher Rebbe he replied: "The Messiah will come and he will take all these troubles and doubts. He could come while I am here. Why postpone his coming?"

When asked by college students "What is the function of the *Rebbe?*" the *Rebbe* replied: " . . . to find the right switch in every Jew to connect him to the powerhouse" and referred them to a reply he had previously given to the same question:

> We can realize what the Baal Shem Tov did by noticing the relationship of an electric powerhouse with a switch that is connected to its wire. In order to connect oneself to a powerhouse, one must find the right switch or push the correct button. The soul of every Jew is connected to the powerhouse, but in order to employ the benefits of the powerhouse, the correct switch must be found or the right button pushed. It was the Baal Shem Tov's merit that he was able to discover the right switch in every Jew, so that through their connection to the powerhouse their lives were

transformed from their dark despair to one of harmony and happiness.
(Discussion of Princeton Students with the Lubavitch *Rebbe*—5720 [1960])

Due to the tremendous demand on the *Rebbe's* time, each Lubavitcher is
granted a private audience with him only once a year, usually around the
time of his birthdate. During this personal audience the *Rebbe* may be
asked for advice or a *brocheh*[9] (blessing). Although restricted to one
personal audience Lubavitcher can ask the *Rebbe* for advice or for his
blessing at any time by "writing in."

As Lubavitcher should strive to listen to and follow the *Rebbe's*
personal advice as well as his general teachings and directions to all his
followers it is essential that the Lubavitcher is aware of these teachings
and directives and understands the *Rebbe's* perspective on particular
matters. This may be accomplished in several ways, the most desirable of
which is by attending as many as possible of the *Rebbe's Farbrengens* which
are celebrated in Crown Heights, New York. Although the Lubavitch
community may listen to the *Rebbe's Farbrengen*, all Lubavitcher agree that
it is far preferable to attend personally. An older student remarked:

> Come on, you've been there. You know what it is. When you're there
> you see the *Rebbe* and you can actually feel what he's saying. You can
> see how holy the man is. Alright, here in the Yeshiva you can listen, but
> it's not the same thing as seeing, my friend.

As expected, Lubavitcher eagerly take advantage of the hook-up and
willingly contribute toward the financial cost. This institutionalized
means of binding the chassidim to their *Rebbe* is more effective than the
previous technique whereby someone present at the *Farbrengen* would,
upon his return, report on the proceedings. Lubavitcher claim that it is
more rewarding and spiritually satisfying to listen to the *Rebbe's* voice and
hear the manner and tone in which he addresses his audience. The
shared experience of listening to the *Rebbe's* discourses is believed to have
a profound impact on those assembled in the Yeshiva's auditorium:

> Look, everyone here (in the Yeshiva) would rather be in New York with
> the *Rebbe*. There's no question about it. It's not always so easy to get
> away. So we have a *Farbrengen* here. And what better way is there than
> to be able to listen to the *Rebbe*. I can't tell you how important the *Rebbe*
> is. I mean everything in Lubavitch involves the *Rebbe*. You name it and
> the *Rebbe* is involved. You want to know how concerned the *Rebbe* is
> about Jews—I mean all Jews, not only Lubavitcher—listen to his voice.
> That tells it all. You see, this is what we all have in common here—the
> *Rebbe*. Believe me, no one here would miss the chance of using this
> hook-up.

The opportunity to listen to a *Farbrengen* holds additional advantages for
the community. As Lubavitcher continually aim to disseminate the *Rebbe's*

teachings to the larger Jewish community, they can freely invite the Jewish public to share in the experience of listening to the *Rebbe*, and their presence in the Yeshiva affords Lubavitcher the opportunity to discuss with them matters related to Judaism. In addition, these hook-ups permit the chassidim to impress upon their children the reverence and respect to be accorded to the *Rebbe*. On these occasions rows of tables and chairs are arranged in the Yeshiva's auditorium and, as on all occasions when men and women are present, a partition (*mecheetzeh*) separates the sexes. If the *Farbrengen* is celebrated on the Sabbath or a holy day when Sabbath restrictions forbid broadcasting, Lubavitcher present at the *Farbrengen* attempt to memorize the *Rebbe's* words so that they can relate them to others when they return. The sight of men huddled around a table in the Yeshiva listening to a Lubavitcher recount the substance of the *Rebbe's* remarks is very common.

The *Rebbe's* discourses, activities, and published letters are Lubavitchers' basis for discussion and argument during their proselytizing activities. Lubavitcher re-listen to and re-read the discourses and other published material and try to memorize their *Rebbe's* words. It is not surprising, then, that their reasoning and discussion with less observant Jews are drawn mainly from them. The accuracy and manner with which the Lubavitcher successfully reiterates the *Rebbe's* message varies from person to person, but the act itself helps root its truths firmly in the individual's mind and to reinforce his self-conception as a Lubavitcher. For example, I once overheard a Yeshiva student stressing the following point to a university graduate:

> What do you think has kept the Jews together throughout history? If you're going to tell me that it was the State of Israel, then I think that you're wrong. I'll tell you what it was. What has united the Jewish people is the Torah and its commandments. This is what the Jews had in common regardless of where they were.

Compare these remarks with those of the *Rebbe*:

> The essential element which unites our "dispersed and scattered people" and makes it "one people" throughout its dispersion and regardless of time, is the Torah and Mitzvoth, the Jewish way of life which has remained basically the same throughout the ages and in all places. The conclusion is clear and beyond doubt: It is the Torah and Mitzvoth which make our people indestructible on the world scene in the face of massacres and pogroms aiming at our physical destruction and in the face of ideological onslaughts of foreign cultures aiming at our spiritual destruction.

On another occasion, a Lubavitcher, discussing Jewish youth with a college student, argued that the older generation compromised their religion, leaving their children to believe that in today's society traditional Judaism is outdated and hence irrelevant—a point frequently presented by the *Rebbe*.

Along with arguments drawn from the *Rebbe's* discourses, stories reflecting the *Rebbe's* foresight and miraculous powers are sometimes offered as sufficient reason for observing a particular precept. The following story is widely circulated in Lubavitch circles:

> ...(An) American soldier in Korea...one day wandered off from his squad looking for a stream in which to wash his hands before opening his can of C rations. A shell struck the squad's position, killing every one of his comrades. Today the young veteran vows he owes his life to a visit he had made, just before he shipped out to Korea, to the rebbe of the Lubavitcher movement. The latter had counselled the young man to observe, even while in combat, as much as he could of the Jewish law, including the commandment to wash one's hands before eating. (Weiner, 1969:141)

Another example of the influence of the *Rebbe's* teaching on all Lubavitcher occurred when a young man, in the Yeshiva for the first time for the morning prayers, was asked when his phylacteries (*Tefillin*)[10] were last inspected. When he replied that they had never been inspected, the Lubavitcher welcoming him stressed the importance of having *Tefillin* inspected by a scribe:

> You know, this is a true story just to show you what I'm talking about. This person was very sick and wrote to the *Rebbe* asking him to wish him a *refooeh shlaimeh* (complete recovery) so he would get better. The *Rebbe* answered that he should have his *Tefillin* checked by a *soifer* (scribe) and that's all. So this guy figures "Well, if the *Rebbe* says so ..." So it was found that in the saying, "You should love God with all your soul and serve Him with all your heart," the word heart was scratched away. And it turned out what was wrong with this guy? Heart trouble. So, you see, it's really important to have the *Tefillin* checked.

Socializing Lubavitch Children

Since the *Rebbe* is so highly regarded by his followers, it is to be expected that they will try to implant their reverence for him in their children. While the community's educational institutions, including the schools, summer camps, and other organized activities reflect the *Rebbe's* teaching, the way in which children are socialized in their homes to become aware of and appreciate his presence and authority is, in many ways, more important.

There is no prescribed sequence of steps by which the family educates its young about the *Rebbe*. Instead, it is expected that the child will be generally influenced by the ever-present Lubavitch atmosphere encountered in the home. In fact, the child's relationship to the *Rebbe* is considered so vital that as soon as the child is born the father will phone the *Rebbe*. References are made so frequently to the *Rebbe's* teachings and activities that his presence directly affects all aspects of family life. As Lubavitcher suggest, through the family's relationship with the *Rebbe* the young child inevitably becomes aware of his presence and importance:

> ... You only have to enter into a Lubavitcher household to see what I mean. I'm not talking about pictures hanging on the wall, but about *sforim* (religious books),[11] letters, collections of what the *Rebbe* said, of what the *Rebbe* is giving out.... I think it's experiences that really matter to a child. There is a lot of things that you experience within Lubavitch almost on a daily basis; that's really where a child is going to take it from.... I don't think there are many days that go by in the house when the *Rebbe* isn't mentioned.... There are any problems? The *Rebbe*. Any *simcheh* (celebration)?[12] The *Rebbe*.

In addition to the chassidic atmosphere encountered in the home, the young child accompanies his family to *Farbrengens* in New York and is taken to personal audiences with the *Rebbe*. Such experiences, claim Lubavitcher parents, inevitably leave an indelible impression in the child's mind.

> Take my three-year-old as an example and I don't think this is an isolated instance. You ask who the *Rebbe* is. He'll tell you: "He lives in 770. He gave me wine when I went up, and he gave me a blessing." He'll tell you exactly what the room looked like and he'll tell you what the *Rebbe* looks like.... Already at three years old when we bring him, he can relate. (Does the child go to New York?) Yes, when he's old enough to understand, the whole family goes. There's no doubt, they take him along. And on special occasions when the family as a group has a particular audience with the *Rebbe*, then the family takes advantage of having everyone come in. Now my married daughter ... had an audience with the *Rebbe*.... Her child is only 7 or 8 months old, and she and her husband and the baby all went in. Now I'm sure that the baby doesn't understand anything at the moment, but if she goes in now, and she'll go in a year from now, it will become a tradition.

As young children mature they are continually brought into contact with events and experiences relating directly or indirectly with the *Rebbe*. Through his upbringing, then, the young Lubavitcher is taught and learns to recognize the *Rebbe* as a special kind of person whom his parents and others around him both trust and revere.

Belief in the Rebbe's Advice

There is a wide range of subjects on which the Lubavitcher may seek the *Rebbe's* advice: moving to a new house, taking a new job, seeking solutions to health problems, or planning a summer vacation. Typically, the *Rebbe* is called on to offer advice whenever the issue is uncertain, for his power is believed to consist not only of foreseeing the outcome but being able to influence future events. One need not be faced with a critical situation to write to the *Rebbe*, and it has become customary to write in to ask for a blessing (*brocheh*) on the occasion of any celebration such as a birthday or wedding anniversary.

No firm guidelines regulate the kinds of problems the *Rebbe* will consider, and each person decides on which matters to seek the *Rebbe's* counsel. Convinced of the *Rebbe's* special powers, which are believed to penetrate to the essence of every matter, Lubavitcher expect his blessing to help ensure the success of an undertaking. For example, when I mentioned to some Yeshiva students that I was preparing for an important examination, one suggested: "Why don't you write in to the *Rebbe* for a *brocheh* (blessing)? It can only help." A newcomer to Lubavitch consulted with the *Rebbe* about whether he should go back to school although he now had a wife and family to support. In another case, a woman asked the *Rebbe* for the kind of advice usually received from a pediatrician. She was nervous about her new baby who was not sleeping or eating well. Although the *Rebbe* only told her to relax more, which is what any pediatrician would have told her, because the advice came from the *Rebbe* she had more confidence in following it.

The above remarks suggest two important features of the *Rebbe's* relationship with his followers. First, it is left to the individual's own discretion to decide on which matters to seek the *Rebbe's* counsel; second, since he is a righteous man, a *Tzaddic*, Lubavitcher believe that he can offer only helpful advice. It is, in fact, the Lubavitchers' belief that the *Rebbe's* advice can only be helpful that is important, rather than the advice itself. This is what a newcomer, not yet totally sharing Lubavitchers' reverence for the *Rebbe*, referred to when he said: "I mean the *brochess* (blessings) have a certain effect and you wonder to what extent the person reads into the situation, rather than the *brocheh* objectively producing something." This attitude reflects W. I. Thomas's dictum: If men define situations as real, they are real in their consequences. (Volkart, 1951) Because the *Rebbe* is perceived by his followers as unable to do wrong, they are willing to claim to have misinterpreted and not "really understood" his advice if it should prove objectively false. Consequently, it is impossible to have a disconfirmation of the *Rebbe's* teachings.[13]

A Threat to Identity Maintenance in Religious Communities—Assimilation

Although the Lubavitch community's effort to maintain a distinctive identity is mainly reached through its relationship with the *Rebbe*, internal unity is not enough. If any religious community is to persist, it must also resist the threat of assimilation into the larger society. Certain common conditions threaten and compromise any community's efforts to maintain its identity, and many of the same features that help to create the identity may also be used to resist assimilative influences from the surrounding society.

Such features as dress and insulation seem to be becoming decreasingly effective as the larger society's assimilative influences begin to penetrate the community's barriers, resulting in a blurring of the boundary between member and outsider. The group's distinctive garb gradually becomes modified by the fashions regulating dress on the outside, especially by the young who are sometimes embarrassed by their parents' old-fashioned clothes. Hostetler reports that among the New Order Amish, distinctive dress and hair styles show a marked modification. These Amish trim their hair and beards shorter and shorter and "with the dwindling of the beard an Amishman may no longer identify himself as an Amish person . . . Secularization in apparel appears to be greater among men than women, and more advanced among the young than the old." (1968:329)

The same trends can be seen in varying degrees in the chassidic communities. A young man, raised in a chassidic milieu, once told me:

> A lot of the older guys wear these baggy pants and the suits they get for their kids don't look too good on them either. But you'll see the younger guys, those who can afford it, buying suits that are in style. OK, they won't be the real fancy stuff, but the suit will be made well, at a good place. All they do is give the guy the material.

It is also becoming increasingly difficult to resist the outside influences penetrating the community's lifestyle and to maintain physical, cultural, and social insulation. In an urban setting, community members are inevitably exposed, both visually and aurally, to influences considered detrimental to the community's special lifestyle, and the elders are especially concerned about the effect on the young. Conversations with the young from different chassidic groups indicate they are aware of the styles and fads in the outside world as well as their elders' concern about this awareness. A Yeshiva student said: "They (teachers and elders) realize it's impossible or very impractical to keep us from seeing things which the *Yaytzer Ho'Ro* (Evil Inclination)[14] puts in our way. It worries some of them a great deal."

One way in which religious communities try to maintain their distinctive identity is to set up strict criteria to distinguish between who is really inside and who is outside. This distinction can only be maintained effectively when the community insulates itself from those conditions in the outside world which are contradictory to its lifestyle. But it is both impractical and in many ways undesirable for a community to isolate itself completely from the influences of outsiders.

Outsiders' Effect on the Community's Identity

Unlike other chassidic groups which attempt to minimize contact with non-orthodox Jews, the Lubavitch philosophy teaches, and the Lubavitcher *Rebbe* continually reminds his followers, that all Jews must be brought into the orthodox fold and that it is their duty to help accomplish this goal:

> However the Jew must not think only of himself. The commandment "Love thy fellow as thyself" demands the same attitude towards the fellow-Jew. No Jew should ever be given up. It is necessary to kindle in him that pure and holy light, even if it appears to be good only for no more than one day; for even that in itself is worthwhile, and more,—it will steadily grow from day to day, and gradually illuminate his whole life. (Teachers Programme:97)

To this end, Lubavitcher organize a series of activities designed especially to be attractive to Jews of varying degrees of religious observance. Outsiders are invited and encouraged to come to the Lubavitchers' Yeshiva, their homes, and other social and religious functions. The Lubavitch aim is to extend a warm welcome to these Jews in the hope of drawing them progressively closer to observing the practices of traditional Judaism. Since outsiders are invited to mingle with Lubavitcher, the boundaries guarding against outside influences are less effective than among, for example, the Satmarer chassidim. Lubavitcher should, therefore, experience difficulty in maintaining their distinctive identity, since the boundaries separating insider from outsider are less clearly demarcated. In fact, however, Lubavitcher are successful at maintaining their identity and, paradoxically, outsiders contribute toward that effort as Lubavitchers' proselytizing serves to reinforce their own beliefs and clarify their definition of themselves as Lubavitcher.

Possible Motives for the Community's Proselytizing

Systems theorists have argued that recruitment for new members is a functional prerequisite of any social system. (Aberle *et al.* 1950) If the community cannot maintain its ranks through internal production, it will seek outsiders as recruits to maintain itself. The purpose of proselytization, then, is to attract new members to enlarge the community or to maintain its size. Although the Lubavitcher proselytize, they do not do so in order to expand, as few members are attracted to the community in this manner. In addition, the community does not lack for members as it has a high enough birth rate to maintain its numbers. As a result, the argument usually mounted for proselytizing does not apply to the Lubavitch community under study.

Another reason many religious groups need to recruit outsiders is that their numbers are depleted by members lapsing from the faith. To help retain a stable population figure, the community has to shop in the larger community for interested people to join it. The size of a community may decline as adults become dissatisfied and disappointed with the community's lifestyle and leave. It has already been argued that the Lubavitch community's ability to provide a tenable way of life for its adult members means that few if any leave the community. The Yeshiva strongly supports this tenability for adult members, and women's interest in the community's way of life is sustained by their social groups and their acceptance of an ideology related to their role as homemakers. These chassidim's frequent contact with one another, added to their common bond with the *Rebbe*, reinforces their identity as Lubavitcher while imposing social barriers for those who are contemplating leaving the community. Lubavitchers' daily affirmation of their way of life, accomplished through prayer, performing *mitzvess*,[15] and contact with the *Rebbe*, enables the community to satisfy those within it and provides them with reasons to remain.

The size of a community may also decline if it is unable to offset the surrounding society's assimilative influences on its young members. The community may easily lose younger members through intergenerational conflict and intermarriage. When exposure to the surrounding culture is not controlled, family disorganization frequently results for the two generations do not share a similar perspective. Several studies have pointed to the kinds of cultural conflicts that develop between parents and their children when the latter are submitted to a secular education which, at points, openly contradicts their parents' living habits. (Gottlieb and Ramsey, 1964; Hapgood, 1902; Shibutani and Kwan, 1965; Wirth, 1928) The kind of socialization offered at home is often at odds with that taught in the school and this often results in serious disagreements between parents and their children over appropriate selection of mates. Lubavitcher, however, do not generally experience such difficulties with their children. Their two schools enable them to screen the secular curricula carefully to avoid students' exposure to ideas contradictory to the ideology of traditional Judaism. In addition, the culture of the community's younger generation does not lead to the development of an autonomous social world that excludes adults. It is, in fact, closely linked to the perspectives and everyday assumptions governing their parents' lives. Finally, the community's proximity to the much larger New York Lubavitch community ensures that young people of marriageable age will have a good possibility of finding suitable partners there, thus lessening the risk of intermarriage.

Although exact figures showing the community's growth rate are not available, it is safe to argue that its size has increased rather than decreased in the last several years. This is based on several comments offered by Lubavitcher who emphasize that the community's growth is primarily due to large family size. As one remarked:

> There's no question that Lubavitch in Montreal has grown in the last few years. You've probably noticed this yourself that Lubavitcher have large families. It's hard to say how many babies are born but it seems that all the time there's someone who's having a baby.

In addition, though not the main source of the community's growth, Lubavitchers' proselytizing activities have attracted several newcomers. Even though they invest considerable time in such activities, the overwhelming proportion of Lubavitcher's contacts with non-observant Jews is fleeting and success at winning such Jews to orthodox Judaism is, in fact, minimal. Since efforts at proselytization do not, apparently, yield benefits commensurate to the time invested, why are they continued? This question is especially relevant as it is mainly the younger people who engage in most of the proselytizing in the larger Jewish community which might be considered potentially harmful to the Lubavitch community's distinctive identity.

Who Does the Proselytizing? A Threat to the Community's Distinctive Identity The actual practice of proselytizing is not officially delegated to a specific age group within the Lubavitch community. Unofficially, however, the community's formally organized activities are primarily co-ordinated and administered by the older Yeshiva students (*bocherim*)[16] studying the *Bays Medresh*.[17] The *Tefillin* campaign is an excellent illustration of the *bocherim's* involvement in proselytizing, for although all Lubavitcher were interested in the campaign's success, the older Yeshiva students were mainly responsible for the actual proselytizing activities. These students also regularly visit college campuses to contact Jewish youth, call on the orthodox synagogues in the city on Saturday afternoons to recount the *Rebbe's* discourses, serve as counsellors in the boys' camp and organize the Encounter program. The organization of these activities entails entering situations with outsiders—both Jewish and Gentile—which may expose them to ideas and appearances contradictory to their way of life. Unlike the *bocherim* of the Satmarer and Tasher chassidim in Montreal, who are strongly discouraged and sometimes forbidden to converse with non-observant Jews, Lubavitcher *bocherim* regularly devote periods of time to befriending Jews whose religious observance is minimal. As outsiders are invited to the Lubavitcher Yeshiva and are welcomed into their organizations and celebrations, the distinction between insider and outsider, so crucial to the very existence of a community, is obscured. It appears that Lubavitcher's proselytizing in the larger Jewish community could threaten the preservation of their distinctive identity by diluting the community's boundaries and the distinction between the insiders and outsiders. This threat does not, however, appear to decrease the Lubavitcher's proselytizing zeal, nor in fact to weaken the community. In spite of theories to the contrary, proselytizing appears to have beneficial consequences to the community that are almost incidental to the professed aims of most proselytization.

Proselytizing Activities—An Unintended Consequence

Our analysis so far has suggested that the usual consequences of proselytizing do not pertain in the Lubavitch community. It is rather the latent consequences that make it important to the community's persistence.

Festinger *et al.*, in their presentation of cognitive-dissonance theory in *When Prophecy Fails*, suggest that a consequence of a group's successful proselytizing is "reduced dissonance." (1956:28) If the group's central beliefs are either questioned or disbelieved by others, proselytizing is an effective means of reaffirming the members' identity with the group. As the writers assert: *"If more and more people can be persuaded that the system of belief is correct, then clearly it must, after all, be correct."* (1956:28) In spite of the fact that they recognize that a large proportion of Jews in Montreal do not share their convictions about orthodox Judaism, Lubavitcher do not become discouraged, and continue to order their lives according to the precepts underlying traditional Jewish law. It is precisely the act of proselytizing in the larger Jewish community that reinforces the members' beliefs and enables the Lubavitch community to retain its identity. When a Lubavitcher attempts to influence and convince a non-observant Jew of the relevance of orthodox Judaism, he is, in fact, becoming influenced and convinced himself. As G. H. Mead noted, this results from the person's ability to act socially toward himself just as he

acts toward others and thus to become the object of his own actions.
(1934:199-246) An important consequence of Lubavitchers' proselytizing
activity, therefore, is that by discussing and arguing with non-observant
Jews about orthodox Judaism, the Lubavitcher *Rebbe's* accomplishments,
or the everlasting significance of Torah observance, they expose
themselves to certain information and reinforce their identity as
Lubavitcher chassidim. As Festinger *et al.*, argue, the increased
proselytizing activities of messianic movements whose prophecies have
been disconfirmed would indicate that, as the larger Jewish community
drifts away from the tenets of traditional Judaism, Lubavitcher's
proselytizing efforts will increase.

In light of this argument, the involvement of older Yeshiva students
in such activities is now understandable. These students, ranging in age
from fifteen to twenty years, are the very people whose beliefs require
strengthening. Their commitment to the Lubavitch way of life is less
intense than that of the adults who have raised families and have chosen
their friends from within the community. As they live with their parents
and are thus exposed to their influence concerning Torah observance, the
identity of the younger children as orthodox Lubavitch Jews is
continually manipulated and reinforced. As the majority of *Bays Medresh
bocherim* come from other cities and reside at a Lubavitch dormitory by
themselves, they are the ones whose self-conceptions as Lubavitcher must
be supported. Co-opting *bocherim* into recruitment is no doubt an
important way to build their own belief systems. By teaching and
becoming witness to their beliefs and by urging them on others, they
learn to think of themselves as Lubavitcher chassidim. Lubavitcher
bocherim, then, are not expected to isolate themselves, but rather to
control the contexts in which they meet with outsiders. The context is
always expected to assume a religious base, emphasizing religious
differences and making religion an explicit focus of attention or barrier.

Another factor contributing to Lubavitchers' interest in
proselytization has already been discussed in the context of the benefits
they derive from their relationship with the larger Jewish community.
Successful proselytization results in the presence of non-Lubavitch
students in the Lubavitch schools and summer camps. Since such
institutions are advantageous to the community and help ensure its
persistence, Lubavitcher are prepared to invest considerable time and
energy in proselytization work. Although attracting newcomers (*baal
tshuvess*)[18] to the Lubavitch community is again not one of the main
purposes of Lubavitchers' proselytizing activities, they do have a
considerable number of recruits who have to go through a period of
instruction while they are becoming members of the Lubavitch
community. In addition to adding to the community's population, these
recruits provide concrete evidence that Lubavitchers' proselytizing efforts

enjoy a considerable measure of success. A more important result of their proselytizing than either support of their institutions or new recruits is the positive effect that their activities have in maintaining the identity and tenability of the community.

NOTES

1. *Yeshiva.* School of religious study; rabbinical school.
2. *Goyish.* Non-Jewish. The word may include derogatory implications for Jews and non-Jews alike.
3. *Rebbe.* The religious leader of a chassidic group. (*Rebbeim.* Plural.)
4. *Farbrengen.* A chassidic gathering.
5. *Tanya.* The book written by Rabbi Schneur Zalman of Liadi, the first Lubavitcher *Rebbe*, dealing with the philosophy of the Lubavitch movement.
6. *Shleeta.* Initials of *sheyeechyeh l'oyrech yomim toyvim, omayn,* meaning he shall live good long years, amen. Referring only to a *Rebbe*.
7. *Yiddishkayt* (Yiddish). Literally, Jewishness. Refers to a way of life within traditional Judaism.
8. Some recent studies about the chassidim deal with the *Rebbe's* importance to his followers. Mintz (1968), for example, tells us that one aspect of the *Rebbe's* role is that he serves as a mediator between his followers and God. Mintz presents an analysis of the *Rebbe's* functions regarding his followers and the interrelationship resulting between the two. Weiner (1969) in his chapter on "The Lubavitcher Movement" describes his personal audience with the Lubavitcher *Rebbe*. For a discussion of the Satmarer *Rebbe*, see Rubin (1972), pp. 56-62. Gutwirth's study (1970) of the Belzer chassidim includes discussion of the Belzer *Rebbe*.
9. *Brocheh.* Blessing. (*Brochess.* Plural.)
10. *Tefillin* (Hebrew). Phylacteries. Religious objects containing excerpts from the Bible worn on the arm and forehead during morning services on weekdays.
11. *Saifer.* Holy book. (*Sforim.* Plural.)
12. *Simcheh.* Literally, joy. Celebration of any kind. (*Simchess.* Plural.)
13. A similar point is suggested by Rubin in his discussion of the Satmarer *Rebbe*:" . . . what is important is the way he is perceived by the members of the community, rather than the way he might score on some objective value scale." (1972:59)
14. *Yaytzer Ho'Ro.* Evil Inclination. Counterpart to the *Yaytzer Tov*—Good Inclination.
15. *Mitzveh.* A Prescribed religious command; a good deed. (*Mitzvess.* Plural.)
16. *Bocher.* A young boy; also unmarried male. (*Bocherim.* Plural.)
17. *Baal Tshuveh.* Literally, repenter. Used in this study to mean a newcomer to Lubavitch. (*Baal Tshuvess.* Plural.)
18. *Bays Medresh.* A place for prayer and study.

BIBLIOGRAPHY

Aberle, D. F. *et al.* "The Functional Prerequisites of a Society," In Demerath III, N.J. and Peterson, Richard A. (eds.) *System, Change, and Conflict.* New York: The Free Press, 1967.

Di Yiddishe Heim. New York: Council *Neshai Un'Nos Chabad.*

Festinger, Leon, Henry W. Riecken, and Stanley Schachter. *When Prophecy Fails.* New York: Harper & Row, 1956.

Gottlieb, David and Charles E. Ramsey. *The American Adolescent.* Homewood, Illinois: The Dorsey Press, 1964.

Gutwirth, Jacques. *Vie Juive Traditionelle: Ethnologie D'Une Communauté Hassidique.* Paris: Les Editions De Minuit, 1970.

Hapgood, Hutchins. *The Spirit Of The Ghetto: Studies of the Jewish Quarter of New York.* New York: Schocken Books, 1966.

Hostetler, John A. *Amish Society.* Baltimore: The Johns Hopkins Press, 1968.

Mead, George H. *Mind, Self, and Society.* Chicago, Ill.: University of Chicago Press, 1934.

Mintz, Jerome R. *Legends of the Hasidim.* Chicago: University of Chicago Press, 1968.

Rubin, Israel. *Satmar: An Island in the City.*

Shibutani, Tamotsu and Kian M. Kwan. *Ethnic Stratification: A Comparative Approach.* New York: The Macmillan Company, 1965.

Teachers Programme. London: Lubavitch Foundation, 1969.

Weiner, Herbert. *9½ Mystics.* New York: Holt, Rinehart and Winston, 1969.

Wirth, Louis. *The Ghetto.* Chicago: University of Chicago Press, 1928.

Occupational Careers & Identity

PERHAPS THE MOST important question we can ask when defining and identifying a stranger and his interests is "What do you do?" The answer usually deals with the person's work, and provides us with a set of assumptions and expectations about the individual. Such identifications give us a preliminary set of understandings about the other person and an idea of the range and limits of any continuing interaction. Occupational identification is one of the chief means by which we define and relate to others.

In the work group or collectivity we undergo one of our most important adult socializing experiences. Through our work associations we not only learn the techniques of a job or jobs, but more importantly, an occupational culture which serves as an important source of meanings and identification. Occupational membership and participation are important spheres of activity which locate and define us *vis-à-vis* others and provide us with a ready-made set of relationships and identifications affecting our self-concept, and the image others have of us.

The work of E. C. Hughes has had a great impact on the sociology of education and occupations. A central feature of Hughes's approach is his insight into the common themes that run through seemingly different occupational roles. In *Men and Their Work*, for example, physicians, teachers, ministers, janitors, realtors, prostitutes, librarians, nurses, factory workers, musicians, personnel officers, quack salesmen, and scientists are all mentioned. In each of these different occupational roles, suggests Hughes, the incumbents are faced with similar kinds of tasks and problems to which they must adapt and respond either as individuals, or collectively, in order to continue their work.

One theme in the study of occupations is that of routine and emergency. A situation that is defined as a crisis and considered an emergency by one person is seen by another as a routine matter. A homeowner may become frantic about a burst pipe in the basement, while a plumber will calmly see the pipe as similar to the others he fixed earlier in the day. And the physician's calm reply to parents' extreme concern over their child's illness indicates that the doctor does not share their view of the situation.

Another theme found in all occupations is the problem of mistakes and failures. All work contains potential problems and there is always the possibility of mistakes and failure. In some occupations mistakes can have more drastic consequences than in others. While the garbageman who forgets to empty a can of garbage, and the surgeon who absent-mindedly leaves a clamp inside a patient's body have both made mistakes, the latter's error is likely to have more serious effects. In occupations where mistakes can be serious, there may be attempts to conceal the inner workings of the occupation from public view, as in the case of medicine. It is also to be expected that those "who are subject to the same work risks will compose a collective rationale which they whistle to one another to keep up their courage, and that they will build up collective defenses against the lay world." (Hughes, 1951:322) The nature of such defenses will vary in complexity and in frequency of use, but the problem of dealing with mistakes and failures is common to all occupational groups.

Yet another theme is that of dirty work. Dirty work of some kind is found in all occupations. "The dirty work of society, whether physically dirty or socially disreputable, must be done. While some occupations specialize in dirty work, almost every occupation includes some such work." (Solomon, 1968:9) For instance, janitors frankly admit that their physically dirty work involves collecting garbage. For the university professor, on the other hand, dirty work may consist in grading term papers and examinations. In all occupations, however, the people involved must, in some manner, come to terms with the fact that some of their tasks are *infra dignitate.* Solomon writes about some alternate ways workers face the problem of dirty work when he says:

> This may involve developing a terminology to make the work seem less dirty, concealing the dirty aspects, referring the dirty work to less-favored colleagues, or sloughing it off onto members of other occupations. If work, or some aspects of work are, or are regarded as, dirty, workers seem to feel the need somehow or other to structure interaction so as to mitigate the impact. (Solomon, 1968:9)

Several of the selections for this section of the book focus on these occupational themes and describe the way workers' perceptions of problems in their jobs lead to collectively derived perspectives. The first article, "Work and Self" by Everett C. Hughes, describes the social psychological adaptations that workers make to attend to a variety of problems in different occupations. Two other articles, one dealing with medical students and the other with high steel ironworkers, center on the common problem of demonstrating competence. These different kinds of occupations are alike in that they bear potentially fateful consequences for other people. This perception leads both medical students and ironworker apprentices to manage convincing performances of competence before concerned audiences, even though these manipulated impressions may not be a true reflection of their personal convictions.

The next article by Peter Letkemann describes the elements common to criminal and conventional work; both criminals and legitimate workers face problems of technological change. Our closing selection deals with the relationship between occupation, life style, and involvement in community affairs. Aileen Ross describes the relationship between the successful business career and philanthropic community activities. Achievement in both the business and community spheres is seen as intimately related to the desire of entrepreneurs to be visibly involved in community matters, hence strengthening their identification and reputation politically and economically.

Work & Self

EVERETT C. HUGHES

THERE ARE SOCIETIES in which custom or sanctioned rule determines what work a man of a given status may do. In our society, at least one strong strain of ideology has it that a man may do any work which he is competent to do; or even that he has a right to the schooling and experience necessary to gain competence in any kind of work which he sets as the goal of his ambition. Equality of opportunity is, among us, stated very much in terms of the right to enter upon any occupation whatsoever. Although we do not practice this belief to the full, we are a people who cultivate ambition. A great deal of our ambition takes the form of getting training for kinds of work which carry more prestige than that which our fathers did. Thus a man's work is one of the things by which he is judged, and certainly one of the more significant things by which he judges himself.

Many people in our society work in named occupations. The names are tags, a combination of price tag and calling card. One has only to hear casual conversation to sense how important these tags are. Hear a salesman, who has just been asked what he does, reply, "I am in sales work," or "I am in promotional work," not "I sell skillets." School teachers sometimes turn schoolteaching into educational work, and the disciplining of youngsters and chaperoning of parties into personnel work. Teaching Sunday School becomes religious education, and the Y.M.C.A. Secretary is "in group work." Social scientists emphasize the science end of their name. These hedging statements in which people pick the most favorable of several possible names for their work imply an audience. And one of the most important things about any man is his

"Work and the Self" by Everett Cherrington Hughes in Social Psychology *at the Crossroads. Edited by John H. Rohrer and Muzafer Sherif. Copyright, 1951 by Harper & Row, Publishers, Inc. By permission of the Publisher.*

audience, or his choice of the several available audiences to which he may address his claims to be someone of worth.

These remarks should be sufficient to call it to your attention that a man's work is one of the more important parts of his social identity, of his self, indeed, of his fate, in the one life he has to live, for there is something almost as irrevocable about choice of occupation as there is about choice of a mate. And since the language about work is so loaded with value and prestige judgments, and with defensive choice of symbols, we should not be astonished that the concepts of social scientists who study work should carry a similar load, for the relation of social-science concepts to popular speech remains close in spite of our efforts to separate them. The difference is that the value-weighting in popular speech is natural and proper, for concealment and ego-protection are of the essence of social intercourse. But in scientific discourse the value-loaded concept may be a blinder. And part of the problem of method in the study of work behavior is that the people who have the most knowledge about a given occupation (let us say medicine), and from whom therefore the data for analysis must come, are the people in the occupation. They may combine in themselves a very sophisticated manipulative knowledge of the appropriate social relations, with a very strongly motivated suppression, and even repression, of the deeper truths about these relationships, and, in occupations of higher status, with great verbal skill in keeping these relationships from coming up for thought and discussion by other people. This is done in part by the use of and insistence upon loaded value words where their work is discussed.

May I, to illustrate the point that concepts may be blinders, tell you briefly of my own experience in the study of occupations. Maybe one reason we social scientists fall into their trap so easily is that many such occupations have higher status than our own.

My first essay into the field was a study of the real estate agents in Chicago. These highly competitive men were just at that point in their journey toward respectability at which they wished to emphasize their conversion from business-minded suspicion of one another to the professional attitude, with confidence in each other and with a demand for confidence from the public. I started the study with the idea of finding out an answer to this familiar question, "Are these men professionals?" It was a false question, for the concept "profession" in our society is not so much a descriptive term as one of value and prestige. It happens over and over that the people who practice an occupation attempt to revise the conceptions which their various publics have of the occupation and of the people in it. In so doing, they also attempt to revise their own conception of themselves and of their work. The model which these occupations set before themselves is that of the "profession;" thus the term profession is a symbol for a desired conception of one's work and, hence, of one's self. The movement to "professionalize" an occupation is thus collective mobility of some among the people in an occupation. One aim of the movement is to rid the occupation of people who are not mobile enough to go along with the changes. There are two possible kinds of occupational mobility. One is individual. The individual makes the several choices, and achieves the skills which allow him to move to a certain position in the occupational, and thus—he hopes—in the social and economic hierarchy. His choice is limited by several conditions, among which is the social knowledge available to him at the time of crucial decision, a time which varies for the several kinds of work.

The other kind of occupational mobility is that of a group of people in an occupation, i.e., of the occupation itself. This has been important in our society with its great changes of technology, with its attendant proliferation of new occupations and of change in technique and social relation of old ones. Now it sometimes happens that by the time a person has the full social knowledge necessary to the smartest possible choice of occupations, he is already stuck with one and in one. How strongly this may affect the drive for professionalization of occupations, I don't know. I suspect that it is a motive. At any rate, it is common in our society for occupational groups to step their occupation up in the hierarchy by turning it into a profession. I will not here describe this process. Let me only indicate that in my own studies I passed from the false question "Is this occupation a profession?" to the more fundamental one, "What are the circumstances in which the people in an occupation attempt to turn it into a profession, and themselves into professional people?" and "What are the steps by which they attempt to bring about identification with their valued model?"

Even with this new orientation the term *profession* acted as a blinder. For as I began to give courses and seminars on occupations, I used a whole set of concepts and headings which were prejudicial to full understanding of what work behavior and relations are. One of them was that of the "code of ethics," which still tended to sort people into the good and the bad. It was not until I had occasion to undertake study of race relations in industry that I finally, I trust, got rid of this bias in the concepts which I used. Negro industrial workers, the chief objects of our study, performed the kinds of work which have least prestige and which make least pretension; yet, it turned out that even in the lowest occupations people do develop collective pretensions to give their work, and consequently themselves, value in the eyes of each other and of outsiders.

It was from these people that we learned that the common dignifying rationalization of people in all positions of a work hierarchy except the very top one is, "We in this position save the people in the next higher position above from their own mistakes." The notion that one saves a person of more acknowledged skill, and certainly of more acknowledged prestige and power, than one's self from his mistakes appears to be peculiarly satisfying. Now there grow up in work organizations rules of mutual protection among the persons in a given category and rank, and across ranks and categories. If one uses the term "code of ethics" he is likely not to see the true nature of these rules. These rules have of necessity to do with mistakes, for it is in the nature of work that people make mistakes. The question of how mistakes are handled is a much more penetrating one than any question which contains the concept "professional ethics" as ordinarily conceived. For in finding out how mistakes are handled, one must get at the fundamental psychological and social devices by which people are able to carry on through time, to live with others and with themselves, knowing that what is daily routine for them in their occupational roles may be fateful for others, knowing that one's routine mistakes, even the mistakes by which one learns better, may touch other lives at crucial points. It is in part the problem of dealing routinely with what are the crises of others. The people in lower ranks are thus using a powerful psychological weapon when they rationalize their worth and indispensability as lying in their protection of people in higher ranks from their mistakes. I suppose it is almost a truism that the people who take the larger responsibilities must be people who can face making mistakes, while punctiliousness must remain in second place. But this is a matter which has not been very seriously taken into account, as far as I know, in studies of the social drama of work.

Of course, the rules which people make to govern their behavior at work cover other problems than that of mistakes. Essentially the rules classify people, for to define situations and the proper behavior in situations one has to assign roles to the people involved. Thus among the most important subject matter of rules is setting up of criteria for recognizing a true fellow-worker, for determining who it is safe and may even be necessary to initiate into the in-group of close equals, and who must be kept at some distance. This problem is apt to be obscured by the term "colleague-ship," which, although its etymology is perfect for the matter in hand, carries a certain notion of higher status, of respectabiity. (In pre-Hitler Germany the Social-Democratic workers called one another "Comrade." The Christian trade-unions insisted on the term "Colleague.")

Allow me to mention one other value-laden term which may act as a blinder in study of the social psychology of work, to wit, "restriction of production." This term contains a value assumption of another kind— namely, that there is someone who knows and has a right to determine the right amount of work for other people to do. If one does less, he is restricting production. Mayo and others have done a good deal to analyze the phenomenon in question, but it was Max Weber who—forty years ago—pointed to "putting on the brakes," as an inevitable result of the wrestling match between a man and his employer over the price he must pay with his body for his wage. In short, he suggested that no man easily yields to another full control over the effort, and especially over the amount of physical effort he must daily exert. On the other hand, there is no more characteristically human phenomenon than determined and even heroic effort to do a task which one has somehow taken as his own. I do not mean to make the absurd implication that there could be a situation in which every man would be his own and only taskmaster. But I think we might understand the social interaction which determines the measure of effort if we are to keep ourselves free of terms which suggest that it is abnormal to do less than one is asked by some reasonable authority.

You will have doubtless got the impression that I am making the usual plea for a value-free science, that is, for neutrality. Such is not my intention. Our aim is to *penetrate more deeply* into the personal and social drama of work, to understand the social and social-psychological arrangements and devices by which men make their work tolerable, or even make it glorious to themselves and others. I believe that much of our terminology and hence, of our problem setting, has limited our field of perception by a certain pretentiousness and a certain value-loading. Specifically we need to rid ourselves of any concepts which keep us from seeing that the essential problems of men at work are the same whether they do their work in the laboratories of some famous institution or in the messiest vat room of a pickle factory. Until we can find a point of view and concepts which will enable us to make comparisons between the junk peddler and the professor without intent to debunk the one and patronize the other, we cannot do our best work in this field.

Perhaps there is as much to be learned about the high-prestige occupations by applying to them the concepts which naturally come to mind for study of people in the most lowly kinds of work as there is to be learned by applying to other occupations the conceptions developed in connection with the highly valued professions. Furthermore, I have come to the conclusion that is is a fruitful thing to start study of any social phenomenon at the point of least prestige. For, since prestige is so much a matter of symbols, and even of pretentions—however well merited— there goes with prestige a tendency to preserve a front which hides the inside of things; a front of names, of indirection, of secrecy (much of it necessary secrecy). On the other hand, in things of less prestige, the core may be more easy of access.

In recent years a number of my students have studied some more or less lowly occupations: apartment-house janitors, junk men, boxers, jazz musicians, osteopaths, pharmacists, etc. They have done so mainly because of their own connections with the occupations in question, and perhaps because of some problem of their own. At first, I thought of these studies as merely interesting and informative for what they would tell about people who do these humbler jobs, i.e., as American ethnology. I have now come to the belief that although the problems of people in these lines of work are as interesting and important as any other, their deeper value lies in the insights they yield about work behavior in any and all occupations. It is not that it puts one into the position to debunk the others, but simply that processes which are hidden in other occupations come more readily to view in these lowly ones. We may be here dealing with a fundamental matter of method in social science, the matter of finding the best possible laboratory animal for study of a given series of mechanisms.

Let me illustrate. The apartment-house janitor is a fellow who, in making his living, has to do a lot of other people's dirty work. This is patent. He could not hide it if he would. Now every occupation is not one but several activities; some of them are the "dirty work" of that trade. It may be dirty in one of several ways. It may be simply physically disgusting. It may be a symbol of degradation, something that wounds one's dignity.

Finally, it may be dirty work in that it in some way goes counter to the more heroic of our moral conceptions. Dirty work of some kind is found in all occupations. It is hard to imagine an occupation in which one does not appear, in certain repeated contingencies, to be practically compelled to play a role of which he thinks he ought to be a little ashamed morally. Insofar as an occupation carries with it a self-conception, a notion of personal dignity, it is likely that at some point one will feel that he is having to do something that is *infra dignitate*. Janitors turned out to be bitterly frank about their physically dirty work. When asked, "What is the toughest part of your job," they answered almost to a man in the spirit of this quotation: "Garbage. Often the stuff is sloppy and smelly. You know some fellows can't look at garbage if it's sloppy. I'm getting used to it now, but it almost killed me when I started." Or as another put it, "The toughest part? It's the messing up in front of the garbage incinerator. That's the most miserable thing there is on this job. The tenants don't co-operate—them bastards. You tell them today, and tomorrow there is the same mess over again by the incinerator."

In the second quotation it becomes evident that the physical disgust of the janitor is not merely a thing between him and the garbage, but involves also the tenant. Now the tenant is the person who impinges most on the daily work activity of the janitor. It is the tenant who interferes most with his own dignified ordering of his life and work. If it were not for a tenant who had broken a window, he could have got his regular Saturday cleaning done on time; if it were not for a tenant who had clogged a trap, he would not have been ignominiously called away from the head of his family table just when he was expansively offering his wife's critical relatives a second helping of porkchops, talking the while about the importance of his job. It is the tenant who causes the janitor's status pain. The physically disgusting part of the janitor's work is directly involved in his relations with other actors in his work drama.

By a *contre coup*, it is by the garbage that the janitor judges, and, as it were, gets power over the tenants who high-hat him. Janitors know about hidden love-affairs by bits of torn-up letter paper; of impending financial disaster or of financial four-flushing by the presence of many unopened letters in the waste. Or they may stall off demands for immediate service by an unreasonable woman of whom they know from the garbage that she, as the janitors put it, "has the rag on." The garbage gives the janitor the makings of a kind of magical power over that pretentious villain, the tenant. I say a kind of magical power, for there appears to be no thought of betraying any individual and thus turning this knowledge into overt power. He protects the tenant, but, at least among Chicago janitors, it is certainly not a loving protection.

Let your mind dwell on what one might hear from people in certain other occupations if they were to answer as frankly and bitterly as did the janitors. I do not say nor do I think that it would be a good thing for persons in all occupations to speak so freely on physical disgust as did these men. To do so, except in the most tightly closed circles, would create impossible situations. But we are likely to overlook the matter altogether in studying occupations where concealment is practiced, and this gives a quite false notion of the problems which have to be faced in such occupations, and of the possible psychological and social by-products of the solutions which are developed for the problem of disgust.

Now the delegation of dirty work to someone else is common among humans. Many cleanliness taboos, and perhaps even more moral scruples, depend for their practice upon success in delegating the tabooed activity to someone else. Delegation of dirty work is also a part of the process of occupational mobility. Yet there are kinds of work, some of them of very high prestige, in which such delegation is possible only to a limited extent. The dirty work may be an intimate part of the very activity which gives the occupation its charisma, as is the case with the handling of the human body by the physician. In this case, I suppose the dirty work is somehow integrated into the whole, and into the prestigious role of the person who does the work. What role it plays in the drama of work relations in such a case is something to find out. The janitor, however, does not integrate his dirty work into any deeply satisfying definition of his role that might liquidate his antagonism to the people whose dirt he handles. Incidentally, we have found reason to believe that one of the deeper sources of antagonisms in hospitals arises from the belief of the people in the humblest jobs that the physicians in charge call upon them to do their dirty work in the name of the role of "healing the sick," although none of the prestige and little of the money reward of that role reaches the people at the bottom. Thus we might conceive of a classification of occupations involving dirty work into those in which it is knit into some satisfying and prestige-giving definition of role and those in which it is not. I suppose we might think of another classification into those in which the dirty work seems somehow wilfully put upon one and those in which it is quite unconnected with any person involved in the work drama.

There is a feeling among prison guards and mental-hospital attendants that society at large and their superiors hypocritically put upon them dirty work which they, society, and the superiors in prison and hospital know is necessary but which they pretend is not necessary. Here it takes the form, in the minds of people in these two lowly occupations, of leaving them to cope for twenty hours, day in and day out, with inmates whom the public never has to see and whom the people at the head of the organization see only episodically. There is a whole series of problems here which cannot be solved by some miracle of changing the social selection of those who enter the job (which is the usual unrealistic solution for such cases).

And this brings us to the brief consideration of what one may call the social drama of work. Most kinds of work bring people together in definable roles; thus the janitor and the tenant, the doctor and the patient, the teacher and the pupil, the worker and his foreman, the prison guard and the prisoner, the musician and his listener. In many occupations there is some category of persons with whom the people at work regularly come into crucial contact. In some occupations the most crucial relations are those with one's fellow-workers. It is they who can do most to make life sweet or sour. Often, however, it is the people in some other position. And in many there is a category of persons who are, so to speak, the consumers of one's work or services. It is probable that the people in the occupation will have their chronic fight for status, for personal dignity with this group of consumers of their services. Part of the social psychological problem of the occupation is the maintenance of a certain freedom and social distance from these people most crucially and intimately concerned with one's work.

In a good deal of our talk about occupations we imply that the tension between the producer and consumer of services is somehow a matter of ill-will or misunderstandings which easily might be removed. It may be that it lies a good deal deeper than that. Often there is a certain ambivalence on the side of the producer, which may be illustrated by the case of the professional jazz-musicians. The musician wants jobs and an income. He also wants his music to be appreciated, but to have his living depend upon the appreciation does not entirely please him. For he likes to think himself and other musicians the best judges of his playing. To play what pleases the audience—the paying customers, who are not, in his opinion, good judges—is a source of annoyance. It is not merely that the listeners, having poor taste, demand that he play music which he does not think is the best he can do; even when they admire him for playing in his own sweet way, he doesn't like it, for then they are getting too close—they are impinging on his private world too much. The musicians accordingly use all sorts of little devices to keep a line drawn between themselves and the audience; such as turning the musicians' chairs, in a dance hall without platform, in such a way as to make something of a barrier. It is characteristic of many occupations that the people in them, although convinced that they themselves are the best judges, not merely of their own competence but also of what is best for the people for whom they perform services, are required in some measure to yield judgement of what is wanted to these amateurs who receive the services. This is a problem not only among musicians, but in teaching, medicine, dentistry, the arts, and many other fields. It is a chronic source of ego-wound and possibly of antagonism.

Related to this is the problem of routine and emergency. In many occupations, the workers or practitioners (to use both a lower and a higher status term) deal routinely with what are emergencies to the people who receive the services. This is a source of chronic tension between the two. For the person with the crisis feels that the other is trying to belittle his trouble; he does not take it seriously enough. His very competence comes from having dealt with a thousand cases of what I like to consider my unique trouble. The worker thinks he knows from long experience that people exaggerate their troubles. He therefore builds up devices to protect himself to stall people off. This is the function of the janitor's wife when a tenant phones an appeal or a demand for immediate attention to a leaky tap; it is also the function of the doctor's wife and even sometimes of the professor's wife. The physician plays one emergency off against the other; the reason he can't run right up to see Johnny who may have the measles is that he is, unfortunately, right at that moment treating a case of the black plague. Involved in this is something of the struggle mentioned above in various connections, the struggle to maintain some control over one's decisions of what work to do, and over the disposition of one's time and of one's routine of life. It would be interesting to know what the parish priest thinks to himself when he is called for the tenth time to give extreme unction to the sainted Mrs. O'Flaherty who hasn't committed a sin in years except that of, in her anxiety over dying in a state of sin, being a nuisance to the priest. On Mrs. O'Flaherty's side there is the danger that she might die unshriven, and she has some occasion to fear that the people who shrive may not take her physical danger seriously and hence may not come quickly enough when at last her hour has come. There may indeed be in the minds of the receivers of emergency services a resentment that something so crucial to them can be a matter for a cooler and more objective attitude, even though they know perfectly well that such an attitude is necessary to competence, and though they could not stand it if the expert to whom they take their troubles were to show any signs of excitement. I have not worked out in any full or systematic way all of the problems of this routine vs. emergency drama. Nor, for that matter, have I worked out systematically any of the problems mentioned in this discussion. My aim has been to call attention to certain problems which lie, it seems to me, on the margin between sociology and psychology, problems on which people of these two disciplines should be working jointly.

THE COMPARATIVE STUDY of people's work "starts with the assumption that all kinds of work belong in the same series, regardless of their places in prestige or ethical rating." (Hughes, 1971:316) It follows, therefore, that different kinds of occupations are likely to be characterized by common themes. One such theme may be described as the demonstration of competence. Much research on the sociology of occupations has focused on the process by which persons learn to do the tasks associated with their work. Incumbents of all occupational groups realize that to be judged competent, they must demonstrate their mastery of a set of skills and techniques. Judgments reflecting capability, however, are also likely to be based on the ability of people to convey an air of competence when in fact these individuals are uncertain of their own skills. A successful demonstration of competence may, then, be substituted temporarily for actual ability.

Socialization into an occupational group and career involves not only learning and adopting certain skills, but more importantly, "a progressive perception of the whole system and of possible places in it and the accompanying changes in conceptions of the work and one's self in relation to it." (Hughes, 1959:456) Such changes in identity accompany the neophyte's immersion into the new work culture, wherein the newcomer learns and acts according to the expectations of the work group.

In order for the newcomers to identify with the occupational group, they must be accepted by the established workers. These interactions often have a career of their own and can be conceptualized as stages of learning and acceptance that are symbolized by the participants as part of the group's rites of passage.

In the following two selections, the relationship of occupational career and identity is examined in two very different fields: medicine and high steel ironworking. Despite the obvious differences in the nature of these two work activities, we observe that the common problem of demonstrating competence in fateful matters leads to markedly similar definitions of the situation. In both fields we see occupational aspirants trying to protect themselves from ridicule and charges of incompetence or failure. To accomplish this, they must give performances that elicit only certain desirable reactions. The exaggerated expectations of competence that are perceived by both sets of newcomers lead them, individually and collectively, to manage these expectations by symbolically defining and controlling their presentations and situations to display an image of competence.

The Professionalization of Medical Students: Developing Competence and A Cloak of Competence*

JACK HAAS/WILLIAM SHAFFIR

Introduction

The cultural study of a population which, unlike that of a small homogeneous community, is of diverse origins and experiences, encounters many special problems. It is necessary to discover what, in the mass of that experience, is the central and consistent element in the life activities of the population under consideration. Dr. Edgerton has found this commonality in the efforts of these people [mentally retarded released into the community from institutions] to envelop themselves in a 'cloak of competence', *in their need to deny themselves the reality of their condition,* and in the closely related requisite *that they hide—or convince themselves they have hidden—the fact that they have been adjudged deficient.* (Foreword by Walter Goldschmidt in Edgerton, 1967:v-vi, emphasis ours)

THE PROCESSES OF covering up personal incompetence, the appearance of incompetence, or feelings of incompetence are not restricted to the mentally retarded but are characteristic of participants in occupations and societies that place high value on cognitive skills and abilities. Edgerton observes that institutionalized retardates, released to the community, face

We wish to express our gratitude to Howard S. Becker, Arlene K. Daniels, Berkeley Fleming, Ronald Keyser and Victor Marshall for their helpful suggestions. We are grateful to the Canada Council and McMaster University for their generous support of the research.

Jack Haas and William Shaffir, "The Professionalization of Medical Students: Developing Competence and a Cloak of Competence." Originally published in Symbolic Interaction, Vol. 1, No. 1. Reprinted by permission of the Society for Symbolic Interaction.

the problem of acting "normally" and not revealing their secret. Goffman has suggested that managing and manipulating impressions, and conveying a competence one would like to be believed and accepted, characterizes interactions where participants desire to be successful. Individuals and groups maintain fronts conveying certain impressions and covering up less desirable aspects of personality or behavior (Goffman, 1959).

Though managing impressions and role playing are basic parts of the sociological drama, they may be more obvious where participants perceive a potentially critical and condemning audience. This is obvious when the audience has high expectations of competence for others and expect, if not demand, displays of competence, particularly when those assumed to be competent control the situation and act or make decisions affecting the well-being of others. The affected parties then look for cues and indications of personal and/or collective (institutional) competence and practitioners organize a carefully managed presentation of self to create and sustain a reality of competence.

This concern about the competence of those granted rights and responsibilities affecting others is very obvious in the case of patient relationships with medical professionals. Patients look for competent advice and assistance and want to believe they will get it. Conversely, medical professionals, particularly doctors, want to convince those they treat that they are indeed competent and trustworthy, and that the patient can confidently allow them to diagnose, prescribe and intervene to affect the patient's condition.[1]

Studies of professional socialization (Becker *et al.*, 1961; Bloom, 1973; Merton *et al.*, 1957; Olesen and Whittaker, 1968; Ross, 1961) have shown how students or trainees adopt a professional image as they proceed through the socialization experience. Sociological studies of non-college school and training situations (Geer, 1974) show that the socialization experience involves learning specific skills and techniques as well as taking on an occupational culture including a new or altered identity. Both describe a process whereby students or trainees are altered and develop a new view of self.

The neophyte medical student leaves the lay world and joins a markedly different one (Hughes, 1958:119). The separation involves an alteration of biography, status and identity. Professional, particularly medical student, socialization, is traumatic because the separation includes not only leaving one's past but moving to a position and role accorded great power and prestige.

This separation or alienation is a social psychological process Davis (1968:237) describes as doctrinal conversion. Students change their own "lay views and imagery of the profession for those the profession ascribes to itself." Coming to medical school with a limited, lay conception of medicine, their socialization includes learning the "institutionally approved" imagery as they adopt the professional role and license. The conversion from lay to professional is not without trauma or perils. Medical students experience profound anxiety during the conversion process (Fox, 1957; Haas *et al.*, 1975).

This paper[2] describes the adoption of a cloak of competence as a critical part of the professionalizing process. We observed medical students in an innovative three-year program attempting to come to grips with the problem of meeting exaggerated expectations.[3] The profound anxiety they feel about learning medicine and becoming competent is complicated by the pressing practical demands of the situation, particularly faculty, staff and institutional expectations.

As students move through the program they are converted to the new culture and gradually adopt those symbols which represent the profession and its generally accepted truths. These symbols (language, tools, clothing, and demeanor) establish, identify and separate the bearer from outsiders, particularly client and paraprofessional audiences. Professionalization, as we observed it, involves the adoption and manipulation of symbols and symbolic behavior to create an imagery of competence and the separation and elevation of the profession from those they serve.

Faced with inordinate expectations, students professionalize by distancing themselves from those they interact with, using the symbols of this new status to distinguish their activity as grounded in mystery and sciences unfathomable to others, and managing their performances to convince others and themselves that they are competent and confident to face the immense responsibilities of their privileged role.

The Expectations of Competence

Medicine is a distinctively powerful and unique profession. Freidson outlines the characteristics of this occupation that set it apart from others. These are:

1. A general public belief in the consulting occupation's competence, in the value of its professed knowledge and skill.

2. The occupational group . . . must be the prime source of the criteria that qualify a man to work in an acceptable fashion.

3. The occupation has gained command of the exclusive competence to determine the proper content and effective method of performing some tasks (1970a:10-11).

Medicine's position, Freidson notes, is equivalent to that of a state religion: "it has an officially approved monopoly of the right to define health and illness and to treat illness" (1970a:5).

Doctors possess a unique authority because of their generally accepted expertise about human health. Their work is believed to constitute a social and individual good. Their authority is further enhanced by the historical unity of medicine and religion; the physician mediates the mysteries of scientific research through a ritual system where the doctor becomes a priest (Siegler and Osmond, 1974:42).[4]

To create the physician's unique authority requires an effective symbol system, shared and accepted by most participants in the drama. The moral authority of the physician is most complete and unassailable when the doctor fights the spectre of death. The fact that death strikes fear in human beings gives impressive, Aesculapian authority to those who are believed able to ward it off or postpone it (*ibid.*:41-52).[5]

Medical practitioners, students and physicians alike, have to deal with the inordinate and exaggerated demands of those they treat. This problem is somewhat less important to the medical student, who is protected from situations which would prematurely or inappropriately demand responsibility. Students, however, realize that the outcome of their socialization will be to meet such expectations, and hope their socialization will prepare them to meet them responsibly, competently, and confidently. According to one student:

> I think you're faced with a problem, that in a large way the public has unrealistic expectations about the medical profession. It puts the doctor in a very difficult position because you know yourself you don't know it all, but the public thinks you know it all and puts you in a position where you have to be a good actor.

While students are protected from meeting the real expectations of patients,[6] they do face the unpredictability of faculty expectations, and faculty become the major reference group or audience that students feel demand and evaluate competence. The teaching staff is responsible for evaluating and determining the progress of students. Students attempt to estimate teachers' demands, although they are ill-defined and sometimes contradictory, and try to meet these expectations. The students' immediate problem is dealing with staff whose medical interests and views differ widely. Faced with such threatening ambiguity, students try to find out the particular biases and interests of those with whom they must interact (Becker *et al.*, 1961). They soon realize that their teachers are both knowledgeable about medicine and convinced of the correctness and validity of their expertise and skill, and find that their competence and learning are assessed in situations in which they are weak, vulnerable and easily reminded of their incompetence.

Students react to the problem of meeting others' competency expectations with collective anxiety.[7] Facing exaggerated and uncertain expectations, and increasingly aware of the complexity of medical knowledge, students strive to develop a working and growing level of competence.

These problems are magnified at the school we are studying because lectures are deemphasized and there are no formal examinations, evaluations or grades. Students are evaluated on problem write-ups by their tutors and by group and self evaluations. Because these innovative forms of evaluation are new to students and more clearly reveal their personal deficiencies and problems, collective student insecurity is heightened. The absence of tests and grades contributes to their anxiety by removing the security of benchmarks of comparison and competence that examinations and grades are believed to reveal. Further, other educational systems, in which these students have been successful, allowed them a protective cloak of anonymity. These students face instead, evaluation which is largely interactional and interpersonal.

With these problems and the resulting severe anxiety, students work feverishly to meet expectations of competence which are never clear or predictable. Student-physicians must attend to their role in a network of uncertain expectations and reactions that surround students and also to the general perspective others have of the medical student position in the social structure.

The remainder of this paper describes how students resolve their uncertainty by enveloping themselves in a cloak of competence, which also includes a distancing and separation from others. The major changes students undergo center around the adoption of a professional perspective. Students become more empathetic to the profession as they begin to identify with their future role. They learn, adopt and begin to use and manipulate the symbols of the profession. They also learn the necessity of objectifying patients and controlling personal feelings and reactions. These changes provide the bases for students to successfully meet difficult expectations, enacting the professional role by adopting a cloak of competence.

Becoming Professional

From the outset, students are impressed by the tremendous responsibility of the physician. During their examination of various "psychosocial" problems, in Phase I,[8] students recognize that the physician's role is very broad. They learn that the medical profession not only deals with medical problems *per se*, but also with many apparently non-medical problems. The small group tutorial sessions, which form the major vehicle for learning at this stage of medical school, help shape students' enlarging conception of medicine and its practise. While early sessions are intended essentially to introduce students to the school's philosophy

—the educational rationale underlying the distinctive structure and organization of the medical curriculum—they also serve to teach students the duties and responsibilities of the medical profession. An excerpt from the Phase I manual for incoming students illustrates this point:

> You are also becoming health professionals—members of an historic community concerned with the alleviation of human illness, the mainte-nance of health and the understanding of disease. You will begin to realize the special nature of the 'doctor-patient relationship'. Some of you will have initial difficulty with some of the physical things—blood, operations, injury, autopsies. Other experiences are more difficult to incorporate into your growth as a health professional—deformity, chronic illness, death, pain. You will see that physicians and other health professionals are ordinary human beings—with tempers, insensi-tivities and varied motivations (Phase I Manual, 1974:25).

The physicians' influence on the way students learn about and define medical situations is critical to the professionalizing process. From the earliest stages of their medical training, and as they advance through the program, students continually watch doctors' working habits, listen to their philosophies of medical practice, take note of their competencies and incompetencies, and reflect upon the nature of their own present and future relationships with patients. The physicians with whom they practice their clinical skills become models after whom students can pattern their own beliefs and behavior:

> certainly there are people who impress me . . . certain aspects of their personality that I would want to incorporate in some way in my prac-tice. It is easy to model yourself after people you see on the wards . . . You don't know anything and you start watching them and before too long you find yourself in a position where you tend to model yourself after these people. . . .

A dramatic shift in the professionalization process occurs when the students are given greater responsibility for patient health care and management. This occurs during the clerkship phase. Students become more integral members of a health care team, are delegated some tasks requiring personal responsibility, and become accountable in ways almost entirely new to them. As they assume increased responsibilities and make medical judgments for which they must account to a variety of professionals, they develop an increasingly sympathetic outlook towards their future profession. The following examples illustrate the point.

> [The conversation centers around clerkship and whether this phase of the program alters one's view of the medical profession.] I think it does from the point of view that you can more or less see other people's

situations much more because you're in their boat . . . . I agree with that. Having been in it [medicine], I can see why some patients are dealt with quickly perhaps.

I remember when we were way back in Phase II and Phase I, we would go see a patient with a clinical skills preceptor, and he might have said something to the patient that seemed rude, and I'd get all very indignant about it and say "My God, you're not being sensitive." While that may have been justified now that I'm on the ward I can see that in a way it's a bit silly to take that one episode, because what you are seeing is one episode in a long history of the relationship between that patient and his doctor. You're taking this totally out of context and it's really not relevant to criticize unless you really know the relationship. Now I'm much less free with those sorts of criticisms. . . .

Through observation, role-taking, imitation and practice, students begin identifying with the organization and practice of the medical profession.

As students observe and experience the problems of medical care and practice, they develop an understanding and identification with the profession and the ways its members confront their problems. Students are less quick to voice criticisms of what they see, as they come to take the role, directly or indirectly, of those they will soon follow. This creeping commitment and identification with the profession is accompanied by their symbolic transformation from lay person to medical student-physician.

The Symbols of Professionalism

The professionalization of medical students is facilitated by symbols the neophytes take on which serve to announce to insiders and outsiders how they are to be identified. During the first weeks of their studies students begin wearing white lab jackets with plastic name tags identifying them as medical students. In addition, since clinical skill sessions are included in the curriculum from the beginning, students participate in a variety of settings with the tools of the doctoring trade carried on their person. This attire clearly identifies students to participants and visitors of the hospital/school setting. Along with their newly acquired identity kit, students begin to learn and express themselves in the medical vernacular. Distinctive dress, badges, tools and language provide the student with symbols which announce their role and activity. They are identified as students learning to be doctors.

The significance of these symbols to the professionalization process is critical. The symbols serve, on the one hand, to identify and unite the bearers as members of a community of shared interests, purposes and identification (Roth, 1957). Simultaneously, the symbols distinguish and separate their possessors from lay people, making their role seem more mysterious, shrouded, and priest-like (Bramson, 1973). The early possession of these symbols serves to hasten their identification and commitment to the profession, while at the same time, facilitating their separation from the lay world.

At this point, their very selection of medicine as a career has produced a set of reactions by friends, family and others which reinforce in the students' minds the idea that they are becoming very special people. Immediately upon acceptance into medical school, students perceive themselves being related to, in typified fashion, as medical students and future physicians. This reaction of others intensifies as students enter training and immerse themselves in it. At the same time, students see that they must devote more and more time and energy to their studies, and less time to past relationships and interests. They find themselves increasingly separated from social worlds outside of medicine; more and more they find themselves either alone or with other medical people. The socialization experience is intense, extensive, anguishing, and exhausting.

One of the first difficult tasks that faces students is to begin to learn and communicate in the symbolic system that defines medical work and workers. Immediately in tutorials, readings, demonstrations and rounds, students are inundated with a language they know they are expected to become facile in. Their task is even more difficult because this exotic language is used to describe very complex processes and understandings. Students are taken aback at the difficulty of learning to communicate in their new language. They begin carrying medical dictionaries to help them translate and define terms and phrases. They complain about the problems of simultaneously translating readings with understanding, and committing to memory such elusive material.

The separation between "we" and "they" becomes clearer to students as they are absorbed into the medical culture. As they move through the culture, they learn how the symbols are used to communicate and enforce certain definitions of the situation. Students learn how practicing physicians use these symbols of the profession to shape and control the definition of the situation.

The ability to use the language symbols of medicine defines members of the profession and creates a boundary that is only occasionally erased. Reflecting on the significance of this technical terminology, a student remarks:

> you just can't survive if you don't learn the jargon. It's not so much an effort to identify as it is an effort to survive. People in medicine have a world unto themselves and a language unto themselves. It's a world with a vocabulary ... and a vocabulary that, no question about it, creates a fraternity that excludes the rest of the world and it's a real tyranny to lay persons who don't understand it. ...

The adoption of the medical symbol system and imagery reinforces students' commitment and identification with medicine. At the same time, the manipulation of these symbols serves to distinguish and separate their users from others. An important and related consequence of this separation is the elevation of the practitioner to a position of control and detachment. The symbols identify their bearers as people who have been prepared and trained to deal coolly, dispassionately, and authoritatively with the most provocative and critical aspects of human feelings and emotion, as people who can transcend the pressures and emotive character of medical situations and act competently.

Turning off your Feelings

Previous research on medical students has shown that a major effect of medical education is to make the medical student more cynical and less idealistic (Beale and Kriesberg, 1959; Becker and Geer, 1958; Eron, 1955). Our data also suggest that as students move through school and develop a professional self-image, and thus begin to take on the identity of a doctor, their views on medicine become transformed from what they describe as an idealistic phase to what they believe is a more realistic one. Accounting for this transition, one student claims:

> . . . first of all, the exposure to what really goes on. You sort of keep your eyes open and you really get an idea of the real world of medicine. . . . The other part of it is when you're allowed responsibility . . . and you really become involved with patients.

Students become less vocal in their questioning and criticisms of the medical profession. They attribute many of their earlier concerns to naiveté, and argue for a more sympathetic view of doctors and the profession as a whole:

> I think I went through a phase, as I went from knowing very little about medicine to a little bit . . . You go through a sort of stage of disillusion in which you sort of expect doctors to be perfect, and the medical profession and treatment and everything else to be perfect. And you find out that it's not. So you sort of react to that. I think now, after about two years, I'm starting to get to the phase now where I'm quite pleased with it really. Part of it is getting into arguments about other professions and this brings out things that you've thought about but not really verbalized. . . . A particular friend of mine is in law and he was talking about malpractice suits and it really makes you think that knowing doctors the way you do, and I've seen them operate, if other professions were as self-critical as doctors were and had a good sense of responsibility to duty, then I think a lot of the professions would be a lot better off. Part of the flack that you hear about medical doctors and malpractice suits, and about things that go wrong, are partly due to the fact that doctors

tend to look after themselves and examine their own profession very carefully.

Though not entirely pleased by the outcome of this transformation, students know that their views of medicine are being altered. They describe these changes as part of their personal and professional growth. They argue that they are becoming more mature personally and developing a clearer and sharper understanding of the world of medicine. Most importantly, they admit a willingness to accept the situation as a small price for becoming more competent. With only minor exceptions they accept the present sacrifice of their ideals as a necessary condition of medical training, and hope to recapture their idealism at a later time:

> There are certain things that I do, and I'm not the only one, that I don't think are right. I don't think I should do them but I don't think I have a choice right now. I've got to play the game. I don't know if this is going to be possible, but I hope that later on after I graduate I'll be able to run my practice the way I'd like, and not like you're supposed to do it.

The hope and belief that they will be in a more opportune position to express and act upon their initial idealism after graduation is coupled, for many, with a more sombre realization that matters are unlikely to change. On the basis of their observations and deliberations many students become resigned to their behavior as physicians always coming under close scrutiny and control from their colleagues. Most students do not have high hopes of being able to change medicine.

Although they are often initially dismayed by how physicians and other hospital staff treat patients, they come to accept that the objectification of patients is a routine feature of doctor-patient relationships. It is the "professional" way to deal with medical situations.[9] In time they accept the view that patients must be objectified and depersonalized or the doctor will be unable to maintain clinical objectivity (Coombs and Powers, 1975; Emerson, 1970). While initially bothered, even offended, by this detachment, they come to see it as part of the professional situation over which they have little control. They believe it is, at least, temporarily necessary if they are to learn clinical symptoms and pathology, thus adding to their medical knowledge and competence.

> I think you realize that there is a structural problem, and there are a lot of demands made on you and you are forced to act in certain ways just to accomplish your work. But right now in the training phase, I find if the clinical preceptor takes me around to listen to six patients with heart murmurs and I only have five minutes with each patient, I don't get concerned that I'm not getting it on with the patient, because I'm trying to learn about heart murmurs.

Striving for competence is the primary student rationale to explain avoiding or shutting off emotional reactions. As they progress through the program students come to express the belief that their relationship with the patient should be governed strictly by the patient's medical problem; emotional feelings are a hindrance. They believe that they do not have time for both learning and caring, and learn to stifle their feelings because of the higher value they and others place on competence.

Students also believe that they are being trained for busy lives. Accepting the hectic pace as inevitable, they recognize that it is not temporary, but will continue throughout their medical career. Their work in the hospitals impresses on them the long hours that physicians devote to their work:

> If you look around at people who are teaching you, they often have a pretty rough life as far as time commitment and work. The work doesn't end when you get out of medical school and you can see somebody who is forty-five or fifty and married and has a couple of kids, in on Saturday afternoons working away, and being on call in the evenings.

Students recognize that many physicians work long and irregular hours. As they embark upon the clerkship phase of the program, they discover that the hospital routine they must fit demands that their everyday lives be organized around medicine. A student comments on the time commitment:

> At the end of Phase III the party's over. In Phase IV your life is not your own already, and that's a very shocking experience when your life is not your own.

The dominant concern with learning medicine leads students to maintain their learning efficiency and productivity. Students come to believe that they have no time for the frills of emotional involvement and quickly learn to close off feelings that interfere with their work (Lief and Fox, 1963). The following statement by a student emphasizes the idea of productivity:

> You can't function if you think about things like that [death and dying]. Everything you see sort of gets in there and turns about in your mind and you aren't productive. The reason you have to shut it off is because you won't be productive.... I think that my prime objective is to learn the pathology and just to know it and then, understanding that, I can go back to these other things and worry about the personal part of it.

During the first ten weeks of the curriculum the students are introduced to, among other things, the psychosocial component of health care. As many students are interested in working with and helping people, and are aware that medical problems have many different causes, the emphasis on the psychosocial issues gives them an opportunity to express their views concerning social, economic, political and moral aspects of medicine. However, even before Phase I is completed, they are eager to start what they consider to be their "real" medical studies. Reflecting the views of others in the class, a student says:

> [In Phase I] you really concentrate on a lot of psychosocial issues. But it becomes really obvious before the ten weeks are up that you are getting tired of talking about that kind of stuff, and you want to get on with it.

The students' concern for the psychosocial aspects of medicine are not entirely ignored when they enter Phase II of their program. As they are gradually introduced to the content and "core" of medicine, they begin to realize that there is too much to know and little time in which to learn it all. Like the religious or political convert who becomes fanatically observant and committed, students devote themselves to the task of learning medicine. Time becomes a commodity that must be spent wisely. They become very concerned about not misusing or wasting their time studying certain topics deemed unproductive. In this context, the psychosocial component becomes less important:

> One thing you have to do at medical school is pick up all the pathophysiology and to pick up all of the anatomy and pick up the clinical histories, the presentations, the clinical skills and so on. So psychosocial time is really a luxury, it can't really be afforded sometimes. Not that it gets pushed out of the way. It's just that in a tutorial group if you are given two weeks and two hours per tutorial group, how do you most profitably spend that time in terms of the task at hand? Do you want to learn a lot of what we call the core material . . . or do you want to rehash a lot of arguments that are of fundamental human importance but really can't be resolved within a reasonable time limit.

Although they put them aside, students continue to recognize that psychosocial matters are important. They believe this area must be neglected, however, in the interests of acquiring as much medical knowledge and competence as possible. They believe that if they feel for their patients and become involved with them they will not become professionally competent:

> When you see someone who is going to die, especially when you're still learning, you're really cut off from that personal level. You just clue into the pathology. You really shut off. You sort of turn it out of your mind that this person is going to die. You just look at the pathology, all of the symptoms, and you have one train of thought. You don't really think,

"What about the family?" what they must be going through.... You can't fall to pieces because you find your patient is going to die in three months or is rapidly going downhill. You have a role to play here. You can't come apart and cry in the patient's room for half an hour every time you see him.

Most students move to the view that personal concerns for the patient should not intrude on the physician's professional responsibility:

This is a really stupid analogy but it probably rings true too. When you go bowling you can't worry about the kinds of problems you have selling your house because you're bowling and you want a good score, yet you're being a human and still bowling. So the point is you're trying to tackle the task at hand and those kinds of emotions are inappropriate to that kind of situation. And I don't think you would feel embarrassed that you didn't think about all the trouble you had selling your house because you're bowling. And it's essentially the same kind of thing you have to deal with at various treatment levels with the patient. If you are talking to the family you've got to bring back all those emotions and you've got to use them. If you are dealing with a nursing staff and deciding how you're going to change the solutions and what type of drug you're going to add to this guy's regimen, you can't be saying "Oh the poor bastard, we're going to stick another needle in him." You can't do that.

Student concerns about learning medicine, making the most efficient use of time, and establishing some bases of certainty and security in their work are all reflected in the selected interest they take in patients with unusual pathology (Becker *et al.*, 1961). Discussing the kind of patients that he looked forward to seeing, a student claims:

A patient who has physical findings. Gees, I don't care what the findings are. It's a fantastic experience to see that physical finding. They may only have two or even one.... In order to do a physical exam you've got to have something there to feel. Someone can tell you this is the way to feel for a lump in the stomach, but if there is no lump there you are not going to learn how to feel it.... I think that's what I get the most out of, getting exposure to the pathology, feeling things that I may not feel.

The high point for students is making a correct diagnosis by sleuthing out relevant material, and knowing with some assurance the diagnosis is valid and the treatment competent. A student hypothesizes about such noteworthy experiences:

I think the magic moments are when someone goes in to see a patient that they haven't seen their records or charts, and they come up with their own diagnosis. And they get the charts and they've discovered some rare tropical disease that they had and they got it on the head. That's the magical moment I've heard of.

Students alter their understanding of how medicine should be practised. Unable to feel as deeply concerned about the patient's total condition as they believe they should, they discover an approach that justifies concentrating only on the person's medical problem. As a student remarks:

> Somebody will say "Listen to Mrs. Jones' heart. It's just a little thing flubbing on the table." And you forget about the rest of her. Part of that is the objectivity and it helps in learning in the sense that you can go in to a patient, put your stethoscope on the heart, listen to it and walk out. ... The advantage is that you can go in a short time and see a patient, get the important things out of the patient and leave.

As students learn to objectify patients they lose their sensitivity for them. When they can concentrate on the interesting pathology of the patient's condition, students' feelings for the patient's total situation are eroded:

> In the neuro unit you can define exactly where the lesion is by deciding on how well you know the conducting system and, of course, if there is a lesion closer to the cortex than to the midbrain, then you will see all kinds of behavioral problems. But then you won't think they are a psychiatric case. They are a neurological case showing an interesting effect.... And you get that kind of approach and you really lose your sensitivity in terms of what's happening in terms of the anxiety of the patient.

The students do not lose their idealism and assume a professional mask without a struggle. But even when they see and feel the worst, students recognize that they do not have the time to crusade. That would interfere with the learning of medicine and impede their efforts to become competent.

Students learn to become objective during their clinical skills sessions in hospital settings. They are introduced to striking examples of how patients' needs, rights and dignities are submerged to the clinical task at hand. The following examples indicate the kind of objectivity the students are exposed to and affected by:

> What I do remember about Phase II that really got me when I did go to a cancer clinic at the Fensteran and I saw the way they were just herding in ladies that had hysterectomies and cancer, and just the way the doctors would walk right in and wouldn't even introduce us as students, and just open them up and just look and say a lot of heavy jargon. And the ladies would be saying, "How is it?", "Am I better, worse?" And

they say in this phony reassuring tone, "Yes, you're fine", and take you into the hallway and say how bad the person was.

They hardly talked to the patient at all. Like this was a big checkup after waiting three months or six months and then the doctor whips in for two minutes to take a quick look and then they're gone. We would get in there and he'd hold the speculum and we'd all take a look and we would just herd right out again into another room and have a look and herd out again. I thought the dehumanization was awful. . . . So that's what got me, what turned me off to a specialty. I didn't tell the doctor how I felt at the time, but when I left other people felt the same way. I remember another student came up to me and he was put off by that whole thing too, and we sort of bitched to each other about how rough it was and how we were going to do something about it and we never did. We let it slide by.

Students often share accounts of such experiences during social occasions. They are affected by these experiences and want to know whether other people have had similar experiences and if they react in the same way. Students discover that such experiences are a routine feature of the hospital setting, regularly accepted by the medical profession. More importantly, however, they learn and accept the rationales usually given. They heed their teachers' reminders that their primary object at this stage of their career is to absorb as much pathology as possible. This end, they are told, is best achieved by examining patients. They are made to realize that the physician's high case load precludes attending to anything but the patient's medical condition.

Students use the pressures of learning medicine and developing competence to rationalize their growing alienation from patients and their willingness to ignore the more extreme examples of objectivity:

You sort of go in and you don't know the people that are under anesthesia. Just practice putting the tube in, and the person wakes up with a sore throat, and well, it's just sort of a part of the procedure kind of thing. "How do you feel about intubating dead on arrivals?" Someone comes in who has croaked, "Well come on, here is a chance to practice your intubation." It seems awfully barbaric.

Though not entirely pleased with how they see medicine practiced, and how they practice it themselves, they elect to put their idealism in abeyance. Their solution to the problem of protecting themselves from becoming emotionally involved with patients is to present themselves as they believe they are expected to behave. Their assessment of the situation is that they are to act professionally (competently and objectively) and they organize their self-presentation to coincide with this expectation.

Acting the Professional Role

Students believe they are expected to act as if they are in the know, not in ways which might put their developing competence into question. The pressure to be seen as competent by faculty, fellow students, hospital personnel and patients narrows the range of alternative roles students can assume. Students recognize their low status in the hospital hierarchy and on hospital rotations. They realize that the extent of their medical knowledge can easily be called into question by fellow students, tutors, interns, residents and faculty. To reduce the possibility of embarrassment and humiliation which, at this stage in their medical career, is easily their fate, students attempt to reduce the unpredictability of their situation by manipulating an impression of themselves as enthusiastic, interested, and eager to learn. At the same time, students seize opportunities which allow them to impress others, particularly faculty and fellow students, with their growing competence and confidence.

Two students describe the practicality in, at times, assuming this demeanor:

> JIM: And you don't want to play the game either of just, I'll be a student and you be teacher.
> JOHN: Yeah, and at the same time, you don't want to come off as appearing stupid. If you happen to believe something and you have good reason for thinking it, you try to defend yourself, but in a very very diplomatic manner, all the time being careful not to step on anybody's toes. And yet, at the same time, nobody is careful not to step on our toes. We have to take it. Residents always will say: "No, it is not like that." But if you say, "Well, it is my understanding according to what I just read in Harrison's, that is what they said. I mean, I don't know if it is right or not. I am just telling you what I read."
> JIM: That's right.
> JOHN: That is literally what we have to say.... This happened with the chief of medicine. He said, "Well you don't get [lost in transcription]" and I said: "Well wait a minute." I said, "Harrison's said you do get it." And the chief of medicine turned to me and said, "I don't give a shit what Harrison's said." ... And I said, "Okay, but that is what I read."

Although a basic objective of the school's philosophy is to encourage learning through problem-solving and a questioning attitude throughout the medical career, the philosophy does not help students' overriding problem of appearing competent. A perspective shared by students to manage an appearance of competence is to limit their initiatives to those situations which will be convincing demonstrations of their competence. Some students decide, for example, to ask questions in areas with which they are already familiar, to cultivate an impression of competence.

> The best way of impressing others with your competence is asking questions you know the answers to. Because if they ever put it back on you: "Well what do you think?" then you tell them what you think and you'd give a very intelligent answer because you knew it. You didn't ask it to find out information. You ask it to impress people.

The general strategy that the students adopt is to mask their uncertainty and anxiety with an image of self-confidence. Image making becomes recognized as being as important as technical competence. As one student remarks: "We have to be good actors, put across the image of self-confidence, that you know it all. . . . "

Two students, referring to the importance of creating the right impression, claim:

> It's like any fraternity. You've got to know. You've got to have a certain amount of basic knowledge before they think it's worth talking to you. If you display less than that basic knowledge their reflexes come into play and they think this person is an idiot. Let's find out exactly how much they don't know, rather than building on what you do know. That's a different maneuver. Being out in the pale, not worth talking to, or within the pale and well worth talking to. There is image management in every profession. It's very unfortunate because the people who precisely need the help are those who are willing to admit their ignorance, and I've been in tutorials where people who are really willing to admit their ignorance tend to get put down for it. After a while they stop asking questions. That's very unfortunate.

> Dr. Jones who was my advisor or boss for medicine, he always came and did rounds on Wednesday mornings. Well he didn't have very many patients on the service, but we always knew that his interest was in endocrinology, and he knew damn well if he had an endocrine patient. Or, if he didn't have an endocrine patient on the ward and knew somebody else had one, we knew damn well that he was going to pick that endocrine patient to talk about. And so, of course, Tuesday night, any dummy can read up Tuesday night like hell on the new American Diabetic Association standards for diabetes or hyperglycemia and you can read up like hell on it, or read it over twice, and you can handle general medicine. So the next day you seem fairly knowledgeable. . . . That afternoon you forget about it because you figure Thursday morning hematology people make their rounds and, of course, you have to read up on hematology. . . .

The pressure to conform is perhaps even more extreme at this school than at other medical schools because its evaluation system is much more pervasive and a large part of it is generated by students. Students observe each other, seeking to establish a base of comparison. A student argues the pervasiveness of evaluation and its consequences when he says:

> I think that what we might find is that we are more controlled and conformist and more alike than students in other programs. In the other programs they are able to be anonymous, to sit in class and say nothing. And to take tests and be evaluated in that way but they don't have to reveal much of themselves. We are constantly subject to the scrutiny of others, and constantly engaged in addressing others who are evaluating us.

The students are acutely aware of the relationship between impression management and successful evaluation. While the evaluation ought to consist of an objective assessment of the students' abilities to conduct a diagnosis and prescribe a course of treatment, the outcome is, in fact, shaped by the students' abilities to behave as if they are able to accomplish these tasks. The following excerpt graphically illustrates a student's attempt to conceptualize the manner in which a successful evaluation is obtained:

> [In clerkship] how does one person get a good evaluation and another doesn't? We made this analogy between feathers and black eyes. Depending on how many black eyes you got and how many feathers, that's what your final evaluation was based on. If you began in the beginning with too many black eyes, you could never get rid of a black eye. A blue and black eye would always stay there and they would always recognize you with the black eyes. It didn't matter how many feathers you got afterwards, but you'd always have a black eye. Whereas, if you started off with feathers, and you got enough feathers in the beginning, so you almost had a full hatband of feathers, it doesn't matter what you did. One may fall off every now and then. . . . And then you'd get to a stage where you'd have all these feathers, shit, a whole roll of feathers, and you couldn't for the life of you, you just couldn't get a black eye. You were invincible. You were the big chief. And that's what clerkship is all about—impressing. And if you impress a person enough, and you impress him at a critical time, then that was it—you got your good evaluation.

Students realize that to be a good student-physician is either to be or appear to be competent. They observe that others react to their role playing. A student describes the self-fulfilling nature of this process when he says:

> To be a good GP, you've got to be a good actor, you've got to respond to a situation. You have to be quick, pick up the dynamics of what is

going on at the time and try to make the person leave the office thinking that you know something. And a lot of people, the way they handle that is by letting the patient know that they know it all, and only letting out a little bit at a time, and as little as possible. I think that they eventually reach a plateau where they start thinking themselves they are really great and they know it all, because they have these people who are worshipping at their feet.

The process of adopting the cloak of competence is justified by students as helpful to the patient. A student summarizes the relationship between acting competently and patients responding to such a performance by getting well when he says:

You know the patients put pressure on you to act as if you are in the know. If you know anything about the placebo effect, you know that a lot of the healing and curing of patients does not involve doing anything that will really help them, but rather creating confidence in the patient that things are being done and will be done. We know that the placebo effect for example has even cured cancer patients. If they have the confidence in the doctor and what doctor and what treatment they are undergoing, they are much more likely to get well, irrespective of the objective effects of the treatment.

Students learn the practical importance of the cloak of competence. It provides patients a "taken-for-granted" situation about the competence of the professional that is important for their confidence in the professional and the treatment process. Students also find it helps them deal with the unpredictable and potentially threatening reactions of those who view or evaluate their work.

Conclusion

Everett Hughes provides all students of occupations with a sound sociological maxim when he says:

I think it a good rule to assume that a feature of work behavior found in one occupation, even a minor or odd one, will be found in others. The fact that it is denied at first by the people in some occupations, or that it has not been revealed by previous research, should not be considered sufficient evidence it is not there (1952:425).

Hughes's principle makes sociological research both exciting and mundane. The basic processes of social life operate throughout the social structure. All social groups create boundaries and differences, view themselves ethnocentrically, and create and manipulate symbols to present themselves in the most favorable ways.[10] All individuals and groups strive to protect themselves from ridicule and charges of incompetence. In this sense, our paper only describes what has been a "taken-for-granted" understanding of social life: much behavior is performance designed to elicit certain reactions. Professional behavior is, or can be, understood as performance.[11]

In this paper we have described the professionalization of medical students. Medical school socialization involves meeting two problematic sets of expectations and reactions, one future and one immediate. The long-term problem is for the aspiring professional to successfully meet the sometimes exaggerated expectations of clients and outsiders who cast the physician in a demi-god role. The more immediate problem of medical students is to successfully negotiate the socialization experience by meeting the variable expectations and reactions of those (students, staff and faculty) who control student reputation and success.

From the very beginning of the socialization experience students are impressed by the responsibility they are preparing for. As students begin to learn the range of competencies expected of them, they develop a powerful and sustained insecurity about their ability to perform competently. Students collectively perceive that there is too much to know and not enough time to learn it all. Their initial reaction is to work feverishly in an attempt to develop a working and growing competency.

As students move through the program, and particularly in clinical situations, they begin to adopt a professionalizing perspective to meet others' expectations. They learn in their contacts with medical staff, faculty and practitioners the beliefs and practices of the profession. They begin to identify more closely with the profession as they grow more separated from the lay culture and more immersed in the new medical culture. They begin to adopt a professional role and identification, using and manipulating the symbols of the profession (clothing, tools, language and demeanor) to enact a set of images defining them as student-physicians.

Medical students learn a new symbol system that not only distinguishes them as neophyte members of a distinctive and powerful community but creates an imagery of authoritativeness and competence. At the same time, students learn that the student role requires an objectification of patients and a covering of personal feelings and reactions. Students initially adopt this professional-scientific posture to help them increase their learning efficiency. They believe they do not have enough time to deal with psychosocial problems because of the dominant concern with learning the "core" of medicine. With more clinical experiences the rationale for objectifying patients and closing off feelings comes to be reinterpreted as professionally appropriate and, even, helpful to patients.

Students focus on the "pathology" of patients as the necessary way of learning medicine. They observe that patient objectification is a *pro forma* part of clinical relationships and they realize that idealistic conceptions of patient care must be shunted aside in order to develop a professionally appropriate competence.

Students observe, particularly in clinical situations, the physician-patient relationship. They come to realize that an important part of becoming a doctor is learning a role or roles that project an image of competence and reduce threats or charges of incompetence. In a situation where too much is expected, professionalism provides a protective shield helping students and practitioners define and exert control over medical situations.

Our findings should be analogous to other professions and their socialization processes. The process of making some expert and more competent separates professionals from those they are presumed to help and serves to create a situation where the exaggerated expectations of competence are managed by symbolically defining and controlling the situation to display the imagery of competence. Impression management is basic and fundamental in those occupations and professions which profess competence in matters seriously affecting others.

Edgerton (1967) believes that the central and shared commonality of the mentally retarded released from institutions was for them to develop themselves in a cloak of competence to deny the discomforting reality of their stigma. The development of a cloak of competence is, perhaps, most apparent for those who must meet exaggerated expectations. The problem of meeting other's enlarged expectations is magnified for those uncertain about their ability to manage a convincing performance. Moreover, the performer faces the personal problem of reconciling his private self-awareness and uncertainty with his publicly displayed image. For those required to perform beyond their capacities, in order to be successful, there is the constant threat of breakdown or exposure. For both retardates and professionals the problem and, ironically, the solution, are similar. Expectations of competence are dealt with by strategies of impression management, specifically, manipulation and concealment. Interactional competencies depend on convincing presentations and much of professionalism requires the masking of insecurity and incompetence with the symbolic-interactional cloak of competence.

NOTES

1. Parsons (1969) argues that the competence gap between doctor and patient and the inherent stratification is bridged by trust. Freidson disagrees arguing that the differential possession of technical knowledge perpetuates the privilege and authority of physicians. He concludes that: "Insistence on faith constitutes insistence that the client give up his role as an independent adult and, by so neutralizing him, protects the esoteric foundation of the profession's institutionalized authority" (1970b:143).

2. This paper is based on data that were collected largely during the first two

years of a three-year study we are conducting on the socialization of medical students at a medical school in Ontario, Canada. The data were collected by means of participant observation and interviews. We have observed students during the full range of their educational and informal activities and to date have interviewed fifty-five of the eighty students in the class. We are presently completing the fieldwork phase of the study as students approach their licensing examination and graduation. We will be writing a monograph, based on the research, in the coming year.

3. Unlike most medical schools, the school we are studying has a three-year program where long summer vacations are eliminated. Admission is not restricted to individuals with strong pre-medical or science backgrounds. The school deemphasizes lectures and has no formal tests or grades. Students are introduced to clinical settings from the very beginning of their studies. Learning revolves around a "problem-solving" approach as students meet in six-person tutorial groups. An analysis of the consequences of such innovations will be described in subsequent writings.

4. Ernest Becker (1975) argues that man's innate and all-encompassing fear of death drives him to attempt to transcend death through culturally standardized hero systems and symbols.

5. The complaint that physicians avoid patient death and dying is partly explained in the basic human fear of death (Becker, 1975). Although they may grow more desensitized to others' death and dying, they are, at the same time, more often reminded of their own mortality. Moreover, the doctor facing such a situation of telling patient and/or family of impending death is vulnerable to charges of incompetence or failure and it is competence or its appearance that defines the doctor's role.
Quint (1965) describes institutionalized practices of information control by medical professionals which protect professionals from unpleasant and emotionally disturbing scenes with terminally ill patients and also cushions involvement with their own identity feelings, both personal and professional, when these are threatened.

6. Students are aware of the exaggerated expectations of outsiders towards the medical profession and the desire to believe in the ability of practitioners to perform miracles of healing and cure. Although the program we are studying provides students contact with patients from the very beginning, patients do not expect such competence from students and students are generally relieved from having to perform credibly, competently and confidently, with them. The situations where students see patients are collectively defined as learning situations and students are not expected, nor allowed, to put their developing competence to test.

7. Although students collectively respond to this uncertain situation with anxiety, the very nature of their problem, performing competently, creates a situation of pluralistic ignorance (Schanck, 1932:102, 130-31; Mayer and Rosenblatt, 1975) where students are reluctant to fully reveal and share their uncertainty with others.

8. The program is divided into five Phases: Phase I lasts ten weeks; Phase II twelve weeks; Phase III forty weeks; Phase IV essentially the last half of the three-year program, is the clinical clerkship. Student electives, vacations and a review phase - Phase V - make up the remainder of the M.D. program.

9. The core of the professional attitude toward the patient is to be found in what Parsons (1951) has termed "affective neutrality". As Bloom and Wilson have written: "This orientation is the vital distancing mechanism which

prevents the practitioner from becoming the patient's colleague in illness. . . . Affective neutrality constitutes the physician's prime safeguard against the antitherapeutic dangers of countertransference" (1972:321). The management of closeness and detachment in professional-client relations is discussed in Joan Emerson (1970), and in Charles Kadushin (1962). For a discussion of the socialization of medical students toward a detached attitude, see Morris J. Daniels (1960). For an insightful analysis of how student-physicians come to manage the clinical role pertaining to death and dying, and learn to retain composure, no matter how dramatic the death scene, see Coombs and Powers (1975).

10. For an example of an occupation where members shroud themselves in a cloak of competence see Haas (1972, 1974, and particularly, 1977). High steel ironworkers, like physicians, must act competently and confidently in fateful matters. Ironworker apprentices, like student-physicians, were observed attempting to control others' definitions of them by acting competently and not revealing their fear or ignorance. In both situations we find neophytes reluctant to reveal their incompetence.

11. Ernest Becker reminds social scientists about their most important question and responsibility when he says: "How do we get rid of the power to mystify? The talent and processes of mesmerization and mystification have to be exposed. Which is another way of saying that we have to work against both structural and psychological unfreedom in society. The task of science would be to explore both of these dimensions" (1975:165). Our analysis suggests that demystification requires an appreciation of the interactive, collaborative and symbolic nature of professional-client relations and definitions of the situation.

BIBLIOGRAPHY

Becker, Ernest. *Escape from Evil.* New York: The Free Press, 1975.

Becker, Howard S. and Blanche Geer. "The Fate of Idealism in Medical School." *American Sociological Review,* Vol. 23 (1958), pp 50-56.

Becker, Howard S., Blanche Geer, Everett C. Hughes and Anselm Strauss. *Boys in White: Student Culture in Medical School.* Chicago: University of Chicago Press, 1961.

Bloom, Samuel W. and Robert N. Wilson. "Patient-Practitioner Relationships," pp. 315-39 in H. E. Freeman, S. Levine and L. G. Reeder (eds.), *Handbook of Medical Sociology.* Englewood Cliffs, N.J.: Prentice-Hall, 1972.

Bramson, Roy. "The Secularization of American Medicine." *Hastings Center Studies,* (1973), pp. 17-28.

Coombs, Robert H. and Pauline S. Powers. "Socialization for Death: The Physician's Role." *Urban Life,* Vol. 4 (1975), pp. 250-71.

Daniels, Morris J. "Affect and its Control in the Medical Intern." *American Journal of Sociology,* Vol. 66 (1960), pp. 259-67.

Davis, Fred. "Professional Socialization as Subjective Experience: The Process of Doctrinal Conversion among Student Nurses," pp. 235-51 in Howard S. Becker *et al.* (eds.), *Institutions And The Person.* Chicago: Aldine Publishing Company, 1968.

Edgerton, Robert B. *The Cloak of Competence: Stigma In The Lives Of the Mentally Retarded.* Berkeley: University of California Press, 1967.

Emerson, Joan P. "Behavior in Private Places: Sustaining Definitions of Reality in Gynecological Examinations," pp. 73-97 in Hans Peter Dreitzel (ed.), *Recent Sociology.* New York: The Macmillan Company, 1970.

Eron, Leonard D. "Effect of Medical Education on Medical Students." *Journal of Medical Education,* Vol. 10. (1955), pp. 559-66.

Fox, Renée. "Training for Uncertainty," pp. 207-41 in Robert K. Merton, George G. Reader and Patricia L. Kendall (eds.), *The Student Physician.* Cambridge, Mass.: Harvard University Press, 1957.

Freidson, Eliot. *Profession of Medicine.* New York: Dodds Mead and Co, 1970a.

————. *Professional Dominance,* New York: Atherton, 1970b.

Geer, Blanche (ed.). *Learning to Work.* Beverly Hills: Sage Publications, Inc, 1972.

Goffman, Erving. *The Presentation of Self in Everyday Life.* New York: Doubleday Anchor Books, 1959.

Haas, Jack. "Binging: Educational Control among High Steel Ironworkers." *American Behavioral Scientist,* Vol. 16 (1972), pp. 27-34.

————. "The Stages of the High Steel Ironworker Apprentice Career." *The Sociological Quarterly,* Vol. 15 (1974), pp. 93-108.

————. "Learning Real Feelings: A Study of High Steel Ironworkers' Reactions to Fear and Danger." *Sociology of Work and Occupations,* Vol. 4 (1977), pp. 147-70.

Haas, Jack, Victor Marshall and William Shaffir. "Anxiety and Changing Conceptions of Self: A Study of First-year Medical Students." Paper presented at the Canadian Sociological and Anthropological Association, May, 1975.

Hughes, Everett C. "The Sociological Study of Work: An Editorial Foreword." *American Journal of Sociology,* Vol. 57 (1952), pp. 423-26.

————. *Men and Their Work.* Glencoe: The Free Press, 1958.

Kadushin, Charles. "Social Distance between Client and Professional." *American Journal of Sociology,* Vol. 67 (1962), pp. 517-31.

Lief, Harold I. and Renée Fox. "Training for 'Detached Concern' in Medical Students," pp. 12-35 in Lief, H. I., V. Lief and N. R. Lief (eds.), *The Psychological Basis of Medical Practice.* New York: Harper and Row, 1963.

Mayer, John E. and Aaron Rosenblatt. "Encounters with Danger: Social Workers in the Ghetto." *Sociology of Work and Occupations,* Vol. 2 (1975), pp. 227-45.

Olesen, Virginia L. and Elvi W. Whittaker. *The Silent Dialogue.* San Francisco: Jossey-Bass Inc, 1968.

Parsons, Talcott. *The Social System.* London: Routledge and Kegan Paul, 1951.

————. "Research with Human Subjects and the Professional Complex." *Daedalus,* Vol. 98 (1969), pp. 325-60.

Phase I Manual, 1974.

Quint, Jeanne C. "Institutionalized Practises of Information Control." *Psychiatry,* Vol. 28 (1956), pp. 119-32.

Ross, Aileen D. *Becoming a Nurse.* Toronto: The Macmillan Company of Canada Ltd, 1961.

Roth, Julius A. "Ritual and Magic in the Control of Contagion." *American Sociological Review,* Vol. 22 (1957), pp. 310-14.

Schanck, Richard L. "A Study of a Community and its Groups and Institutions Conceived of as Behaviors of Individuals." *Psychological Monographs,* Vol. 43, No. 2 (1932).

Siegler, Miriam and Humphry Osmond. "Aesculapian Authority." *Hastings Center Studies,* Vol. 1 (1973), pp. 41-52.

Learning Real Feelings: A Study of High Steel Ironworkers' Reactions to Fear and Danger

JACK HAAS

SIDEWALK OBSERVERS WATCH in a mixture of respect and awe as, high above the ground, hardhat construction workers perform their dangerous ballet. They watch silently as the high steel ironworkers maneuver into place the tinker-toy-like sections of steel that form the skeletal framework of today's high buildings and bridges. High above the workmen, cranes dangle steel beams that must be caught and fixed into place; far below loom enormous chasms of empty space. These workers are protected from certain death only by their skill in balancing on slender beams, a skill theatened by swirls of weather and wind. One cannot but ask how, when faced with such danger, the high steel ironworker can so casually ignore the perils of his occupation? The confidence and quickness of the workers is bewildering to onlookers who well note the hazards that beset such an occupation; how can these men walk the emerging structures with such confident aplomb? Are we considering brave men, or are these workers foolhardy, challenged by the very nature of their occupation; alternatively, does the answer to the enigma lie in the fact that these men are innately gifted, specially trained, or culturally conditioned so as to enable them to remain calm in the face of such danger? Questions like this are raised in the observer's mind because he cannot relate to the workers' situation; to most of us, such displays, such defiance of risk and the certain consequences of error are inexplicable.

In this paper I shall describe how high steel ironworkers feel and act toward the dangers inherent in their occupation. I shall explore the seemingly inconceivable attitude and behavior of the workers by a juxtaposition of my own reactions when exposed to the same dangers. I will describe how I came to understand the high steel ironworkers' perspectives toward fear and danger. I found myself (in spite of myself) beginning more and more to act as they did. As I came to know these men they admitted to sharing my fear-laden assessment of their occupational situation. We came to share a definition of the situation, a

"Learning Real Feelings: A Study of High Steel Ironworkers' Reactions to Fear and Danger" by Jack Hass *is reprinted from* Sociology of Work and Occupations *Vol. 4, No. 2 (May, 1977), pp. 147-170 by permission of the Publisher, Sage Publications, Inc.*

situation they had developed a perspective[1] for dealing with that I had yet to learn.

During the nine months of observation of the construction of a 21 storey office building I was a participant observer in a variety of work and recreational settings. I observed union activities, participated in a formal training program for ironworker apprentices, and ate and drank with them. I focused upon the apprentices and attempted to understand the processes by which they were socialized.[2]

The analysis of the data takes two forms. First, the natural history of the research is described as I came to learn the attitude of the workers toward their perilous work. I found that the ironworkers' perspective toward danger was not revealed in their words or actions, but remained an important, although not overtly communicated, part of their everyday methods of coping with their occupational situation. Workers were expected to act in ways which would convince others that they were not afraid. Second, I describe how ironworkers act out their implicitly accepted perspective about danger, and how, through a variety of mechanisms, both individual and collective, they manage to maintain a control of with whom and when they work. The element of danger depends on the trust they are able to afford their fellow workers, the nature and predictability of the weather, the location of their work activity on the emerging structure, and the risks their particular specialty requires.

A Natural History of My First Days in the Field

My traumatic introduction to the workday realities of high steel ironworking came the day the construction superintendent passed me through the construction gate, gave me a hard hat, and wished me good luck. Directly ahead were five incomplete levels of an emerging 21 storey office building. From my vantage point I observed a variety of workers engaged in the construction process. The most visible and immediately impressive group of workers were those on the upper level who were putting steel beams into place. These were the ironworkers I had come to participate with and observe. This chilling reality filled me with an almost overwhelming anxiety. I began to experience a trepidation that far exceeded any usual observer anxiety encountered in the first days of field research. It was the first time I felt this since attempting to gain entree to do a study of apprenticeship training. I watched the men at the top, the precariousness of their position, and the risks of firsthand observation were profoundly obvious. It was with fearful anticipation that I moved toward the job site.

I had anticipated this day but never so directly and profoundly. I had taken out a $50,000 accident policy to protect my family—just in case. I had not told my wife about the research. She found out when a fellow graduate student blurted it out at a party. I protected her and hid my true feelings from my colleagues. Long before the research started I had expected to convince parties to the agreement that I do the research, by writing a letter forgiving them any liability. In these ways I prepared. But as I looked up, I knew I was not prepared for this. These were the people I had come to study and they were up there, and as I watched them I was dumbfounded and awe-struck by their aplomb. They "ran the iron" with seeming abandon. It was apparent from the ground that workers moving so confidently across and up and down beams were unafraid.

There I stood, with work shoes, levis, work shirt, and a borrowed hardhat, in controlled terror. I noticed two apprentices at the ground level getting out of a trailer van. My strategy had been to locate those apprentices I had met two days previously at an apprentice welding class and follow them on the job.

I yelled to them: "Hi, how are you doing?"

An apprentice said, "What's up?"

I told him that I had just got on the job, and that I would like to follow some of the guys around. By this time another fellow, Bob, came up behind us. We stood and talked for awhile. I said, "I just saw the superintendent of slippery structural steel. I had to see them before I could get on the job. How are things up there? Safe enough?"

He answered, "Yeh, it's all right, they've got planking all over. Why don't you come up with us? We'll show you around."

"Fine, let's go." (Believe me what follows were tense moments. We walked past workmen putting rods in and setting concrete foundations to a ladder.)

Tom, using only one hand, while carrying welding rods on his shoulder, went up ahead of me on the ladder and climbed to the second level of the building. The ladder was some 20 feet high; tied securely at top and bottom. I climbed up behind Tom, my apprehension growing in direct proportion to my height above the ground. It appeared that large sections between the girders were planked, but others were not. Many places were exposed and one had to be extremely careful with his footing. Scared but "poised," I carefully and exactly followed Tom. A large quantity of cable was apparent, most of it running diagonally from beam to beam. I followed up another ladder to more planking and over to a planked work area.

This was my introduction to "running the iron," a traumatic experience I somehow survived. In retrospect it was a critical first step in my understanding of how ironworkers perceived and reacted to danger. Needless to say, it was a most important beginning for developing rapport with the ironworkers. I was an outsider beginning to meet their career-long challenge. I earned some credibility as a person who could begin to appreciate and empathize with the problems of their work situation.

For the first few weeks I was very scared. On the steel (or as I now knew "iron") I was cautious, but not too visibly. I knew I was on stage. We were all on stage and I was concerned about developing rapport and not being defined and mocked as the weak deviant. But, I was really scared. I was afraid but trying not to show it. They were boisterous, boastful, and continually demonstrating, by their actions, a lack of intimidation about the same situation of which I was most apprehensive. The discrepancy between my personal reactions to "running the iron" and their unified and contrary reaction to the same situation raised the first important question of the research—why did they act this way?[3] I thought it possibly a difference between them and me (never a matter of genetics, culture, or the Mohawk Indian stereotype, but more likely a matter of experience). I had been told before I went on the steel that ironworkers were in fact a very different and unique group of workers.[4]

The actions of ironworkers from the very first day were quite disconcerting; my feeling was one of great fear, yet their actions belied this approach. I felt, and this proved correct, that in order to establish rapport with these workers I would have to demonstrate a certain willingness to participate in the situation and indicate that I could, and would, accommodate myself.

The discrepancy between my feelings and the lack of meaning of their unusually confident behavior raised a question in my mind; was I attempting to interpret their actions according to my relevance structure? I had assumed that, sharing the same experience, we would have the same feelings about it; their actions, however, suggested we were not defining the situation similarly, and, in fact, they had overlooked what was, in my assessment of the situation, frightening. This perplexing discrepancy between the meaning of their behavior and my own definition of the situation led me to attempt to understand why their behavior would be appropriate to such a situation.

Schutz (1967:174-175) describes three different approaches for understanding the motives of others. The observer can search his memory for similar actions and can assume his motive for such an action holds true for another's actions. If this approach is unsuccessful, the observer can resort to what he knows about the person's behavior and deduce his motive. Finally, if he lacks information about the person he is observing, he can ask him whether one or another motive would be furthered by the act in question. In this situation, I was not able to compare actions in my past with those I observed, nor did I know much about those I was observing except what I had been told by the contractors' representative. The third approach, of attributing different motives, was immediately relevant, but not immediately obvious to me.

In questioning their behavior, I asked myself whether it could be possible that these workers had gained an immunity to fear because of their constant exposure to dangerous situations. It seemed plausible. The more I walked the high steel, to some degree, the more confident and assured I became. This was relative. Whenever I went up on the steel, fear was a strong emotion but there were peaks and valleys depending on what I was on, and where. If ironworkers' actions belied any indications of fear, I suspected they might, nevertheless, talk about it and also about ways of handling it. I was disappointed. They did not talk about being afraid, although they did talk a great deal about danger.

This questioning process was essentially a process where on the basis of my own experience and perceptions I was attempting to understand the actions of others and to a point it didn't make sense until I realized, I was doing what they were doing. I was attempting in this sense to reconcile my reactions with the reactions of others. The consistency of ironworker actions on the high steel and their total lack of discussion about fear (a problem I considered paramount), led me to suspect that they had developed a shared perspective for dealing with the problem of which these particular actions were a part. This was a perspective I was beginning to learn, as I came to realize I was acting like they were.

Shared Perspective: The Disavowal of Fear

I had developed a perspective: fear was a reaction to walking the steel, but it was controlled when running the iron. Either ironworkers were immune to the fear of heights and danger, or as I had, they hid their fears when they went up on the steel. Was this perspective peculiar to me or was it one shared by the workers also?

The working hypothesis was that fear was part of their definition of the situation, and that the collective way they dealt with the problem was to treat it as if it did not exist. Individual workers concealed fear from each other. Collectively these reactions produce a situation of pluralistic ignorance (Schanck, 1932:102, 130-131; Mayer and Rosenblatt, 1975) in which each worker tended to think he was more frightened than coworkers who convincingly controlled their fears. To test this hypothesis is difficult, particularly if workers feel reluctant to talk about their fear— their reticence both confirms the hypothesis and denies the testing of the hypothesis.

Faced with this methodological problem, the provisional explanation was that workers cannot express their fears, because such expression would raise doubts of their trustworthiness. In a work situation, where the actions of one can affect the safety and lives of others, workers must inspire trust and confidence. Showing fear is exactly contrary to the development of this kind of trust.

One hint that workers did indeed have the perspective that I was beginning to develop, was their discussion about workers who were afraid. They were extremely critical of such workers, and part of their criticism was that they added to the danger of the situation.

While working near the top of the emerging office building, a journeyman ironworker reveals the problem a fearful worker presents. I say, "I guess you have to watch out for the other fellow."

Abe answers, "That's right, most of these guys know what they're doing, but you get some of the fucking apprentices, like that guy over there (he points to Roy) who's scared up here, and you have really got to watch yourself, because you don't know what the hell they're liable to do."

The journeyman points out that a worker who is afraid has to be watched. He warns me that a worker who acts afraid is unpredictable. This instruction helps me to learn his perspective about fear. The process of developing shared beliefs and actions about a problem was expressed even more clearly by a journeyman teacher at the apprentice class. He warns apprentices about assumed trust of their coworkers by saying:

> There's one thing I want you guys to remember, because in so many ways your life depends upon not doing things in a stupid way. Think out what you're going to do beforehand. Make sure that the guy that you're working with knows what the hell he's doing too.
>
> There's no sense working with a dummy, because you can never trust them, you've always got to watch out for them and you're not learning a damn thing. If something's been done by another guy, say he's hung a float for you, or done this or done that for you, and you've got to get out on it, you're a damned fool if you don't check it yourself. Now I don't say this is always the case, if you work with someone, say you're paired up with a guy and you've been working with him for awhile and you know him well, and you can trust him and he's no dummy, then you don't have to be that thorough. But if you come on a new job, you are doing the most foolish thing that you could ever do by not making sure.

In this quote, one may perceive the process by which a group (apprentices) come to learn this shared perspective. Apprentices are told the importance of guarding themselves against untrustworthy workers. They are told how to act by thinking out what they are going to do and making sure that their coworkers do too. Later, the instructor presents a number of possible situations. Each situation is interpreted for the apprentices and the proper action for each situation is described. Interpreting situations and actions for others is part of the process of sharing this perspective about fear and threatening coworkers.

Oftentimes a group will develop a special language or argot that focuses on special problems or experiences that the group may face. During the research, I was struck by the vivid phrases ironworkers used to describe actions that revealed fear. The phrases ironworkers used are "to coon it," "to seagull it," or "to cradle it." Cooning it or cradling it (it being the steel beam) involves walking on all fours across the steel, or holding onto the steel while traversing it. Seagulling refers to walking the steel with arms outstretched, as in flight, to provide balance. These phrases are only used criticizing the actions of others.

The importance of this relationship of personal danger to the actions of work associates is reflected in the following conversation with a journeyman ironworker. High up on the steel, I look down and say to the journeyman, "Pretty scary up here, eh?"

The journeyman responds, "It really isn't that bad, just depends on who you're working with. If you're working with a guy that knows what the hell he's doing up here, it's safe as can be. It's only when you get a guy that doesn't know what's going on that you have to watch out."

A fearful or unknowing worker adds a measure of unpredictability to the work situation and makes it potentially even more dangerous. One who is afraid cannot be trusted to act correctly; he may act rashly, being concerned about his own protection or unsure about how to respond. The worker who is afraid may, moreover, neglect or avoid his responsibilities, and, as a consequence, endanger others. One who reveals his fear cannot be trusted to put his responsibility to others in priority to his emotions.

Considering this, it is obvious that one of the crucial tests one must pass to gain acceptance by his ironworker colleagues is to manage his impressions and to hide his fear. Workers act confidently on the steel and do not express their fears because to do so would damage their prospects for gaining the confidence of others and acceptance as a colleague. Their reputation and employability depends upon being defined as trustworthy.

Fear is taken for granted in that it is not talked about or revealed. It is, however, a personal reaction that ironworkers feel. Worker fear is hidden, controlled, and privately lived. Beyond that, there is little one can do about it. A journeyman at the union hall describes what can be done and, given that, how one must accept danger and fear without allowing it to control or adversely affect his behavior.

> I think it [danger] is something you realize as soon as you step foot on it [the steel]. It is a dangerous situation or at least it can be made so. So in a sense you take every precaution you can, and make the job as safe as you can. And then you don't worry about it. You really don't worry about it. I know that sounds funny with you, but no one is going to make it that sits there and stands there and worries about it all day. You recognize it and you respect it, but you don't let it get to you.

The journeyman explains how each ironworker must deal with this reality. Workers take all the precautions possible. After doing so, they must attempt to submerge their feelings and go about their job.

The journeyman's closing statement is instructive. It is important that the worker doesn't allow his fear to bother him and, hence we might assume, his colleagues. Workers must act as if there was nothing to fear. Hughes (1958:90-91) makes this same point when he says:

> It is also to be expected that those who are subject to the same work risks will compose a collective rationale which they whistle to one another to keep up their courage, and they will build up collective defenses against the lay world. . . . These rationales and defenses contain a logic that is somewhat like that of insurance, in that they tend to spread the risk psychologically (by saying that it might happen to anyone), morally, and financially.

The collective "whistle" suggests Goffman's (1959) dramaturgical analogy of front and backstage behavior—workers maintain a front of confidence and lack of fear before their audience. In this case, the audience is composed of fellow workers, and consequently there are few backstage areas where their front breaks down. One such backstage area was in private conversation with the observer. Alone and in my confidence, workers would tell me of their fear.

Verifying this perspective—that ironworkers deliberately pretend to be unafraid—was a continuing research interest. Ironworkers I observed throughout the research acted almost with disdain to the dangers surrounding them. As a way of proving themselves to their work fellows, many seemed deliberately to flaunt the situation by taking risks—they showed off by volunteering for the most dangerous work activity, as a way of demonstrating their trustworthiness and enhancing their reputations. The very few who acted afraid were treated as deviants, threats, and objects of ridicule to be driven out of ironworking before they allowed their fear to disrupt the shared perspective.

There were only two occasions where advertently or inadvertently ironworkers revealed their fear-laden feelings. The confessions that were made to me privately and personally were most important. These confessions were made when some ironworkers came to trust me as one who would not betray their confidence to fellow workers. Many of them wanted to quit ironworking but they were hopelessly bound into a network of relationships and a career that was difficult if not impossible to terminate. Leaving ironworking would be tantamount to admitting they were afraid, and that would mean total expulsion from a way of life they had become bound and committed to, despite its anxiety provoking consequences.

The most touching example I encountered was when a highly regarded Indian ironworker literally begged me to open university doors to a new career. We both agreed, in a boozy and emotional stupor, that he could not leave ironworking because his whole life, particularly his honored status among ironworkers and reservation Indians, would be forever altered. Competing with his young brother on the high steel, he knew he was pushing the limits. It was only a matter of time before that competition, and the veneer of fearlessness, would be shattered by one or the other's fall.

The other graphic breakdown of front which corroborates the underlying but conscious suppression of fear is when a worker falls "in the hole" and is killed. Although I fortunately never directly experienced such a situation, an Indian journeyman recounted his first dramatic confrontation with the underlying reality. He says:

> I remember one time when a guy fell in the hole. He hit his head on a piece of steel on the way down, so he was killed instantly. Well anyways, this has an effect on you. Most times you stop work and quit for the day. I didn't feel too bad. I guess death has got to hit closer to home, like if your brother or father gets it. Maybe, I was too new then, but anyways the older guys up there just froze. They wouldn't move, and they wouldn't come off the iron. I had to go up there and bring them down one by one, and some guys were so scared I had to bring them down almost by carrying them.

When a worker falls and is killed, ironworkers leave the job. They go drinking and reminisce about their lost colleague. The next day, seemingly adjusted once more to the dangers, they return to work.

The above story indicates how their managed impressions and assumed behavior were dramatically confronted. The accident and loss of a colleague stimulates a reevaluation of the workers's socially constructed reality. Contrary to the way they were expected to act and the behavior supposedly consonant with their definition of the situation was the fact there was much to fear. It is not difficult to understand their complete breakdown of front. They are reminded—in the most personally affecting way—there is much to be afraid of.

Testing Fellow Workers

Although one should conceal fear, workers do agree that the relativity of danger allows a worker to define for himself situations which are too dangerous. Part of their perspective about fear is the recognition that workers should protect themselves and others from situations which increase their common danger. One way to do this is to test the trustworthiness of their fellow workers.

Workers recognize that running the iron is a managed performance and may not reflect one's true feelings. It is important for workers to know whether a confident front (Goffman, 1959) will break down in a crisis. Workers believe it is important to know as much as possible about the trustworthiness of fellow workers in all sorts of situations, and they test this by binging,[5] a process similar to styles of interaction observed in black ghetto youth (Kochman, 1969), white lower-class gang members (Miller *et al.*, 1961), hospital personnel (Goffman, 1951:122), and perhaps as Berne (1964) suggests, North Americans in general. These studies indicate the many purposes of this form of interaction. Hughes (1945:356) points out an important use of binging in testing newcomers when he comments:

> To be sure that a new fellow will not misunderstand requires a sparring match of social gestures. The zealot who turns the sparring match into a real battle, who takes a friendly initiation too seriously, is not likely to be trusted with the lighter sort of comment in one's work or with doubts and misgivings; nor can he learn those parts of the working code which are communicated only by hint and gesture. . . . In order that men may communicate freely and confidently, they must be able to take a good deal of each other's sentiments for granted.

In the following quotation, a journeyman, three apprentices, and I engage in a sparring match on top of an emerging 21 storey building. Abe, the journeyman says, "These fucking apprentices don't know their ass from a hole in the ground." The journeyman turns to me and says, "I hope you don't think these guys are representative of the whole apprenticeship. They're a pretty sad lot."

Joining in with the kidding, I say, "Yeh, I've noticed that."

Bud, an apprentice adds, "Don't listen to him. He's just a fucking Indian."

The journeyman responds, "Yeh, and he's a fucking nigger."

Abe yells down to the apprentice below, "What the fuck are you doing down there, playing with yourself? For Christ's sakes get up here and bring that machine up here with you."

The example demonstrates how repartee tests relationships and exchanges information. The style is characteristically earthy, there is little regard for amenities, and the jibes seem deliberately provocative—a verbal challenge. In a dangerous work situation where we expect workers to try to ease conflict, we find deliberate provocation. An Indian journeyman sums up the importance of this form of interaction as he and I drink beer in a bar:

> You see, I don't get upset often. And when I do I forget right after. You've got to figure, if you're going to work with the guy, you can't hold something against him, because he could kill you and you could kill him. You forget fast when you're in this business. What you do is try to see what the guy is made of, because if he gets agitated, and

wants to fight over something like this, then you don't know what he's going to do up on the steel if something goes wrong. A lot of times you're responsible for that other guy up there and you can either make him or break him.

Workers use binging to test trustworthiness and self-control—will a man keep cool when subjected to such personal abuse? If he loses his poise, it indicates he may lose control in other threatening situations, e.g., high above the ground. If he takes such kidding too seriously, he may carry a grudge into a situation where revenge could be easy. Binging also conveys information about expected relationships among participants; relationships characterized by constant redefinition, indicated by subtle cues from the participants. Such interaction permits the apprentice to experiment by binging back in anticipation of a favorable response, which shows journeymen consider him acceptable.

The one-sided nature of binging between journeymen and apprentices was apparent throughout the study. New apprentices are called "punks," and their role involves carrying out the most demeaning tasks and the acceptance of the deliberate castigation of veteran workers.

On the top of the building, I talked with a journeyman about his constant kidding of new apprentices. I say, "Looks like you were busting Jerry, the firewatch, the other day."

Abe, the journeyman answers, "That's all right. I used to take it even worse than that. You see, I started pretty young. I used to work summers at this, and they had me doing all sorts of punking, and everyone was on my ass, all the time. I remember one summer, I carried bolts around, and that's all. I got so fucking sick of looking at those bolts, I was about ready to go out of my nut. If I took it these guys can take it. You've got to take it and dish it right back."

This journeyman makes it clear that binging is an institutionalized part of the apprentice's career; it is an initiation all must pass through before acceptance as a peer who can "dish it right back." The process is used by ironworkers to test the trustworthiness and loyalty of coworkers, and apprentices are most subject to it. The mechanism is used to test the self-control of coworkers; ironworkers believe it is useful in measuring a man's ability to handle himself in a dangerous situation. Ironworkers also believe that an apprentice's willingness to accept disparaging and hostile attacks on his person provides predictable evidence that he will commit himself to the interests of the group, over and above any self-interests.

Worker Autonomy to Reduce Danger

In an attempt to reduce the threats to their safety, ironworkers try to control factors they perceive that add to their danger. Such factors include superiors who have little regard for worker safety and unsafe weather conditions. Ironworkers try to limit the effects of both.

It is not difficult to imagine the kind of havoc the wind can play in the high, open areas where ironworkers frequently work. The wind complicates the worker's problem of keeping his balance on steel beams, which range in width from four to 12 inches. The wind is particularly dangerous when workers are carrying equipment across the steel. For example, the heavy wooden "floats" of plywood, on which the welders sit or stand, act as sails when caught by the wind and workers must take special care not to be blown off the beams. Two workers are usually required to carry a float. In a strong wind they will drag the float across the steel. They carry the float away from the wind, then if a sudden breeze stirs up the float does not push them off for they can let it give and reduce the sail effect. If the wind blows very hard, they can drop the float, grab the ropes, and sit or stand on them while the platform swings free in space. Their other alternative is to drop the float completely, endangering workers below—a last and rarely considered option.

Workers frequently were observed telling stories about unusual and extremely dangerous working situations. The following is an example of a story about the wind told by an ironworker journeyman to other journeymen, three apprentices, and myself:

> I remember when I was on this job putting this bridge over the seaway, and this stupid son-of-a-bitch is up there on the bridge and he had his hat on backwards, so this wind comes and lifts the peak up and the hat starts flying off his head. So this guy comes and reaches up with both hands and grabs his hat and goes overboard with it. I mean this fucking guy should have known better and let the goddamned hat drop. So there he is falling down through the air about 100 feet still holding on to the goddamned helmet. And then you look down below and there he is swimming and he still has one hand on that goddamned helmet. I don't know how stupid guys can be.

The journeyman warns the others of the problem that the wind presents and suggests that they ensure their safety first, and then worry about their clothing or equipment. In addition to the wind, snow, sleet, rain, and ice reduce the workers' visibility and/or make the steel beams and wood planking slippery. Walking the iron is difficult enough without these added imponderables.

Work, however, continues despite difficult weather; snow is shoveled off the steel beams and wood planking and ice is melted from the beams by a portable heater. During the winter, workers dress as warmly as possible and carry on the work activity. The weather is always a problem because it affects not only workers' safety but also their wages. The values of money and safety are sometimes in conflict. The worker is paid by the contractor for showing up in the morning, whether he works or not. If the weather is too inclement, he is paid two hours "show up time." Oftentimes, there is a difference of opinion between the workers and the foreman as to whether work should continue. Sometimes the workers want to work to increase their wages, and the foreman tells them to take the day off; other times the workers feel the weather has made working too dangerous, but the foreman believes the work should go on. The following discussion by a group of apprentices at the apprentice class indicates some of the problems the weather presents.

Nine apprentices stand around talking about their work week.

DICK: "How many hours you guys get? I got forty again this week."

BILL: "Twenty-eight hours, can you imagine that? Friday we came in and we worked up there in that fucking blizzard until quarter of ten and then the blizzard starts to stop and then they tell us to go home. That pisses me off. I mean, I'm willing to work, I say fuck the weather. You know what they have me do, they go and give me a broom and have me go out and sweep the beams off so the welders can go out there. Friday was a bastard, you couldn't even coon it to get out there. Tell 'em Roy."

ROY: "Well I only got twenty-two hours. They put you up there and you work your show-up time and then things start to clear up and they tell you to go home. You see, you get all these guys from Connecticut. We haven't worked a Friday in the last five weeks. Fucking guys are all getting an early start home, so they tell us to get off."

JOHN: "I only had twenty hours. I didn't even get in Wednesday. Did you work Wednesday, Bill?"

BILL: "Damned right, about froze my balls, but I got in four hours until lunchtime. You know that welder, Joe Walker? Christ he was hanging out in the front of the building. What do you think of this, Ralph [teacher-journeyman]? There he is on the goddamned float and the wind's blowing like hell and it's cold as hell up there and the float is banging away up there. So he's got to hold on to the steel with one hand to keep the float from banging away, and try welding with the other. So he just said "fuck it" and got off of it, and went down to the Cartel [bar] and got himself some brews."

DICK: "I don't know about you guys. All the decking crews got their forty hours this week. All the rodmen were down there working. Structural guys, they always drag up. What's the matter with you guys, can't you take it up there?"

BILL: Oh, fuck you. You go up there and walk around in that shit. Goddamn wind's blowing so hard and it's snowing and you can't see your foot in front of you. It's all right, you guys are down on the bottom. That stuff was starting to freeze on Friday. It's all right if it's slushy. I mean it's still not good, but it's not as bad as when that stuff is freezing up on you. Then you're really on your ass."

These comments point out the varied definitions of safe working conditions. Under ordinary conditions workers are expected to handle their fears and accept the problem of danger. In unusual conditions workers decide for themselves whether or not to work. There are, however, other considerations which they may take into account in defining the situation. Some of the factors which influence their decision are the loss of pay, leaving early, and determining how their action will affect the ability of their coworkers to continue working.

At the end of the apprentices' discussion, an apprentice (Bill) indicates that the problem of danger is a relative one. He commented, "It's all right if it's slushy. . . . It's not as bad as when the stuff is freezing up on you." Some kinds of foul weather are more dangerous than others, and some places and jobs on the steel structure are more dangerous than the others. For example, the tops and sides of the structure are more dangerous than the center and lower areas of the building. The top is more dangerous because it is higher; the sides because there is nothing to break a fall.

The relativity of danger in ironworkers' thinking sometimes leads to different interpretations of the situation. Some workers may choose to leave work while others may stay. The important point is the collective support given to workers to choose freely, excepting occasions when their refusal to work affects the group. If the group is burdened by a member's decision to "drag up," he is criticized; otherwise, his action is not rebuked.

In the next example, an apprentice describes how the decision to work or not to work is made. At the apprentice class an apprentice says to the rest of the group including myself, "I will always go up and take a look at what it is like. . . . I usually go up like I did Wednesday, when it was 26° below—I went up there, and went all the way to the eighth floor and looked around and it was too cold. So, I came back down." It is the apprentice who goes up to the floor where he will be working and who checks out for himself the working conditions; his decision not to work is an independent one, not relying on the judgments of others. The decision to work or not may be a group one; when a decision is made to thwart the foreman or contractor's usurpation of their autonomy the group will then invariably act together. On one occasion I followed Ray (apprentice) up to the top level which was almost completely planked. Because of the planking, this floor had accumulated between two or three inches of hardpacked snow. It was quite slippery and treacherous because of open spaces and planking that was insecurely based. Ray said, "Most of the guys aren't in today, they all took off."

"You mean they came in earlier?"

Ray answers, "Yeh, but Bill didn't come in."

"Who decides whether they're to leave?"

"They do. Mac [the foreman] asked a couple of them to go and shovel snow and they said 'no' and took off."

In this example, the foreman directs the workers to shovel snow; the group chooses not to, and the men leave the job. Other workers remain free to decide for themselves whether or not to work. The perspective of worker autonomy is enacted and reinforced.

Conclusion

This paper outlines the major problems ironworkers face in their work environment. The first problem, fear of the work setting, is described in terms of the author's changing awareness of the problem and the seeming contradiction between my personal reaction and the observable reactions of the men of the high steel. I thought my reactions to be different at first, even though I acted as if I shared their definition of the situation.

Their reaction to danger I saw as being unusual and unexpected, but later more obvious reasons for their behaving in this way became an important question for the research. The questioning process resolving these contradictory reactions to danger was important for coming to understand why ironworkers act the way they do. Indeed, despite my trepidation of the situation, I found myself acting unafraid, because I was also interested in developing rapport with the workers and proving my mettle to them. The fact that they didn't talk about their fears, if they had any, was suggestive itself of the possibility that an important understanding was not to reveal one's fear. This reticence was complimented by acts of bravado on the steel, which were viewed by me as calculated performances for the audience of fellow workers.

I developed a concept that when workers are subjected to an environment where they heavily depend on the trustworthy and competent actions of others, it becomes necessary for them to make continuous demonstrations of their fearlessness in their work situation. To act afraid increases the dangers and reduces trust among workers whose security depends on such trust being developed. Thus I came to learn and act out the same perspective toward fear shared by the group, a perspective in which workers deny fear in front of others, but live privately.

The processes of social control I have described—testing and controlling fellow workers and maintaining and enhancing individual and collective control over the work setting—are processes characteristic of occupations where danger is a perceived worker problem. The careful surveillance and testing of colleagues, particularly newcomers, the controlled actions belying any fear, and the unified efforts to increase worker autonomy are sociologically relevant outcomes in situations where workers face extreme danger. The processes ironworkers have derived for controlling and directing the behavior of apprentices, as well as journeymen, in many ways parallel those described of pipeline construction workers (Graves, 1958), lumberjacks (Haynes, 1945), miners (Gouldner, 1954; Lucas, 1969), combat personnel (Grinker and Spiegel, 1963; Stouffer, 1949; Weiss, 1967), and ghetto social workers (Mayer and Rosenblatt, 1975).

In dangerous occupations participants are described as engaging in a great deal of horseplay, joking and banter, or, as I refer to it—binging. This form of interaction supports worker efforts to maintain control of their work environment and to evolve rigorous sets of expectations about appropriate behavior and shared worker attributes. This suggests that the perception of danger leads to very similar processes and expectations in very disparate occupational groups. The single characteristic they all share is their perception of danger; this perception produces a set of perspectives around the problem of danger that is rigorously and continuously enforced.

The workers' attempt to increase their control over their work environment and lessen the dangers is the second and related theme of this paper. This perspective emphasizes the ironworkers' commitment to increasing worker autonomy and thus a control over their environment. They strive to maintain control by collectively supporting individual and group decisions to judge for themselves safe and unsafe working conditions. They support the actions of fellow workers who decide whether or not to work in inclement weather. Fellow workers accept or reject the judgments of work superiors who may not give precedence to ironworkers' considerations and who could consequently pose a threat to their personal and collective security. Workers who perceive physical danger develop mechanisms to control their reactions and the reactions of others. Individually and collectively they struggle to enhance the security of their situation. Symbolic or real threats bind workers together in an effort to protect themselves. Part of the defense, however, lies in controlling one's personal trepidations and insecurities and maintaining an appearance of fearlessness.

These reactions, I believe, are characteristic of many groups and are only more obvious and dramatic in the observation of high steel ironworkers. Behind the calculated performances and fronts of much social activity is the underlying insecurity and threat of failure. These fears are contained and controlled, because to do otherwise is to admit personal failure and to face ridicule or ostracism.

NOTES

1. The concept perspective is taken from Becker *et al.* (1961) and refers to a set of beliefs and actions an individual or group has towards a perceived problem. In this case the perspective is a shared or group one, which has developed out of the interactions ironworkers have about their mutually defined problem.

2. After each observation I dictated in as complete a form as possible all that I

had seen and heard in the course of the observation. These near verbatim dictations were typed in full as field notes and later coded and categorized and serve as the basis of this analysis.

3. An important point is that as a stranger to the situation I did not share the expectations of others. This estrangement on my part made the actions of others more profound and dramatic. See Garfinkel (1957: 37), where he point out that such estrangement is helpful for bringing into view the background expectancies of the participants. See also Simmel (1950: 405), where he makes the point that the stranger role carries with it a certain objectivity, i.e., he is not committed to the "unique ingredients and peculiar tendencies of the group."

4. During the interview phase of the study, when the decision to study ironworkers had not yet been reached, respondents provided me with a preliminary set of expectations which affected my thinking. Having had no experience or contact with ironworkers, their comments provided me with the framework of understanding about ironworkers even though subsequently they were found to be incorrect or exaggerated.

In this example, the contractor's representative tells me about Indian ironworkers:

> You know they're the damnest ironworkers (Indians). I don't care what you say, they can go out Saturday night and get a real toot and Monday morning have the jumping jeepers. But, by gosh, you get them up there and they're not afraid of anything.

This statement by the contractor's representative suggests that Indians are unafraid and that there is indeed something to fear, a very important point for me.

5. The term "binging" was, I believe, first used and described by Roethlisberger and Dickson (1934). They describe workers binging each other by punching others on the shoulder. This action served as a means of social control, a warning to the worker that he had exceeded the work group's informally agreed upon standard of production.

REFERENCES

Becker, H. S., B. Geer, A. Strauss, and E. Hughes (1961) *Boys in White.* Chicago: Univ. of Chicago Press.

Berne, E. (1964) *Games People Play.* New York: Grove.

Garfinkel, H. (1957) *Studies in Ethnomethodology.* Englewood Cliffs, N.J.: Prentice-Hall.

Goffman, E. (1959) *Presentation of Self in Everyday Life.* New York: Doubleday Anchor.

———. (1951) *Encounters.* Indianapolis, Ind.: Bobbs-Merrill.

Gouldner, A. (1954) *Patterns of Industrial Bureaucracy.* New York: Free Press.

Graves, B. (1958) "'Breaking out': an apprenticeship system among pipeline construction workers." *Human Organization* 17 (Fall): 9-13.

Grinker, R. R. and J. P. Spiegel (1963) *Men Under Stress.* Philadelphia: Blakerston Co.

Haas, J. (1974) "The stages of the high steel ironworker apprentice career. "*Soc. Q.* 15 (Winter): 93-108.

———. (1972) "Binging: educational control among high steel ironworkers." *Amer. Behavioral Scientist* 16 (September/October): 27-34.

Haynes, N. (1945) "Taming the lumberjack." *Amer. Soc. Rev.* 10 (April): 217-225.

Hughes, E. C. (1958) *Men and Their Work.* New York: Free Press.
———. (1945) "Dilemmas and contradictions of status." *Amer. J. of Sociology* 5 (March): 353-359.
Kochman, T. (1969) "'Rapping' in the black ghetto." *Trans-action* 6 (February): 26-34.
Lucas, R. (1969) *Men in Crisis, A Study of Mine Disaster.* New York: Basic Books.
Mayer, J. E. and A. Rosenblatt (1975) "Encounters with danger: social workers in the ghetto." *Sociology of Work and Occupations* 2 (August): 227-245.
Miller, W. B., H. Geertz, and H. S. G. Cutter (1961) "Aggression in a boy's street-corner gang." *Psychiatry* 24 (November): 283-298.
Roethlisberger, F. L. and W. J. Dickson (1934) *Management and the Worker.* Boston: Harvard University Graduate School of Business Administration.
Schanck, R. L. (1932) "A study of a community and its groups and institutions conceived of as behaviors of individuals." *Psychiatry Monographs* 43, 2.
Schutz, A. (1967) *The Phenomenology of the Social World* [trans. by George Walsh and Frederick Lehnert]. Evanston, Ill.: Northwestern Univ. Press.
Simmel, G. (1950) *The Sociology of Georg Simmel* [trans. and ed. by Kurt H. Wolff]. New York: Free Press.
Stouffer, S. (1949) *The American Soldier: Combat and its Aftermath.* II. Princeton, N.J.: Princeton Univ. Press.
Weiss, M. (1967) "Rebirth in the airborne." *Transaction* 4 (May): 23-26.

WORK IS AN important indicator of social and moral worth, and so people try to present their jobs in favorable terms. This is commonly done either by placing their work in a recognized prestigious category, or by giving a favorable description of what they do, often focusing on the importance of their job within the organizational hierarchy. For example, a janitor may tell others that he is a building administrator and involved in personnel work, while a printer working at a particular machine may remark "If we don't do our job right, no one else can get their work done properly." Individuals' descriptions of and discussions about their work are often intended to make others recognize them as certain kinds of people.

To paraphrase Everett Hughes, every occupational group does its work in some social matrix in interaction with the people it defines as its clients, with fellow members of the occupational group, and with members of related occupations. (Hughes, 1971:353) This suggests that while working, a person comes into contact with and performs for different audiences. Although one audience may be more important than another, or better able to recognize a person's worth, and although the individual's reputation may be judged differently by these separate audiences, the recognition and judgments given are central to the worker's self-image and personal identity.

Though analytically separable, our occupational self-image, derived from others' recognition and judgments, is closely linked to our self-perception. We appreciate it when others commend us for our good work and feel slighted when our labor passes by unnoticed, or is criticized. Other people's reactions to our work, whether favorable or unfavorable, are important to us for we often believe they are also telling us something about ourselves.

While research on the sociology of occupations has focused on such matters as the kind of work that people do, the way they do it, the learning techniques involved, the types of problems that arise, and the solutions to these problems, virtually all the research has dealt with the legitimate worker and legitimate work. There is very little descriptive material available dealing specifically and analytically with deviant or criminal behavior and about those individuals who think of such activities as their work. Our knowledge about criminals is derived from research that focuses mainly on the " ... characteristics of the criminal and on the ways in which the official agencies come to define certain persons as being criminal." (Letkemann, 1973:1)

Not long ago, in his study of poolroom hustlers, Ned Polsky wrote:

> Criminologists stand to lose little and gain much in the way of sociological understanding if, and when studying people dedicated to an illegal occupation, they will overcome their fascination with the "illegal" part long enough to focus on the "occupation" part. After all, any theory of illegal occupations can be but a special case, albeit an important one, of general occupational theory.
>
> Criminologists following the lead of the late Edwin Sutherland, recognize that one hallmark of the criminal career—be he engaged in major crime or, like the hustler most of the time, in violating generally unenforced criminal law—is that the illegal activity in question constitutes his regular job. Yet their researches seem thoroughly untenanted by what occupational sociologists have learned about how to look at someone else's regular job. (Polsky, 1967:101)

The following selection is taken from Peter Letkemann's excellent study of experienced criminals, *Crime as Work*. One of the arguments presented by Letkemann is that " ... the various dimensions of work appear to be as applicable ... to the illegitimate as to the legitimate worker." (Letkemann, 1973:6) The author gives examples highlighting the similarities between crime as an occupation and ordinary work. For instance, both criminals and non-criminals must develop certain skills to be successful at their work and neither are immune to the effects of technological change on the organization of their work. Letkemann also points out that criminals are concerned with "recognition and reputation", especially as these features of social life affect their place in the social organization of the criminal world.

Recognition & Reputation

PETER LETKEMANN

THE EVERYDAY LEGITIMATE world includes a variety of public *rites de passage* by which the public ratifies the right of a certain individual to assume a certain role. This may include the right to use certain public symbols (such as the wedding ring), or it may consist of a private document or license that can be produced if necessary. On the other hand, some persons (for example, leaders) may be acknowledged informally, without formal ratification of that role.

These matters, complicated enough in the legitimate society, are even more complex when applied to criminals. The criminal is a part of at least three worlds or defining communities—namely, his fellow criminals, square-johns, and law enforcement personnel, particularly the police. He recognizes the evaluations of each as important, even though they may differ radically from each other.

For most citizens the courts provide a highly useful simplification process. Certain officials are assigned the task of differentiating between the criminal and noncriminal (just as psychiatrists do with reference to mental health). The ritual associated with court processes adds the stamp of legitimacy and validity to the decisions made. The difficulties the exconvict has in being socially accepted indicate the irreversible character of such a definition. This suggests that the lay person who defines criminals as "those convicted by the courts" is unlikely to reverse this definition; he also prefers to believe that persons not so convicted are not criminals.

1. On Being "Known"

As numerous studies indicate, policemen are not as readily impressed by the decisions of the courts as are lay people. They "know" before such decisions are made who is guilty or innocent, and are not likely to change their opinion as a result of the court decision.[1]

The lay person may be content to distinguish between a criminal and a noncriminal, but the police are interested in more specific subcategories. Some of these might correspond to those already discussed as relevant categories used by criminals themselves, but since policemen were not interviewed, this must be left to speculation. It does seem reasonable to suppose that police are interested in imputing some degree of consistency and predictability to the criminals they encounter so that

Peter Letkemann, Crime as Work, © *1973, pp. 41-48. Reprinted by permission of Prentice-Hall, Inc., Englewood Cliffs, New Jersey, U.S.A.*

they can be more easily recognized as having done a particular "job." This is seen by the criminals:

> Once you are known as one who does B & E's the police can pick you up and charge you with anything[2] on the slate. (no. 33)

This suggests the establishment of a line by a criminal is useful to the police, but involves a danger for the criminal in terms of unwanted recognition. This avenue of recognition is also useful to those business institutions most vulnerable as victims of criminal activities, for it is in their interest to be able to differentiate between legitimate and illegitimate customers. For example, no. 33 doesn't seem very choosy as to where he would boost. When he mentions the Bay, I ask whether the clerks at the Bay would recognize him, since I heard they studied pictures of known shoplifters:

> I'm not known as a shoplifter. The Bay knows the shoplifters. WHAT ARE YOU KNOWN AS? Just an ordinary drunken thief, that's all. (no. 33)

Because he is not "known" as a shoplifter, he will not be suspected as one.

To become known as a specialist invokes the danger of police recognition and suspicion; on the other hand, we have noted that criminal specialization is not particularly restrictive. That is, one may leave one's line occasionally to do different jobs. None of my respondents indicated that such movement was consciously designed to frustrate police, though one may reasonably deduce that this is one of the consequences.[3]

As a criterion of status it is not as important to be known for any particular line, as it is to be known as someone who has a line. To be known implies recognition of rounder qualities; it does not seem to matter much what one's particular line is. One qualification should be added—the young kids, or punks, appear to pay more attention to the specific line itself than do the older fellows. It may be that they carry over to the criminal world some of the square criteria for assigning status. They are not yet socialized to the new value system.

Also important is the matter of reputation. If to be known is more important than to be known *as a pete-man*, then to be known as a *good* pete-man is more important than to be known as a pete-man. The level of performance within one's line forms the basis for the criminal's reputation. My respondents appeared to assign equal status to the good B & E man and the good safecracker. Expertise is more admired than the form of its application.

> I know of two particular fellows that were very good safecrackers—they

were very good. I've worked with them and done time with them and
everything else. But I know these two in particular have gone in for
hotel thefts, like room-prowling, I guess you would call it. And it really
pays off—big money. (no. 14)

2. How One Becomes Known

As indicated earlier, there are some obvious reasons why it is hazardous
to become known; it was generally assumed that if one is known to one's
peers, one is also known to the police. All my respondents took for
granted that there was a steady flow of information from the larger
criminal culture to the police agencies. Information that was not to get to
the police had to be kept from this culture as well—and, conversely, it is
possible to communicate with the police via this culture. An apartment
burglar stated:

> Nobody in this area knew what I was doing—I wouldn't, as I said
> before, flash around a roll, because I never hung around with anybody.
> You see, this is the trouble with most people in here (prison)—they all
> drink at the same place. So you walk into there—let's say it's a bar or a
> pub or something. So you walk into there, and you sit down and these
> people all sitting around, and you can tell who is making out all right
> and who isn't. By who is flashing the roll around and who is buying the
> rounds, and stuff like this. Well, I never hang around with the criminal
> element when I'm on the street and all. For instance, if I hire a partner
> who goes on scores with me from time to time, then I wouldn't hang
> with him. (no. 35)

The above person would not become known until he does time. If the
trial indicates a consistency in his history of crime, this reputation will be
ascribed to him by other inmates. From then on he is known.

Criminals, particularly those who are known, seek their social
rewards within the criminal element. As one known safecracker put it,
"What's the point of scoring if nobody knows about it?" (no. 32) In his
case, he tended to celebrate a good "score"[4] by buying the drinks for
everyone. Others are more subtle, but manage some social recognition as
well:

> Well, actually that's kinda hard to answer because when you rob banks
> you don't actually—I don't come around telling you—I don't tell the guy
> next door. I didn't tell this guy. I didn't tell anybody, because it was
> none of their business. But little by little people around town know that
> "this guy—he don't work; man, he's doin' somethin'!" You see what I
> mean—it's just supposition. You hear it somewhere along the line,
> somewhere along the grapevine—they think, but they don't know, you
> see. (no. 7)

Further:

> SO YOU CAN'T REALLY ENJOY YOUR STATUS? No, you can't. The only part
> you can enjoy is when you pick up the paper and you read that such
> and such a gunman tore off such and such a bank. That's all you get out
> of it, see?[5] But then again, in a place like this here, you're right at the
> top.
> HOW DO ANY OF THE OTHER GUYS IN HERE KNOW THAT YOU EVER DID ANY
> BANKS BESIDES THE LAST ONE THAT YOU WERE CAUGHT ON? Oh, they don't
> know. But when you organize that like that, they know darn well that
> you just haven't done one—you've probably done several more before
> that. (no.7)

It should not be assumed, however, that the criminal's display before
his peers is entirely a matter of seeking status, or that it constitutes a
weakness on the part of the criminal. Instead, it is more useful to view it
as a "demand characteristic" of the criminal's trade; a display in the
sense that the term is used by Turner, who points out that "work is not
merely done, but oriented to as a display," and that each occupational
setting is oriented in part to "particularly significant audiences" which
must be taken into account by the worker.[6] For the criminal, one such
significant audience is his peer group of fellow criminals. He relies on
them for vital information that determines the course of his daily
activities—which parts of the city are "hot," which fence is in need of
what at any one time, and so on. Since by definition his work is secret, it
is he who must communicate his successes and competence to others.
(Also, by definition, failures are highly visible, being made public via
numerous agencies.) Communication of competence may well be
necessary for him to find or be offered continued work.

It would seem paradoxical to suggest that one of the criminals'
"significant audiences" is the police and that he would think of his work
as a "display" for them. By this I mean more than the fact that the
criminal knows the police will see his work. It is to suggest that the
criminal is sensitive to the police as an important reference group; he
wants them to think highly of his workmanship as a criminal. Besides his
fellow criminals, the police are the only other persons capable of
evaluating and, therefore, "appreciating" criminal work skills. Such
display orientation is possible if we recall our earlier "experienced"/
"amateur" distinction. It was noted that the experienced criminal is
concerned with lack of *evidence* rather than with secrecy. Providing that
his display does not include evidence it is possible for him to orient his
work with a police audience in mind.

The burglar quoted below feels he would lose status in the opinion
of the police should he miss some money in a house burglary:

The police even. They—police will say that, like "What a sucker—he

missed five-hundred dollars—how the hell'd you miss five-hundred dollars?" See? "If he took forty to fifty dollars, why didn't he take the
others?" That's what they're going to say. But if you can't find it, how
the hell you goin' to take it? See—that's the whole trouble. A smart
crook—a smart crook, he'll look into these things, and say, "Well, he's
got some stashed here, some stashed there, some stashed on the floor"—
you look all over, and you clean him, and then when they come to
investigate, the police say, "Well, there was a smart aleck, eh? He took
everything! He knew the layout!" You got to work that layout out. (no.
16)

Becoming known is not entirely a matter of choice. The police have
developed a system of clues that indicate to them the probability of
criminal involvement, as will be illustrated by the following account.
When no. 35 was seventeen years of age he frequently travelled with a
friend who delivered food for a Chinese restaurant. The police stopped
them one night, and successfully charged them with possession of house-
breaking instruments. These "instruments" consisted of a tire iron, a pair
of pliers, and a screwdriver. No. 35 claimed they were innocent at the
time but, acknowledged that the police had reason to be suspicious: "In
their eyes I was well-heeled at the time, so in their eyes I was doing
something." (no. 35)

3. *The Implications of Being Known*

It is interesting to note that the clues used by policemen bear striking
similarity to those used by criminals themselves. It has already been
noted that the experienced criminal is not particularly worried about
being known, as such, to the police. In contrast to the amateur, whose
concern is with concealment, the experienced criminal's concern, as we
have seen, is with evidence. He is satisfied when the police "have
nothing on me."

In this sense also, the criminal who is known poses quite a different
problem to the police than the criminal who is not known. For the latter,
it is a question of "Who did it?"; for the former, the question is, "What
have we got on him?":

Criminals are inclined to talk shop all the time. (FOR THIS REASON POLICE
OFTEN FIND OUT WHAT'S GOING ON, AND INMATES IN PRISON ALSO KNOW
WHAT IS GOING ON.) When a bank's been done, we know pretty soon
who done it. The police, they know half the time who done it, but they
can't prove it. (no. 36)

To be accorded "known criminal" status results in the redefinition of
everyday events. Respondents frequently spoke of "bum beefs," "phony

beefs," "bum raps," and so on. Such beefs were defined as "a traffic beef or something." That is, a phony beef may be a legitimate charge, which is, however, made for other than the stated reasons. Both the police officer and the criminal understand the act as being symbolic. To the criminal it is a "sneaky way" for the police to apprehend someone, and such behavior is not considered entirely fair by the criminal, although he must play along with the game.

A phony beef is to be distinguished from what is referred to as "not getting a fair shake." The latter is perceived of as lack of justice, discrimination, and a violation of the rules of the game. Criminals have strong notions as to what constitutes a just sentence, and also what consitutes valid evidence. Although I have little evidence to this effect, there is reason to believe that to be known as a criminal may, in the courtroom, be beneficial rather than detrimental to the accused. That is, it is known by both prosecutor and magistrate that the accused is not ignorant of precedent, and has a fairly accurate notion of what sentence the bench may reasonably impose.

On the other hand, a criminal's reputation may effect a legal redefinition of his behavior. The example below indicates how the act of B & E may be reinterpreted by the judge in a way that would be consistent with the criminal's reputation—in this case, as an act leading toward an intended safecracking. The criminal is aware that his reputation places additional meaning on his behavior:

WHAT HAPPENED AFTER THESE TWO YEARS OF SAFEBLOWING? Went to the pen. Got caught and went to the pen. HOW DID YOU GET CAUGHT? Uh— let's see—it was during—I was going in to blow a safe and I ran into a burglar alarm, just before I started getting into burglar alarms. I ran into a burglar alarm, and naturally, before I got out of there they were there and they pinched me and they charged me with B & E. This is all they can charge me with, in a spot like this, 'cause I've already got rid of the —as soon as I saw them coming I got rid of the fuses one way—I pored the nitro glycerine down the sink. They don't know what I had, or, you know—so they charge me with B & E and I got three years for that. As much as they suspect—like I told you, they've got to have evidence, definite evidence.

NOW, WHEN THE POLICE KNOW THAT YOU ARE OBVIOUSLY GOING TO BLOW A CAN, AS THEY WOULD HAVE IN THAT CASE—DOES THE JUDGE ALSO KNOW THAT? Officially he doesn't, but he—the prosecutor usually gets to him and talks to him. NOW, IN FACT THEN YOU ARE SENTENCED AS IF YOU WERE GOING TO BLOW A CAN? Oh yes, sure. It isn't what you did, it's what you know. Another man could come along right behind you and get charged with B & E and get six months where I get three years—for the very fact that I was a known—that I was involved in this.

WOULD YOU HAVE GOT MORE TIME IF THEY HAD FOUND ALL THE STUFF ON YOU? Oh yes, oh yes. You see, they've got an excuse now, to give you more time. You see, certain sections of the code call for—ah—breaking and entering calls for, I forget—six months to five to ten years. FOUR-TEEN YEARS? Yeh—it's fourteen now, but at that time is was either six to five years. Six months to five years. Explosives, carrying explosives was considered a more serious crime in their eyes, you know. (no. 29)

Being known may also provide immunity from some types of police informers. One of the interesting factors in the career of a thief is the role of the fence, particularly when the fence is also a bootlegger. There is evidence to suggest that bootleggers need police protection in order to operate—they also depend on the illegitimate order for a mandate. With reference to this, a respondent suggested that the bootlegger acts as an informer for the police, but informs only on those thieves who have no status in the criminal subculture. (no. 18)

NOTES

1. This is documented in Skolnick, *Justice Without Trial*.

2. The context of this statement implies that the "anything" refers to any type of B & E, rather than any type of crime.

3. It would be useful to determine how rigid the policeman's "typing" proves to be. That is, having typed someone as a B & E man, is such a person ruled out as a potential booster?

4. A successful property offence. "Score" refers both to the event (also known as a "caper") and to the money or property stolen.

5. This suggests an unacknowledged consequence of newspaper reporting. For example, for some criminals it provides the only source of social recognition.

6. Roy Turner, "Occupational Routines: Some Demand Characteristics of Police Work," (unpublished paper presented to the Canadian Sociology and Anthropology Association, June 1969), pp. 6 and 7.

THE WORK THAT people do is related to other aspects of their lives. Occupations tend to make certain life styles mandatory by the limitations they impose or the expectations they involve. Our ways of life, and their patterns of spending, saving, and consumption, are directly linked to different levels of income. The amount that we can spend on entertainment, travel, health, food, and clothing is connected to the amount of money that we earn. Our income level, in turn, is directly linked to the kind of reward we get for the work we do.

The nature of our work may also determine our role and involvement in the community. The area in which we live, our membership in clubs and associations, our consumption and entertainment patterns, and the education of our children are closely related to, and often dictated by, our work. They may even be related specifically to the company or corporation in which we are employed. For example, in order to maintain and manipulate its public image in the community, a corporation will ensure that its executives live in certain residential neighborhoods and belong to selected social clubs and voluntary associations. The employee's social activities may be channeled by his particular work, and his wife and children may also be expected to act in certain appropriate and responsible ways. In writing about the corporation wife, Whyte says:

> One year she may be a member of a company community, another year a branch manager's wife, expected to integrate with the local community —or, in some cases, to become a civic leader; and frequently, as the wife of the company representative, to provide a way station on the route of touring company brass. (Whyte, 1951:87-88)

Various sociological studies have pointed to the relationship between position in the occupational structure and place in the community power structure (Mills, 1956; Veblen, 1940). Such studies make explicit the relationship between occupation and life style. Expectations of involvement in community life may arise from the nature of people's work, but their success at work may also be contingent on successful integration and performance in the community. In the next selection, Aileen Ross highlights the way this relationship pertains to the successful businessman's involvement in philanthropy, particularly the organization of financial campaigns, and the way this involvement helps a business career. Philanthropy, Ross suggests, is seen as an important area for individual and corporate power and prestige. Charity work is no longer left to the employee's initiative, but companies insist that their managerial personnel engage in philanthropic and community functions because they see achievements in these spheres as an indication of status level in the community. As the relationship between status in charitable organizations and status in the community is thought to be a direct one, philanthropic activities increasingly provide new opportunities for the businessman and the company to strengthen their economic positions.

Philanthropic Activity
and the Business Career

AILEEN D. ROSS

THIS ARTICLE ATTEMPTS to set forth the various ways in which participation in philanthropic activity influences the career of the businessman. It is the contention of this study that philanthropy, most particularly the organization of financial campaigns, is a substantial activity of the successful businessman. Moreover, such activity not only facilitates business careers in ways well recognized by the fraternity of successful businessmen, but also enters as a substantial ingredient in the public relations programmes of modern corporations.[1]

The analysis of the material on which the study is based falls under three main headings: A) business position and the demands of financial campaigns; B) major facets of the philanthropic career; and C) some background characteristics of men who have held important positions in campaigns.

A. Business Position and the Demands
of Financial Campaigns

As money-raising campaigns for charitable purposes have increased in number and scope on the North American continent, it is now essential for most businessmen to take part in them. In fact, it is very difficult for a man to avoid canvassing once he is well started in his business career.[2] The individual usually begins as a door-to-door canvasser, and from there advances in the campaign hierarchy to team captain, then to divisional captain, and then to a low position on an executive committee. From this position he moves up to vice-chairman and is finally made chairman of a campaign. After that he will be put on the Special Names committee,[3] and eventually may become chairman of that committee, which is the pinnacle of campaign positions.[4]

As many of the important businessmen of Wellsville have moved up to important executive positions in campaigns in some such manner, we can now talk of "philanthropic careers" as well as "business careers". However, a career in philanthropy is dependent on the business career, for a man must be high up in the business world before he is in a position of sufficient influence to take over the top philanthropic positions.

So much publicity is necessarily attached to the large city-wide

Reprinted from Social Forces *Vol. 32 (March 1954), pp. 274–280. "Philanthropic Activity and the Business Career," by Aileen D. Ross. Copyright © The University of North Carolina Press.*

money-raising campaigns that the success or failure of a canvasser is clearly visible, and he may therefore become a marked man in the business world. Success will mean that other positions of importance in the community will open out to him, such as membership in important clubs, executive positions on welfare agencies, hospitals, or universities, as well as further advancement in business. This relationship between advancement in business and philanthropy is outlined in the following interviews:

Public-relations head of large retail firm: If you study the lists of campaign workers, you will find an amazing parallel between the level a man holds in his place of business and the level he holds in the campaign. Thus, if you are working at the bottom part of some business organization you will be ringing doorbells. You can't possibly head a campaign and deal with people who are the heads of large corporations. As you go up in the business world you go up in philanthropy. If you are at the top in a business or financial corporation you will appear at the top of the campaign.

President of firm: You will find that when a man first gets into this game he will be given some sort of minor campaign position depending on his business position. My own men have taken these positions, but as they have progressed with the firm so they have taken on more responsibility in these campaigns. Furthermore, they are helping themselves, since I am watching them to see how they get along. They are ambitious, which is all to the good. They realize that we want them to do this work, and they will do a good job when we set them to it.

It is these minor executives whom it is important to bring into the campaigns, because they will later on become important men if they are any good.

I think other businessmen try to do the same thing with their own men. They see to it that they take over these campaign responsibilities and if they do a good job they keep them in mind for the future. I think these young men realize this, and now they are trying to get into the campaigns without anyone asking them. Now I have a letter here from a young lawyer who has only been out in the field for about five years, but already he is into all these campaigns. That young fellow is going to make a name for himself!

Another point to be noted is that as a man advances in the campaign hierarchy he becomes better trained for its higher positions, and also comes more and more into contact with men who are influential in business.

Lawyers: The top leaders have participated from year to year in the campaigns. They become part of it, and each year they become more and more experienced. They are just moved up to the vacancy above. Of course there is a sort of screening process which takes into account the respectability of the person and the type of occupation that will permit him to hold the position. The whole organization of philanthropic activity is arranged like a ladder. Once you start in the system you slowly climb up—and if you have real and vital interest you reach the top rungs.

Through coming to know these men, both as friends and as business associates, he becomes still more powerful in the philanthropic structure. For it is only influential men who can elicit the large individual and corporation subscriptions essential for the success of any large campaign.

Occasionally a man of exceptional qualifications will be put into a top philanthropic position without working his way up in the structure, but as participation in philanthropy has become more and more an essential part of the business career, this is the exception rather than the rule.

The few businessmen who refused to take part in the Wellsville campaigns were criticized by interviewees, who thought that such behaviour would eventually react on their careers.

> *General Manager, Bank Y:* It's *very* important for a man to take part in campaigns. Just as important for a lawyer or an accountant as for a businessman. It's important for their firms too. A man who won't take his share is thought a lot less of—and probably it affects his business.

Hence, although it was impossible to find a direct correlation between the business careers and the philanthropic careers of all the men studied, records and interviews showed that there is a decided relationship between the rise of a man to the top executive positions in charitable campaigns and his rise in the business hierarchy.

B. Major Facets of the Philanthropic Career

The Importance Of Sponsorship   Since business institutions have gradually taken over the control of the collection of money for all large city-wide campaigns,[5] an "inner circle" of important businessmen has gradually come to control the top executive positions in these campaigns. This inner circle chooses either one of its own members for important campaign positions or a man whom it wishes to see advance in the business world.[6]

> *Head of publishing firm:* Stewart Black was the logical man to choose to head the Z Campaign. He was a man well known in the city, he had done a lot of this sort of thing over the years, and he had a good family name. But perhaps most important of all he was *au fait* with the important people around here. He travelled in the same circle with

them, and could talk to them in their own language. He didn't have to get to know the important people in Wellsville—he was one of them. By choosing him, the organizers knew what they were doing: they were choosing a good sponsor, someone whom the important people would accept without hesitation. I don't think this campaign system could continue without this sort of thing. The only way to get the important people behind you is to have someone leading the campaign who is one of them.

This sponsorship of participants in philanthropy can be seen as a way in which the inner circle manages to perpetuate itself. For, through their ability to control the incumbents of the top positions, they are able to pass on the control of philanthropy to a group which will carry it on in the way of which they would approve.

The choice of executives for the large campaigns is taken very seriously by the inner circle, and a careful selection of candidates is made. Interviewees said that they often sat "for hours" to be sure that they got the "right" person. Not only must they perpetuate their own group, but they must be sure that their man will be able to make a success of the campaign.

Sponsorship of the inner circle is in fact so important that a man cannot possibly attain a top position by volunteering his services. Rather, he must wait until he is approached by one or more of the inner circle and asked to take the position.

General Manager, Trust company: You don't just volunteer for these positions—it isn't done; you wait until you are asked. In fact, I don't know what would happen if you *did* volunteer! When asked, you are expected to say "Yes", but it is considered bad to show any eagerness. I am sure that if someone volunteered to be chairman of the next campaign he would be turned down.

Reasons for Participating The pressures that can be exerted on people to participate in philanthropy coming from friends, business associates, and members of the inner circle have been described in another article.[7] Pressures also come through family and religious training, which may instil a sense of duty and responsibility to the community. This training may exert great influence on men whose families have been engaged in philanthropy for several generations.

Pressures to participate also come from one's business firm, for philanthropic activity is now such an important part of the public relations of business concerns that in most cases a man is automatically expected to canvass when he reaches a certain business position.

General Manager, Retail Firm D: My interest in philanthropy arose because I was at the head of a large firm. In this position it is just part of your job. I suppose that there are families who have a tradition along these lines, but I think that most of us are active in philanthropy because we are doing the particular jobs that we are.

Hence, at certain levels of business, active participation is expected of the *business position*, regardless of who the incumbent may be.

Indeed, participation has become so essential that many business enterprises now include "training" for these community responsibilities as part of the regular training of their staff.

> *General Manager, Bank Y:* Training for philanthropy is a very important part of the training in our bank. It's our policy to drill into our men from the very beginning that they *must* take an interest in the community they're working in. Even if they're just a manager in a small town they *must* take an interest in the new hospital, or school, or whatever it is. We get reports each year on every clerk in every branch, and this shows whether they take an interest in their community affairs or not. They're reprimanded if they don't show this community interest. Stress right through is on this. And it's all for public relations. We *have* to do it —the competition between banks is so great. So we are all trained to take community responsibility. We expect to see the result of it somewhere in our balance sheet!

There is also a growing realization on the part of ambitious young men that participation is important to their careers, so directly or indirectly they may seek these positions.

> *Professional Organizer B:* G told someone in his firm to get on with the job of canvassing, and he did it because he thought he was pleasing the boss, and that it might mean something for him if he did a good job. That's the way it works.

> *Department Head, Retail Firm D:* Each person along the line resents being asked to canvass, but on the other hand is glad that he is singled out. He knows that his name will appear on a sheet in the main office, meaning that his name comes to the attention of top management.

Many, too, recognize that through participation they are able to meet people and make contacts which may eventually be of business or "social" use.

> *Professional Organizer A:* Even the ordinary volunteer canvassers get to know people whom they would not ordinarily meet. I can give you an example of this. There was a cocktail party at a particular home here in Wellsville a few days ago for the various team captains and vice-chairmen. Many of these men would never have gone to that house for a cocktail party, and they probably never will again. But the campaign

gave them a chance to see the inside of the house and meet other people whom they would not usually meet. That sort of thing goes on a lot. People know they will rub elbows with a lot of important people. They will make friends and contacts. A man makes acquaintances in his work and maybe at his club, but these campaigns are an opportunity for him to meet a lot of other people, and make a lot of friends. That's the way it works. You can see the friendships being made all around you.

These contacts are of particular importance for the broker, lawyer, insurance agent, and others whose success in business depends on personal contacts.

Lawyer: A man in the selling field has much to gain from philanthropic work. Each contact that he makes in this group will widen his clientele. A great many sellers probably depend a great deal on this activity for their business careers.

Finally, some corporations feel that philanthropy can serve as an important training in salesmanship, so they urge their men to take part.

The reasons for participation are therefore complex, and include pressures which the individual cannot escape, rewards and the hope of reward, and training which will improve the man's business position.

Testing the Individual It has been pointed out that philanthropic activity is an exceptionally good way in which to test a man's ability, as the success of any canvasser is clearly marked in terms of dollars and cents. Many corporations realize this, and consciously use campaign activity to test a promising young man.[8]

Professional Organizer E: He is the centre of all publicity. The spotlight is on him for a long time and he is placed before people's eyes. It certainly helps him in his business or profession.

Hence, a man's success or failure will receive a great deal of publicity in the business world, particularly if he is in a high position in an important campaign. This means that some men may try to avoid high positions because they feel that the risk of failure is too great and would be detrimental to their careers.

President of firm: If you are given a job in a campaign you simply *cannot* fail. It would be a reflection on your business and organizational ability. It is taken for granted that you will succeed. And people are apt to remember you because your name has been prominent. But no one is sure that their name will not be remembered equally well as a person who has done a poor job.

So important is success that the head of a campaign may try to arrange the objective of the campaign for an amount of money which he is reasonably sure that he can collect.

> *Professional Organizer F:* I don't think that the chairman of the last Q Campaign wanted an objective that was too high. It's a feather in his cap if he can make it. . . . It helps him a lot and people take note of him. Once a person heads a campaign that goes over, he is a marked man. He will be asked to do it again and again.

Failure to achieve the campaign objective is felt to be such a stigma on the executive of a campaign that some of the smaller campaigns may not publish their failures.

> *Professional Organizer G:* Mr. X [professional organizer] says that for some reason a number of campaigns don't make their objective, but say they do. He knows positively of several that didn't this year, and yet wouldn't admit it. Mr. X thinks that perhaps they think that it will be a stigma against them if they don't make it.

Another fear comes from the angle of personal competition. A man may not wish to take over a high executive position for fear that he will not be able to come up to the standard set by a personal or business rival in another campaign.

> *President, Bank Y:* The Z Campaign was a terrible strain right up to the end because we really didn't think we'd make it. They hadn't made their objective for a number of years. But I was *bound* that I would! I nearly killed myself doing it! You always want to do better than the other fellows! John Brown [member of a rival firm] is chairman this year. I bet he'll try to outdo me!

Hence, philanthropic activity can now serve as a testing-ground on which corporations can judge the abilities of participants. Failure may entail so much harmful publicity that some men are loath to take over the executive positions.

C. Background Characteristics of Men in Important Positions in Campaigns

The first two sections have shown that a relationship exists between participation in business and participation in philanthropy. This section extends this analysis to show the relationship of family background, positions in other philanthropic agencies, and club membership to campaign participation and economic success.[9] This information was obtained for a random sample of 67 men who had held high executive positions in the annual Community Chest Campaigns of Wellsville. All of these men had held high positions in business or the professions, and together held 458 directorships of corporations. By type of business affiliation, the 67 men were distributed as follows: finance, 23; industry, 15; professions, 8; transportation and communication, 7; insurance, 3; merchandising, 3; publishing, 3; wholesale, 2; real estate, 1; machinery repair, 1; and capitalist, 1. The positions in business held by these 67 men included: chairman of board, 3; president, 17; vice-president, 11; general manager, 8; assistant general manager, 1; manager, 3; assistant manager, 2; associate treasurer, 1; secretary, 1; proprietor, 1; partner, 13; general counsel, 1; and unknown, 5.[10]

Family Background   As the ethnic composition of the top social classes of Wellsville is largely of English and Scottish origin, it is not surprising to find that the tradition of *noblesse oblige* is still strong among the old wealthy families. Many of these families were early community benefactors through their donations of hospital or university buildings. The names of their descendants are still identified with the prestige attached to these concrete symbols of benevolence. If descendants of these families hold high executive positions in business, and especially if the business concern still bears the family name, then these men are "naturals" for high executive positions in philanthropy.

> *President of large wholesale firm:* Jim Reid was the natural person to head the last hospital campaign. The Reids have been interested in the hospital for generations. Jim's father was Chairman for years. Then the Reids are one of the great Wellsville families. And Jim is popular and has lots of friends whom he could get to help. And he has energy and lots of time because he works in a firm that could allow him time to do it.[11]

However, as philanthropic activity has changed from the control of the religious institutions and upper classes to the control of business, it was not unexpected to find that family position is not now as important in obtaining high positions in philanthropy. Today it is more essential to have a business organization behind the incumbent of a top executive position, for his business firm can assist him by looking after his work during the campaign and loaning additional staff, and as their representative he can use their name as a lever to get subscriptions and personnel.

Hence, although high family position still serves an important function for philanthropic activity through inculcating ideas of responsibility to the community, and family names can act as symbols of prestige in the campaign, they are only additional assets for acquiring high positions. It is now more essential for the incumbent to have an important business position in a firm which will back him in his money-raising efforts.

> *President, Bank Y:* No, I don't agree that your family background is all-important, because anyone that runs a campaign *must* have an organization behind him who can help. For example, when I took over the chairmanship of the Q Campaign I wrote to each of our branch bank managers. I told them that I didn't insist at all that they should work in the campaign, but that I would be very glad for any assistance that they could give me. And everyone of them worked terribly hard to help. But families are important in giving a sense of responsibility. It's born into some families—like the L family. Of course the first L was one of the biggest crooks, but he managed to pass on a sense of responsibility to others to his children.

Social Agencies   Executive positions on boards of social agencies have traditionally been the prerogative of the top social classes.[12] These positions identify the incumbents with the leisured class, and are another important medium for gaining community recognition. It was not possible to get completely accurate information for board memberships for the sample of 67 men. However, data found for 46 of the 67 men show that they held executive positions on 146 boards of charitable agencies.

While universities and hospitals are not usually included in the category of "social agencies", they are so dependent on private financial support in Wellsville that, for the purpose of this paper, they can in fact be placed in this category. Executive positions on the boards of these two institutions are the pinnacle of the prestige positions in Wellsville. Of the 67 men included in the same, 12 had been Governors or Chancellors of universities, and 41 had held executive positions on the boards of local hospitals.

These figures indicate that executive positions in social agencies are another important adjunct to the business career. Moreover, these positions mark the incumbent as a person ready—and fit—for further philanthropic responsibilities and higher business positions.

Club Membership   Many studies have shown the growing importance of club membership as a distinctive mark of social class position. In this study records and interviews showed a relationship between the individual's rise in the business hierarchy and his rise in the "club hierarchy". That is, many of the men studied were able to join the top-ranking clubs in Wellsville only after they had obtained certain positions in business.

Interviewees claimed that clubs have a distinct relationship to philanthropy for they "provide meeting-places to discuss strategy". In other words, as one of the important functions of clubs is to provide a locale for cliques, many of the informal decisions about personnel and subscriptions are carried out in their milieu, and friends are recruited.

Partner, Accounting firm: Bill drew a lot of clubmen into the F Campaign when he became Chairman of the Special Names Committee.

It is perhaps as difficult for the club member to resist the pressures to participate in philanthropy coming from fellow clubmen as it is for businessmen to resist the pressure coming from business associates. If this is so, it follows that participation in campaigns is expected of certain "club memberships" as such, in much the same way that it is expected of certain business positions.

The sample of 67 men had held 38 club memberships in *the* top-ranking club of Wellsville, 186 memberships in second-ranking clubs, and 104 memberships in third-ranking clubs. As no record of club membership could be found for 7 men, this means that the 60 men included in the sample had held 382 memberships in Wellsville's top 19 clubs. Club membership can thus be said to have a distinct relationship to a man's philanthropic career as well as to his business career.

Conclusions

Two important results have ensued from the gradual monopolization of money-raising campaigns by the business world.

On the one hand, philanthropic activity now serves as a means by which the modern businessman can strengthen his position in a highly competitive world by taking over as many philanthropic positions as possible. On the other hand, business firms must now engage in philanthropic activity in order to compete with rival firms and in order to enhance their relations with the public. This means that ambitious men will recognize the importance of philanthropic participation for their new careers, and business enterprises will see that their men participate in order that they may benefit from the reflected publicity.

Before the development of organized philanthropy in Wellsville, church membership and activity in church work were important adjuncts to the businessman's career. Now, however, it is much more important for the businessman to identify himself with philanthropic activity. This is largely due to the fact that the competitive nature of the campaigns displays the skills of the participants, and the publicity given the campaigns places the participant visibly before the public. In fact, participation in the large city-wide campaigns now gives a man and his firm more publicity than many of the usual advertising channels.

This paper has tried to show the relationship that now exists between business, philanthropy, and other community prestige-positions. It can be summed up in the words of an interviewee:

> *Manager of Trust Company*: There is a definite way up the business ladder in Wellsville. The bottom rung is to be Chairman of the G [lunch] Club. The top rung is to be Chairman of the Chamber of Commerce. In between you are on the executive of the Community Chest Campaigns, and join the A [top-ranking] Club. I've seen it happen again and again! If you make the Chairmanship of the G Club, you're made! Then "THEY" will see that you get to the top. But you *have* to be good or "THEY" won't back you!

NOTES

1. I am indebted to Professor Everett C. Hughes for stimulating discussion on this topic, and to Mrs. Nancy Brooks for assistance in gathering and analysing data.

   The materials of the paper were drawn in part from interviews with seventy men who had held prominent positions in the large city-wide money-raising campaigns of Wellsville, an Eastern Canadian city. Supplementary data on their careers were accumulated from a variety of sources, including complete records for thirteen city-wide campaigns held in Wellsville from 1909 to 1922; records for Community Chest campaigns from 1930 to 1951; and all published volumes of *Who's Who in Canada, The Canadian Who's Who, Canadiana*, and *The Directory of Directors*. Additional material was taken from the back and current files of the two leading newspapers in Wellsville and from records of many other Wellsville campaigns.

2. Throughout this article the term "canvassing" will be used to describe time given to any kind of campaign activity.

3. Since the Special Names committee is responsible for canvassing the largest individual and corporation subscribers, it is composed solely of influential businessmen.

4. This advancement does not necessarily take place in one particular campaign. The individual may take part in a number of different important city-wide campaigns such as the Community Chest, Red Cross, Salvation Army, Y.M.C.A., hospital or university campaigns, during his philanthropic career. Smaller campaigns are not important to his career.

5. Aileen D. Ross, "Organized Philanthropy in an Urban Community," *Canadian Journal of Economics and Political Science*, XVIII (November 1952), pp. 482-85.

6. Four aspects of the inner circle are of importance when considering its implication for philanthropy: its importance in sponsoring campaigns; its control of philanthropy; its importance as a vehicle for careers; its importance as sponsoring individuals for campaign positions. It is this last function of the inner circle that will be dealt with here.

7. Aileen D. Ross, "Social Control in Philanthropy," *American Journal of Sociology*, LVIII (March 1953), p. 451.

8. Norman Miller, "The Jewish Leadership of Lakeport," in Alvin W. Gouldner (ed.), *Studies in Leadership* (New York: Harper and Brothers, 1950), p. 213: "Functionally the [campaign] organization serves for the prestige-candidate as a stage from which he can make a regular and conspicuous show of his efforts."

9. Everett C. Hughes, "The Institutional Office and the Person," *American Journal of Sociology*, XLIII (November 1937), p. 411: "The interlocking of the directorships of educations, charitable and other philanthropic agencies is due . . . to the very fact that they are philanthropic. Philanthropic, as we know it, implies economic success; it comes late in a career. It may come only in the ground generation of success. But when it does come, it is quite as much a matter of assuming certain prerogatives and responsibilities in the control of philanthropic institutions as of giving money. The prerogatives and responsibilities form part of the successful man's conception of himself, and part of the world's expectation of him."

10. The random sample was drawn from the Campaign Chairmen, and men on the Special Names Committee of the Community Chest Campaigns from 1930 to 1951. The information given here was obtained from the sources outlined in footnote 1. The figures cannot claim to be accurate; they only represent the positions found in the available sources. It is therefore highly probable that the men represented in the sample have held many more directorships in corporations and executive positions in social agencies, hospitals, and universities than indicated.

11. Jim Reid is in the firm which still bears the family name. It should be noted that there is a double pressure to engage in philanthropy for such men, coming from both their business and their family positions.

12. Everett C. Hughes, "The Institutional Office and the Person," *loc. cit.*, p. 411. Professor Hughes quotes a survey in New York City that showed that the governing boards of settlement houses in that city were made up of people with prestige in business and professional life. This pattern has also been traced in Warner's studies of Yankee City; see W. L. Warner and P. S. Lunt, *The Social Life of a Modern Community* (New Haven: Yale University Press, 1941).

Social Structure & Identity

The consciousness of men does not determine their material existence; nor does their material existence determine their consciousness. Between consciousness and existence stand meanings and designs and communications which other men have passed on—first, in human speech itself, and later, by the management of symbols. These received and manipulated interpretations decisively influence such consciousness as men have of their existence. They provide the clues to what men see, to how they respond to it, to how they feel about it, and to how they respond to these feelings. Symbols focus experience; meanings organize knowledge, guiding the surface perceptions of an instant no less than the aspirations of a lifetime. (Mills, 1963:405-406)

MILLS'S STATEMENT EXPRESSES the importance of interpretation and symbolism in the construction of social activity and identity. Selectively and subjectively, out of life's experiences, we take into account the objective world, giving some features prominence, overlooking and ignoring other aspects of the situation.

Our biographies and social position link us with some groups and separate us from others. Our experiences with specific others, and the meanings we learn and share are focused by the symbols that have developed to communicate collective meanings. These meanings are the bases for human action and may or may not reflect other interpretations or objective circumstances. Our identification, membership, and participation with others is essentially symbolic.

Symbolic action is an act of identification. Our manner of self-expression and the symbols we adopt indicate how, and with whom, we identify ourselves. Our networks of symbolic communications and understandings depend on the use of conventional symbols which allow us to share certain perspectives. The framework within which we act—those patterns of symbolically communicated meanings and definitions of the situation—is the social organization or structure of the situation.

The dynamic quality of social relationships (social structure) justifies the symbolic interactionist emphasis on the process by which we create and recreate the social order. The perceptions, meanings, and understandings that we develop and operate out of are most affected by our evolving relationships with others.

One characteristic found in many of our relationships is inequality. The unequal distribution of opportunities and rewards in society creates social hierarchies, in which people are distinguished by their social position. Social inequality is a source of group-defined differences because certain factors physically and symbolically separate various groups. Individuals who belong to the same social class and have similar educational backgrounds and occupations will likely share perspectives about their situation, and see themselves as different from the others in the social hierarchy.

Social inequality restricts and oppresses some people, while it benefits others. In our society for example, social position, as strongly affected by economic condition, is associated with personal worth. Individuals or groups who are economically superior are believed to be "superior" on a personal level as well; society attributes certain valued qualities to these people. Inferiority, then, consists of a lack of these subjectively defined or culturally biased attributes. The poor are typically cast as the "fallen", deficient, or lacking in character, ability, or motivation. Objective inferiority of material condition, poverty, is a positive attribute only when it is accepted in a vow by religious members of the society.

The relationship between economic condition and personal worth is both reflected by symbols (status symbols) and internalized in terms of images. The imagery we learn, including the connotations, assumptions, or typifications of superiority and inferiority, is insidiously incorporated in definitions we make about other people's characters. Social status and social class conceptions are reinforced by the breakdown of communication between the members of different classes. The symbolic communication that takes place is primarily controlled and directed by the more powerful individuals in the relationship, thus reinforcing the symbolic inequity.

One of the major problems in applying sociological theories to the study of identity is the difficulty involved in expressing the relationship of the individual to concepts of structure (group, organization, role, values, status group, institution, social class, etc.), which themselves are relationships in process. This book tries to emphasize both structure and process. The dynamic quality of social relationships or social structure has dictated our stress on understanding the importance of symbolic interaction processes which create and recreate the ongoing social order.

The readings in the last section of the book examine the way social class differences are reflected in different group-based definitions of the situation. In the first essay, Herbert Blumer describes and analyzes the relationships of human beings constructing and sharing their social worlds; he puts a symbolic interactionist emphasis on understanding the interpretations made symbolically by participants. Blumer's essay is followed by two articles that discuss elites. It is hoped that a structural and historical study as presented by Lawrence Felt and Stephen Berkowitz will complement the more intimate, firsthand glimpse of Canadian elites by Peter Newman, to provide a better picture of the relationship of social class and identity.

In the last section, James Lorimer and Myfanwy Phillips study the class-based identity of working people. The article also helps dramatize the contrast in life style and self-perceptions of working people and the elites described by Newman. The importance of such contrasts to the formation and maintenance of a class-based identity is reinforced by the working people presented in the study, who describe themselves and their identity in relation to the groups above and beneath them in the social hierarchy.

Society as Symbolic Interaction

HERBERT BLUMER

A VIEW OF human society as symbolic interaction has been followed more than it has been formulated. Partial, usually fragmentary, statements of it are to be found in the writings of a number of eminent scholars, some inside the field of sociology and some outside. Among the former we may note such scholars as Charles Horton Cooley, W. I. Thomas, Robert E. Parks, E. W. Burgess, Florian Znaniecki, Ellsworth Faris, and James Mickel Williams. Among those outside the discipline we may note William James, John Dewey, and George Herbert Mead. None of these scholars, in my judgment, has presented a systematic statement of the nature of human group life from the standpoint of symbolic interaction. Mead stands out among all of them in laying bare the fundamental premises of the approach, yet he did little to develop its methodological implications for sociological study. Students who seek to depict the position of symbolic interaction may easily give different pictures of it. What I have to present should be regarded as my personal version. My aim is to present the basic premises of the point of view and to develop their methodological consequences for the study of human group life.

   The term "symbolic interaction" refers, of course, to the peculiar and distinctive character of interaction as it takes place between human beings. The peculiarity consists in the fact that human beings interpret or "define" each other's actions instead of merely reacting to each other's actions. Their "response" is not made directly to the actions of one another but instead is based on the meaning which they attach to such actions. Thus, human interaction is mediated by the use of symbols, by interpretation, or by ascertaining the meaning of one another's actions. This mediation is equivalent to inserting a process of interpretation between stimulus and response in the case of human behavior.

The simple recognition that human beings interpret each other's actions as the means of acting toward one another has permeated the thought and writings of many scholars of human conduct and of human group life. Yet few of them have endeavored to analyze what such interpretation implies about the nature of the human being or about the nature of human association. They are usually content with a mere recognition that "interpretation" should be caught by the student, or with a simple realization that symbols, such as cultural norms or values, must be introduced into their analyses. Only G. H. Mead, in my judgment, has sought to think through what the act of interpretation implies for an understanding of the human being, human action, and human association. The essentials of his analysis are so penetrating and profound and so important for an understanding of human group life that I wish to spell them out, even though briefly.

The key feature in Mead's analysis is that the human being has a self. This idea should not be cast aside as esoteric or glossed over as something that is obvious and hence not worthy of attention. In declaring that the human being has a self, Mead had in mind chiefly that the human being can be the object of his own actions. He can act toward himself as he might act toward others. Each of us is familiar with actions of this sort in which the human being gets angry with himself, rebuffs himself, takes pride in himself, argues with himself, tries to bolster his own courage, tells himself that he should "do this" or not "do that," sets goals for himself, makes compromises with himself, and plans what he is going to do. That the human being acts toward himself in these and countless other ways is a matter of easy empirical observation. To recognize that the human being can act toward himself is no mystical conjuration.

Mead regards this ability of the human being to act toward himself as the central mechanism with which the human being faces and deals with his world. This mechanism enables the human being to make indications to himself of things in his surroundings and thus to guide his actions by what he notes. Anything of which a human being is conscious is something which he is indicating to himself—the ticking of a clock, a knock at the door, the appearance of a friend, the remark made by a companion, a recognition that he has a task to perform, or the realization that he has a cold. Conversely, anything of which he is not conscious is, *ipso facto*, something which he is not indicating to himself. The conscious life of the human being, from the time that he awakens until he falls asleep, is a continual flow of self-indications—notations of the things with which he deals and takes into account. We are given, then, a picture of the human being as an organism which confronts its world with a mechanism for making indications to itself. This is the mechanism that is involved in interpreting the actions of others. To interpret the actions of another is to point out to oneself that the action has this or that meaning or character.

Now, according to Mead, the significance of making indications to oneself is of paramount importance. The importance lies along two lines. First, to indicate something is to extricate it from its setting, to hold it apart, to give it a meaning or, in Mead's language, to make it into an object. An object—that is to say, anything that an individual indicates to himself—is different from a stimulus; instead of having an intrinsic character which acts on the individual and which can be identified apart from the individual, its character or meaning is conferred on it by the individual. The object is a product of the individual's disposition to act instead of being an antecedent stimulus which evokes the act. Instead of the individual being surrounded by an environment of pre-existing objects which play upon him and call forth his behavior, the proper picture is that he constructs his objects on the basis of his on-going activity. In any of his countless acts—whether minor, like dressing himself, or major, like organizing himself for a professional career—the individual is designating different objects to himself, giving them meaning, judging their suitability to his action, and making decisions on the basis of the judgment. This is what is meant by interpretation or acting on the basis of symbols.

The second important implication of the fact that the human being makes indications to himself is that his action is constructed or built up instead of being a mere release. Whatever the action in which he is engaged, the human individual proceeds by pointing out to himself the divergent things which have to be taken into account in the course of his action. He has to note what he wants to do and how he is to do it; he has to point out to himself the various conditions which may be instrumental to his action and those which may obstruct his action; he has to take account of the demands, the expectations, the prohibitions, and the threats as they may arise in the situation in which he is acting. His action is built up step by step through a process of such self-indication. The human individual pieces together and guides his action by taking account of different things and interpreting their significance for his prospective action. There is no instance of conscious action of which this is not true.

The process of constructing action through making indications to oneself cannot be swallowed up in any of the conventional psychological categories. This process is distinct from and different from what is spoken of as the "ego"—just as it is different from any other conception which conceives of the self in terms of composition or organization. Self-indication is a moving communicative process in which the individual notes things, assesses them, gives them a meaning, and decides to act on the basis of the meaning. The human being stands over against the world, or against "alters," with such a process and not with a mere ego. Further, the process of self-indication cannot be subsumed under the forces, whether from the outside or inside, which are presumed to play upon the individual to produce his behavior. Environmental pressures, external stimuli, organic drives, wishes, attitudes, feelings, ideas, and their like do not cover or explain the process of self-indication. The process of self-indication stands over against them in that the individual points out to himself and interprets the appearance or expression of such things, noting a given social demand that is made on him, recognizing a command, observing that he is hungry, realizing that he wishes to buy something, aware that he has a given feeling, conscious that he dislikes eating with someone he despises, or aware that he is thinking of doing some given thing. By virtue of indicating such things to himself, he places himself over against them and is able to act back against them, accepting them, rejecting them, or transforming them in accordance with how he defines or interprets them. His behavior, accordingly, is not a result of such things as environmental pressures, stimuli, motives, attitudes, and ideas but arises instead from how he interprets and handles these things in the action which he is constructing. The process of self-indication by means of which human action is formed cannot be accounted for by factors which precede the act. The process of self-indication exists in its own right and must be accepted and studied as such. It is through this process that the human being constructs his conscious action.

Now Mead recognizes that the formation of action by the individual through a process of self-indication always takes place in a social context. Since this matter is so vital to an understanding of symbolic interaction it needs to be explained carefully. Fundamentally, group action takes the form of a fitting together of individual lines of action. Each individual aligns his action to the action of others by ascertaining what they are doing or what they intend to do—that is, by getting the meaning of their acts. For Mead, this is done by the individual "taking the role" of others —either the role of a specific person or the role of a group (Mead's "generalized other"). In taking such roles the individual seeks to ascertain the intention or direction of the acts of others. He forms and aligns his own action on the basis of such interpretation of the acts of others. This is the fundamental way in which group action takes place in human society.

The foregoing are the essential features, as I see them, in Mead's analysis of the bases of symbolic interaction. They presuppose the following: that human society is made up of individuals who have selves (that is, make indications to themselves); that individual action is a construction and not a release, being built up by the individual through noting and interpreting features of the situations in which he acts; that group or collective action consists of the aligning of individual actions, brought about by the individuals' interpreting or taking into account each other's actions. Since my purpose is to present and not to defend the position of symbolic interaction I shall not endeavor in this essay to advance support for the three premises which I have just indicated. I wish merely to say that the three premises can be easily verified empirically. I know of no instance of human group action to which the three premises do not apply. The reader is challenged to find or think of a single instance which they do not fit.

I wish now to point out that sociological views of human society are, in general, markedly at variance with the premises which I have indicated as underlying symbolic interaction. Indeed, the predominant number of such views, especially those in vogue at the present time, do not see or treat human society as symbolic interaction. Wedded, as they tend to be, to some form of sociological determinism, they adopt images of human society, of individuals in it, and of group action which do not square with the premises of symbolic interaction. I wish to say a few words about the major lines of variance.

Sociological thought rarely recognizes or treats human societies as composed of individuals who have selves. Instead, they assume human beings to be merely organisms with some kind of organization, responding to forces which play upon them. Generally, although not exclusively, these forces are lodged in the make-up of the society, as in the case of "social system," "social structure," "culture," "status position," "social role," "custom," "institution," "collective representation," "social situation," "social norm," and "values." The assumption is that the behavior of people as members of a society is an expression of the play on them of these kinds of factors or forces. This, of course, is the logical position which is necessarily taken when the scholar explains their behavior or phases of their behavior in terms of one or another of such social factors. The individuals who compose a human society are treated as the media through which such factors operate, and the social action of such individuals is regarded as an expression of such factors. This approach or point of view denies, or at least ignores, that human beings have selves—that they act by making indications to themselves. Incidentally, the "self" is not brought into the picture by introducing such items as organic drives, motives, attitudes, feelings, internalized social factors, or psychological components. Such psychological factors have the same status as the social factors mentioned: they are regarded as factors which play on the individual to produce his action. They do not constitute the process of self-indication. The process of self-indication stands over against them, just as it stands over against the social factors which play on the human being. Practically all sociological conceptions of human society fail to recognize that the individuals who compose it have selves in the sense spoken of.

Correspondingly, such sociological conceptions do not regard the social actions of individuals in human society as being constructed by them through a process of interpretation. Instead, action is treated as a product of factors which play on and through individuals. The social behavior of people is not seen as built up by them through an interpretation of objects, situations, or the actions of others. If a place is given to "interpretation," the interpretation is regarded as merely an expression of other factors (such as motives) which precede the act, and accordingly disappears as a factor in its own right. Hence, the social action of people is treated as an outward flow or expression of forces playing on them rather than as acts which are built up by people through their interpretation of the situations in which they are placed.

These remarks suggest another significant line of difference between general sociological views and the position of symbolic interaction. These two sets of views differ in where they lodge social action. Under the perspective of symbolic interaction, social action is lodged in acting individuals who fit their respective lines of action to one another through a process of interpretation; group action is the collective action of such individuals. As opposed to this view, sociological conceptions generally lodge social action in the action of society or in some unit of society. Examples of this are legion. Let me cite a few. Some conceptions, in treating societies or human groups as "social systems," regard group action as an expression of a system, either in a state of balance or seeking to achieve balance. Or group action is conceived as an expression of the "functions" of a society or of a group. Or group action is regarded as the outward expression of elements lodged in society or the group, such as cultural demands, societal purposes, social values, or institutional stresses. These typical conceptions ignore or blot out a view of group life or of group action as consisting of the collective or concerted actions of individuals seeking to meet their life situations. If recognized at all, the efforts of people to develop collective acts to meet their situations are subsumed under the play of underlying or transcending forces which are lodged in society or its parts. The individuals composing the society or the group become "carriers," or media for the expression of such forces; and the interpretative behavior by means of which people form their actions is merely a coerced link in the play of such forces.

The indication of the foregoing lines of variance should help to put the position of symbolic interaction in better perspective. In the remaining discussion I wish to sketch somewhat more fully how human society appears in terms of symbolic interaction and to point out some methodological implications.

Human society is to be seen as consisting of acting people, and the life of the society is to be seen as consisting of their actions. The acting units may be separate individuals, collectivities whose members are acting together on a common quest, or organizations acting on behalf of a constituency. Respective examples are individual purchasers in a market, a play group or missionary band, and a business corporation or a national professional association. There is no empirically observable activity in a human society that does not spring from some acting unit. This banal statement needs to be stressed in light of the common practice to sociologists of reducing human society to social units that do not act— for example, social classes in modern society. Obviously, there are ways of viewing human society other than in terms of the acting units that compose it. I merely wish to point out that in respect to concrete or empirical activity human society must necessarily be seen in terms of the acting units that form it. I would add that any scheme of human society claiming to be a realistic analysis has to respect and be congruent with the empirical recognition that a human society consists of acting units.

Corresponding respect must be shown to the conditions under which such units act. One primary condition is that action takes place in and with regard to a situation. Whatever be the acting unit—an individual, a family, a school, a church, a business firm, a labor union, a legislature, and so on—any particular action is formed in the light of the situation in which it takes place. This leads to the recognition of a second major condition, namely, that the action is formed or constructed by interpreting the situation. The acting unit necessarily has to identify the things which it has to take into account—tasks, opportunities, obstacles, means, demands, discomforts, dangers, and the like; it has to assess them in some fashion and it has to make decisions on the basis of the assessment. Such interpretative behavior may take place in the individual guiding his own action, in a collectivity of individuals acting in concert, or in "agents" acting on behalf of a group or organization. Group life consists of acting units developing acts to meet the situations in which they are placed.

Usually, most of the situations encountered by people in a given society are defined or "structured" by them in the same way. Through previous interaction they develop and acquire common understandings or definitions of how to act in this or that situation. These common definitions enable people to act alike. The common repetitive behavior of people in such situations should not mislead the student into believing that no process of interpretation is in play; on the contrary, even though fixed, the actions of the participating people are constructed by them through a process of interpretation. Since ready-made and commonly accepted definitions are at hand, little strain is placed on people in guiding and organizing their acts. However, many other situations may not be defined in a single way by the participating people. In this event, their lines of action do not fit together readily and collective action is blocked. Interpretations have to be developed and effective accommodation of the participants to one another has to be worked out.

In the case of such "undefined" situations, it is necessary to trace and study the emerging process of definition which is brought into play.

Insofar as sociologists or students of human society are concerned with the behavior of acting units, the position of symbolic interaction requires the student to catch the process of interpretation through which they construct their actions. This process is not to be caught merely by turning to conditions which are antecedent to the process. Such antecedent conditions are helpful in understanding the process insofar as they enter into it, but as mentioned previously they do not constitute the process. Nor can one catch the process merely by inferring its nature from the overt action which is its product. To catch the process, the student must take the role of the acting unit whose behavior he is studying. Since the interpretation is being made by the acting unit in terms of objects designated and appraised, meanings acquired, and decisions made, the process has to be seen from the standpoint of the acting unit. It is the recognition of this fact that makes the research work of such scholars as R. E. Park and W. I. Thomas so notable. To try to catch the interpretative process by remaining aloof as a so-called "objective" observer and refusing to take the role of the acting unit is to risk the worst kind of subjectivism—the objective observer is likely to fill in the process of interpretation with his own surmises in place of catching the process as it occurs in the experience of the acting unit which uses it.

By and large, of course, sociologists do not study human society in terms of its acting units. Instead, they are disposed to view human society in terms of structure or organization and to treat social action as an expression of such structure or organization. Thus, reliance is placed on such structural categories as social system, culture, norms, values, social stratification, status positions, social roles and institutional organization. These are used both to analyze human society and to account for social action within it. Other major interests of sociological scholars center around this focal theme of organization. One line of interest is to view organization in terms of the functions it is supposed to perform. Another line of interest is to study societal organization as a system seeking equilibrium; here the scholar endeavors to detect mechanisms which are indigenous to the system. Another line of interest is to identify forces which play upon organization to bring about changes in it; here the scholar endeavors, especially through comparative study, to isolate a relation between causative factors and structural results. These various lines of sociological perspective and interest, which are so strongly entrenched today, leap over the acting units of a society and bypass the interpretative process by which such acting units build up their actions.

These respective concerns with organization on one hand and with acting units on the other hand set the essential difference between conventional views of human society and the view of it implied in symbolic interaction. The latter view recognizes the presence of organization to human society and respects its importance. However, it sees and treats organization differently. The difference is along two major lines. First, from the standpoint of symbolic interaction the organization of a human society is the framework inside of which social action takes place and is not the determinant of that action. Second, such organization and changes in it are the product of the activity of acting units and not of "forces" which leave such acting units out of account. Each of these two major lines of difference should be explained briefly in order to obtain a better understanding of how human society appears in terms of symbolic interaction.

From the standpoint of symbolic interaction, social organization is a framework inside of which acting units develop their actions. Structural features, such as "culture," "social systems," "social stratification," or "social roles," set conditions for their action but do not determine their action. People—that is, acting units—do not act toward culture, social structure or the like; they act toward situations. Social organization enters into action only to the extent to which it shapes situations in which people act, and to the extent to which it supplies fixed sets of symbols which people use in interpreting their situations. These two forms of influence of social organization are important. In the case of settled and stabilized societies, such as isolated primitive tribes and peasant communities, the influence is certain to be profound. In the case of human societies, particularly modern societies, in which streams of new situations arise and old situations become unstable, the influence of organization decreases. One should bear in mind that the most important element confronting an acting unit in situations is the actions of other acting units. In modern society, with its increasing criss-crossing of lines of action, it is common for situations to arise in which the actions of participants are not previously regularized and standardized. To this extent, existing social organization does not shape the situations. Correspondingly, the symbols or tools of interpretation used by acting units in such situations may vary and shift considerably. For these reasons, social action may go beyond, or depart from, existing organization in any of its structural dimensions. The organization of a human society is not to be identified with the process of interpretation used by its acting units; even though it affects that process, it does not embrace or cover the process.

Perhaps the most outstanding consequence of viewing human society as organization is to overlook the part played by acting units in social change. The conventional procedure of sociologists is (a) to identify human society (or some part of it) in terms of an established or organized form, (b) to identify some factor or condition of change playing upon the human society or the given part of it, and (c) to identify the new form assumed by the society following upon the play of the factor of change. Such observations permit the student to couch propositions to the effect that a given factor of change playing upon a given organized form results in a given new organized form. Examples ranging from crude to refined statements are legion, such as that an economic depression increases solidarity in the families of workingmen or that industrialization replaces extended families by nuclear families. My concern here is not with the validity of such propositions but with the methodological position which they presuppose. Essentially, such propositions either ignore the role of the interpretative behavior of acting units in the given instance of change, or else regard the interpretative behavior as coerced by the factor of change. I wish to point out that any line of social change, since it involves change in human action, is necessarily mediated by interpretation on the part of the people caught up in the change—the change appears in the form of new situations in which people have to construct new forms of action. Also, in line with what has been said previously, interpretations of new situations are not predetermined by conditions antecedent to the situations but depend on what is taken into account and assessed in the actual situations in which behavior is formed. Variations in interpretation may readily occur as different acting units cut out different objects in the situation, or give different weight to the objects which they note, or piece objects together in different patterns. In formulating propositions of social change, it would be wise to recognize that any given line of such change is mediated by acting units interpreting the situations with which they are confronted.

Students of human society will have to face the question of whether their preoccupation with categories of structure and organization can be squared with the interpretative process by means of which human beings, individually and collectively, act in human society. It is the discrepancy between the two which plagues such students in their efforts to attain scientific propositions of the sort achieved in the physical and biological sciences. It is this discrepancy, further, which is chiefly responsible for their difficulty in fitting hypothetical propositions to new arrays of empirical data. Efforts are made, of course, to overcome these shortcomings by devising new structural categories, by formulating new structural hypotheses, by developing more refined techniques of research, and even by formulating new methodological schemes of a structural character. These efforts continue to ignore or to explain away the interpretative process by which people act, individually and collectively, in society. The question remains whether human society or social action can be successfully analyzed by schemes which refuse to recognize human beings as they are, namely, as persons constructing individual and collective action through an interpretation of the situations which confront them.

SOCIAL STRATIFICATION INVOLVES the ranking of social participants and each stratum includes those who have similar chances to gain highly valued experiences or possessions. The characteristics of any stratum of society are perhaps best determined by noting the ways it differs from other strata. To appreciate the difference between groups at various levels of the social structure we begin by describing the elites of Canadian society. Later in this section, the working class is examined, and the contrasts between this class and the elites serve to emphasize the importance of social class location and participation to people's views of reality, others, and themselves.

There are a number of characteristics that distinguish the elites from other groups in the society. The chief distinction of elites is money, which in turn means power; our elites are composed of rich men (with few exceptions) of enormous power. Because of their wealth and power, they are in the unique position of being able to make decisions that profoundly affect others. Their decisions to expand, move, or redirect factories and industries have tremendous implications for Canadian workers, towns, and cities. Their power in economic decision-making is accompanied by influence in political decision-making. This combination of powers helps guarantee that their version of reality is dominant.

The following selections by Felt and Berkowitz and Newman present both a historical and present-day picture of the elites. These readings provide us with a picture of the influence and ways of our most powerful members of society.

Elite Structure and Identity in Canada: A Historical Overview

LAWRENCE F. FELT/S. D. BERKOWITZ

Introduction

A CENTRAL CONCERN of symbolic interactionist sociology is the study of various social identities. By identity is meant that complex of symbols, values, and structured relations with others that provides both the collective and individual answer to the rhetorial query "Who am I?" The research procedures and theoretical constructs employed in the study of

Lawrence F. Felt is an Associate Professor, Department of Sociology, Memorial University, and an Associate Director of the Institute for Social Research.

S. D. Berkowitz is an Assistant Professor, Department of Sociology, University of Toronto, and a Research Associate of the Institute for Policy Analysis.

social identities are well known. A stabilized collectivity, be it a delinquent gang or a highly professionalized occupational group such as doctors, is selected. The collective identity of that group is sketched and then the processes that allow that group to survive, such as recruitment, socialization, and identity management *vis-à-vis* other groups and the society at large, are examined. This is usually accomplished by focusing upon an individual's passage through various stages of group participation from the status of an outsider to that of a fully accepted member. The concept of "career" is often used to link the various stages and the problems of moving from one stage of participation to another.

The routine methodology for studying social identities has consisted of field work and semistructured interviewing. The size of the group selected has also been reasonably small. Thus, although generalizations regarding larger groupings in a society are frequently made, such research has been defined as micro-sociological in its focus.

There is no necessary logic in the study of social identities, however, that requires a micro-focus. In this essay we offer some initial efforts toward bridging the gap between discrete, concrete identities and a vaguer concept of a Canadian national identity. At the same time, we hope to suggest some ways in which historical structural data can be integrated with social psychological factors in the study of Canadian identity. Specifically, we will attempt to integrate historical material on Canadian elites with contemporary aspects of Canadian identity.

Elite Identity and Canadian Identity

The ingredients that contribute to a national identity are numerous and complex. One significant ingredient, however, is the identity (or identities) of various national elites. Elites contribute to national identity formation in a number of obvious and not-so-obvious ways. By virtue of their position at or near the top of institutional areas important to the functioning of the society, elites make decisions about the specific values and goals that their institutions will pursue. Insofar as such institutions are considered to be national, elite decisions help to articulate a national image. Consider federal political institutions and their elite. Decisions made in the Ministry of External Affairs convey to non-Canadians an image of "who we are and what we stand for". Once this image has been internalized abroad, it becomes a major determinant of the way foreigners respond to us. Through media, diplomatic contacts, and even ordinary citizen contact, the image created by national political institutions is reflected back upon us as if by a mirror. This reflected image is then incorporated into our national image.

Elites can affect identity formation in more complex and subtle ways as well. An interesting example of this is found in the unintended influence of the Canadian financial elite. Historically, the values and behavior of the elite in charge of our chartered banks have been cautious and conservative with respect to providing risk capital to Canadian industrial entrepreneurs. This orientation is said to be a result of the Scottish Presbyterian origins of the early bankers, and the fact that our banks were modeled after Scottish institutions. This policy consequently forced many Canadian entrepreneurs to move south to the United States. Another effect was the penetration of foreign direct investment, first by the British and in the twentieth century by Americans; this investment produced the industrial infrastructure. At the level of a national Canadian identity, American investment has played an important part in the rather paradoxical attitude many businessmen and the public at large display toward American cultural, economic, and political influence in our society: a wariness coupled with a thankful attitude for the many economic benefits that have resulted from the "branch plants".[1]

The examples discussed above oversimplify the relationships between elite actions and identities and the formation of a national identity, but nevertheless they demonstrate the advantages of using a focus upon elites to elucidate certain aspects of our national identity. In the remainder of this essay, we shall present a historical overview of the structure of Canadian elites and some of the more salient aspects of their identity. Our primary concern will be with both providing some descriptive information on these elites and introducing individuals with little sociological background to some theoretical tools for analyzing the elites. Once this is accomplished, we shall conclude with a brief discussion of some ways in which our elites have affected and continue to influence our collective self-conception.

Elites and Power

Despite frequent legal equality, no modern society has ever been observed in which all persons participate equally in the making of decisions that affect them as members of that society. This is particularly true if we consider only those higher level decisions which have the most pervasive impact on the society such as law-making, the policies of large economic firms, or the creation of national cultural symbols. Most of us are receivers rather than initiators of such decisions.

Sociologists use the term "elite" to describe a group of individuals participating in higher level decision-making in a society. To the extent that they are able to enforce their decisions effectively, such elites are said to possess power. Because of the extreme importance of these two terms to our presentation, it may prove helpful to develop a better understanding of their meaning before proceeding.

In every area of human activity, some individuals (for a variety of reasons that we need not discuss here)[2] are more successful than others and thus provide leadership and direction to the activity. This is as true of horseshoe pitching as the practice of law. In everyday language, many people use the word "elite" to distinguish these successful individuals from the more ordinary ones engaged in the same activity. A society then, to follow this usage, possesses a vast multitude of elites corresponding to the various activities going on in that society (a horseshoe-pitching elite, a legal elite, a canoeing elite, a business elite, etc.). The use of "elite" in this manner does not assist us very much in understanding how higher level decisions are made, because the term is far too general. For that reason, sociologists describe as elites only those groups of individuals at or near the top in certain general categories of activity thought to be most important to society. These activities include politics, economic enterprise, religion, education, media, and the arts. Some writers have added a few areas, such as labor,[3] to the list. Taken collectively, these areas of activity represent the source of most major decisions in a society. It is in this restricted sense that we will use the term "elite".

Power is the capacity to enforce a decision. The specific forms of such power may vary considerably. In its most primitive form, power is the ability to put a decision into effect through the use of physical coercion. Normally, however, power is utilized in more complex, subtle ways. Some individuals, because of the positions they occupy in a society, are mandated by the other members of that society to make and enforce decisions on their behalf. Elected representatives of government are the most obvious examples of persons entrusted with power. When individuals acquire such a mandate, sociologists refer to their resulting power as legitimate or legal power. This form of power is the inverse of sheer physical coercion.

Between these extremes, many additional forms of power exist. For example, under certain conditions, control over information may be used as a form of power. Consider the case of a public utility company wishing to raise prices. A governmental regulatory board must approve the raise and so requests the firm to provide it with information on the firm's profitability. Insofar as the firm can withhold damaging information (for example, because of its complex auditing system which only its personnel can decipher), and present evidence supporting its requested increases, it is exercising a very subtle form of power and is highly likely to be able to enforce its decision to raise prices.

Frequently, friendships or business relationships with an individual possessing power may be used by other parties to increase their own power. Sociologists use the term "influence" to describe such indirectly acquired power.

The application of the terms "elite" and "power" to an

understanding of decision-making in Canadian society is more complex than our rather simple definitions imply. Not all areas of activity mentioned earlier as being important to societal functioning have, in fact, equal importance. In contemporary western societies, institutions of government (elected bodies and the appointed civil service in particular) and private economic organizations stand out as affecting the citizenry in the most far-reaching ways. Sociologists agree that the institution of religion, on the other hand, is no longer as powerful as it once was. As governments grow larger and economic power continues to be concentrated in a smaller number of firms, the importance of elites in these two sectors of society will increase even further.

The examples of the increasing power of government and large private economic firms suggest an important characteristic of power. Power is, to a very large extent, an institutional and not a personal phenomenon. While some of the differences in the power between various members of an elite may be related to the personal characteristics of the elite member (personality or intelligence, for example), the primary sources of power are the institutional resources that may be mobilized to enforce a decision. The clearest example of this occurs with the government, where extensive resources (courts, police, jail) exist to ensure compliance with a decision. If a prime minister is defeated in an election, he may retain some of his former power in the form of personal influence; he relinquishes most of his power, however, when forced to vacate the position of leader of the government.

If it is great enough, power in one area of activity may be extended to other, seemingly unrelated activities. In many cases, the power of the external elite may be greater than that of the elite controlling this other area. Consider the newspaper industry (part of the media) and its elite. Countless examples of direct and indirect extensions of power (through out-right purchase, withholding of advertising, etc.) by non-media, economic elites are available in the briefs presented to the recent Royal Commission on the Media[4] and in the evidence presented at the hearing on the Irving newspaper monopoly in New Brunswick.[5]

What accounts for this tendency of elites to attempt to expand the scope of their power to other activities? In some cases, it is simply a question of power corrupting the individuals' desires; the more power they have, the more power they want. In most cases there is an additional, more practical explanation as well. In an advanced society, virtually all important activities are likely to be highly interrelated. Thus, the extension of power into another area may actually increase the amount of power in the original activity. In our example, control of newspapers by a member of the economic elite serves the interests of that elite by reducing outlets for criticism of the group, or by reducing the marketing ability of economic competitors through control of newspaper advertising.

Figure 1: Elites in Society

Elites are groups of individuals at or near the top of societally important institutions. Power is the varying ability to enforce decisions by individual collective elites.

Institutional sector elite. Economic and governmental elite most important.

Each sector elite divided into more specific elites that possess varying degrees of power and may either cooperate or conflict.

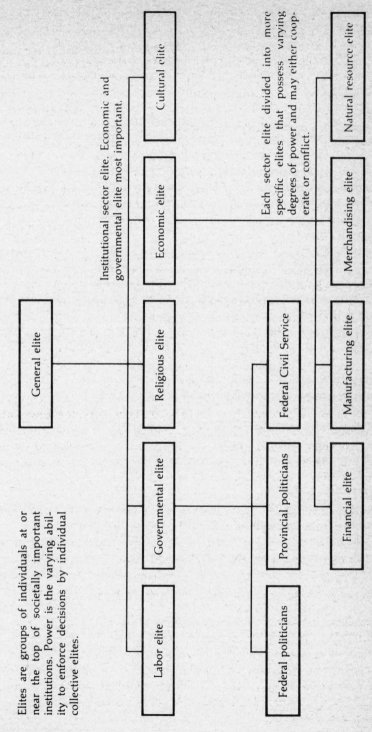

In addition to our observation that not all elite activities are equally important in the society and that, therefore, not all elites have equal amounts of power, two further comments should be made. First, not all elites within the same general activity are exactly equal in power; second, we cannot assume that elites within the same general activity are unified and cooperative.

Our first point should be obvious. Few would consider a parliamentary backbencher equal in power to a prime minister even though both would be considered members of the political elite as we have used the term. The prime minister can draw upon many more resources as head of the government. Often, however, it is very difficult to rank members of the same elite according to the power they possess. Is a federal cabinet minister more powerful than the premier of Ontario? Is the president of a large manufacturing firm more powerful than a member of the board of directors of a chartered bank? The evaluation of positions in terms of their relative power in a society is difficult. Rather than developing some specific ranking of elites within the same area, sociologists have been content to talk more generally about the approximate amount of power possessed by a particular member of an elite.

When social activities are placed in a few general categories, each with its own elite, the diversity of these activities is overlooked. When speaking of an economic elite, sociologists refer to individuals who, in reality, are involved in many different economic activities—from banking to manufacturing to mining to merchandising. Thus there is no reason to assume that such an elite is unified on all issues. Indeed, there is frequent conflict among members of this or any other elite; provincial politicians often fight with federal politicians and bankers frequently clash with manufacturers over credit policies.

We have examined the terms "elite" and "power" to gain a basic understanding of the way sociologists attempt to explain the complex processes of decision-making in a modern society such as Canada's. Figure 1 attempts to summarize what we have thus far argued. With this formal presentation of elites and power behind us, let us turn to a more specific discussion of Canadian society.

Canadian Elites: Past and Present

The particular types of elites centrally involved in a society's decision-making vary over time. As the structure of the society changes, new types of elites gain prominence while others become obsolete. Thus, for example, a merchant elite (within the economic elite) plays a central role in decision-making in a society where there is little industrial activity but much trading; as industrialization proceeds, however, manufacturing elites will evolve and challenge the merchant elite. Similarly, a civil service elite will evolve to challenge an elected political elite as a society modernizes. In short, at any point in the development of a society, some types of elites are powerful and others not.

Canada has passed through five general stages of development since its founding as a colony. In each stage, a different configuration of elite types was important. While we will restrict our most thorough discussion to the fifth and present stage, some comments on earlier stages will provide a perspective from which to view the present.

1. Early Colonial Stage (to 1840)   Canada was a rural, lightly populated colonial society. A great many important decisions affecting the colony were made abroad. The decision-making elite in Canada was organized into two small groups of no more than thirty or forty individuals each. The group in Upper Canada (Ontario) was called the "Family Compact" while that in Lower Canada (Quebec) was termed the "Chateau Clique". Three specific types of people comprised each group; wealthy merchants (economic elite), religious leaders (religious elite) such as Strachan in Upper Canada, and colonial administrators (political elite) appointed from England. While the official power to make decisions was vested in the colonial administrators and their staff (termed the "executive council"), members of the merchant and religious elite unofficially played equal parts in determining the course of the young society. In some cases, individuals used influence to gain this power (Bishop Strachan had earlier taught a large number of the Family Compact members at the prestigious Anglican school in Toronto and was thus in an excellent position to influence them); in others, wealthy merchants or religious leaders were officially made members of the executive council. Military force was used to enforce decisions. Membership in the groups was further reinforced through frequent intermarriage—hence, the meaning of "family" in "Family Compact". Finally, membership appears to have been perpetuated through inheritance, with many male offspring inheriting positions in groups previously helped by their fathers or close relatives.[6]

2. Merchant Colonial Stage   Between 1840 and 1880, new forces changed the structure of Canadian society. Immigration increased Canada's population from a few hundred thousand to roughly three million; dominion status was secured from England; canals and railroads were built to link distant regions together; industrial activity began to increase dramatically; and, by the end of period, settlement schemes were being developed to populate the barren western prairies. The Compact and the Clique gave way to wider, less tightly knit clusters of different elites. Upon close examination, however, two specific types of elites emerged as most powerful in this period. One was the merchant elite of Montreal and, somewhat later, of Toronto, which grew larger and stronger as the population of the society increased. The other important elite was the elected political group (initially at the provincial level and after Confederation at the federal level).

Some of the members of these elites were descendants of the Compact and Clique elites. In most cases, however, they came from the new middle classes of moderately "well-to-do" individuals who grew up during the period. Although it is difficult to specify the total number of persons most centrally involved in important decision-making, Myers places the number at no more than 200 to 300 individuals.[7]

The attempts at development undertaken during this period were not without considerable controversies. Outrageously generous grants were often made to canal and railroad builders; the famous "Grand Trunk" and "CPR" scandals were only two of the numerous controversies centering on these grants. Such largesse from different levels of government, and particularly the federal government, was perhaps understandable when we consider a rather intriguing fact of the period. The federal politicians, the officers of the railroad companies, and the prosperous merchants were often the same individuals! Both Myers[8] and Ryerson[9] have shown the startling extent to which the same individuals were involved in all three activities simultaneously without any apparent sense of conflict of interest. If different individuals participated in these activities, they were frequently related either by blood or marriage. It is perhaps not surprising to discover, therefore, that some of the largest private family fortunes ever amassed in Canada were made at this time.

3. Early Industrial Stage (1880-1910)   Commencing with the National Policy programs of 1879, industrialization in Canada accelerated greatly. Montreal, Toronto, Moncton, St. John, and other cities became manufacturing centers, since they were aided by a protective tariff on foreign manufactured goods, the extension of railroad service, and a population increase through immigration which provided both a labor force and a market for goods. Additionally, the development of limited liability, joint stock companies allowed the assembly of greatly expanded capital and labor resources for production (most firms until then had been either family-owned or based on partnerships).[10] Privy council decisions in England clarified the scope of provincial and federal power as well. Countless new elites emerged to challenge the established groups in commerce, federal politics, and religion; perhaps the most important new groups were the provincial politicians and the regional manufacturing elite.

Because the society was now more complex than in earlier periods, any attempt to understand the distribution of power among these old and new elites is difficult. Social scientists themselves are at odds over the exact configuration of elites and power in this era.[11] One point is clear, however; the power used to direct the society's development was considerably more diffused. The number of individuals within any particular elite as well as the number of different types of elites grew larger.

A further change that many researchers have noted is the beginning of elite specialization. We have said that in earlier periods, individuals frequently and without difficulty moved from one type of elite to another, or even held positions in different elites simultaneously. This pattern continued into the early part of the industrial period. A considerable number of merchants or lumber entrepreneurs moved into manufacturing activities or had close kin—generally sons or brothers— who did so. If they were successful in this new endeavor, they moved into another field, usually politics. Many became successful in all three areas simultaneously and used their expanded resources to establish themselves firmly and guarantee further success.

By the 1890s, such movement became restricted to particular elites within a general category (such as economics or politics). Movement between different general areas of important activity (from politics to economics, for example) became much less common. By the early 1900s, even movement within a general elite (from manufacturing to banking) became more difficult. The restricting of individual careers to one rather specific activity resulted, according to sociologists, from the great expansion in technical knowledge and time required to gain and retain any type of elite position. One major consequence of such specialization, and the increasingly bureaucratic form that firms acquired as they expanded, was that a greater number of individuals than previously could gain access to elite positions.

It should not be construed from what we have said that access to both established and emergent elites was available to most members of the society. The distribution of power was relatively wider than in the 1850s; nonetheless, a large number of people belonging to the new elites were relatives of older elite members. Those who achieved elite positions for the first time were nearly always Anglo-Saxon and middle or upper middle class in origin and socioeconomic background. In Quebec, religious elites and rural-based political elites at the provincial level retained firm control despite the encroachment of industrialization.

Decision-making involved numerous participants. The colonial relationship with England was still an important factor in structuring the society. Privy council decisions in the 1870s, 80s, and 90s played a very important part in shaping the society—particularly in establishing areas of responsibility for federal and provincial governments. Within Canada, a large number of different elites cajoled and bargained with each other for the power to enforce their decisions. Researchers disagree on the types of elites, if any, that were most powerful. Our own research suggests that the merchant-industrial elite (those individuals who began in merchandising and successfully expanded into industrial activity while retaining some of their merchant activities) and the elected political elite at the federal level had somewhat greater power throughout most of the period.[12] In some regions, bankers and local politicians were also important, especially at the beginning of this period. Considerable negotiation and compromise among these and the emergent elites in the government civil service and in manufacturing comprised the standard pattern for decision-making. This is reflected in the avalanche of conflicting legislation passed federally and provincially at the time dealing with immigration, tariffs, reciprocity with the U.S.A., and labor legislation.

4. Financial Hegemonic Stage (1910-1930) The period we have termed financial hegemony saw two particular types of elites overshadow all others in directing the society. These two elites were the federally elected political elite and an elite that we have termed the financial elite. This latter group consists of those individuals in control of the financial institutions in the society, such as banks, trust companies, and insurance companies.

The financial elite acquired such enormous power because of the critical role its institutions played in later stages of the industrialization process. As industrial enterprises became larger, the requirements for capital to buy machinery, acquire raw materials, or pay labor increased greatly. These requirements soon became too high for even the largest firms to meet by using their profits. Since the primary function of the financial elite was the mobilization of large amounts of capital, it soon came to play a decisive role in industrialization. A financial elite had always existed in Canada to facilitate merchant activity, but now it began to overshadow the other groups.

Who belonged to the financial elite? The owners and high level managers of the financial institutions, and particularly of the chartered banks, were usually descendants of successful merchant families. Many of the banks had originally been incorporated by merchants to provide the necessary capital for their activities (the Bank of Montreal being the classic example). In terms of ethnicity, they were almost exclusively Anglo-Saxon. As the capital requirements for Canadian development increased (from the railroad boom of the 1850s onward) the financial elite grew larger and more powerful.

Financial hegemony had some important consequences for the structure of Canadian society: one in particular merits attention. From

Canada's first days as a colony, power had been possessed by a relatively small number of people and centralized geographically. This occurred first in the Compact period in Toronto and Montreal and later during the merchant period in the same cities. During the industrial period this pattern was somewhat altered. Regional industrial elites arose, particularly in the Maritimes, to challenge those of "central" Canada. As this happened, regional political elites also began to challenge central Canadian political elites. The rise to power of the financial elite reintroduced the highly concentrated and centralized nature of decision-making in Canada, since by 1910, the largest banks were located in Ontario and Quebec. By the outbreak of World War I, virtually all Canadian financial institutions were under the firm control of the Montreal or Toronto financial elites. As these banks loaned money to industrialists, they frequently took shares in the firms either as payment or collateral. Gradually, they assumed control. So complete was this process that, according to Acheson,[13] the central Canadian financial elite had assumed effective control over most manufacturing in Maritime Canada by 1910. As these regional economic elites lost power, so did their counterparts in the political arena.

5. Contemporary Stage (1930 to present) Since the Second World War, new forces have dramatically altered Canadian society. In the economic sphere, many new elites have evolved, and compete with merchant, financial, and manufacturing elites. Consider for example, the new managerial elite. According to social scientists such as John Kenneth Galbraith,[14] as economic organizations have become larger, a new type of economic elite has emerged—the managerial elite. Significant amounts of economic power have passed from the traditional elites who owned the firms and participated directly in their operation, to a new non-owning managerial elite which effectively utilizes modern marketing and technical knowledge to direct the firm. Ownership and control have thus become separated. Considerable power still remains with the traditional elite, but much is shared by the managerial elite.

In politics, a body of appointed civil servants appeared as governmental activity expanded. Frequently, this civil service elite has played a very important role in decision-making. Lipset,[15] for example, outlines some of the ways in which the Saskatchewan civil service was able to subvert the intentions of the first elected NDP government in that province.

According to popular opinion, new elites outside the traditional areas of economics and politics have become important in decision-making as their numbers have increased along with their public visibility. Scientific, labor, academic, and general culture elites (writers, poets, composers) serve as examples.

With this seeming abundance of elites, how does decision-making occur in contemporary Canada? In truth, sociologists have not yet arrived at a consensus regarding the answer, but two explanations are generally offered. These explanations, or "models" as they are termed by social scientists, are the "elite accommodation model" and the "Neo-Marxian model". Among the advocates[16] of the first are Robert Presthus, John Porter, and Peter Newman, while proponents[17] of the second include Stanley Ryerson, Libbie and Frank Park, Thomas Naylor, and Wallace Clement. While these authors differ on certain technical points, each can be associated with one of the two models. Clement is the most difficult to categorize, since his work reflects both models.

ELITE ACCOMMODATION MODEL   According to the elite accommodation model, important decision-making occurs as a result of negotiation, compromise, and continual lobbying among a few different elites, each of which is pursuing interests related primarily to its specific activity. No one type of elite has substantial and continuous power over any of the other types. Different elites come to know what they can and cannot expect to get from the negotiations. Because of the stability and predictability of this procedure, they accommodate themselves to one another. The main categories of persons involved in this decision-making routine are elected politicians, senior civil servants, financiers, owners and high level managers of manufacturing firms, and lawyers who, through their directorships, are actively involved in large-scale economic enterprise. Groups of such people meet frequently and informally. Other types of elites may be asked to attend meetings as well if the decision to be made directly affects them. Thus, for example, government, economic, and labor elites will meet to discuss a wage and price freeze needed to combat inflation. Any decision reached will reflect the relative power of the participants.

Two conditions facilitate this process of negotiation and accommodation. One is the rather small number of individuals who make up the elites. It is estimated that there are three or four thousand people involved, a number small enough to ensure that many participants know one another well and that most at least share some friends.

The second condition that makes negotiation easier is a certain similarity of background—the sharing of a similar subculture. An overwhelming majority of members of the elites come from upper middle and upper class Anglo-Saxon backgrounds. In some cases, there is considerable intermarriage among them as well. Despite Porter's assertion that there are few, if any, kinship ties between different general types of elites, such as the political or economic elites, examples of these ties can be found: Robert Bourassa, John Turner, and other important political figures are related through marriage to influential families of the economic elite.[18] Regardless of their kin relationships, members of different elites have similar socioeconomic backgrounds and are thus likely to share certain subculture orientations which will assist negotiations. This orientation may be nothing more than a certain sense of community *vis-à-vis* the Canadian masses, or it may be something more specific such as agreement on certain "rules of the game" to be followed in bargaining among fellow elite members.

This similarity in background has more concrete implications as well. Given the relatively small size of the upper middle and upper classes in Canada, many members of the different elites are likely to have gone to the same "right" school or belong to the "right" social club—a favorite place, incidentally, for negotiations to occur.

The elite accommodation model can be summarized as follows: different types of elites representing the interests of their particular activities negotiate with one another. Because of the predictability and stability of such negotiation, plus the fact that power is fairly evenly apportioned thereby preventing one elite from dominating the others, different elites accommodate themselves to one another and maintain the pattern of decision-making. Due to their importance in the society, certain political and economic elites are continuously involved; depending on what areas a decision will affect, other types of elites may be included as well. A common socioeconomic background facilitates negotiation.

NEO-MARXIST MODEL   The Neo-Marxist model for understanding power and decision-making differs in some important respects from the one we have just summarized. First, this model emphasizes the primacy of the economic elite over the other general elites. Within this general economic elite, the financial elite is the most powerful because of its control over a wide range of economic activities. Second, this economic elite constitutes an entire class. Rather than seeing each specific type of economic elite as defending its particular interests *vis-à-vis* other economic elites or other general elites, this model asserts the coordination, cooperation, and fundamental similarity of interests of groups within the economic elite. When such cooperation is found among a number of different elite groups, such groups are said to form a class. The similarity of interests results from the groups' ownership of the means of production in the society.

There is evidence to support the contention that, in Canada, a class, rather than various elite groups, makes the important economic decisions. For example, the same individuals are found on the boards of directors of a wide range of different economic organizations; also, there is a high concentration of stock ownership among a relatively small number of Canadians.[19]

This class (called a capitalist class because of its ownership of the capital resources), while more powerful than the different elites representing the other parts of the society, does not possess the power to control other groups. It frequently needs to negotiate; such negotiation, however, takes place from a position of strength. Moreover, given the democratic cultural orientation of the society, the power of this class must be camouflaged to avoid antagonizing the general populace. These facts place some constraints on its strength, and force it to exercise its power in intricate, highly subtle ways.

There is a third way in which the Neo-Marxist model differs from the elite accommodation one. The Neo-Marxist model argues that the distribution of power and decision-making in Canada cannot be completely understood without understanding the way in which Canada is integrated into a worldwide economic system of private enterprise. Many decisions which profoundly affect Canadian society are made beyond our political borders; given our colonial legacy this should not sound strange. What the Neo-Marxist model argues, however, is that after a period of relative independence, from 1870 to 1930, Canada is now entering a new period of colonization. The cause of this new colonial status is the multinational corporation, particularly the American-based multinational corporation. Because of the expansion of these corporations in Canada (through their branch plants), decisions on what products are produced, where they are produced, what price they are sold for, and a wide range of other issues are made outside the country's political boundaries. Moreover, this economic power may be, and is, used to influence decisions in the political arena as well.

To some extent, this foreign presence restricts the power of what we have termed the Canadian capitalist class, but the degrees and types of restrictions are very hard to determine. Equally difficult to define are relationships, if any, between this Canadian class and its foreign counterparts, particularly its American counterpart. Some social scientists have even argued that it is senseless to talk about a Canadian capitalist class because it has been almost completely absorbed into foreign capitalist classes.[20] Further research is needed to determine the validity of this statement, and the implications of such a situation.

One interesting effect that foreign firms have had on decision-making in Canada has been noted in several studies.[21] The presence of foreign corporations has provided opportunities for Canadians from lower socioeconomic backgrounds and various ethnic groups to rise into managerial elite positions in the multinational corporation. Although this managerial elite does not, in the Neo-Marxian view, have nearly as much power as the owners of the corporations, it is nevertheless able to participate in intermediate levels of decision-making. In promoting individuals who are not Anglo-Saxon and do not come from upper class backgrounds, foreign corporations are breaking quite dramatically with the traditional pattern of the Canadian economic class, with its restricted access to high positions. What is happening, then, is that while higher level decision-making is being moved beyond our borders, opportunities for intermediate levels of decision-making are being spread throughout the society.

Conclusion

Five significant trends which have important consequences for the content of a Canadian identity can be seen from our discussion of the historical structure of Canadian elites. These five are: elite continuity in Canadian development; the highly centralized and concentrated nature of elites throughout most of Canada's history; the central position of the financial elite; the absence of significant French Canadian elite members; and the rise of a parallel economic elite based on mobility within foreign-owned businesses operating in the society. A discussion of the relevance of each observation to national identity formation will conclude our study.

White Anglo-Saxon Protestants (WASPs) have dominated Canadian elites since the British conquest. This is particularly striking if we consider only economic and political elites—the most powerful types in a democratic, capitalist society such as Canada's. This continuity and the resulting stability allegedly explain certain important "core" cultural values such as conservatism, respect for traditional authority, and pragmatism. We have had no revolutions; the British tie has remained strong (at least until very recently). In some cases, a family has been able to retain its elite position throughout the six or seven generations since Canada became a British colony.

In addition, except for the period 1880-1910, Canadian elites have been heavily concentrated in Montreal and Toronto. Thus their relatively small size, geographical concentration, and common background have led to a club-like organization among elites. Peter Newman uses the term "establishment" to describe this well-developed internal organization. These characteristics of the various members of the elite have retarded the development of a truly national elite. All too frequently, the elite acts as if Canada begins in Hamilton and ends in Montreal. The fact that other Canadian regions are ignored and that ethnic groups generally have no access to elites has led to the growth of regional social identities at both the local elite and popular cultural levels. Moreover, because of the frequently exploitative ways in which the central Canadian elite has used its power, regional identities have frequently been (and continue to be) militant, and opposed to central Canada since they reflect the hinterland status of both regional local elites and the general public.

The extent to which descriptions of our national values and the values of our financial elite overlap is striking. Whether this elite is just one of many powerful elites the country as the accommodation model suggests, or whether it is the ruling class proposed by the Marxist model, the elements that constitute the social identity of the financial elite almost summarize our national identity.[22] In an introductory study we can only suggest one or two possible reasons for this. One partial explanation is the peculiar role chartered banks have played in our economic development. Unlike American financial institutions, for example, Canadian banks have not been highly competitive. Six chartered banks dominate our financial sector; historically they have cooperated and coordinated their efforts with respect to development strategies. In the United States, on the other hand, roughly fifteen thousand banks (most with much smaller assets than their Canadian counterparts) have competed to provide capital for economic development. The gigantic coordination of effort in Canadian society has meant that the financial elite has been able to wield enormous power. Nor, as we suggested earlier, has this power been restricted to economic fields alone; as societies have become more technologically advanced and integrated there has been a corresponding tendency for elites to influence decisions outside their own particular institutional area.

A second partial explanation for the similarity between financial elite identity and Canadian identity results from the continuity and stability of financial institutions and their elite. More than any other institutional sector of the society, financial organizations have been the stronghold of the WASP elite. Given this continuity of values (and even of specific WASP families) within the financial institutions and the powerful role such institutions have played in our development as a nation, it is perhaps not surprising that this particular elite has had considerable impact on national values.

The fourth observation made from our study helps to understand events of the late 1970s in Quebec. Historically, French Canadians have had very little access to economic elite positions and only slightly more access to the national political elite. This had led to the "two solitude" character of English-French relations in the country. Since the Quiet Revolution of the early 1960s, new economic and political elites have developed. In the classical tradition of ethnic rivalry, however, this emergent Quebec elite is setting up its own Establishment, with little or no integration with the English elite. Although the separatist movement is more complex than the rise of an independent French elite in search of greater control over Quebec's destiny, this new elite is yet another group within Quebec wanting autonomy. It is also no accident that the list of the influential people in the separatist movement reads like the *Who's Who* of the emergent elite.

Our final observation results from the increased involvement of foreign, now largely American, subsidiaries operating in Canada. These foreign plants provide a new set of opportunities for non-WASP ethnic groups to advance. Historically, non-WASP groups have had limited access to positions within the Canadian economic elite. To a slightly lesser extent this has also been true of their access to political elite positions. Foreign firms have been much more willing to hire from a wide variety of ethnic backgrounds insofar as individuals possessed the required abilities. Perhaps the clearest illustration of this is found in Alberta, where Poles, Ukrainians, and Japanese of Canadian citizenship hold upper management positions in foreign owned and controlled oil firms. While somewhat less visible, the pattern prevails in other industrial sectors as well.

While it may be unfair to call individuals in such positions members of an elite, since a great deal of the decision-making power is usurped from them and placed in the head office in Houston or New York, the power and influence they are able to exert is still significant in the society. As suggested in the introductory statement about elite identity and Canadian identity, these improved opportunities for mobility have led to rather ambiguous feelings toward foreign investment in general and Americans in particular. This ambiguity is shared by rank and file workers as well since many of them believe that if Americans had not come into Alberta to develop the oil industry, the oil would still be in the ground and the workers without jobs. Simultaneously there is a considerable amount of resentment displayed toward those Canadian firms and their elite who denied them opportunities in the first place. Such attitudes are particularly common in formerly "have not" regions—Alberta and British Columbia in particular—that became wealthy through the infusion of foreign capital.

In this essay we have not attempted to equate elite identity with national identity; rather we have tried, through a historical analysis, to suggest some ways in which an understanding of elites can provide valuable insights into the structure and content of the present Canadian national identity. Our relatively small population, stable political institutions, and the continuity of many families within elite groups since the country's beginnings have meant that such elites have had a pronounced effect upon the society. Unfortunately, our observations suggest that Canada's elites have seldom, if ever, considered themselves national. Ethnically Anglo-Saxon Protestant and residing in Toronto and Montreal, the members have been either unwilling or incapable of providing the leadership necessary for creating national symbols and institutions. To a considerable extent, then, Canadians' ambiguity regarding their national identity parallels the weak national consciousness of the country's past and present elites.

NOTES

1. Philiip Perry's book, *Galt; USA* (Toronto: Maclean-Hunter, 1973), captures better than any other work we know this complex, often contradictory set of feelings experienced by Canadians.

2. The major terms of reference of this debate have to do with "social" versus "biological" explanations. For an example of the social explanation, see A. Cicourel and J. Kitsuse, *The Educational Decision Makers* (New York: Bobbs-Merrill, 1963). For the biological, see Arthur B. Jensen "Social Class, Race, and Genetics: Implications for Education," *American Educational Research Journal*, Vol. 5 (1968), pp. 1-42. For a good review, consult Christopher Jencks, *Inequality* (New York: Basic Books, 1972).

3. John Porter adds this elite. See J. Porter, *The Vertical Mosaic* (Toronto: University of Toronto Press, 1965), Ch. 11.

4. Senate of Canada, *Report of the Special Commission on the Media* (Ottawa: Information Canada, 1971).

5. The Canadian Wire Service has covered these hearings over the last year. The reports have appeared in a large number of Canadian newspapers.

6. See J. L. Granatstein, ed., *The Family Compact: Aristocracy or Oligarchy?*, Issues in Canadian History Series (Toronto: Copp-Clark, 1968).

7. G. Meyers, *A History of Canadian Wealth* (Toronto: James Lorimer and Co., Ltd., 1972).

8. *Ibid.*

9. Stanley Ryerson, *Unequal Union* (New York: International Publishers, 1967).

10. See T. W. Acheson, "The National Policy and the Industrialization of the Maritimes," *Acadiensis*, Vol. 2, No. 1.

11. For a review, see T. W. Acheson, *ibid.*; S. D. Clark, *The Developing Canadian Community* (Toronto: University of Toronto Press, 1972); and R. T. Naylor, *The History of Canadian Business* (Toronto: Lorimer, 1975).

12. See T. W. Acheson, *ibid.*

13. *Ibid.*

14. John Kenneth Galbraith, *The New Industrial State* (New York: New American Library, 1971).

15. S. M. Lipset, *Agrarian Socialism* (New York: Anchor Paperbacks, 1964).

16. Robert Presthus, *Elite Accommodation in Canadian Politics* (Toronto: Macmillan, 1973); John Porter, *op. cit.*, Peter Newman, *The Canadian Establishment* (Toronto: McClelland and Stewart, 1975).

17. Libbie and Frank Park, *Anatomy of Big Business* (Toronto: James Lewis and Samuel, 1973); Stanley Ryerson, *op. cit.*; Wallace Clement, *The Canadian Corporate Elite* (Toronto: McClelland and Stewart, 1975).

18. For more information, see S. D. Berkowitz and L. Felt, "A Structural Analysis of the Canadian Financial System," Report to the Ministry of Consumer and Corporate Affairs, Ottawa, May 1975.

19. See Libbie and Frank Park, *op. cit.*

20. This is based on conversations with a number of sociologists studying the history of the capitalist class in Canada.

21. L. F. Felt, "The Development of an Industrial Bourgeoisie in Southern Ontario," paper given at the annual meeting of the North Central Sociological Association, Windsor, May, 1974. See also, D. Craig McKie, "An

Ontario Industrial Elite," Ph.D. thesis, University of Toronto, Department of Sociology, 1974.

22. See S. M. Lipset, *op. cit.* Also J. Porter, *The Vertical Mosaic* (Toronto: University of Toronto Press, 1965), Chs. 16 and 17; and S. D. Clark, *The Developing Canadian Community* (Toronto: University of Toronto Press, 1962), Ch. 15 for a discussion of Canadian core values and a Canadian identity. The reader will find that there is little said about the essence of such an identity.

Elites

PETER NEWMAN

WHENEVER CANADA IS examined as a society it is almost always considered in terms of its identity crisis, bicultural problems, or agonies as a pygmy nation in thrall to one or another overdeveloped empire. The country is rarely viewed through the prism of its status as one of the world's most successful capitalist states. Yet, that's what we are—a capitalist society run by clusters of interlocking elites.

The men who operate this system are much more interested in exercising power than in any process of self-analysis. Attempts at introspection throw most of them into inarticulate confusion. But whenever they hear the catch phrase "free enterprise," something inside them clicks to attention. The real buzzword, of course, is "business," which is said reverentially, as in "Well, that's business . . . " or "But it's *good* for business . . . "—statements that leave ignored the most flamboyant distortions of how any egalitarian society should operate.

The businessmen's faith is more a collection of attitudes than any carefully conceived theology. But it does follow a catechism of sorts. All men and the actions of all men, the orthodox believe, are essentially a product of the marketplace; everyone therefore and everything has its price.[1] Pure free-enterprisers hold that man can be motivated to help society only by helping himself; they regard any form of incentive not based on the profit motive as hopelessly romantic. Adherents of the creed genuinely believe that virtue can be certified by wordly accomplishments, that success is tangible evidence of holy favour. They have limited tolerance for the meaning of heaven or hell, recognize little logic in pain or compassion. The real enemies are chaos and Big Government.

Power is no judge of values, but it acts instinctively to create order because no order can exist without power and no power exists without order. That's why businessmen place so much emphasis on institutions

---

From The Canadian Establishment, *by Peter Newman, pp. 143-160. Reprinted by permission of* The Canadian Publishers, *McClelland and Stewart Limited, Toronto.*

and hierarchies in which people know and keep their place. It is this deeply felt faith in institutions that is at the heart of the capitalist ethic.

According to this creed, freedom has about it an indivisible quality. Since economic freedom and political freedom are inseparable, it follows that democracy and capitalism necessarily reinforce each other. Private property thus becomes not only the basis for the free enterprise system but also the source of individual freedom. (The link here seems to be that if the individual has private property, it is more difficult for the state to deprive him of liberty.) This doctrine holds that dynamic capitalism has the best chance of producing the higher living standards in which democracy can flourish; that the free enterprise system must always triumph because it builds on individual and collective self-interest.

Out of such dogma emerges the businessman's stoutest conviction: that every piece of social legislation proposed by any government constitutes a potential affront to future liberties and must be opposed by all available means. To most members of the Canadian Establishment, the idea of a tolerable social reformer stops well short of Pope John XXIII.

The shout that David Kilgour, president of Great-West Life, directed in 1963 at Ottawa's pension plan ("Let's raise a storm! Let's make it a good one! The strongest, most lightning-packed, angry wind that has blown around Parliament Hill for a long time!") finds strong echoes among Canadian business leaders:

Ian Sinclair, chairman, Canadian Pacific Limited: "We need to counter the raucous clamour that the private sector is not performing, that it is 'ripping off' exorbitant profits, that it is a relic of the past. A weak and indecisive government is not prepared to stand up and be counted and present the true facts.... Every dollar removed from the capital market, because it has been taken by taxation from the pocket of the would-be investor, is a dollar denied to Canadian business. It is the volume of expenditure of governments which limits the range of private business activity."

Bill McLean, president, Canada Packers: "Being a businessman has a negative influence when dealing with the government. Business has become impotent. In a sense there's been a revolt against all established institutions—they've gone out of style. My views are coloured by my background and upbringing but I think we are moving left too fast. I'm especially concerned by the barrage of rules and regulations. If business doesn't prosper, governments will not have the taxes to provide the economic base for transfer payments."

Bud Willmot, chairman, Molson Companies: "As government legislation and regulations encroach on the economic system, affecting such prerogatives as financial resource allocation, investment in underdeveloped areas, executive compensation, and the quality-of-life restrictions, we will see a gradual narrowing of the decision-making parameters for corporate executives. It would appear that if, and I say *if*, the death of corporate enterprise occurs, it will not be as a great cataclysmic event such as a revolution or the election of an avowed socialist government but simply through the interplay of trends which are already at work. Indeed, there are those who would argue that 'free enterprise' as it is called has already expired in a historical sense and that it will simply become a label associated with the industrial era through which we have already passed."

Bud McDougald, chairman, Argus Corporation: "Governments should just run the affairs of the country. They shouldn't be buying their seats back in the Commons by spending taxpayers' money just to get themselves elected and they shouldn't be trying to kill off the people who are creating the nation's wealth."

Leo Kolber, president, Cemp Investments: "Our political leaders seem to go out of their way to discourage the formation of pools of capital. In every which-way: first of all, the Foreign Investment Review Act won't let foreign capital in. Then, our laws militate against accumulating capital yourself. It's virtually impossible to get a top executive motivated to the point where he accumulates capital. It's nice that our government is on a great big giveaway program, and it's very difficult for a guy in my position to say that people shouldn't have benefits. It doesn't come out sounding properly, I understand that. But I also understand that the government doesn't seem to know where the hell the money's going to come from. It's nice that they're going to have a guaranteed wage and free medicine, free this and free that, and at the same time discourage pools of capital. Where does it come from? It's a difficult subject to discuss because, God knows, I have benefited greatly from the free-enterprise system. I started off with two cents in my pocket, but everything I've earned I've earned on my own. And I've contributed—in my opinion anyhow—a hell of a lot. I've helped make the wheels go round. You need literally hundreds of guys like myself, who are willing to work long hours and weekends and nights and holidays and push, because we just happen to have the drive and ambition. Whether it's ego or sickness or neurosis, it doesn't matter. But you've got to make the achievers of this world live in an ambience that allows them to fulfil their particular pretension. And in doing that, they benefit the country greatly. Look, we have a bloody welfare system here where in many, many instances people at the low end of the scale are well advised to stay home and do nothing. That's not good for mental health. I'm not trying to become a great psychiatrist here, but it's not good, and it's also terrible for business."

Stephen Jarislowsky, Montreal investment counsellor: "We're going through a change in class structure. The meek are not just inheriting the earth, they are grabbing it. While our capitalist system, to work properly, doesn't permit this, the politicians must inevitably look at the vote. About 90 per cent of Canadian households earn under $14,000, so the vote of the rest doesn't count. Socialism is happening, whether we agree with it or not, and it's probably irreversible. The 10 per cent of the people with funds to invest are locked out of the democratic process."

Alf Powis, president, Noranda Mines: "Ideally the government should set the rules under which business operates in a reasonably stable way, rules that aren't subject to violent, year-to-year change. What business complains about are very rapid shifts in what the rules are, and shifts for reasons that we don't consider very good ones. Politicians have to be political. But they also have a responsibility to give leadership. The terrible problem we've got in Canada is that everybody is preoccupied with the distribution of wealth and nobody is paying enough attention to the fact that you first have to create the wealth you're trying to distribute. . . . The average businessman is a rotten politician. Even C. D. Howe, in the end, was a rotten politician and brought a government down. If you're in business, you're used to getting on with things, doing things, and to hell with compromise, you go straight down the road. Politicians have to be a lot more flexible."

David Collier, president, General Motors of Canada: "What the people of North America need to realize is that with the loss of a free-choice, competitive market, it is only a step away from the loss of a free-political-choice society. Government today often tells business not only what it must not do, but what it must do, and—more than that—how to run business. Corporate responsibility becomes meaningless in that atmosphere."

Roy Thomson, press lord: "The welfare state robs people of incentive. If, in my early days, there had been family allowances and old age pensions and all the rest of it, I wouldn't have done what I did. They say business is the law of the jungle. I think it's the law of life. If you want to live and you want to prosper, you've got to be ambitious. You've got to be ready to sacrifice leisure and pleasure, and you've got to plan ahead. I was forty years old before I had any money at all. But these things don't happen overnight. Now, how many people are there who will wait that long to be successful, and work all the time? Not very many. Maybe they're right. Maybe I'm a bloody fool. But I don't think I am."

Lord Thomson's oath of allegiance to the Protestant ethic is deep within the Canadian business tradition. It is a view of life that stresses the more sombre virtues, the quiet good feeling of a hard day's work well done, the idea that the good man always more than earns his pay, a kind of fierce pragmatism in which the hard-and-fast, here-and-now aspects of life alone deserve reality.

The idea of the Protestant ethic as state religion appeals to most businessmen. They have little trouble stretching their creed toward heaven. It is a view of life reflected in the prayers repeated at Junior Chamber of Commerce meetings ("We believe that faith in God gives purpose and meaning to human life; that economic justice can best be won by free men through enterprise . . . ") and the invocation at monthly gatherings of one of the organizations of geological scientists in Calgary ("O Lord, who put the treasures beneath the earth, help us, Thy servants, to find them. . . . ").[2]

It is one of the deep paradoxes of Canada's economic history that more often than not government provided the fiscal answer to some of the most rugged free-enterprisers' prayers. Our businessmen have loudly touted the capitalist ethic without really believing it. A true capitalist tradition requires faith in free enterprise unhindered by any sense of sin, something like the way Eskimos must have felt about sex before the missionaries came. But the founding economic class in Canada, as R. T. Naylor has pointed out,[3] had *mercantile* roots, accumulating its wealth through circulation rather than production. This has led not to independent capitalist development, but to the perpetuation of a colonial mentality and risk-free *under*-development. The men who have prevailed in the running of the country's private sector since Confederation have persisted for their own purposes (mostly the desire to attract foreign capital on which to get rich) in seeing economic development as desperately risky, feeling always the need of a protector in the form of either outside investment or government aid.

"At a time when American conservative intellectuals were freeing the individual for the progressive Darwinian struggle, Canadian thinkers, owing more to Burke than to Darwin, insisted that the state should provide some measure of moral direction for the society," wrote Viv Nelles in a recent analysis of Ontario's mixed economy.[4] "For them, loyalty to the British crown signified more than just a choice of a particular set of representative institutions; it implied as well an organic view of society within which the crown and the institutions of government moulded the character of the individual, measured wealth against commonwealth, and presided over just and orderly social change." Crown ownership of natural resources was a joint heritage from French seigneurial and British freehold systems.

The idea of developing a joint economy with public money backing private enterprise was initially forced on Canada by the threat of American dominance. "The public involvement in canals and railroads took place step by step to protect the Canadian political economy (indeed Confederation itself) against American expansionism," according to Herschel Hardin, a British Columbia playwright who has probably come the closest to defining the Canadian identity.[5] "Only by publicly organized investment could a country like Canada, with its small domestic market and lesser population, keep within hailing distance of the great U.S. spectacle and defend itself. . . . The public enterprise tradition in Canada has sustained the culture of private enterprise. When we undertook the Pacific railroad, and during the Second World War when public enterprise flourished, we felt we had come into our own, which indeed we had. By contrast, in the one period when creating new Crown enterprises was largely neglected – the post-war years – Canadians' entrepreneurial will disintegrated. It was a period not simply of sell-out, of abject lack of confidence, and of blind giving of concessions to others in the desperate hope they would provide us with industry and jobs. It was also a period when, despite the impact on the national psyche of the Second World War, Canadians began to talk morosely and endlessly about an identity crisis. Public enterprise and financing are at the core of what Canada is all about, economically speaking."

This two-way partnership between business and government has resulted in some strange alliances. Probably the most ostentatious admission of a businessman's political dealings came out in the last will of Lord Strathcona, the former Hudson's Bay factor who wound up heading both his old company and the Bank of Montreal, as well as being one of the chief financiers (and beneficiaries) of the building of the CPR. His will, distributing an estate of $17 million (an amount that didn't truly reflect his wealth because most of his money had already been given away to his heirs), included provisions for cancelling the debts owed to him by Sir Richard Cartwright and Sir George Foster, formerly the ministers of finance in Liberal and Conservative governments.

The trouble some of the less ethical entrepreneurs have in dealing with governments is that politicians tend not to stay bought; they can at best be rented. Politicians generally find that the best way to solicit funds from businessmen is to anchor their campaigns to specific causes. When Ross Thatcher became Saskatchewan's Liberal leader in 1959, for example, he had no war chest and asked his friend Mel Jack, the supreme backroom-stager of the Conservative party, for help. (When Thatcher had been with the CCF in the federal House, he, Jack, and

Jimmy Sinclair of the Liberals ran a floating bar in each other's homes during the early fifties.) Jack set out to organize two dinners, one at the National Club in Toronto, with Bob Winters as host, and the other at the Mount Royal Club in Montreal, put on by Bill Bennett, the former assistant to C. D. Howe. Thatcher made a simple pitch: if they gave him enough money, he would go out and fight socialism. From the ninety men at the two meals, he raised $189,000 in cash.[6]

The lines between business and government became blurred during World War II, when dollar-a-year men swarmed into Ottawa and set out (along with C. D. Howe) to run the economy. The business creed became, for a while at least, the official standard for defining the national interest. For the next decade, the same men drifted between Cabinet and business board rooms. When Louis St. Laurent entered the government, for instance, he resigned as a director of Metropolitan Life Insurance; when Brooke Claxton left the Liberal cabinet, it was to take over as president of the same company. Governments saw themselves as creators of a climate in which free enterprise could prosper. "I think all of us recognize," St. Laurent told the Commons on May 14, 1953, "that there are some things which it is more appropriate to have done by public authorities than by free enterprise. But I think we are all most happy when free enterprise does what is required to be done and public authorities do not have to intervene."

But starting with the fiery Prairie populism of John George Diefenbaker, economics became, quite simply, a branch of politics. The nation's legislators, sensing that business was losing public support, decided that the acquisitive impulse was not necessarily man's noblest instinct, that businessmen weren't the best brains or the most enjoyable company, that they constituted a faction to be propitiated, not a force to be followed. Then, during the mid-seventies, business itself seemed confused, losing its access to capital, misjudging its markets, battered by a recession it did not foresee and could not handle.

Too many businessmen had distorted their own system of values by subscribing to the notion that they could be ethical without being moral, that the main operative restraint was to show maximum profits without going to jail. The environmental devastation of the Sudbury basin by Inco and Falconbridge, for example, had become so complete that U.S. astronauts used the area to practise moon-walking before the Apollo flights.

The $135-million Atlantic Acceptance scandal tainted 286 corporations, shaking the whole North American capital market. (Although it wasn't known at the time, Atlantic's collapse came so close to causing a credit panic that in the first two months of the company's default, the Bank of Canada had to increase the money supply by $1

billion.) The "Harbourgate" affair that came to light in the spring of
1975, in which charges of conspiracy to defraud the public of $4 million
were laid against fourteen chief executives of dredging companies,
including some pillars of the Establishment, further eroded public faith in
Canadian capitalism.[7]

"The only alternative to the further expansion of government to fill
the vacuum of economic leadership," wrote Professor Abe Rotstein, an
associate professor in the Department of Political Economy at the
University of Toronto, "is a renaissance of Canadian business, willing
and able to step into the breach and reassert control as proximate
representatives of the Canadian interest. Canadian business should
understand that it is its own failure to fill the power vacuum which is at
the heart of the emergence of the new government corporations and
initiatives with which it feels itself suddenly surrounded."

Part of the trouble businessmen have in dealing with Ottawa is the
character of the city itself. It is a place of corridors, with everyone
constantly on the point of arrival or departure. Bureaucrats rich in
caution, clever, industrious, curiously cool, their desks neat, their clothes
inconspicuous, their haircuts inoffensive, pass their days poring over fat
dossiers. Their decisions have a provisional air, like commutation orders
that the intended victim is never quite certain will really be signed. It all
seems like a huge paper factory with a negative purpose, where the right
things are usually done for the wrong reason, an environment
unequipped for an overdose of anything natural. The total effect is that
of an upside-down insane asylum, with most of what is publicly
presented adding up to fantasy and much of what is privately transacted
being real.

The businessmen and the bureaucrat-politicians view each other
across a chasm of misunderstanding. They are not only different men,
they are different *kinds* of men. The denizens of Ottawa see corporate
executives essentially as marauders, selfish plutocrats who wear cutaways
and have dollar signs for watch fobs. Neanderthal creatures who walk
around with raw knuckles, because they keep scraping the ground.[8] The
executives who fly into the capital on uncomfortable forays regard the
government men as misguided quasi-radicals who could never meet a
payroll, don't understand very much about anything, and never seem to
realize that their only purpose in life should be to provide custodial care
for those whom the private sector rejects.

They complain that more and more money is being spent by the
federal government, but what really concerns them is the shift of more
and more *power* from private to public hands. They resent the myriad
regulations,[9] the length of time it takes for regulatory agencies to hand
down rulings, and the fact that their decisions can't be appealed.[10]

"Anything where the government has got you by the balls, I think your chance of getting rich out of it is very bad," Lord Thomson complains. "As soon as you start to make more money than they think is good for you, they'll put in more restrictions."

The government-business feud broke into the open with the debate in 1970 on Ben Benson's White Paper on Tax Reform, which coincided with Ron Basford's new competition bill and Bryce Mackasey's revised labour code. Even though Pierre Trudeau is the first Canadian prime minister to come out of an affluent urban background,[11] he has become the chief target of every businessman's anger. Since he is also being attacked by most of the country's social reformers, it may be that he has been more successful than any of his predecessors since Mackenzie King in attaining the ideal state of Canadian political grace: he is occupying the political centre while moving simultaneously both to the left and to the right.[12]

Trudeau has acquired few genuine friends inside the Canadian financial community.[13] Only three important members of the business Establishment feel particularly close to him: John Aird and John Godfrey, the Toronto lawyers who are his former and present chief fund-raisers, and Paul Desmarais, the Power Corporation chief. But there are other businessmen with whom Trudeau has friendly relations. They include Allen Lambert, chairman of the Toronto-Dominion Bank, Bill Wilder, chairman of Canadian Arctic Gas Pipeline, Harrison McCain of New Brunswick, and Stu Keate, publisher of the *Vancouver Sun*. Urged on by Senator Keith Davey and James Coutts, the P.M. has repeatedly tried to establish closer rapport by meeting businessmen in small groups, but somehow the chemistry isn't there.[14]

In mid-December of 1974, when the economy had turned sour, a two-hour lunch at 24 Sussex Drive was organized at the business community's request, with James Coutts acting as the middleman. Only five senior business ambassadors were invited: Bill Wilder of Canadian Arctic Gas, Jake Moore of Brascan, Peter Gordon of Stelco, Paul Desmarais of Power, and Doug Gibson, the Toronto corporate consultant.[15]

To document their conviction that Trudeau is really a socialist in pragmatist's clothing, his critics quote from an article he wrote in *Vrai* during the late fifties, attacking the role of the church in Quebec's economic development: "They told us that the Popes were against state ownership, with the result that Ontario Hydro got fifty years' head start over Quebec."

Under Trudeau, Ottawa's interventionist grip on the economy has been tightening.[16] The retroactive legislation preventing the sale of Denison Mines to a Canadian subsidiary of the U.S.-owned Continental Oil Company, the institution of export taxes on petroleum products, the monitoring of food and steel prices, the tax increases on mining profits, the financing of Panarctic Oils Limited as a joint public-private venture, and, particularly, the growing vigilance of the Department of Consumer and Corporate Affairs in attacking the monopolistic practices of large Canadian corporations – these are some of the specific targets for the complaints levelled at Trudeau from inside Corporate board rooms.

They find his anti-monopoly drive especially galling. Despite their unqualified allegiance to free enterprise, most Canadian businessmen don't, in fact, like to compete. When they extol the virtues of capitalism, they are really describing an oligarchic economy with little scope or need for competition.[17]

Ever since 1888, when a group of Toronto undertakers was discovered to be keeping coffin prices artificially high, Canada's anti-combines investigators have provided some spectacular illustrations of firms that overcharge consumers if they can escape into the economic no-man's land where prices are set by clandestine intercompany dealings. Ottawa's justice department agents have uncovered price-fixing agreements among the manufacturers and distributors of such commodities as oatmeal, fruits and vegetables, car accessories, matches, sugar, wire fencing, galoshes, quilted goods, eyeglasses, tires, flour, gasoline, bread, coal, cigarettes, toilet paper, false teeth, and cement.

Canada became the first nation to legislate against the modern type of industrial combine by adding a section to the Criminal Code directed at flourishing monopolies in oatmeal, stoves, barbed wire, coal, and coffins. The Combines Investigation Act was written and guided through Parliament in 1910 by Mackenzie King, then minister of labour. A further revision of the act in 1923 set up a permanent investigating organization, headed by King's private secretary, Fred McGregor. One of the most rigid combines was in the rubber industry. The manufacturers of rubber footwear, for example, not only agreed to observe identical prices but also set up elaborate sales-quota arrangements. Companies exceeding their allotments paid their surplus profits to firms that failed to meet sales quotas. Every manufacturer had to make a substantial deposit at a central office as proof of his allegiance. During the rubber companies' trial, the Toronto fire department complained that it had just received four identical tenders for rubber hose.

The case that focused the most national attention on the work of the Combines Investigation Branch was the report charging a price conspiracy among Canadian flour millers. When Ottawa took the wartime controls off flour on September 15, 1947, the millers immediately raised prices by identical amounts. McGregor impounded their files and found undeniable evidence of price-setting.[18] The law at that time required anti-monopoly reports to be made public within fifteen days of their printing. The yellow-covered 121-page copies of the findings (charging that eleven milling companies, controlling 70 per cent of the market, were operating an illegal combine) landed on the desk of justice minister Stuart Garson on April 22, 1949. Parliament had prorogued on April 20 for a general election without action on the report. Cabinet had split on the issue, with C. D. Howe insisting that the millers' decision was in keeping with the orders of the Wartime Prices and Trade Board. When the government refused to release the investigation's findings even after the election, McGregor resigned in protest, on October 29, 1949. The report was finally tabled in the House of Commons nine days later. The Opposition benches exploded. George Drew demanded that the Liberals dissolve Parliament because of the delay. "In 1649," proclaimed M. J. Coldwell, the leader of the CCF, "an English king was beheaded for doing exactly what the government has done." The flour millers were never prosecuted.

An even more rigid cartel was the wooden-match monopoly, formed by companies associated with Ivar Kreuger, the Swedish millionaire who at one time owned a hundred and fifty factories in twenty-eight countries producing 65 per cent of the world's matches. In 1923 Kreuger bought a match plant at Berthierville, Quebec, from the Rockefeller family and five years later merged it with the match business of the E. B. Eddy Company at Hull, then controlled by R. B. Bennett. This made the Swedish financier's newly formed Eddy Match Company Canada's only producer of wooden matches. As competing plants were established, Eddy flooded their sales areas with under-priced brands. Columbia Match Company, which set up a large factory at St. Johns, Quebec, in 1929, for a while was the most successful competitor. "No doubt you will watch their efforts and see that they are carefully attended to if they attempt to take any of our business," G. W. Paton, the president of Eddy, instructed A. G. Woodruff, one of his vice-presidents, in a confidential interoffice memo soon after Columbia's incorporation. After three years of battling Eddy's low-priced "fighting brands," Columbia was forced into bankruptcy. Eddy executives secretly purchased the plant and operated it as the Commonwealth Match Company.

Eddy was tried and convicted as a monopoly in 1951. Because the company had maintained the firms it absorbed as separate corporations – to give the appearance of competition within the industry – the fine totalled $85,000 instead of a meaningful amount. Eddy's grasp on the Canadian market was hardly splintered, because a section of the law providing for the break-up of monopolies was not yet in force.

One problem with combines cases is that prosecution of charges takes so long. In the fall of 1948, for instance, the combines investigators noted that the prices of Canadian writing, blotting, and book papers were remarkably similar and that since 1935 only three new companies had joined the fine-paper industry. A full-scale inquiry was launched. Three years of searching through the files of forty-five paper mills were followed by two years of private hearings to gather oral evidence and allow the firms to state their defence. The transcript of these sessions amounted to a million words. The report, charging Canada's fine-paper industry with having maintained a competition-restraining combine over the past seventeen years, was issued in 1952. The trial of the companies in the Supreme Court of Ontario began on January 11, 1954. It lasted seventy-one days; more than twenty million words of evidence were taken. The judge took five hours to read his ruling, which found most of the companies guilty. After a hearing before the Ontario Court of Appeal, the case reached the Supreme Court of Canada in the fall of 1956. This court delivered its judgement on May 13, 1957, confirming the decision in a twenty-four-page single-spaced document. Twenty-seven of the fine-paper companies were fined a total of $242,000 in November, 1957 – almost a decade from the beginning of the investigation.

The effectiveness of past combines prosecutions has been fatally weakened by the insignificance of fines imposed. In January, 1958, for instance, eleven shingle manufacturers paid the courts the maximum fine of $10,000 each for having operated a combine in the $30-million-a-year asphalt-roofing industry since 1932.

Until recently, the pace of anti-monopoly prosecutions has been hesitant, almost lackadaisical. The conviction of the Electric Reduction Company of Canada by the Supreme Court of Canada in 1970 for its 1959 merger with Dominion Fertilizers was the combines branch's first monopoly conviction in seventeen years. The fine of $150,000 imposed in 1974 on the Irving newspaper interests in New Brunswick was for the first conviction under the section of the law that prohibits mergers from harming the public since the Eddy Match case.[19] But the Trudeau government has raised the fines,[20] and under proposed new legislation, guilty executives would not only have to pay personal penalties of up to a million dollars but could also go to jail for five years.

Faced with these and other onslaughts on their profits, a few business leaders have been making tentative efforts to don a mantle of corporate responsibility. Even though the *status quo* is quaking beneath their feet, only a tiny enclave within the Canadian Establishment is yet aware of the need for a fresh response. This enlightened minority recognizes the approaching disappearance of *laissez-faire* capitalism and with its passing the need to reach an appropriate accommodation with the new forces that are grabbing a larger share of society's powers, particularly the various levels of government administration. "Business now clearly must hitch its wagon to the rising star of social capitalism in this country," wrote Don Carlson, the publisher of the *Financial Times of Canada*, who first tried to define the new ideology. "This would be a more constructive response, more contemporary than entrenchment against the unfolding political and economic system, alien though this system is to the past experience of business.... Social capitalism as charted by our public leaders is increasingly blessed by public mandate. The only sensible reaction by the private sector is to use its considerable expertise to help build self-restraint into the Canadian Grand Plan. Elected and bureaucratic planners need to be inspired – or embarrassed – into providing this missing component in their avant-garde programming.... But business can accomplish more – in the public interest and in its own self-interest – by going beyond mere submissive adaptation to the new roles being planned for it. Some perceptive Canadians believe that new kinds of business initiatives can contribute to practical economic policy within the broader context of Canada's unfolding social capitalism."

Whether they realize it or not, even some diehard adherents of free enterprise are becoming converts to the philosophy of John Maynard Keynes (a concept nearly forty years old), accepting the function of government as the chief energizer and stabilizer of the economy. "It is in the national interest for government and business to get closer together to solve the problems at hand," Peter Gordon, the president of the Steel Company of Canada, told the Hamilton chapter of the Financial Executives' Institute in the spring of 1975. "I'm not suggesting that the public and private sectors can be completely compatible. But there are obvious areas for mutual co-operation and joint enterprise, which combine the ability of industry to get things done in the most efficient way with the responsibility of the government to uphold the legitimate public interest."[21]

No one has tried harder to reconcile the two factions than Bob Wisener, a graduate of the Royal Canadian Naval College and a former governor of the Toronto Stock Exchange. For two weekends every autumn since the mid-fifties, Wisener has thrown open Rosehill, his summer compound on Sturgeon Lake (near Bobcaygeon, Ontario), to groups of business executives and top-level bureaucrats, three dozen at a time, for off-the-record, free-for-all confrontations.

These unstructured occasions allow the ambassadors of both sides to exchange intuitions, deceptions, and obsessions while lounging around Wisener's Italian gardens, golf course, and private beach. The 1973 gathering, just after Ottawa had implemented its capital gains tax measures, was highlighted by a noisy argument between Alf Powis, the Noranda president, and Simon Reisman, then the finance deputy, who ended the exchange by shouting, "You fat cats will just have to pay more taxes!" and diving into Sturgeon Lake. "There have been some moments that have been sort of fun," says Wisener, a large man with a sardonic sense of humour. "But it isn't what's discussed during the weekends that creates something. It's the phone calls that go on for the next year between the people who meet there. They see that the other fellow doesn't have horns. The businessmen realize that the Ottawa guys have real problems. They've just got to do things that are politically acceptable, because if they don't, they aren't going to be there anymore."

The concept that most clearly separates the two groups, no matter how friendly their plenipotentiaries may become, is the idea of profit as the ultimate measure of individual achievement and happiness. "Capitalism revolves around profit," says Jack Clyne, the former MacMillan Bloedel chairman. "If you do away with the profit motive you are acting in a manner totally contrary to the human instinct. Money in itself doesn't bring happiness. But often the *pursuit* of money does." According to this bottom-line philosophy, there can never be too much profit,[22] and pursuit of profit excuses almost everything, even idealism (Canadian industrial profits run to about $10 billion a year). Walter Gordon, whose nationalistic measures made him the devil incarnate along Toronto's Bay Street during the sixties, found that by the early seventies businessmen who had studiously avoided him for years were suddenly crossing the street to greet him. "At first," he says, "I thought they might be changing their minds on the foreign ownership issue. But then I quickly discovered that it was because my company, Canadian Corporate Management, was making a good profit, and they must have figured that anyone who can make money can't be all bad."

The shift in position of a few businessmen does not amount to a reformation. The typical Establishmentarian's search for understanding begins not in wonder but in the reduction of an increasingly confusing world to safe old values. Outlining what he considered to be the typical career pattern for ambitious young Canadians, Harry Jackman, the head of Dominion and Anglo Investment, told a parliamentary committee hearing on the Benson White Paper in 1970: "He begins by learning his trade; he saves his small stake, borrows from the bank, starts a business and, if successful, creates employment and provides goods and services for the people. In his forties he may start making some money. In his fifties his standard of living is pretty well established. Because of the general affluence, domestic servants are almost impossible to get. Probably corporatewise or personally he becomes an automatic saver or provider of capital. . . . "

It's been a while since the average Canadian youngster saw his future in quite this Horatio Alger spirit. But Jackman and most other members of the business Establishment continue clinging to the notion that somehow, at some dim time in the not too distant future, society will return to what they like to think of as normal. However unlikely this is to happen, their faith that it is still possible feeds their souls and keeps them from the wind.

NOTES

1. At the same time, they reject both the cold-blooded approach of old-line capitalists such as Sir James Dunn who was reported to have been ecstatic when fire destroyed the CSL vessel Noronic in Toronto harbour on September 17, 1949, because he was in the process of accumulating the company's stock and the catastrophe drove down its price, and the antics of New Rich buccaneers like Harold Ballard, president of Maple Leaf Gardens, who was charged with forty-seven counts of theft and fraud and was convicted in 1972 of defrauding his company of $82,000 and taking part in the theft of another $123,000.

2. Some American entrepreneurs tailor their appeals to more individual requirements. In 1948, when Wallace Johnson, who was to become a founding figure in Holiday Inns, was fighting a rezoning battle with the municipality of Memphis, he used the following text for his daily prayers: "O Lord, make us one of the greatest leaders of the nation in the building of men and homes, and help the city officials of Memphis to understand that this is our goal, so they will help us instead of hinder us. O Lord, help me to be one of the biggest businessmen in the country and if it be Thy will, let me be a vice-president of the National Home Builders' Association. Amen."

3. R. T. Naylor. "The Rise and Fall of the Third Commercial Empire of the St. Lawrence," in *Capitalism and the National Question in Canada*, edited by Gary Teeple (Toronto: University of Toronto Press, 1972).

4. H. V. Nelles, *The Politics of Development: Forests, Mines and Hydro-Electric Power in Ontario, 1849-1841* (Toronto: Macmillan, 1974).

5. Herschel Hardin, *A Nation Unaware* (Vancouver: J. J. Douglas, 1974).

6. Such appeals don't always work. When Senator Grattan O'Leary was collecting funds for the Tory leadership campaign of Robert Stanfield as a way of saving the two-party system, he went to see Neil McKinnon at the Commerce and was given $5,000. J. Grant Glassco, then head of Brazilian Light and Power, also donated $5,000 but reminded O'Leary that in the same building there was a man (Henry Borden, nephew of Sir Robert Borden, the former prime minister and a fellow Nova Scotian) who was much richer than either he or McKinnon. O'Leary went to see him and a week later he received Borden's cheque. It was for $100.

7. Among the accused were Hugh Martin, chairman of Marwell Dredging and Canadian Dredge & Dock Co., a high-ranking Liberal stalwart and director of the Canada Development Corp.; Harold McNamara, chairman of Bovis Corp. and McNamara Corp.; Gérard Filion, former president of Marine Industries Ltd. and former head of the Canadian Manufacturers' Association; and Jean Simard, a part-owner of Marine Industries and director of twenty other companies.

8. Lord Keynes caught this mood in 1938 when he wrote in a private letter to Franklin Delano Roosevelt: "You could do anything you liked with businessmen if you could treat them (even the big ones) not as wolves and tigers, but as domestic animals by nature, even though they have been badly brought up and not trained as you would wish."

9. There is rumoured to be one civil service regulation that states: "If you are absent from work owing to illness or injury on the date on which you joined the Pension Plan (or if this is a non-working day, then the next

preceding working day), you will not be entitled to death benefits until you return to work."

10. For example, TransCanada Pipelines requested a 4½ per cent rate increase, in August of 1969. It took the National Energy Board forty-five months to put it through, involving 156 days of hearings that took 15,000 pages to transcribe.

11. Only two prime ministers are usually thought of as having favoured big business. But one of them, Arthur Meighen, came from a Western Ontario hamlet (Anderson, near St. Marys) and an Ulster Presbyterian background, sustaining himself by a belief in hard work and plain living; the other, R. B. Bennett, didn't become rich until he was an adult.

12. To tag Trudeau with any recognizable ideology, it is probably necessary to move into the existentialism of the French philosopher Jean-Paul Sartre, who claims that each individual is what he makes of himself—that "man invents himself through exercising his freedom of choices."

13. Lester Pearson's network was a bit wider, including Jack Clyne and John Nicholin Vancouver, Philip Chester and Brig. Richard Malone in Winnipeg, Bill Harris, John Aird, and Tony Griffin in Toronto, and Charles Bronfman and Hartland Molson in Montreal.

14. At a private meeting on April 18, 1972, Trudeau's guests were Roy Bennett of Ford Canada, W. J. Cheesman of Westinghouse Canada, R. J. Richardson of Du Pont Canada, W. O. Twaits of Imperial Oil, Robert Bonner of MacMillan Bloedel, Paul Leman of Alcan, W. F. McLean of Canada Packers, Alfred Powis of Noranda Mines, A. A. Thornbrough of Massey-Ferguson, Marcel Vincent of Bell Canada, and D. G. Willmot of Molson Industries.

15. On May 15, 1975, a much larger group met Trudeau and finance minister John Turner: J. C. Barrow of Simpsons-Sears, T. J. Bell of Abitibi Paper, Thomas G. Bolton of Dominion Stories, John F. Bulloch of the Canadian Federation of Independent Business, Fred Burnet of Cominco, J. W. Burns of Great-West Life, R. J. Butler of Eaton's, J. W. Cameron of Alcan, Alistair Campbell of Sun Life, Arthur Child of Burns Foods, William Clerihue of Celanese Canada, David C. Collier of General Motors of Canada, George Crompton of the Retail Merchants' Association, George Currie of MacMillan Bloedel, Peter Gordon of Stelco, L. Edward Grubb of Inco, Alex D. Hamilton of Domtar, Eric Hamilton of CIL, William Hamilton of the Employers' Council of British Columbia, Jean-Claude Hébert of Bombardier, Samuel Hughes of the Canadian Chamber of Commerce, J. Taylor Kennedy of Canada Cement Lafarge, Harrison McCain of McCain Foods, W. Earle McLaughlin of the Royal Bank, Fred McNeil of the Bank of Montreal, W. K. Mounfield of Massey-Ferguson, David Nichol of Weston's, Charles Perrault of the Conseil du Patronat du Québec, Alfred Powis of Noranda, Henry de Puyjalon of the Canadian Construction Association, Charles Rathgeb of Comstock International, R. G. Reid of Imperial Oil, Michael Schurman of Schurman Construction, F. H. Sherman of Dofasco, E. R. Turner of the Saskatchewan Wheat Pool, and Walter G. Ward of Canadian General Electric.

16. The federal initiatives have been accompanied by more direct nationalization measures sponsored by various provincial governments. This has included not only the NDP administrations of British Columbia, Saskatchewan and Manitoba but also the Conservative regimes of Alberta (which took over Pacific Western Airlines) and Newfoundland (which nationalized the power assets of Brinco). Dealing with provincial governments, even those

headed by unabashed free-enterprisers, is difficult for businessmen who have a different interpretation of what political mandates mean and require. "People seemed to have trouble seeing W.A.C. Bennett when he was premier of B.C., though I never did," recalls Jack Clyne, the former chairman of MacMillan Bloedel. "But I never saw him for very long. If I stayed more that half an hour, either he'd get mad or I'd get mad, so we always used to limit our conversations to about twenty minutes."

17. The difference between a monopoly and an oligopoly is that several large firms instead of one company control the price system of a service or commodity. History's most savage monopoly was probably the quinine cartel. Before the invention of synthetic substitutes during World War II, the world's 500 million malaria sufferers depended on quinine made from the bark of Javanese chichona trees. To maintain its high price, the quinine cartel's hired arsonists regularly burned half the harvest of the life-giving substance.

18. One of the more bizarre practices was documented in a file seized from the Quaker Oats Company of Canada. It contained a description of the tendering procedure for a U.S. Army contract during the building of the Alaska Highway. The American colonel in charge of purchasing found that six Canadian flour mills had submitted identical bids. Using a deck of cards, he eliminated four of the six millers in a series of high-low cuts. Then he and a lieutenant cut the deck again; the king of diamonds won the round for Quaker Oats by beating out the ten of spades, which had turned up representing Lake of the Woods Milling Co. Ltd.

19. The Irving conviction was reversed on appeal in 1975.

20. In the spring of 1974, seven cement companies, including Canada Cement Lafarge Ltd., whose B.C. operations were headed by Jimmy Sinclair, Pierre Trudeau's father-in-law, were fined $432,000 for conspiring to fix base mill cement prices.

21. An independent government investigation of Stelco's operations found the company not guilty of having unduly increased its profit margin during recent price increases.

22. "If I had unlimited wealth and the CRTC would let me have all the electronic media I wanted," John Bassett, president of Baton Broadcasting Inc., told the *Windsor Star*, "I'd be a real pig. I like it. And if you're in business, you want more, you want to be a real pig."

SOCIOLOGISTS ATTRIBUTE DIFFERENT life styles, world views, and concepts of self to individuals and groups according to their position in the social hierarchy. Class circumstances, however, do not necessarily affect our conceptions of reality because we are subjective and social. That fact critically affects the way in which lives are perceived and explained. We can, for example, observe seemingly inexplicable reactions to the most extreme of life's circumstances. We have all seen individuals in excess comfort or deprivation react contrarily to their objective circumstances. As C. Wright put it:

the fact that men are not 'class conscious', at all times and in all places does not mean that 'there are no classes' or that 'in America everybody is middle class'. The economic and social facts are one thing. Psychological feelings may or may not be associated with them in rationally expected ways. (Mills, 1963:317)

This fact of social life has become a sociological dictum, most aptly expressed by W. I. Thomas when he said "What men define as real, is real in its consequences." In other words, reality is constructed by the individual.

There is evidence that interacting individuals who face similar circumstances will evolve similar perspectives about their reality. Peter Newman's article provides us with an example, at one extreme in the Canadian class system, of a perspective or world view predicated on the combination of class circumstances, interests, and interaction in a common situation.

The following article heightens our awareness of the important relationship between class position and group identity by describing the perspective(s) of Canadians in a markedly different class situation. The article by Lorimer and Phillips shows that Canadians who define themselves as "working people" create that identity by distinguishing themselves from those who they believe do not work.

Working people's definitions of themselves and other social groups reveal important incongruities in perception. These people seem to invest the act of working with a sacred quality all its own; thus they see themselves as a special and valued group. On the other hand, the working people interviewed in the study readily attribute negative characteristics to other social groups. Such biased perceptions support our thesis that identity formation does not depend on an objective reality but on "social facts", which are constructed by individuals to maintain their self-worth.

Attitudes

JAMES LORIMER/MYFANWY PHILLIPS

THE WAY PEOPLE think of themselves and other people is a subtle, ambiguous and complicated matter. People east of Parliament often say things—like "Of course we're only working people"—whose apparent meaning, especially to outsiders, is the exact opposite of their real meaning, but which are purposely framed in such a way as to ensure that they will be misinterpreted by outsiders. Determining their real attitudes is not simple.

From Working People *by James Lorimer and Myfanwy Phillips, pp. 106-117. Toronto: James Lewis and Samuel, 1971.*

Consider, for instance, the question of whether working people east of Parliament have a sense of themselves as a distinctive group on any basis other than that they live in the same general area. This is not a subject people often talk about, and it has come up only on the quite rare occasions when it was necessary for area residents to describe themselves. This happened once or twice in the residents' association, when long-standing area residents tried to define exactly what kind of people live east of Parliament. Once Robert Smith was trying to make the distinction between long-time area residents and recent middle-class town-house owners. He used four terms interchangeably to describe the long-time residents: "working people," "working class" (this term only once, and without any special stress), "the ordinary working Joe," and "the working Joe." "Working people" and "the ordinary Joe" were the terms favoured most by other long-time residents in the discussion.

After I noticed that these terms are used on occasion by area residents to describe themselves, gradually it became clear that they express a concept which is familiar to most people even though it is rarely aggressively asserted. Most residents in the area who have manual blue-collar jobs and who share the general patterns of life described here seem to regard themselves as "working people" with characteristics which distinguish them from other people with different kinds of jobs and different patterns of social, economic and political life. They do not use the term "working people" to distinguish themselves from people who do not work. Neither are they prone to use it often. It does not come into play quickly in discussions or in explanations. Other distinctions, like those of age, attractiveness, wealth, and friendliness (only some of which suggest class distinction) are more commonly made. At the same time, however, the category is a perfectly natural one for people to use. They way in which it comes up gives the impression that one reason people do not use it more often is that the facts and circumstances it refers to are taken as obvious.

The characteristics which determine whether someone belongs to the category of "working people" are reasonably clear from the way the term is used. The work a man does is a primary consideration. Blue-collar occupations are the jobs of working men; white-collar jobs, even relatively low-paid and unskilled ones, are felt to be different and to remove most men from the "working people" category. Basic characteristics of the way people live and dress are also considered. A working man wears work clothes on the job and drops his g's in words like "doing" and "thinking."

What the exact differences are between them and other people, however, does not seem to be clear-cut to most working people. Many of the basic patterns of their life appear to be the same as those of other people. The differences which exist surface individually and often appear to be oddities. John and Diane, for instance, remarked from time to time on their astonishment that, while there were always lots of empty gin and scotch bottles in the garbage of one of the new middle-class families on Minster Lane, the family showed none of the usual signs of heavy drinking common to Minister Lane's previous drinkers; they didn't have noisy fights or kick each other out onto the street. When it appeared that a wife-swapping arrangement had been developed by some of the new middle-class couples elsewhere in the area, Diane, John, George and Betty were fascinated; they couldn't conceive of such an arrangement, where all the individuals could be unfaithful but the marriages could go on as before. The working people in the residents' association found it odd and amusing that I or some other town-house resident in the group should get so agitated about situations—like the city's failure to plow our street after a snow storm—which they took for granted as the neighbourhood's due.

To summarize, working people east of Parliament do have a sense of themselves and people like them as being a distinct and separate category of people. The way they use the term "working people" to distinguish people on the basis of objective characteristics, particularly as holders of blue-collar jobs, and on the basis of overall patterns of family, social, political and economic life suggests that they are making the same kind of distinction which sociologists make in their discussions of objective social classes. But because working people tend to draw a line between themselves and other people does not mean that they make any simple evaluation of themselves. In fact, very often when people identify themselves as "working people," they do so in a context which appears to belittle people in this general category. This is clear, for instance, in the phrase *"ordinary* working people" or *"ordinary* working Joe," where "ordinary" serves to communicate the view that working people have nothing special or valuable or important about them. Thus a working man may—and often does—extricate himself from a situation where he finds his views clashing with those of a middle-class individual by saying, "I'm only an ordinary working Joe." There is still more to this extremely common expression. Used by working people in discussions with non-working-class individuals, it enables—in fact it encourages—the non-working-class person to express, or at least assent to, his own superiority and to the inferiority of working people. His assent is obtained if this phrase provokes him to murmur so much as a word of sympathy to the self-confessed ordinary working man, and his assertion of his own superiority is invited. If someone says, "Of course, I'm only an ordinary working Joe," he is asking a middle-class person to reply, "Oh, yes, of course, well in that case . . . ," and so reject or ignore his views not on any grounds of substance but rather on the grounds of the inferiority of the person who formulated them. The device traps the non-working-class person into expressing the sense of superiority he is automatically assumed (and usually accurately so) to feel, while at the same time it establishes for the working man not a sense of his inferiority, but rather his awareness of the fact that non-working-class people consider him inferior. Where he himself stands on this issue he is able to leave unstated.

Amongst themselves working people use similar expressions. "We're only working people," members of the residents' association would on occasion say, "you can't expect city hall to pay any attention to us." In this kind of situation the belittling qualification of *"only* working people" is not being used to express a deeply-felt, sincere appreciation of inferiority. It is being used ironically. It is attributing to the outside world, in this case to city hall, a view which everyone recognizes the outside world holds: that working people are inferior. The tone in which it is said, however, implies the general view that this opinion is ridiculous —that of course working people have interests which should be protected, that of course they should receive fair and equitable treatment, that of course they are important and deserve the same consideration as other social classes. But the fact of the matter is that they are treated as inferior by city hall and the rest of the outside world. When one working man says to another, therefore, "We're only working people," he is saying that while there is no legitimate ground for being treated as inferiors because of this, in fact working people are.

Most working people have a strong sense of their own value and worth. Rarely, however, do they come right out and express it in a clear and uncompromising way. Instead, they assert it in a left-handed way, as for instance in the self-belittling speech just discussed. Another example of this is to be seen in the way people discuss specific aspects of their life, as for example when east of Parliament residents talk about their neighbourhood. Most seem to hold the view that their neighbourhood is basically a good and desirable place to live and has a value which should be respected and protected. At the same time, however, they are aware that most outsiders, particularly middle-class people, extend their general negative view of working people to a specific negative evaluation of working-class neighbourhoods like east of Parliament. Yet area residents know that these middle-class outsiders usually feel that the area could be redeveloped into some valuable alternative form, such as privately-developed high-rise apartments. In these circumstances area residents assert vociferously the value of their area, but they talk about the area not as a neighbourhood but as valuable real estate for redevelopment. "We're sitting on the most valuable land on the North American continent" is the way they put it. Some who express this opinion are in fact people who, like Robert Smith, are anxious to see private developers operating in the area so they can sell their homes and make a substantial windfall profit on the sale. But the assertion of the value of the land on which the area stands is far more general than is the desire to sell out. When city planners, therefore, talked about urban renewal, the residents worried about expropriation didn't say to them, "We know the value of our neighbourhood," but "We know the value of our land."[1]

Within this general sense of their own worth and respectability, however, there is an appreciation of some specific matters on which working people differ from other individuals, particularly from middle-class people. On some of these matters, working people come off better in the comparison. Thus, for instance, all the people we knew well in the neighbourhood, particularly Betty and Diane, consider middle-class people to be much less friendly and easy to get along with as neighbours than are working people. There is also an appreciation of how middle-class individuals often lose touch with or sever connections with their families in their efforts to become successful, a matter on which they are judged inferior to working people who have continued close contact with parents and relations. In other specific respects, however, working people consider themselves inferior. They judge their general economic position, for instance, to be inferior to that of wealthy middle-class families. What a set of specific judgements of this kind reveals is that the changes of circumstance required by a normal working-class family to make their life match their ideals would not amount to a transformation to a middle-class life style, but rather to an improvement of the life they already lead by means of removing its insecurities and inconveniences without altering its positively-judged elements. An improvement of the working-class style rather than a transformation into middle-class living is, interestingly enough, exactly the pattern adopted by certain successful entertainers from working-class backgrounds, particularly country and western singers, whose success is based mainly on an audience of working people.

Another left-handed way in which working people express a feeling of their own worth and respectability is in their passionate denial of worth and respectability to working people who have gone wrong or who have moral weaknesses. In analysing this attitude of working people, I am asserting a broader definition of working class than many sociologists use, though I think my use of the category conforms to the implicit views of working people east of Parliament. It is common for sociologists to distinguish the working class from the lower class, both on the subjective grounds that people in general draw this distinction and on the objective grounds that there are major differences in economic life and other patterns of life between working-class and lower-class people.[1] Apparently closely corresponding to this distinction in sociology is the line which respectable working people east of Parliament draw between themselves and "welfare bums." "Welfare bums," working people feel, spend their life drinking; they neglect their children; they are promiscuous; they spend their money foolishly; they don't keep their homes clean; they show no respect or concern for their neighbours, for other people, or for other people's property. The crucial and single defining characteristic of "welfare bums" is an economic one: their income is unearned, and comes in the form of government welfare payments. The impression one gets on first encountering this distinction between working people and "welfare bums" is that, for working people, it represents a far more important gap than any they might picture between themselves and middle-class people.

Gradually during the time we lived on Minster Lane we encountered facts which led me to wonder whether this is what the "welfare bum" category is really about. The first, most important of these was the discovery that a large number of respectable working people have been what they would describe as "welfare bums" at some point in their lives. The Smyrchanskis were on welfare for several months during the winter of 1967-68 and, though their outward conduct changed hardly at all, that short period was enough for them to be categorized as "welfare bums" by some of the people who knew them fairly well. Betty with her two daughters was on welfare from the time her first husband died until she got together with George; and though the subject has never come up, I would be surprised if there was never a time in Diane's childhood or in John's when their families had to rely on government assistance of some kind. Most of the time we lived on Minster, John's sister Sally, previously respectable and happily married, was on her own with her two kids in an apartment a couple of streets away, supported mainly by welfare.

It is easy, then, to move back and forth between the category of respectable working family and "welfare bum," as the Smyrchanskis did in 1967-68. It could happen to any of the other families we know if the father found himself out of work. Being out of work and on welfare in turn can lead to family tensions and drinking, to a break-up of the family and to a mother on her own with her kids and welfare her only source of income. Finding a job can often put a fast end to this situation and enable a family to return to normal, respectable patterns.

I also gradually realized that people who are living on welfare and who are regarded as "welfare bums" rarely seem to embody more than two or three of the life style characteristics universally attributed to "welfare bums." Their lives are obviously affected by the circumstances which have led them to become dependent on welfare; if a husband stays with his wife, he often drinks a lot, and if a woman is abandoned and can afford only very bad housing, she is a less careful housekeeper than she was in happier and better circumstances. Although some welfare recipients come to worse straits than others, however, few if any achieve the totally desperate pattern of life attributed to them.

I learned too that most welfare recipients seem to hold exactly the same opinion of "welfare bums" as do respectable working people. Proposals fashionable in some political circles that people on welfare have a right to government assistance and are not morally tainted by exercising this right have made no dent in the views of welfare recipients themselves. They condemn their fellow recipients as "welfare bums" just as vigourously as their most respectable neighbours do.

The conclusion I arrived at is that the working-class -"welfare bum" distinction is not a distinction between two different social classes. Rather it is a distinction drawn between people all of whom are working-class, and its function is partly to affirm the value of the characteristics of respectable, worthy working-class people by condemning their opposite. It is simultaneously an expression of fear and disapproval for what happens to working-class individuals whose lives go wrong. Just as the key to respectable family life for working people is a steady, secure job by which the father can support his home, so the single largest threat to this way of life in all its respects is the situation where a man cannot find work and his family is forced to live as dependents on government welfare assistance. From this basic threat of economic dependence all other evils flow. "Welfare bums" are the dark twin of the working class, in much the same way as Heather Robertson suggests Canadian Indians are the dark twin of the urban Canadian middle class.[2]

As well as asserting their superiority to "welfare bums," working people east of Parliament often make distinctions between themselves and other people who share an overall working-class life style on racial and ethnic grounds. Any noticeable racial or ethnic difference is the basis for distinction and a judgement of inferiority. For example, white Anglo-Saxon native residents east of Parliament draw distinctions between themselves and people of a different colour, between themselves and people of different ethnic background like Italians, French, Germans, Ukrainians, and Poles, and between themselves and people of different regional background, particularly Maritimers and Newfoundlanders. The measure of inferiority attributed to people different in one or more of these respects is considerable, though it is not of the same order as that attributed to "welfare bums." It tends to be expressed in milder ways, too, particularly in jokes. And it is partly by means of jokes and stories that children absorb these attitudes. George told us this one: Question: Why does a Newfie always eat baked beans on Friday? Answer: So he can take a bubble bath on Saturday. Mike told us an anti-Jewish joke which he understood vaguely to be funny, even though at his age he probably had very little notion of what a Jew is. Question: What did the Jewish Santa Claus say when he came down the chimney? Answer: Want to buy some Christmas presents?

To sum up, the view which working people take of themselves is not easy to define, nor is it an attitude which asserts the positive value of everything and everyone that is working class. Respectable working people quite clearly judge themselves superior to sub-groups of less respectable working people and to groups with inferior ethnic, national, racial or economic characteristics. While such judgements assert the value and worth of working people as a whole, at the same time they create distinctions and divisions of major importance amongst different groups of working-class people, distinctions on which working people are much more likely to dwell than they are, for example, on the vague but evident distinction which they recognize to exist between themselves and non-working-class people.

There is, then, amongst working people east of Parliament a general recognition of themselves as a broad group with some basic similarities, as well as a general appreciation of themselves, which is almost never expressed in a direct and outright form, as a group just as worthy as any other of respect and, in some matters, admiration. But though they have this general sense of themselves, they refer to it much less commonly than they do to more specific, concrete categories of people with more specific, easily identified characteristics. The category of working people comes up much less often than the categories of wops, frogs, newfies, and niggers.

This same preference for the specific and concrete applies to the way in which working people see the outside world and to the attitudes, which they take to it. There is a relatively vague and infrequently referred-to sense of another large general category of people which embraces most or all of the people who are not working people. The only general term I have encountered for this group is "the better classes," where "better" carries the same irony and double meaning that "ordinary" does in the term "ordinary working Joe." There is, however, a host of more specific and concrete categories, which come up frequently. Area residents talk about "professional people," the young, middle-class professional couples who are buying up and renovating houses in the neighbourhood. They refer to "educated people," people who have university degrees and generally hold well-paid, fairly powerful jobs. "People from Rosedale" refers to the concentration in that area of rich, upper-middle-class and upper-class people who control the politics of the provincial and federal constituencies in which east of Parliament falls, who play a major part in controlling city politics and who are a good part of the city's social, political and economic elite. "The E. P. Taylors" is a similar category, E. P. Taylor being a wealthy Toronto-based Canadian industrialist, used to refer to the few rich and powerful Canadian businessmen. "Pencil pushers" is a term I have encountered once or twice as a reference to the lower-middle-class ranks of clerks and middle-level employees of bureaucracies with whom working people have most of their dealings in their encounters as clients with public bodies and agencies.

The attitudes which are taken to these categories vary considerably and reflect an ironical awareness of the difference between the general superiority attributed by all middle-class people to themselves in comparison to working people and the specific judgements of superiority and inferiority made by most working people. They also reflect a pattern of evaluating individual characteristics of the outside world by the values and preferences of working-class life, so that for example the sense in which both "educated people" and "pencil pushers" are often considered to have "better" jobs is not that these jobs are more interesting to do, more variable, or more demanding than most blue-collar jobs, or even necessarily that they are better paid, but rather that they offer the certainty of steady, reliable work and virtually put an end to the uncertainty which is attached to most blue-collar jobs. In this judgement, however, is implied an awareness of the conventional middle-class judgement that a white-collar job is preferable in all respects; to a working man, the "better job" of a white-collar worker is by no means better in every respect, nor in fact is it usually to be preferred to a good blue-collar job.

Working people east of Parliament have very concrete notions about how life could be better for themselves. Virtually everyone we know, for example, thinks wistfully about how he would like to live on a farm in the country. Life on the farm is considered healthier, happier, better for kids. Once when we were speculating on what we would do if we won the Irish Sweepstakes, John and Diane said they would buy a farm and raise horses. Tom and Peggy had worked out in careful detail how they could buy a small farm northeast of Toronto and do some farming on the side, while Tom kept a job in Toronto driving a truck or a taxi. Living in the suburbs is considered halfway between east of Parliament and a farm. All the young couples we know think that, if they could afford it, they would be better off living in the suburbs than in the city. John and Diane looked long and hard at new suburban houses before choosing one in an older suburb built 40 or 50 years ago but with many of the same features. The biggest attraction of suburbs and farms is the better life they afford young kids.

Long-time residents east of Parliament seem more attached to the area and more conscious of its qualities, but even they always express their feelings as a hard-headed weighting of advantages versus disadvantages, for instance that you don't need a car if you live downtown but that you have to put up with the tenants on the block and with the drunks wandering around on the streets. They have none of the romantic enthusiasm which outsiders sometimes affect for the "colourful," "intensive" life of neighbourhoods like east of Parliament. It is perhaps not so surprising as it first appeared to us that the resident with the strongest feeling for the area as a physical place and for its houses and streets is Allan Hammer, who is a bricklayer by profession. He more than anyone else is conscious of the craftsmanship and elegance in the construction of the houses in the area. When he returned from holidays in the United States, he talked in glowing terms about similar old neighbourhoods there which have been restored and preserved, usually of course by the kind of middle-class renovators moving in east of Parliament.

The attitude which people east of Parliament have to Toronto is difficult to sort out. The evils of city living are worse in Toronto than in other cities in the country, because Toronto is so large and because it is growing so quickly. There are advantages, however, to living in the wealthiest and most prosperous city in the country; wages are better than in the Maritimes or Montreal or Winnipeg, and, more importantly, jobs are usually easier to get in Toronto than in the rest of the country. In an important sense, of course, working people who live in Toronto have little choice in the matter: the jobs are there, the money is there, their connections and friends are there, and they cannot afford to leave.

The point of view which working people east of Parliament take to the political and economic system reflects their awareness of the fact that it is largely controlled and run by other people. They are conscious that these people feel that working people are basically inferior, less worthy of respect, less desirable, and less deserving of fair and equitable treatment than other groups. Working people analyse the way the economic and political system works as in keeping with their general view that people act in the economic and political sphere solely on the basis of their real material interests, from a desire to promote their own immediate ends, usually power, wealth and prestige. Most working people take the position that other factors—a concern for propriety or abstract ideals like justice, virtue and honesty—have little or nothing to do with influencing the actions of people, especially the people running the political and economic system.

This analysis is constantly being applied to political and economic reality, and it is the experience of working people that it serves them well in understanding and predicting how the political-economic system operates. The general view taken of politicians, for example, leads working people east of Parliament to become well-informed about the economic interests of local politicians, to know what businesses they are in and where they have money invested. Even many people who take little interest in city politics know, for example, that Fred Beavis, alderman for the next ward to the east and a powerful long-time city hall politician who is one of the most consistent friends land developers have in Toronto politics,[3] is in the roofing business. They are much more likely to know this than to know what political party claims Fred Beavis's allegiance. In the same way, working people east of Parliament often are quite well-informed about who the powerful members of the economic elite are and how these individuals often appear to have virtually no scruples and encounter no difficulties in bending and manoeuvring the political system and the economy to suit their own interests.

Their analysis of the political and economic system is quite different from that of many middle-class people, who generally take the view that the conduct of people in power is not just the result of the desire to further their own immediate interests, and who feel that values, ideals and propriety play a considerable part not only in the way people explain what they do but in the way they act. Similarly, the working-class analysis of the functioning of the political-economic system is quite different from accounts which stress the system's fundamental basis in values and ideals like the view that all individuals have the same basic rights and should be free to act as they choose, and which assert that the politicians act in a responsible way to represent as best they can the interests of their constituents, that it is the opinions of the public that determine the actions of governments, that businessmen are in business to make a profit and to serve the public at the same time, that the economic system is regulated to ensure fair wages and working conditions for working people and fair profits for businessmen, and so on. The experience of working people is that their analysis of the political and economic system usually explains what is going on and predicts what will happen very effectively, and that it is constantly being confirmed as accurate.

So the attitude which is taken toward the political and economic system is that the system is being run for the benefit of the people with the power and wealth to control it. The standards for judgement which are used, however, are the ideals which are proclaimed by the system itself: equality, justice, freedom. Judged in those terms, and on the basis of the experiences of working people in their economic and political life, the political and economic system is profoundly unsatisfactory.

This view does not, however, draw people to an inevitable conclusion that the economic and political status quo, because it does not meet the ideals which it proclaims and which working people assert in judging it, should be radically and fundamentally changed. This constellation of attitudes of working people leads to quite different evaluations than might be expected both of proposals for radical political and economic change and of their advocates. The view that the status quo is so firmly entrenched that any substantial changes in the distribution of power and wealth are highly unlikely makes "radical" political activity on its face rather an irrelevant and futile activity. This judgement is combined with the view that men—any men—in politics have only one kind of goal, advancement of personal ends like lining their own pockets and making themselves into important individuals, and is further driven home by the view that the achievement of any other kind of result is virtually impossible. Such thinking leads working people to discount the claims of reformers and radicals to seriousness and honest commitment to their stated goals, and makes the claims of a political party like the NDP far less compellingly attractive to them than might otherwise be the case. Also, much of what is described as "radical" politics is being generated from groups of people who are the outcasts of the middle class, the children of respectable people who without losing their basic middle-class style are nevertheless considered to have gone badly wrong. Long-hair hippie radical freaks stand in much the same relation to the urban Canadian middle class as do welfare bums to working people. They are prone to being categorized by working people along with niggers, newfies and welfare bums. This reaction is of course often encouraged by advocates of the status quo, who worry about the dangers which could be posed by combined political action from working people and from critical middle-class people.

This distrust of reformists and political radicals has a firm basis both in the past experience of working people and in the real attitudes and values of the reformers. It is hard to describe as misplaced a cynicism about the possibilities of real change in the political and economic status quo for working people in the light, for instance, of the policies of NDP provincial governments in Canada or of the Labour party in power in Britain, or of the changes brought about by advocates of the interests of the workers in Eastern Europe. Also to be considered is the fact that adoption by middle-class people of what they consider to be left-wing radical political views and greater concern for the interests of working people than the present political system offers does not automatically bring with it an end to the usual middle-class patronizing of working people. Just as common among the new left as among the old is the attitude that the educated and enlightened people should lead and that the workers, once they have been brought to understand their situation properly, should fall in behind their new leaders. Thus, for example, when a caucus of left-wing and mostly young people inside the NDP met in Toronto to discuss the significance for them of community organizing and citizens' groups in working-class areas like east of Parliament, the unquestioned assumption common to everyone in the group about the real function of community organizing was not that it is a means of encouraging people to get together to discover their common interests and to take political action on what they decide to be their most pressing common problems, but that it is a means of getting people together so that they can be educated about the real nature of their situation (which it is assumed they do not understand) and the real possibilities for action.

The view of the world taken by working people east of Parliament is confusing and surprising. On the surface, they see more differences than similarities amongst groups of people who, in fact, they consider to be working people like themselves. They express a negative, belittling attitude towards working people in general which is at once an ironic comment on the fact that this attitude is held by most other people and at the same time an assertion of exactly the opposite evaluation of themselves. A conventional respect is expressed for the conventionally superior social status attached to more powerful and wealthier social groups, like professional people and wealthy businessmen, but this turns out to be an assertion that working people should command at least the same respect and value and are in no general sense inferior to anybody. The political and economic system, judged by the experiences which working people have in their own life, is compared to the fundamental ideals the system itself proclaims and is considered to perform in a completely unsatisfactory way. The actions of people who control the system are considered to flow from exactly the motives which they themselves are most anxious to disclaim. Yet this system is not considered to be so corrupt or so exploitative that any move to change it will be welcome. Rather, at the present time, it is accepted, and in fact considered likely to be superior to available alternative kinds of economic and political organization. The strongest hate and detestation of people east of Parliament are directed not against this system but against people who are in fact mostly working people themselves and who share most of the characteristics of working-class life, but who differ and are inferior in some concrete characteristics of their background or who lack the essential economic element of a father working and earning enough money to support his family.

This view of the world, examined on its own independent of the circumstances of the family, social, economic and political life from which it arises, would certainly seem cynical in its view of government, politics and the economic system, hypocritical in its evaluation of the middle class and of working people on welfare, and absurdly conventional in its self-abnegation and its easy assumption of inferiority. It would no doubt also appear to have only a tenuous link with reality. Yet, examined in the context of the life of working people and interpreted with the care which is required by its explicit respect for the known views of outsiders and its ironies, it emerges as unusually close to the realities of the situation of working people, assertive of the worth and respect due working people, and inventive in the way it denies the world view of middle-class people while at the same time it appears to be confirming it.

NOTES

1. See for instance David Matza, "The Disreputable Poor," p. 290, in R. Bendix and S. M. Lipset, *Class, Status and Power*. New York: Free Press, 1966, second edition.

2. In *Reservations are for Indians*. Toronto: James Lewis and Samuel, 1970. See especially pp. 270-298.

3. See the information on Beavis's 1970 voting record in the 12 January, 1971, issue of the newsletter *City Hall* written by Aldermen Sewell, Crombie, Kilbourn and Jaffary.

Conclusion

Canadian Identity

SOCIAL BEHAVIOR AND identity, as we have discussed it, have a group base, and the group therefore becomes the sociologist's most important focus of study. Sociologists examine social processes and relationships within the cultural and historical context in which people find themselves. Within a framework of tradition, custom, and mutual expectations, individuals and groups interact and create understandings that guide their participation, roles, and identifications. Social life, then, is observed as a dynamic process wherein participants are shaped in interactive relationships with others. The sociological study of human behavior and identity, as we have observed, is a complex process requiring an appreciation of the historical or biographical context and the social structural relationships within which social action takes place.

In this book we have presented an integrated theoretical framework for describing and understanding human behavior and identity. We have outlined the major concept of a specific orientation, symbolic interactionism, and observed its applicability in a wide range of situations and with a variety of participants; such a study increases our understanding of the way people symbolically communicate definitions of situations and expectations about appropriate behavior. This final section of the book applies the central tenets of symbolic interactionism to an analysis of the time-honored problem of Canadian unity and identification.

The development of a national identity, a sense of a society's location and attributes, always requires a direct or implied reference to others. Each group or society distinguishes itself from others through the medium of language. Each society develops a set of shared conventional symbols (flags, crosses, uniforms, monuments, music) as an expression of its particular point of view, interests, culture, and way of life. Such symbols of national identification develop out of the interactions that members have with each other.

Canadian society has struggled to find a common identity because it has lacked the unifying goals and ideals that would provide the country's peoples with a sense of shared culture and fate. (Alford, 1963; Hiller, 1975; Manzer, 1974; Morton, 1965; and Schwartz, 1967) This point is expressed in a newspaper column by journalist Anthony Westell:

> What we lack on this 110th national birthday is a clear idea of what it
> means to be a Canadian. We have no great national idea or goal for

which our symbols stand and to which we can all rally emotionally even when divided by politics, religion, class or language . . .

We can sing O Canada with a catch in our throats but we don't really know what we mean by "true patriot love," and obviously a lot of Canadians don't feel the country is glorious. Other countries know what their symbols represent and what they are celebrating on national days— or at least they think they know. The fact that their beliefs may be myths, denied by reality, does not weaken their power to inspire patriotism.

The Americans are sure that theirs is the land of freedom and opportunity, the world's greatest democracy and most advanced society.

The British find pride and confidence in their history which is enshrined in the monarchy and in parliamentary traditions.

The French still respond to their revolutionary slogan: Liberty, equality, fraternity.

To take a rather different example, the Swedes seem to have accepted as their unifying idea the notion of social justice to be achieved through the welfare state.

What idea, what set of values, can unite Canadians and diffuse the crisis of unity? (*Toronto Star*, 1 July 1977, p. C4.)

Unifying goals and symbols commonly emerge out of crisis when attentions focus on shared problems or threats. When these perceived threats come from outside the society, they serve to unify its members. The threats are symbolized—given collective meaning—by the menaced individuals, who develop a common perspective about the problem and its possible solutions.

Historically we observe Canadians identifying with each other in periods of national crisis, and splitting up when internal divisions are more immediately perceived. Canadian identity depends, then, on the perceptions of Canadian citizens. When Canadians sense an external threat, Canadian identity is strong; if, however, the threats are perceived as internal, the national identity is weakened.

The processes that are most critical for understanding Canadian society and identity involve economic, political, and sociocultural relationships within the society, and between Canadian groups and outsiders. The most impressive external relationship that has historically deterred Canada from developing a national autonomy and identity has been its colonial relationship to imperialist nations. Canada has never been truly independent, economically, politically, or culturally. This fact, as well as the exploitation resulting from its dependence on other countries, has prevented Canada from developing a distinct identity.

Canada has been the colony or dependency of two empires, and historically, has always faced the problem of external control and domination. The shift away from Great Britain was accompanied by greater influence, control, and domination by U.S. interests. The multinational ownership of Canadian industry sources, and trade relationships presently link and integrate her with the U.S. in one continental economy. (Clement, 1977)

As Canada is a producer of raw materials and resources for the multinational corporations, it remains economically dependent. The heavy demand for Canadian resources produces a colonial-like relationship between this country and the most powerful capitalist nation, the United States. In classic mercantilist fashion, Canada's resources and the profits from those resources flow outward. Multinational corporations, as a consequence, have excessive influence over Canadian economic, political, and cultural life.

Those who control economic power ultimately control the rest of the society. Directly or indirectly in Canadian society, there is general agreement that both an external and internal elite make important decisions which largely serve their own interests. In his classic study, *The Vertical Mosaic*, John Porter boldly expresses the implications of external decision-making in Canadian life when he says:

> It has been suggested that this external decision-making affects such things as the development of research, the location of plants, the rate of expansion, marketing policies, purchasing policies, the rate of resource development, and the pricing policy of the parent firm, particularly if the parent operates in many other countries as well as in the United States. There is also the effect on the distribution of earnings. The main benefit to Canadians as labourers within this increasingly foreign dominated economy could be in the form of higher average wages which are being paid in United States controlled firms. By the middle 1950s close to half the profits of Canadian corporations accrued to non-residents, further reducing the possibility of Canadian savings being the source of future investment. To all of these effects must be added the general social effect of cultural uniformity between the two countries, resulting from the uniformity of product, advertising, and sales promotion. It may even be argued that economic integration is the fore-runner of full cultural integration, and that when the latter stage is reached the sense of economic domination will disappear. (Porter, 1965: 268-69)

The economic and social consequences of external control that Porter describes are impressive in themselves. His concluding remark about the related consequences of cultural uniformity has direct bearing on the issue of Canadian identity.

Clement's analysis of class and power in Canada (1975), while updating and adding to Porter's contribution, considers the role of the elite in shaping the structure and organization of Canadian society. Clement asserts that Canada was and remains a society controlled by elites and claims that:

> Between 1951 and 1972, there has been a marked tendency for an increasing centralization and concentration of capital into fewer and larger firms, and secondly, an increasing penetration of the economy by foreign, especially U.S., direct investment. (Clement, 1975: 168)

Analyzing the media elite, Clement summarizes, in diagrammatic form, "the interlocking directorships between dominant corporations and selected media complexes" and concludes that "together the economic and media elite are simply two sides of the same upper class; between them they hold two of the key sources of power—economic and ideological—in Canadian society and form the corporate elite." (Clement, 1975: 325) The relationship between such control and its influence on our self-image is summarized by Clement:

> The media, through the ideology they present, reinforce the existing political and economic system. The mass media are not the pillars of capitalist society; they do, however, add important support to the structure and serve to reinforce the continuation of existing inequalities.... Under the existing system of concentrated and capitalist dominated media, the corporate elite will continue to maintain control over the means of mental production. (Clement, 1975: 343)

Such economic domination and control directly affect the way Canadians see themselves because the economic system is the foundation of society. It affects and shapes other institutions, cultures, and identities within the society. The pivotal importance of economic relations to other features of the society is expressed by Karl Marx when he says:

> In the social production of their life, men enter into definite relations that are indispensable and independent of their will, relations of production which correspond to a definite stage of development of their material productive forces. The sum total of these relations of production constitutes the economic structure of society, the real foundation, on which rises a legal and political superstructure and to which correspond definite forms of social consciousness. The production of material life conditions the social, political and intellectual life processes in general. (Marx, 1968: 182)

The same processes of concentration and exploitation that characterize multinational-Canadian relations are found internally in the relations between urban-developed areas and hinterland-underdeveloped areas. The flow of resources and profits that creates a situation of economic dependency for Canada as a whole is reflected internally by the impoverishment and dependency of certain regions in this country *vis-à-vis* wealthier ones. These real and perceived inequities between provinces and regions in Canadian society create another crucial barrier to conceptions of Canadian unity, and serve to frustrate the development of a shared national identity.

The most critical internal impediment to the development of a national identity is the existence of two language groups in Canada. This fundamental barrier to communication reinforces group perceptions of difference, irrespective of objective reality, and creates a situation in which the development of shared symbols of identification is impossible. In order for individuals to participate and identify with each other they must be able to cooperate and communicate with each other, share each other's points of view, and see themselves as sharing a common tradition and fate. The absence of a shared symbol system prevents these two groups from coming together as participants sharing the same reality.

Language is the most powerful medium of integration and separation. The existence of at least two culturally distinct language groups (the Native People constitute a third, and the large immigrant population representing many different cultures is a fourth force) prevents the development of a unitary set of symbols and identifications. The inability to communicate creates and reinforces distinctions made out of unfamiliarity and discomfort. Unable to share the same meanings, the groups see each other as outsiders.

Ironically, one of the key ways in which individuals join together and see themselves as similar is by distinguishing themselves from others. Identity is formed by incorporating other people's reactions into definitions of self. In order for a society to know what it believes and agrees on, it must define and react to those ideas that are not acceptable. Groups define themselves by contrasting themselves with others. English Canadians and French Canadians are being driven apart, while at the same time members of each group band together. As the conflict between the two groups intensifies and they grow further apart, the individuals of each language group unite against the other.

The Quebec crisis, an internal threat to national unity and identity, has caught the attention of the rest of the country, and strengthened English Canada's loyalty to Canada as a nation. This trend is reflected in a widely reported national survey which states:

> In response to the question of whether people consider themselves as Canadian or Easterners, Westerners, Ontarians, Quebeckers or Maritimers, the vast majority prefer to think of themselves as Canadians (76 per cent overall, from 56 per cent in Quebec to 91 per cent in Ontario). This suggests that a majority of Canadians have a commitment and a pride in Canada. There is a natural association to the reference "Cana-

dian" and a security in its use. It gives people an identity. That same sense of pride, however, is lacking in Quebec relative to the rest of Canada.... (Goldfarb, 1977: 12)

November 15, 1976, the day that the Parti Québecois was elected to power in Quebec, marks a historical watershed in Canada's history. The real threat of internal division has recast Canada's problem around a theme of unity and has effectively dampened concern about external influence. The legacy of the original French and English colonies living peacefully as distinct communities in one nation is threatened as never before, and the question of Canadian identity has been put aside as Quebec seeks sovereignty. Canada faces a new crisis and Canadian identity has become a moot question of dismemberment and survival.

The theoretical separation of Quebec poses a most profound threat to the concepts of Canadian society and identity. As Quebec moves toward becoming a single-language society, the symbolic and psychological estrangement of French and English Canada grows more complete. This breakdown of communication portends a future of social conflict between these groups.

Regional disparity and the growth of multiculturalism are additional important internal constraints to the development of a Canadian identity. Combined with the inordinate influence of outside interests, these constraints blur any sense of unity and collective identity. No wonder, then, that it is difficult for all Canadians to share a sense of oneness, a common identity and fate.

The future of Canadian identity rests with society's participants and the interpretations and meanings that develop, or fail to develop, around shared symbols. It is the development of shared symbols that provides groups and their individual members with distinctive and meaningful identifications.

BIBLIOGRAPHY

Alford, R. R. *Party and Society: The Anglo-American Democracies.* Chicago: Rand McNally, 1963.

Anderson, E. L. *We Americans.* Cambridge: Harvard University Press, 1937.

Becker, H. S. *Outsiders: Studies in the Sociology of Deviance.* New York: The Free Press, 1963.

—————. "The Self and Adult Socialization," in *The Study of Personality: An Interdisciplinary Appraisal,* eds. E. Norbeck, D. Price-Williams, and W. M. McCord. New York: Holt, Rinehart and Winston, 1968, pp. 194-208.

Becker, H. S. and B. Geer. "The Fate of Idealism in Medical School." *American Sociological Review,* Vol. 23 (February 1958), pp. 50-56.

Becker, H. S., and A. L. Strauss. "Careers, Personality and Adult Socialization." *American Journal of Sociology,* Vol. 62 (1956), pp. 253-263.

Becker, H. S., et al. *Boys in White: Student Culture in Medical School.* Chicago: University of Chicago Press, 1961.

Bell, R. R., and M. Gordon, eds. *The Social Dimension of Human Sexuality.* Boston: Little Brown, 1972.

Bendix, R., and S. M. Lipset, eds. *Class, Status and Power,* 2nd ed. New York: Free Press, 1966.

Berger, P. L., and B. Berger. *Sociology: A Biographical Approach.* New York: Basic Books, 1972.

Bettelheim, B. "Feral Children and Autistic Children." *American Journal of Sociology,* Vol. 64 (1959), pp. 455-467.

Blankenship, R. L. "Organizational Careers: An Interactionist Perspective." *Sociological Quarterly,* Vol. 14 (1973), pp. 88-98.

Blishen, B. R. "A Socio-Economic Index for Occupations in Canada," in *Canadian Society: Sociological Perspectives,* 3rd abbrev. ed., eds. B. R. Blishen, F. E. Jones, K. D. Naegele, and J. Porter. Toronto: Macmillan, 1971.

Blumer, H. "Psychological Import of the Human Group," in *Group Relations at the Crossroads,* eds. M. Sherif and M. D. Wilson. New York: Harper and Row, 1953.

—————. "Society as Symbolic Interaction," in *Human Behavior and Social Processes: An Interactionist Approach,* eds. A. Rose *et al.* Boston: Houghton Mifflin, 1962, pp. 179-192.

—————. "Sociological Implications of the Thought of G. H. Mead." *American Journal of Sociology,* Vol. 71 (1966), pp. 535-548.

Boissevain, J. F. *The Italians of Montreal: Immigrant Adjustment in a Plural Society.* Ottawa: Queen's Printer, 1970.

Boocock, S. S. *An Introduction to the Sociology of Learning.* Boston: Houghton Mifflin, 1972.

Breton, R. "Institutional Completeness of Ethnic Communities and the Personal Relations of Immigrants." *American Journal of Sociology,* Vol. 70 (1964), pp. 193-205.

Brim, O. G. "Socialization through the Life Cycle," in *Socialization after Childhood,* eds. O. Brim and S. Wheeler. New York: John Wiley and Sons, 1966, pp. 1-49.

Cahan, A. *The Rise of David Levinsky.* New York: P. Smith, 1951.

Chinoy, E. "The Traditional Opportunity and the Aspirations of Automobile Workers." *American Journal of Sociology,* Vol. 57 (1952), pp. 453-459.

Clement, W. *The Canadian Corporate Elite: An Analysis of Economic Power.* Toronto: McClelland and Stewart, 1975.

—————. *Continental Corporate Power: Economic Linkages between Canada and the United States.* Toronto: McClelland and Stewart, 1977.

Clemmer, D. *The Prison Community.* New York: Holt, Rinehart and Winston, 1958.

Cooley, C. H. *Human Nature and the Social Order.* New York: Schocken Books, 1964.

Cressey, D. R., ed. *The Prison: Studies in Institutional Organization and Change.* New York: Holt, Rinehart and Winston, 1961.

Davis, F. "Deviance Disavowal: The Management of Strained Interaction by the Visibly Handicapped." *Social Problems,* Vol. 9 (1961), pp. 120-132.

Davis, K. "Final Note on a Case of Extreme Isolation." *American Journal of Sociology,* Vol. 52 (1947), pp. 432-437.

Davis, K. and W. Moore. "Some Principles of Stratification." *American Sociological Review,* Vol. 10 (1945), pp. 242-249.

Deutscher, I. "Words and Deeds: Social Science and Social Policy." *Social Problems,* Vol. 13 (1966), pp. 235-254.

Dewey, J. *Democracy and Education.* New York: Macmillan, 1921.

Durkheim, E. *Education and Society,* trans. Sherman Fox. New York: Free Press, 1956.

Ehrlich, H. J. *The Social Psychology of Prejudice.* New York: John Wiley and Sons, 1973.

Elliott, J. L., ed. *Minority Canadians 2: Immigrant Groups.* Scarborough, Ontario: Prentice-Hall, 1971.

Erikson, E. H. "Identity and Totality," *The Behavioral Sciences at Harvard.* Report by a committee of the faculty. Cambridge: 1954, p. 293.

Festinger, L. "The Influence Process in the Presence of Extreme Deviates." *Human Relations,* Vol. 5 (1952), pp. 327-346.

Festinger, L., H. W. Riecken, and S. Schachter. *When Prophecy Fails.* New York: Harper and Row, 1956.

"Full Text of White Paper on Language," a translation of the Quebec government's White Paper on Language. *Montreal Star,* April 2, 1977, p. B1.

Gagnon, J. H., and W. Simon, eds. *The Sexual Scene.* Chicago: Aldine, 1970.

Gans, H. J. *The Urban Villagers.* New York: The Free Press, 1962.

Gardner, R. "Working Class Consciousness and the Structure of Power in Canada," in *Proceedings of the Workshop Conference on Blue-Collar Workers and Their Communities,* ed. A. H. Turritan. Toronto: York University, 1976.

Garfinkel, H. "Conditions of Successful Degradation Ceremonies." *American Journal of Sociology,* Vol. 61 (1956), pp. 420-424.

Geer, B., ed. *Learning to Work.* Beverly Hills, California: Sage Publications, 1973.

Gerth, H., and C. W. Mills. *Character and Social Structure.* New York: Harcourt, Brace and World, 1953.

Glazer, N., and D. P. Moynihan. *Beyond the Melting Pot.* Cambridge, Massachusetts: The M. I. T. Press, 1963.

Goffman, E. "The Nature of Deference and Demeanor." *American Anthropologist,* Vol. 58 (1956), pp. 473-502.

———. *The Presentation of Self in Everyday Life.* Garden City, New York: Doubleday Anchor Books, 1959.

———. *Asylums.* Garden City, New York: Doubleday, 1961.

———. *Stigma: Notes on the Management of Spoiled Identity.* Englewood Cliffs, New Jersey: Prentice-Hall, 1963.

Goldfarb, M. "Canadians want Quebec to stay but refuse sacrifices for unity." *Toronto Star,* September 24, 1977, p. 12.

Gordon, M. M. *Assimilation in American Life: The Roles of Race, Religion, and National Origins.* New York: Oxford University Press, 1964.

Gottlieb, D., and C. E. Ramsey. *The American Adolescent.* Homewood, Illinois: The Dorsey Press, 1964.

Haas, J., and W. Shaffir. "The Professionalization of Medical Students: Developing Competence and a Cloak of Competence," *Symbolic Interaction*, Vol. 1 (Fall 1977), pp. 71-88.

Hacker, H. "Women as a Minority Group." *Social Forces*, Vol. 30 (1951), pp. 60-69.

Hall, O. "The Informal Organization of the Medical Profession." *Canadian Journal of Economic and Political Science*, Vol. 12 (1946), pp. 30-44.

Handlin, O. *The Uprooted*. New York: Grosset and Dunlap, 1951.

Hapgood, H. *The Spirit of the Ghetto: Studies of the Jewish Quarter of New York*. New York: Schocken Books, 1966.

Hawthorn, H., ed. *A Survey of the Contemporary Indians of Canada: A Report on Economic, Political, Educational Needs and Policies*, Vol. 2. Ottawa: Indian Affairs Branch, 1967.

Heller, C., ed. *Structured Social Inequality*. New York: Macmillan, 1969.

Hewitt, J. P. *Self and Society: A Symbolic Interactionist Social Psychology*. Boston: Allyn and Bacon, 1976.

Hiller, H. H. *Canadian Society: A Sociological Analysis*. Scarborough, Ontario: Prentice-Hall, 1976.

Hodges, H. M., Jr. *Conflict and Consensus: An Introduction to Sociology*. New York: Harper & Row, 1971.

Hostetler, J. A. *Amish Society*. Baltimore: The John Hopkins Press, 1968.

Hughes, E. C. "Personality Types and the Division of Labor." *American Journal of Sociology*, Vol. 33 (1927/28), pp. 754-768.

———. "Dilemmas and Contradictions of Status." *American Journal of Sociology*, Vol. L (1945), pp. 353-359.

———. "Mistakes at Work." *Canadian Journal of Economics and Political Science*, Vol. 17 (August 1951), pp. 320-327.

———. "Work and the Self." in *Social Psychology at the Crossroads*, eds. J. H. Rohrer and M. Sherif. New York: Harper and Row, 1951, pp. 313-323.

———. *Men and Their Work*. Glencoe, Illinois: The Free Press, 1958.

———. "The Study of Occupations," in *Sociology Today: Problems and Prospects*, eds. R. K. Merton, L. Broom, and L. S. Cottrell, Jr. New York: Basic Books, 1959, pp. 442-458.

James, W. *The Philosophy of William James*. New York: Random House, 1925.

Jamieson, S. M. *Times of Trouble: Labour Unrest and Industrial Conflict in Canada 1900-1966*. Task Force on Labour Relations, Study 22. Ottawa: Privy Council Office, 1968.

Johnson, L. A. "The Development of Class in Canada in the Twentieth Century," in *Capitalism and the National Question in Canada*, ed. G. Teeple. Toronto: University of Toronto Press, 1972.

Katz, D., and K. W. Braly. "Racial Stereotypes of 100 College Students." *Journal of Abnormal and Social Psychology*, Vol. 33 (1933), pp. 280-290.

Kinsey, A. C., W. B. Pomeroy, and C. E. Martin. *Sexual Behavior in the Human Male*. Philadelphia: W. B. Saunders, 1948.

Kinsey, A. C. et al. *Sexual Behavior in the Human Female*. Philadelphia: W. B. Saunders, 1953.

Kluckhohn, C. *Mirror for Man*. Greenwich, Connecticut: Fawcett World Library, 1964.

Komarovsky, M. "Cultural Contradictions and Sex Roles." *American Journal of Sociology*, Vol. 52 (1946), pp. 184-189.

Kramer, J. R. *The American Minority Community*. New York: Thomas Y. Crowell, 1970.

Kurokawa, M. *Minority Responses*. New York: Random House, 1970.

Lagasse, J. H. *A Study of the Population of Indian Ancestry in Manitoba*. The Department of Agriculture and Immigration, Manitoba: 1955.

Lemert, E. *Social Pathology*. New York: McGraw-Hill, 1951.

Letkemann, P. *Crime as Work.* Englewood Cliffs, New Jersey: Prentice-Hall, 1973.

Lewin, K. *A Dynamic Theory on Personality.* New York: McGraw-Hill, 1935.

————.*Resolving Social Conflicts.* New York: Harper and Row, 1948.

Lindesmith, A. R., and A. L. Strauss. *Social Psychology,* 3rd ed. New York: Holt, Rinehart and Winston, 1968.

Lipton, C. *The Trade Union Movement of Canada 1827-1959.* Montreal: Canadian Social Publications, 1968.

Lofland, J. *Doomsday Cult: A Study of Conversion, Proselytization, and Maintenance of Faith.* Englewood Cliffs, New Jersey: Prentice-Hall, 1966.

Manzer, R. *Canada: A Socio-Political Report.* Toronto: McGraw-Hill Ryerson, 1974.

Marden, C. E., and G. Meyer. *Minorities in American Society.* New York: American Book Company, 1962.

Marx, K. "Preface to 'A Contribution to the Critique of Political Economy'," in K. Marx and F. Engels, *Selected Works.* Moscow: Progress Publishers, 1968.

Masters, W. H., and V. E. Johnson, *Human Sexual Response.* Boston: Little, Brown and Co., 1966.

McCall, G. J., and J. L. Simmons. *Identities and Interaction.* New York: The Free Press, 1966.

Mead, G. H. *The Philosophy of the Present.* Chicago: University of Chicago Press, 1932.

————. *Mind, Self, and Society,* ed. C. W. Morris. Chicago: University of Chicago Press, 1962.

Merton, R. K. *Social Theory and Social Structure.* Glencoe, Illinois: The Free Press, 1957.

Mills, C. W. "Situated Actions and Vocabularies of Motive." *American Sociological Review,* Vol. 5 (1940), pp. 904-913.

———— *The Power Elite.* New York: Oxford University Press, 1956.

———— "The Sociology of Stratification," in *Power, Politics and People,* ed. I. L. Horowitz. New York: Oxford University Press, 1963, pp. 305-323.

Morton, W. L. *The Canadian Identity.* Madison: University of Wisconsin Press, 1965.

Newman, P. *The Canadian Establishment,* Vol. 1. Toronto: McClelland and Stewart, 1975.

Park, R. E. *Principles of Human Behavior.* Chicago: The Zalaz Corporation, 1915.

———— *Race and Culture,* eds. E. C. Hughes *et al.* Glencoe, Illinois: The Free Press, 1950.

Peters, V. *All Things Common: The Hutterian Way of Life.* New York: Harper and Row, 1971.

Petras, J. W. *Sexuality in Society.* Boston: Allyn and Bacon, 1973.

Pike, R. M., and E. T. Zureik, eds. *Socialization and Values in Canadian Society.* Toronto: McClelland and Stewart, 1975.

Pineo, P. C., and J. Porter. "Occupational Prestige in Canada." *Canadian Review of Sociology and Anthropology,* Vol. 4 (1967), pp. 24-40.

Podmore, C. J. "Private Schooling in English Canada." Ph.D. Thesis, McMaster University, 1976.

Polsky, N. *Hustlers, Beats, and Others.* Chicago: Aldine, 1967.

Porter, J. *The Vertical Mosaic.* Toronto: University of Toronto Press, 1965.

Ray, M. "The Cycle of Abstinence and Relapse Among Heroin Addicts." *Social Problems,* Vol. 9 (1961), pp. 132-140.

Redekop, C. W. *The Old Colony Mennonites: Dilemmas of Ethnic Minority Life.* Baltimore: The John Hopkins Press, 1969.

Reiss, I. R. *The Family System in America.* New York: Holt, Rinehart and Winston, 1971.

Riesman, D. *The Lonely Crowd: A Study of the Changing American Character.* New Haven: Yale University Press, 1966.

Royal Commission on Bilingualism and Biculturalism. *Report of the Royal Commission on Bilingualism and Biculturalism,* Book IV, *The Cultural Contribution of Other Ethnic Groups.* Ottawa: Queen's Printer, 1969.

Salaman, G. "Some Sociological Determinants of Occupational Communities." *American Sociological Review,* Vol. 19 (1971), pp. 53-74.

Sartre, J. P. *Anti-Semite and Jew.* New York: Grove Press, 1960.

Schutz, A. *The Phenomenology of the Social World.* Evanston, Illinois: Northwestern University Press, 1967.

Schwartz, M. A. *Public Opinion and Canadian Identity.* Berkeley: University of California Press, 1967.

Shaffir, W. *Life in a Religious Community: The Lubavitcher Chassidim in Montreal.* Toronto: Holt, Rinehart and Winston, 1974.

Shibutani, T. "Reference Groups and Social Control," in *Human Behavior and Social Processes: An Interactionist Approach,* ed. A. Rose. Boston: Houghton Mifflin, 1962, pp. 128-147.

Shibutani, T. and K. M. Kwan. *Ethnic Stratification: A Comparative Approach.* New York: Macmillan, 1965.

Simpson, G. E., and J. M. Yinger. *Racial and Cultural Minorities.* New York: Harper and Row, 1965.

Singh, A. L., and R. M. Zingy. *Wolf-Children and Feral Men.* New York: Harper and Row, 1942.

Solomon, D. N. "Sociological Perspectives on Occupations," in *Institutions and the Person,* eds. H. S. Becker *et al.* Chicago: Aldine, 1968, pp. 3-13.

Stonequist, E. V. *The Marginal Man.* New York: Russell and Russell, 1961.

Stouffer, S. A. "An Analysis of Conflicting Social Norms." *American Sociological Review,* Vol. 14 (1949), pp. 707-717.

Strauss, A. L. ed. *The Social Psychology of George Herbert Mead.* Chicago: University of Chicago Press, 1956.

———. *Mirrors and Masks: The Search for Identity.* San Francisco: The Sociology Press, 1969.

———. *The Contexts of Social Mobility: Ideology and Theory.* Chicago: Aldine, 1971.

Sykes, G. M. *The Society of Captives: A Study of a Maximum Security Prison.* New York: Atheneum, 1965.

Thomas, W. I. "The Definition of the Situation," in *Symbolic Interaction: A Reader in Social Psychology,* eds. J. Manis and B. Meltzer. Boston: Allyn and Bacon, 1967, pp. 315-321.

Tumin, M. "On Inequality." *American Sociological Review,* Vol. 28 (1963), pp. 19-26.

Vallee, F. G. "Multi-Ethnic Societies: The Issues of Identity and Inequality," in *Issues in Canadian Society: An Introduction to Sociology,* eds. D. Forcese and S. Richer. Scarborough, Ontario: Prentice-Hall, pp. 162-202.

Veblen, T. *The Engineers and the Price System.* New York: The Viking Press, 1940.

Walsh, G. *Indians in Transition: An Inquiry Approach.* Toronto: McClelland and Stewart, 1971.

Ward, D. A., and G. Kassebaum. *Women's Prison: Sex and Social Structure.* Chicago: Aldine, 1965.

Weber, M. *Max Weber: Essays in Sociology,* eds. and trans. H. H. Gerth and C. W. Mills. New York: Oxford University Press, 1946.

Westell, A. "Beginnings of national goal for Canada may be emerging." *Toronto Star*, 1 July 1977, p. C4.

Whyte, W. F. *Street Corner Society*. Chicago: University of Chicago Press, 1943.

Whyte, W. H., Jr. "The Wives of Management." *Fortune*, October, 1951, pp. 86-88, 204, 206, 207, 210, 213.

Williams, R. M., Jr. *The Reduction of Intergroup Relations*. Social Science Research Committee, No. 57, New York: 1947.

Williams, R. M., et al. *Strangers Next Door*. Englewood Cliffs, New Jersey: Prentice-Hall, 1964.

Wirth, L. *The Ghetto*. Chicago: University of Chicago Press, 1928.

———— . "Race and Public Policy." *The Scientific Monthly*, Vol. 58, No. 4 (March 1944), p. 303.

Wray, D. E. "Marginal Men of Industry: The Foremen." *American Journal of Sociology*, Vol. 54 (1949), pp. 298-301.

Young, P. V. *The Pilgrims of Russian-Town*. Chicago: The University of Chicago Press, 1932.

Zangwill, I. *The Melting Pot*. New York: Macmillan, 1909.

Zorbaugh, H. *The Gold Coast and the Slum*. Chicago: University of Chicago Press, 1929.